W9-AIP-967

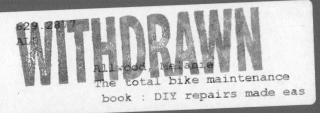

THE TOTAL BIKE MAINTENANCE BOOK

DIY REPAIRS MADE EASY

The following companies very kindly supplied bikes, tools and photoshoot props; without their help this book would not have been possible.

2Pure Ltd.
www.2pure.co.uk

Bicycle Magic *(with special thanks to Scott Stanners)*
www.bicyclemagic.com

Fisher Outdoor Leisure Ltd.
www.fisheroutdoor.co.uk

Genesis Bikes
www.genesisbikes.co.uk

Hope Technology Ltd.
www.hopegb.com

Just Riding Along
www.justridingalong.com

Madison
www.madison.co.uk

First published in 2004

This revised and updated edition published in 2016

10 9 8 7 6 5 4 3 2 1

Copyright © Carlton Books Limited 2016

A CIP catalogue record for this book is available from the British Library.

ISBN 13: 978-1-78097-785-0

Printed in Dubai

THE TOTAL BIKE MAINTENANCE BOOK

DIY REPAIRS MADE EASY

Mel Allwood

CARLTON
BOOKS

Contents

1 Kitting out 8–19
What to wear

Safety gear

2 Setting up 20–39
Choosing saddles and pedals

Choosing handlebars

Locks and locking up

Luggage, racks, bags and trailers

Lights and mudguards

3 Basic tools and repairs 40–79
Tools and equipment

Fixing punctures

Fixing chains

Transmission and gear cable failures

Safety checks

4 Brakes 80–127
Setting up V-, cantilever and calliper brakes

Changing cables and brake blocks

Installing and adjusting disc brakes

Changing disc brake pads

Bleeding hydraulic brakes

5 Transmission 128–185
Installing chains and cassettes

Installing and adjusting derailleurs

Fitting new gear cables

Replacing chainrings

Singlespeed riding

Maintaining hub gears

6 Wheels 186–217
Servicing cup-and-cone hubs

Truing wheels

Inserting new spokes

Building wheels

7 Suspension 218–243
The language of suspension

Setting up and servicing front forks

Setting up and servicing rear suspension

8 Bottom brackets and headsets 244–269
Checking bottom brackets

Installing new bottom brackets

Adjusting headsets

Servicing headsets

9 Components 270–285
Installing handlebars and stems

Installing and servicing seatposts

Servicing pedals

Fitting accessories

10 Conclusion 286–304
Glossary

Index

Introduction

There are plenty of really good reasons for using a bicycle to get around. It's good for you, it helps keep the air clean and it's good for the planet. All of these notions are very worthy and, no doubt, provide the impetus for many people to get out of their cars and back onto two wheels. But I'm sure there are plenty of others like me carrying around a guilty secret. We don't cycle because we're virtuous. We do it because it makes us smile.

I became a cyclist originally because I live in a big crowded city, and I'm an impatient traveller. Bikes are the quickest way to get around and mean you're travelling under your own steam. I can't be doing with sitting in a tin box in traffic, or waiting for another piece of non-existent public transport to arrive. I love being out and about, able to stop and start whenever I fancy as well as being close to the way the city changes with the seasons.

Even wet, miserable days are worth it because I know they'll be balanced by that great feeling of riding around when spring's just arrived, or when you get pushed all the way home after a long day by a miraculous autumn tailwind. Sitting in a car, with the heating on and the windows sealed, you're divorced from the weather and every journey is much like any other.

But once you own a bicycle, it doesn't take long to find that you'll enjoy it more if you've got an idea how it works. A little bit of knowledge means you're more self-sufficient, so that if something goes wrong by the side of the road or when you're just about to set off on a journey, you can sort it out and get on with your life. It's not all about emergencies though: if you've got a few tools and a bit of time to tinker, you can set your bike up so that it's comfortable to ride. And finally it's not just about fixing things that don't work. If you spend time keeping your bike clean and in good working order, the parts will last longer, saving you time and money. Regular, mild care and attention is much more effective, and cheap, than occasional guilty servicing frenzies.

None of the procedures listed in the mechanics section of the book are difficult, but that's not to say they're easy if you haven't done them before. However carefully you follow the instructions, they always take longer the first time than you expect. But each time you return to the same job – and some will become quite familiar, as city roads give you plenty of practice at punctures – it will get a little bit quicker and easier. You'll find yourself having to collect tools quite rapidly at first; each new job you tackle will require another gadget or two. Don't panic about this. The rate of acquisition tails off after a while and you'll find you can rely on a relatively small toolkit to cover most eventualities.

Part of what I love about bicycles is their simplicity. Bicycles rely on your energy to keep them moving, so there's a big incentive to make them as light as possible. This leads to almost zero tolerance for anything that's not essential to rolling you along – the bicycle is no 'kitchen sink' means of transport. Although appealing from an aesthetic perspective, this has its disadvantages. If everything's essential, then anything that goes wrong by the side of the road will stop you getting where you're going. This is why you should learn to tackle problems in an emergency. As a side benefit, since most bicycles work in similar ways, if you've learned to fix your own steed, chances are you can make yourself useful if somebody else has a problem, too.

Like so many bike mechanics, most of what I've learned about how to make bikes feel nice and work efficiently comes from just taking things apart and putting them back together. Bikes seldom need complex or expensive tools, but respond magically to a bit of care and attention – a nurtured bicycle feels better than a neglected one that cost twice as much. I've been very lucky to have had a job that I really loved, working for Brixton Cycles Co-op in south London. Everything in this book comes from having spent that time trying to keep a startling range of different kinds of bicycle on the road for a sensible amount of money.

This book is particularly useful for people new to cycling, new to using their bicycle to get about town and those who love mountain biking, a maintenance-heavy part of the cycling world and the one this book concentrates on, though most of the principles will apply to any bike. There's plenty of mechanics, starting with how to fix a puncture and maintain your transmission, all the way up to servicing suspension units and building your own wheels. Hopefully, there are also some useful tips for the people who've had experience of tinkering with their bicycles, but want to expand into more involved procedures. Either way, what I hope you'll learn from it is how to understand your bicycle better and to feel more confident about working on it.

Whether you're completely new to cycling or have been riding for ages and want some tips on fixing a variety of different types of bike, this book should help you get out there and enjoy your riding. I like the way cycling helps you see the world in a different way. Slightly more slowly, perhaps, but much more clearly.

Mel Allwood

1 – Kitting out

For short trips on a warm sunny day, you need very little kit to enjoy cycling. You can get away with wearing normal clothes: sling a bag over your shoulder and you're off. But don't let the threat of bad weather put you off as, with the right protective clothing, you can be warm and dry whatever the sky throws at you. Don't be put off by the expense either. You definitely don't need to rush out and buy everything in this chapter all at once – just pick up what you need when you need it.

What to wear: jackets

Your raincoat is your first line of defence against the elements. Unless you live somewhere with year-round sunshine, you'll need something that stops you getting cold, wet and miserable. Cycling around town makes an extra demand on your cycling clothing as you're usually going somewhere, rather than cycling around in circles just for the fun of it.

This means you have to consider what the jacket looks like off the bike too – a skintight tube of fluorescent yellow might be very efficient, but it's not an attractive item to wear to the pub at the end of the day. Jackets perform three functions. They keep you dry when it's raining and warm when it's windy or cold. Also, since purpose-made cycling jackets are so often used as an outer layer in the wet, they often have reflective stripes or tabs. These are especially valuable in the rain, since that's when car drivers seem to concentrate least on who they're sharing the road with.

While any jacket will provide you with protection, something bike-specific will do the job better, simply because it's made for the job. These are some of the features you'll want to look out for:

Cut
Cycling clothes are designed to fit you properly when you're sitting on the bike, so they often look odd when you're standing up. A cycling jacket will have a longer back to ensure your kidneys don't get cold and wet. It will also help protect your bottom from the spray that comes off the road if you don't have mudguards. The arms are slightly longer than normal since you're generally reaching forward to the bars. If the sleeves were of normal length, your wrists would be exposed and get cold and wet quickly. The front of the jacket should be cut short so your legs can move freely. If the jacket reaches down as far as the front of your thighs, you'll find your legs lift up the jacket with every pedal stroke, sucking cold air in.

Sealing
The neck, wrists and around the waist need to be draughtproof. Best of all are toggles that you can pull tighter and release with one hand so you can keep your ventilation and warmth balance just right.

Pockets
There's a conflict here. When you're wandering around off the bike, you definitely want pockets at the front of your jacket. You can put your keys in them or your hands to keep them warm. However, front pockets are a bit of a pain when you're riding along. Anything in them weighs the front of the jacket down, misshaping it so that it creates a big draughty space inside the jacket instead of fitting warmly and snugly with no gaps. You may also find that precious things drop out of your pocket as you ride along. A good solution is to put the pockets on the back. It goes against your instincts at first, but means that anything you put in your pocket will stay there.

Features
Pockets, storm flaps, extra zips and hoods are all good, but any features you add to the jacket make it more bulky. This is fine if you know it's definitely going to rain, because you will sling your jacket on anyway. Trouble starts on 'just-in-case' days. A jacket with fewer features that packs smaller is more likely to be used. A larger, bulkier one is more likely to get left at home in a dose of optimism where it will be no good to anyone.

Safety is more important than vanity: bright clothing is essential on dark days since it will keep you visible on your bike; reflective piping and tabs are more than useful at night since they help you stand out in headlights

Colour

If you're going to be riding in town, then anything that helps drivers to see you is an advantage. Bright yellow is obviously the best in terms of visibility, although some people struggle with the idea of riding around looking frighteningly like a banana. Jackets need to be versatile enough to cope with being worn off the bike as well as on it and sometimes that means compromise in the visibility department.

Fabric

There is a bewildering array of different fabrics available. Generally, all claim to be the best at everything. There are a few key things you need to look out for. The level of waterproofing is often the deciding factor. There are two distinct types: waterproof and water-resistant. Water-resistant will protect you from showers. Waterproof is more expensive and will keep you dry for longer. In fact, better fabrics, such as Gore-Tex, will keep you dry all day. Water-resistant jackets will keep you dry on shorter journeys – up to about 40 minutes in a shower or 20 in heavy rain. After that, they'll start to leak, usually through the seams first. But if your average commute is 20 minutes or so, a water-resistant jacket will do the job just fine, saving you a large chunk of money. It's essential that the fabric of the jacket is breathable. However casual you are about cycling, there will be times when you're working hard enough to get hot and sweaty. Breathable fabrics are made so that the moisture you generate can easily pass out of the jacket, stopping you from ending up swimming in a puddle of your own making.

Windproofing

This is more important than it sounds. You're constantly moving through the air, so effectively when you're cycling it's always windy. On hot days this is great as it keeps you cool. On cold, damp days, you'll get cold very quickly and the faster you move, the colder you'll get, especially on long downhills when you're not working hard enough to keep you warm. Luckily, windproof fabric can be made very thin and light. A shell that you can throw on during chilly days won't take up much room in your bag and will even fit in your pocket.

Hoods

Generally, they're rare on cycling jackets since many people wear a helmet. A better option is usually a hat as it turns with your head. The experience of glancing back at traffic before a perilous manoeuvre and getting a clear view of the inside of a hood puts people off them quite quickly.

What to wear: lower half

Weather protection depends on the length of your journey and the climate. In mild weather you can cycle around in whatever you normally wear – high heels can be a little unstable and jeans are quite sweaty, but pretty much anything will work. Trouser legs need to be either rolled up or strapped out of the way of chain oil with a trouser clip. But if it's hot, cold or wet, you'll need to think through your lower-half options.

Proper cycling shorts look ridiculous on the rail in the shop and feel ridiculous the first time you try them on as the padding makes it feel like you're wearing a nappy. But they're not designed to be hung on a rail or stood about in. They only make sense when you realise that you can happily sit in the saddle all day, then go on to sit on something more conventional like a chair without wincing. More expensive shorts are specifically designed for men and women's different anatomies, although even the most basic will make your saddle more comfortable. Your saddle should be comfortable. Don't listen to anyone who tells you that you should 'break a new saddle in' or that 'you'll get used to it'. If it's not comfortable, get some proper cycling shorts or a new saddle, or both.

Choosing shorts can be quite confusing. The expensive ones look almost identical to the ones that cost a quarter of the price, so it's difficult to understand what you're getting for the extra money. One of the major differences is the fabric – pricier shorts are made of more breathable material, like Coolmax, which keep you cool and dry. They will also be made up of more, smaller panels, so that the shape of the short will follow your contours as you cycle. Padding is more sophisticated in expensive shorts and can be more supportive and comfortable without being too thick.

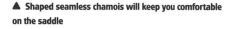

▲ **Shaped seamless chamois will keep you comfortable on the saddle**

If you're commuting on hot days you'll probably want to change when you arrive. It's a good thing to share the warm glow of your commute with your colleagues, but you don't want to become a health hazard. And unless you work in a particularly casual environment, cycling shorts don't make you look professional. Enlightened employers provide showers, lockers and changing facilities, but

▲ **Grippers round the bottoms of the legs stop fabric from riding up**
◄ **Baggy shorts are more flattering**

even a lavatory can be pressed into temporary service.

Good, comfortable shorts are made of Lycra, Coolmax or similar stretchy materials. This works well, but for most of the population it isn't particularly flattering as it emphasises every curve in ways most of us would rather not. However, there is absolutely no law against wearing whatever you want over your cycling shorts such as baggy shorts, a skirt or whatever you fancy.

Nobody need ever know that you're sporting a skintight layer underneath. You can even get bike shorts that have a baggy outer layer concealing a proper pair of cycling shorts underneath. There's a final thing about cycling shorts that nobody ever tells you: they're designed to be worn next to the skin, with nothing underneath.

Cold weather

In some ways, very cold weather is easier to deal with than in-between days. You can just put on everything you own and then cycle as fast as you possible can to keep warm.

Tights should go over shorts, not the other way around for the Superman look. Tights always have a seam in the middle, which you don't really want to be sitting directly on as the shorts are there to protect you from that.

Once it gets colder, choose tights with a fleecy lining. This traps the heat generated by the work your legs are doing and keeps everything snug. Make sure you choose a pair that are long enough to cover your ankles even when your legs are bent. As with your wrists, this is where your blood is carried close to the surface of your skin, so once it gets chilled you tend to get really cold. The same goes for the waistband at the back and, when you're sitting on your bike, this should come up high enough to overlap your jacket as exposed skin will chill quickly.

Knees are complex joints and need to be taken care of as much as possible. Cycling is rarely bad for knees on its own, but it can aggravate other injuries if not treated with care. Keeping your knees warm on chilly days makes a big difference. If you hurl them out into the cold and expect to be able to stamp up hills without any warm-up, they'll protest. If you've had a history of knee injuries, wear leggings until it's really warm or get three-quarter length shorts as these come right down over your knees.

Wet weather

Rain causes a bit of a dilemma about what to wear on your legs. Your legs are the part of your body that's working the hardest, which will mostly keep them warm even if they're wet. So getting your legs wet shouldn't be as much of a problem in the rain as not having a proper jacket. This is fine if your trousers fit fairly close and you don't have to spend the rest of the day standing around in them. But wet, loose trousers that flap about never warm up, no matter how hard you work. Waterproof trousers, therefore, are useful for keeping your normal trousers dry, even if your legs don't need it. But, unless you have very breathable waterproofs, they get horrible and sweaty inside and you'll end up wishing you hadn't bothered to try and keep dry. Waterproof trousers over shorts seems like an odd combination, but they work much better than you expect as long as you have somewhere to change out of your shorts at the other end.

Choose a pair of waterproof trousers with reflective tabs. If it's cold the chances are it will be wet and dark as well. They should be baggy enough so that there's room for your knees to bend and so that you can pull them on over your shoes by the side of the road – if you have to take your shoes off you will probably step in a puddle, which spoils the point of putting on waterproof trousers to stay dry. Long zips that come most of the way up your calves or a wide pleat at the bottom that can be cinched in tight with Velcro tabs both work well, especially if you can get them open and closed without taking your gloves off.

**Overtrousers should be wide enough to fit easily over your shoes: but make
sure they are breathable or your legs will get horrible and sweaty inside them ▶**

What to wear: shoes

Many people who cycle as their main form of transport prefer to wear as many of their normal clothes as possible. This makes it easier to arrive at and leave places without spending half an hour fiddling around with gadgets and gear.

However, it's often the shoes that give people away as more serious cyclists than they'd care to admit to being. The realisation that cycling kills normal shoes is often a major push towards specialist shoes. Any pedal that's got enough grip to keep you securely connected to your bike will tear away at the soles of your shoes. It also makes cycling shoes appear much cheaper when you realise how much longer they last than trainers.

The other reason for choosing shoes that have been specifically designed for cycling is that they have very much stiffer soles than ordinary shoes, making you more efficient. All of the precious energy that you use to push your feet around goes into turning the pedals, rather than being wasted scrunching up the soles of your feet.

Cycling shoes also support your feet much better across the whole width of the sole, so that you don't get sore patches under the balls of your feet where the pedals sit. You don't need to ride around looking like you've got crisp packets on your feet, however. There are plenty of options that look very much like trainers so you can get away with wearing them without looking overdressed.

There's also a real advantage to having stiff soles in very hot and very cold weather. If the whole sole of your foot is supported, you can relax it. In cold weather this means that blood can flow freely all the way to your toes, keeping them a bit warmer. In hot weather, air can flow around your skin, keeping your feet cooler.

▲ **Good shoes needn't be ugly**

Clipless pedals

Clipless pedals lock securely into cleats on the soles of your shoes, yet release instantly when you twist your feet. The cleat is a metal key, fitting precisely into the release mechanism of the pedal. The cleat will only fit onto the bottoms of shoes that have been specifically designed to take them and you cannot fit them onto ordinary shoes. Luckily, there is something that approximates to a universal standard for attaching cleats to cycling shoes so you're not stuck with using pedals, shoes and cleats from the same manufacturer. The most usual set-up is that used by Shimano, which consists of two bolt holes deeply recessed into the sole. A range of different manufacturers make pedals and cleats that fit into this shoe pattern.

This universal standard applies only to shoe/cleat combinations, however. It doesn't apply to pedal/cleat combinations. A set of clipless pedals will come with its own cleats and is only designed to work properly with those cleats. This means that, once you've fitted your cleats to your shoes, you can't automatically jump onto somebody else's bike and use their clipless pedals unless they're the same make and, in some cases, the same model.

Be sure to try on a range of shoes before you choose, especially if you have, or are thinking of using, clipless pedals. You need a pair that fits snugly around your feet. It's important that your feet can't twist around in the shoes, otherwise, when you come to try and release your shoe from the pedal by twisting the shoe, you'll find that your foot will slide around inside the shoe without releasing.

The SPD-type clipless pedals are by far the most common. Their biggest advantage is that the cleat is recessed into the sole so that you can walk easily. There is another type of pedal, typically used on racing bikes. These have a larger cleat that protrudes out from the surface of the sole. However, they're not a great idea for using round town as the cleat makes the shoes very slippery to walk on, especially if it's wet.

▲ **Specialized trail boots**

▲ **Cleats must be bolted to the soles of the shoe**

What to wear: overshoes and gloves

Cold weather makes extra demands on your feet as they're stuck way out on the end of your body, a position which tends to leave them exposed when the temperature plummets. As you pedal, they're spinning around as well as moving along so the wind chill factor is exaggerated.

The most obvious solution is overshoes. These are booties made of neoprene, Gore-Tex or nylon that you pull on over your shoes. They have a cut-out window in the sole for the shoe to grip the pedal or, if you're using clipless, for the cleat to poke out. Velcro secures them tightly around your shoes and they usually have some retro reflective strips on the back.

These keep the wind and water off your feet and have the added advantage of keeping your shoes dry, essential if you have to spend the rest of the day walking around in them. They do look a bit daft, but that seems like quite a small price to pay for comfy toes. Take them off as soon as you get off the bike. If you walk around in them, the soles wear quickly and once they're torn they don't stay on your feet properly. They're especially useful if you don't have a front mudguard. Water from the road gets picked up by your front tyre and carried a little way around the wheel by its rotation. Soon enough, however, it sprays off the back of the tyre and gets dumped all over your feet.

If you really can't imagine yourself being seen in overshoes, you can get waterproof socks. There are a few different brands, but the best are made by SealSkinz. You wear them instead of ordinary socks. They're a little bit stiffer than normal socks and so feel a bit strange, but keep out both the wind and the water. They're thicker than normal socks too, so make sure there's enough room in your shoes. If it's too much of a squeeze, you'll restrict the circulation of warm blood down to your feet, which will then get cold anyway. Wear your largest shoes.

Cycling shoes come with variable amounts of ventilation. Some are almost all mesh, which is great for hot weather, but useless in winter. If you're mainly dealing with the cold, look for a pair that has few or no mesh areas.

▲ **These overshoes have plenty of reflective piping, front and back**

Gloves

Keeping hands warm is a number one priority from the beginning of autumn to the end of spring. There are a few things to look out for in winter gloves. The material obviously needs to insulate your hands. But windproofing is equally important as your hands are really exposed, sitting up out front on your bars in the full force of the wind. If they're wet as well, the wind will strip the heat from your skin. Even if your gloves aren't waterproof, choose something windproof. Fully waterproof gloves tend to be expensive as the complicated shape of your hands tends to mean lots of seams, all potential routes for water to get in.

The thickness of the material is also an issue and you'll always find yourself in situations where you have to operate keys or fumble for your phone. It's no good having a lovely warm pair of gloves and then having to rip them off every time you want to do something. You'll also appreciate padding on the palms to absorb vibration from the road. Cycle-specific gloves have padded palms, to protect hands from vibration. This is especially worthwhile if you work at a computer for hours on end as jumping onto the bike at the end of the day can leave you with sore wrists, elbows and shoulders.

Summer gloves with short fingers fit quite snugly.

Try on a few pairs since different manufacturers put the padding in different places and they seem to suit different people. What's comfortable depends on how your hands approach your bars.

▲ **Full-finger gloves keep you warm**
▼ **Mitts protect your palms even on really hot days**

What to wear: thermals, layers

This page is primarily about cold weather. Warmer weather is usually easier to deal with, but there's something satisfying about bundling yourself up against the elements and cycling around all snug in your cocoon. Sometimes, if the weather's really bad, you cycle past a bus queue and you can see that someone in it has seen you and feels sorry for you. But if you've got the right gear, the chances are you're warmer than they are. You'll probably get where you're going first as well.

The basic problem with very cold weather is that you need to be able to change the amount of insulation you're wearing quickly and constantly. When you first step out of the front door on a cold day, you need enough on to keep you from freezing until you've jumped on your bike and got moving. Halfway up the first hill you come to, especially if it's a little bit steep, you'll be all hot and bothered. The first downhill after that is always the moment when you find out if you've managed to dress yourself appropriately. You head downhill and suddenly it gets easier so you don't have to pedal. You're not working yourself warm, but you're moving faster so the wind starts cutting into you and all that sweat that you worked up getting up the hill suddenly starts freezing onto your skin. That's when you get really cold.

The key to beating this scenario is layers. Layers are good for two reasons. The first is that it's vital to be able to remove and replace thin layers, so that you can regulate your temperature precisely, and not get too hot going uphill. The second good reason for layers in cold weather is that each layer serves a different purpose.

Base layer

The layer directly next to your skin is there to make you comfortable. Its most important task is to wick moisture away from your skin, keeping it dry and comfortable. For anything other than really relaxed cycling, cotton T-shirts just aren't up to the job. They absorb and hold sweat, which means that the layer next to your skin is always damp. If any draught can get to it, the damp cotton will feel instantly chilly. Modern fabrics, like Coolmax, wick moisture away from your skin, keeping you warmer and dryer. Coolmax summer jerseys make great winter vests. There's no need for a completely new wardrobe for the winter – you just have to make more use of the stuff you've already got.

Another great fabric for this is merino wool, which is making a comeback after years of being thought of as an old-fashioned fabric. Wool has another great advantage – it's evolved over millions of years protecting sheep to become an unappealing environment for the kind of bacteria that make you smell after exercise, and so won't retain odour in the same way as synthetic fabrics. It's great for arriving at the office without foisting the full joy of your breakneck commute upon all your work colleagues. This doesn't, however, mean that it never needs to be washed. Catalogues for merino cycling clothing frequently carry tales of epic adventures by intrepid explorers, who boast about how many months they survived in the jungle/Antarctic/mid-ocean with no change of shirt. Merino wool will smell less after this kind of punishment than Lycra, but it's not the kind of boast that your work colleagues are likely to appreciate. Modern wool garments don't need outrageous amounts of washing care – they survive fine on normal 40° washes in the washing machine.

Mid layer

Your mid layer is purely for warmth. If it's below freezing, a fleece is a great idea as you'll need to choose something that's not too bulky. For in-between days, a long-sleeved jersey – in Coolmax o r similar – over your vest is fine. It doesn't have to be cycling-specific as any breathable fabric will do. Just make sure that the cut is generous enough so that you can stretch out over your bicycle without exposing flesh at your wrists and across the bottom of your back.

A full zip is always a better idea than a short zip or no zips at all as you can open it easily while riding along for instant ventilation. Again, cotton fabrics are no good; they will just get wet and then cold. They're much better saved for putting on when you're home, warm and dry. Several thinner layers will always be better than one thick one so that you can regulate your temperature easily. The annoying thing about cycling in

◀ **Wicking base layers keep you dry**

cold weather is that you actually spend a fair amount of time trying to keep cool when you find yourself suddenly working hard to overtake a bus or sprint up a hill. Full zips make instant ventilation much easier. As long as they fit, your mid layers don't have to be cycling-specific. If you've already got gear from another sport or exercise, it'll probably do a fine job – as long as the fabric is breathable.

Outer layer

Your final layer of clothing is all about the weather. It's there to keep the wind and the rain off your body. Jackets with full zips are best as again, like mid layers, they allow instant blasts of ventilation. Your jacket is also an essential place for keeping keys, wallet and so forth, so choose one with pockets. These are often positioned at the back to stop the weight of items inside dragging the jacket out of shape. Hoods are rare as it's generally assumed that you'll be wearing either a helmet or a hat anyway. Hoods can be really tricky too as, however well designed they are, they still tend to cut down on your all-round vision.

When you're choosing a jacket, it's best if you can try it on while you're actually sitting on the bike. If you can't, try stretching out in your riding position. Make sure the arms are long enough to cover your wrists and that the material isn't stretched tightly across your shoulders. The back should come down low enough so that your kidneys aren't exposed. The front of the jacket shouldn't sag forward too much. If there's too much space, the wind will get in underneath, exposing you to a constant draught.

It's not always so cold that you'll need a full jacket. Autumn and spring bring days when you can easily get away with a sleeveless gilet, which keeps your torso warm while leaving your arms free. These usually have windproof panels at the front and thinner fabric or mesh – and perhaps some reflective tabs and a pocket – at the back.

▲ **A base layer keeps your skin dry, while a mid layer insulates you. Outer layers protect you from the elements. You need to make a judicious selection of layers if you want to stay warm and dry without getting sweaty**

Layer compatibility

Your layers will only work if they fit together well. A warm fleece that pokes out below the bottom of your jacket at the back will act like a wick, soaking up moisture from the cold outside air and drawing it slowly up your back into the warm gap between your body and your jacket. The same goes for sleeves that poke out of the ends of your jacket. Bulky layers won't fit properly underneath others, restricting your movement and making you feel colder than you are.

Breathable jackets will only work if all the layers underneath the jacket are also breathable. The jacket fabric is designed to rapidly transport moisture from its inside surface to the world outside, but it can only do its job on moisture that reaches the inside surface, which is another thing to think about.

Safety gear: helmets

There are always arguments for and against using safety gear. There's a point of view that says that cycling is so good for you anyway that you can survive the occasional prang. However, if you do end up coming off your bike occasionally, that argument begins to look very unconvincing, so stay safe in the saddle.

Consider your options, but don't get so wrapped up in thinking about cycling as dangerous that you start to treat your journey to work as an extreme sport. Essentially, it's just a way of getting about. Helmets are the most obvious piece of cycling-specific safety gear. There are many convincing arguments for wearing one and they will protect your head in certain types of collisions. Helmets are a legal requirement in a lot of countries. Kids, in particular, should always wear one, even in countries where they are not legally required to, because they have softer skulls and can often make inexperienced decisions. It is also important to remember, however, that helmets won't stop you having accidents.

One of the reasons people used to cite for not ever wearing a helmet was that they were heavy, sweaty and uncomfortable. This just isn't true any more. Modern lids are light enough to wear without you noticing them and have good big vents, which let in plenty of air. There's no need to use comfort as a reason not to wear one. It's essential to go to a shop and try on a few different types before you buy one as they are all different shapes. It's not until you start trying helmets on that you realise some people's heads are very round, while others' are much more oval. Just knowing whether your head is small, medium or large will not be enough to secure you the right helmet. Within each size, there will always be some adjustment to make, but if the basic shape doesn't match your head, try another make.

Big vents in the helmet make it a lot more comfortable, but you lose most of your heat through your head and a helmet without vents will stop this from happening.

If you've got a particularly large or particularly small head, your helmet choice will be rather more restricted and generally involve more expensive makes. The cheaper versions tend to restrict themselves to medium sizes. Giro make a huge range of helmets and their size range for adult helmets goes from 51 to 63cm (20 to 25 in), which should be enough to cover most people's heads.

Before you use a new helmet for the first time, take a bit of time to fit it properly. There's a single strap under your chin, which splits into four parts – two on each side, one leading forwards, the other backwards. There needs to be even tension in each strap with the helmet sitting level on your head. Check this in a mirror as a common mistake is to position the helmet too far back on the head. This makes it fairly useless as a safety device since, if you hit something hard, it will just get pushed off backwards, leaving the strap still wrapped around your neck. Similarly, to work properly, the strap under your chin needs to be reasonably tight so that, if you open your mouth, you feel the helmet pressing down onto the top of your head. When you first try this, you'll probably find it too uncomfortable to wear. But when you get on your bike, you'll find that you generally ride around looking forwards and upwards, which loosens off the strap to a point where it should feel comfortable. The straps are a little bit fiddly but you only have to set them up the first time. After that, the helmet will only need an occasional tighten as the straps work loose. It's essential to get it right, however, as a badly set up helmet won't stay on your head and protect you in a collision.

If you don't like riding around with a smelly head, you may want to know that the pads inside the helmet are generally secured with Velcro. This means you can pull them out and stick them in the washing machine. You can also buy replacement pad sets and use them to customise the fit of your helmet.

Helmets are ideal for increasing your visibility. Go for a bright one ▶

Safety gear: be safe, be seen

Visibility gear is one of the things that really mark you out as a cyclist. Reflective strips on your body or your bike use the light given off by car headlamps and bounce it back into the driver's eyes. Any time lights are pointed in your direction, you give everybody a chance of noticing you're there.

Reflective bands and strips don't need batteries and don't usually get stolen. Reflective strips worn on your body pick out your silhouette so that you stand out clearly as a person. Even if this only makes it a little bit harder for car drivers to cut you up too close, it helps. If you're sticking reflective strips or stickers onto your bike, remember to give them a quick wipe occasionally as they don't reflect light when they're dirty. Reflective trouser clips are especially effective from behind because they bob up and down as you pedal, making them and you much more visible.

Nothing marks you out as a cyclist more than a Sam Browne belt. There's no mistaking your mode of transport with one of these about your person. They're more expensive than you'd expect, due to the high cost of the reflective material. The combination of Sam Browne belt and a rucksack doesn't work at all since you're covering up the important bit at the back. If you're going to wear a rucksack, make sure that it's got its own reflective strips or tabs. Even better, get yourself a rucksack cover with visibility strips on it. They slip over your bag like a shower cap, and also keep the rain off.

In traffic, your helmet is one of the best places for a little extra sparkle. Your head is above the level of much of the traffic, so if it's bright enough, people will be able to see you weaving about in a line of stationary cars. Light-coloured helmets are easier to pick out than dark colours and those designed for use round town will have silver reflective stickers or logos. You can supplement these with a reflective band that sits around the widest part of the helmet like those made by Respro. For extra visibility, many LED lights are small enough to ziptie onto the back of your helmet, without the weight dragging it out of balance.

The above are the obvious bits of protective gear and probably the ones you need most, but there's a couple of other bits of kit that are more useful, less often. As well as keeping your hands warm and dry, a pair of gloves will protect your palms if you have a spill. It's amazing how much a single layer of fabric will help.

Sun cream is an accepted part of being outdoors now, but you burn in odd places on a bicycle. The tops of your thighs and the backs of your calves get more exposure than you'd expect, as do the backs of your hands, which is another good reason for wearing fingerless gloves. If you're not wearing a helmet, be careful with the top of your head, the back of your neck and your ears.

Contact lens wearers – and many other cyclists – find that a bit of eye protection stops grit getting stuck onto their eyeballs, especially on windy days. Sunglasses are fine for the summer, but are a bit gloomy for the winter. Try a pair of light-enhancing lenses instead. They're like sunglasses, but make everything just a little bit brighter on gloomy days, dark evenings and early mornings.

▲ **Pause for reflection with the Sam Browne belt**

▲ **Glasses for light relief**

▲ **Make yourself visible: small, neat extra lights can be hung from your rucksack or bag straps**

2 – Setting up

This chapter explains how your bicycle can be adjusted so it's comfortable and kitted out so that it's fit for purpose. Riding your bike should be fun, and make you feel great. If sitting on it makes you miserable, you'll soon find excuses to avoid using it. Everybody is different, so it can take a little time to find the right set up to adapt your machine to suit your needs. You may need to swap saddles, pedals or handlebars or add some useful accessories.

Choosing a saddle

One thing that stops people who cycle a little from cycling a lot is an uncomfortable saddle. If it's not comfortable, it's not likely to suddenly get any more comfortable. You're just going to find it unpleasant to ride around and it will put you off.

The solution is to swap your saddle for one that matches your own shape. If you're buying a new bike, the saddle it comes supplied with was chosen to make the bike look appealing on the shop floor. This might mean that the manufacturer has fitted some lean, mean strip of hard plastic to make the bike look racy and weigh as little as possible. If they're aiming for the leisure market, the bike might well come with a big squashy cushion that gives when you press your thumbs into it. That's all very well if you're going to practise handstands on your bike, but bottoms are a very different shape to thumbs – something that feels forgiving to your thumb will be far too soft and unsupportive to ride far on. Just as if you were going to buy a mattress, don't trust any judgement other than how a saddle feels when you're sitting on the bike. It doesn't actually matter at all what it looks like – nobody can see much of it while you're riding along. And, if you find a saddle that suits you, there's no reason not to take it with you if you decide to get a new bike.

Men's and women's saddles

Men and women have different-shaped pelvises, so your saddle is one part of your bike that it's absolutely essential to get right. New bikes generally come fitted as standard with a men's saddle. On request, any bike shop with any sense will swap this for a women's one if you ask them to when you buy the bike. Women's saddles are slightly wider and slightly shorter. The extra width is necessary because women have wider 'sit bones'.

▲ **Brooks leather saddle**

You need enough padding on a saddle to cushion you from road shocks without it being so soft that you sink into it and wallow around. This is a very personal choice and depends on your mileage, your position on the bike and your shape. Softer saddles are better for short trips. If you're sitting very upright, you'll also need a softer saddle and may also want to consider a suspension seat post, since your bottom will be taking most of your weight. The better types have gel cushions under each sit bone, supporting you exactly where you need it most.

In a longer, more stretched-out position, your weight is shared out more equally between bars, saddle and pedal, so your saddle can be firmer without being uncomfortable. A thin layer of gel will reduce vibration from the road and a narrow cutaway shape will allow you to pedal efficiently without the sides of the saddle chafing on your thighs.

Extra comfort can come from having hollow or titanium saddle rails. These flex just enough to give you just a little bit of suspension. A leather upper is more expensive than standard synthetic covers, but will breathe better, which you'll appreciate on hot days or when you're working hard.

Although almost everybody uses a foam- or gel-covered saddle now, some people swear by old-fashioned leather ones. They're rock-hard to begin with, but once you've ridden them for a few hundred miles, the leather breaks into your shape and they fit you perfectly. They need a little more care than normal saddles, but will last for years if not decades.

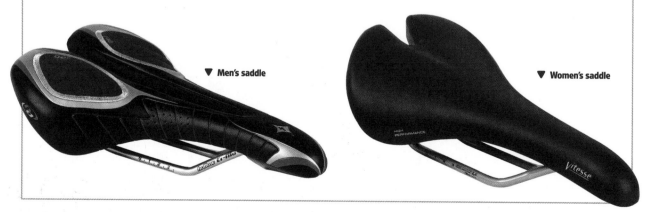

▼ **Men's saddle**

▼ **Women's saddle**

Saddle position

You can make a saddle at least twice as nice to sit on by spending a little time getting the position exactly right. You get to play with three different adjustments – its height, its angle and the length between the bars and the front of the seat. Try to change one at a time, rather than fiddling with everything at once, so that you can pinpoint which adjustments make your bicycle more comfortable.

Saddle height

You would imagine that getting the seat height adjusted correctly would be everyone's first port of call, but the streets are full of people wobbling about because they're perched atop their bicycle as if they were on stilts or because they've got their knees wrapped around their ears. There's no excuse for this and it just makes your entire journey much less comfortable than it should be.

To check your seat height, find a place where you can sit still on your bike in your normal cycling position, leaning against a wall. Look down at your feet. When you're cycling normally, you'll find that the most efficient position for your feet to be in is with the ball of your foot directly over the pedal axle. But just for the purposes of measurement, sit with the heel, rather than the ball, of your foot over the axle. If your seat is at the ideal height, your leg will be almost straight – not locked out, just extended.

Seat height is adjusted at the bottom of the seat post using either an Allen key (4mm, 5mm or 6mm) or a quick-release lever, which you loosen until you can move the post freely.

Fore-and-aft positioning

This is quite a subtle adjustment and it can take a fair amount of fiddling about to find the right place. The fore-and-aft position of the saddle determines how much length there is between the saddle and the bars, and so how upright your sitting position will be when you're holding the bars.

Bringing the saddle forwards will make you more upright and is in many ways equivalent to raising the handlebars. A forward position is often favoured by triathletes – it makes use of similar muscles as running, and so makes the change from one to the other less of a shock. Women also often favour a saddle in a more forward position, placing the pelvis more directly over the pedals. A further aft position will stretch you out more, which you may find more comfortable on long journeys. Change the position of the saddle by loosening the clamp bolt until you can free the saddle rails enough to slide it along in the clamp. Tighten the clamp bolt firmly when you've finished. You'll find that quite small adjustments to the position will make your bike feel quite different, so change it a little at a time.

SADDLE ANGLE

Step 1: In almost all cases, the most comfortable angle for your saddle will be with the top of the saddle either horizontal, or very close to horizontal.

Step 2: If your saddle tips backwards, you'll be pulling yourself forwards with your arms every pedal stroke to counteract the tendency to slide off the back. This can lead to sore shoulders.

Step 3: There can be times when tipping the front of the saddle downwards relieves unpleasant pressure, but an exaggerated angle indicates that either your saddle is the wrong shape for you or your bicycle is too long or just too big. If the saddle tips too far forwards, you'll have to be pushing yourself up and back with your feet constantly, making journeys much more tiring than they need otherwise be.

Choosing pedals

Pedals usually get the shortest shrift when you're thinking about comfort on your bicycle, but remember, along with your hands and your bottom, your feet are in contact with the bicycle all the time. Choosing pedals needs a little care since they have to perform two opposing functions.

Most of the time pedals have to grip your feet firmly so that you stay securely attached to the bicycle. If you stand up off the pedals to sprint up a hill and the soles of your feet slip, you're really going to hurt yourself. If you're stumbling to find a secure position when you set off from the lights, you're going to struggle to accelerate into the stream of traffic. But equally, as soon as you stop, you need to be able to get your feet down and onto the ground as bicycles only hold you upright as long as you're moving along.

Traditionally, this dilemma was solved in two ways. If you considered getting off, safety was paramount which meant you stuck with a pair of flat plastic or rubber pedals that gripped your feet well enough, but assumed you were never going to try to do anything unexpected or sprint about, so the perils of your feet slipping off were low. If you wanted a little more power or were touring and so didn't expect to be getting on and off your bike all day, you strapped yourself into toe clips and straps. These did a great job of keeping your feet attached as long as you cranked the straps tight, but meant that you needed a moment to anticipate stopping so that you could reach down and loosen the straps as you slowed down.

Neither of these two options is ideal for commuting since occasionally you need to be able to get up off the pedals and sprint, knowing you'll stay up off the pedals. But you can't always anticipate stopping, which means a couple of new solutions had to be pinched from different areas of cycling.

BMX-style pedals are designed for an extreme version of the same purposes as commuting – you need your pedals to stick securely to your shoes even if you're six feet off the ground and upside down. But you need to be able to get your feet free in an instant as soon as it becomes apparent that the whole six-feet-off-the-ground-upside-down thing isn't panning out as well as you'd hoped. The pedals, therefore, have big wide platforms so your feet grip only as long as they're anywhere near the pedals. Studs or pins stick upwards, stopping your feet from sliding sideways. In theory, this is perfect for commuting, but in practice, a toned-down, BMX-lite version is a better option as the spiky grip surfaces are just too harsh. If you happen to catch your shins on the pedals, they'll really hurt – BMXers don't seem to care about this as they often wear shin pads – but they're also so sharp they'll rip up the soles of your shoes in no time at all – BMXers don't seem to care much about this either; you wouldn't want to be seen in last year's shoes anyway. But the influence of BMX means plenty of wide, flat pedals with enough pins to keep you attached are available now.

Pedal design has also been stolen from mountain biking. Clipless pedals emerged first in road racing, but there you generally don't have to get off your bike until after a road race has finished so there was never any reason to design the pedals in order to walk in the shoes. Mountain biking created a different need as people wanted to stay securely attached to their pedals, but they also wanted to be able to get off the bike and walk or run or lift it over things they couldn't ride past. This prompted the development of clipless pedals where the cleat is recessed into the sole of the shoe so that it's safe to walk on. The cleat on the sole locks into a sprung mechanism on the pedal, but is shaped so that the action of twisting your feet sideways will unlock the cleat from the pedal instantly. The unlocking movement is an easy, natural twist of your foot, but has to be learned. Once you've got the knack, you don't have to think about it, but during the learning curve there is certainly potential for situations where you don't get your feet out in time.

BMX-style pedals ▶
A normal pedal surface on one side and a clip on the other make these perfect for city riding ▶▶

Pedals: learning to ride clipless

Learning to ride with clipless pedals takes you right back to learning to ride your bike in the first place. Before you can do it, it's impossible to imagine yourself succeeding in this, but after you've worked it out, it seems so simple that you can't remember what it was like not to be able to.

▲ **Ensure that the bolts are greased and tightened securely**

First, fit the new pedals. The left and right pedals are different, and marked 'l' and 'r'. The left-hand pedal has a reverse thread so undoes clockwise and is refitted anticlockwise. The right-hand pedal has a normal thread. Tighten both pedals securely into the cranks. Pedal spanners are thinner than normal ones in order to fit into the gap between crank and pedal, and longer to give you enough leverage to tighten the cranks firmly.

Since you need to have the right size shoes for your feet, you usually have to commit yourself to the clipless pedal idea before you've really had a chance to try them. You'll need a pair of shoes in your size and a pair of clipless pedals. The clipless pedals come with the cleats, which need to be attached to the bottom of the shoes – almost always with a 4mm Allen key.

When new, shoes often (but not always) have a cover hiding the attachment holes on the sole of the shoe. If you're lucky, the cover comes off with a couple of Allen keys. More typically you have to cut a chunk of the sole out of your new shoes – which always seems a bit bizarre. It's also a little tricky – take good care as you do this since you'll need a sharp knife to cut through the rubber and it's all too easy to cut yourself. You'll see the patch to be cut off as soon as you turn the shoe over. Cut neatly around the edge with a sharp knife, then pull off and discard the cover.

Next, it's time for cleat positioning. It's essential that you take a bit of time and care to get the cleat position right. If you ride around with your feet strapped into awkwardly positioned cleats, you can damage your knees. This seems to be particularly problematic for people who've played sports like football which involve lots of knee twisting. If you find yourself getting pains in your knees after fitting cleats, take yourself back to your bike shop and get some advice about cleat fitting. Fit the cleats when you've got enough time to test and readjust them – not just before you set off on a big ride.

The cleat should fit just under or just behind the ball of your foot. It can be tricky to locate where this is on the sole of the shoe, so put your shoes on and have a feel around where your feet fit inside the shoe. Use a bit of tape to mark on the top of the shoes where the middle of the ball of your foot fits and then line the centre of the cleat up with the tape. You'll be able to slide the fitting plate backwards and forwards along the sole of the shoe to find the right place.

It's essential that the cleats point in the right direction. Sit yourself on the edge of a table so that the lower halves of your legs hang vertically and your feet dangle above the floor. Look carefully at the angle your feet hang at as they won't necessarily both point the same way. A good starting point is to set the direction of the cleats so that your feet replicate the angle that they naturally hang at.

Once you've chosen the angle, pop the greased bolts through the cleats including any washers that came with the pack and tighten firmly. Since you'll have to test the cleat position, it's tempting to leave the bolts loose while you do this, but don't because, if the cleats aren't properly tightened into the sole of the shoe, they'll tear out as you try to release your feet.

Then the hard part – you have to teach your feet to get into and out of the cleat. Take a look at the cleat and pedal before you start so that you know what you're trying to do. Lean your bike up against a wall, then try one foot at a time. At first, it takes ages to find the right place for your foot – you have to feel about to engage the front of the cleat and then push down hard to click the back in. Once you're locked in, twist your heel outwards to release. Practise this with both feet separately before you even think about going anywhere. You have to get to a point where you can release your feet without looking or thinking. Once you're confident, take yourself to the park and practise clipping out and then coming to a stop. Don't venture out into traffic until you can come to an emergency stop and get your feet out every time. You'll probably want to readjust the cleat position. Take an Allen key with you on your first few rides and remember to tighten the cleat securely every time. This may seem long-winded, but once you've taught your feet how to do it, they never forget.

Handlebars

Getting the shape and height of your bars right is essential to your comfort. If you're sitting in a position that doesn't suit your body, this will soon make itself known through a sore neck, shoulders, wrists or back.

It can often take a bit of time and a few alterations to the saddle, stem and bars to work out what's wrong. It might be enough simply to change the angle, or height, of the bars. If that doesn't do the job, it may be worth looking at changing bars for a different-shaped pair, although it's difficult to imagine what another pair will feel like until you've had a chance to try them. Part of the problem with positioning is actually aesthetics. People who make and sell bicycles tend to have a fairly clear idea about what a bike should look like: they use words like 'sleek' and 'streamlined'. So they fit flat, straight bars that make the bike look like the kind of thing you want to buy, but isn't necessarily best for your riding style. Bar shape is just as important as position, although the two are intimately connected. If you're looking for an upright position with your back relatively straight, the most comfortable shape for the bars is usually with the grips swept backwards at 30–45°. This means you can grip the bars comfortably without sticking your elbows out. It may seem like a straight bar would be ideal, but the shape of your hands means they grip best at an angle. To see what I mean, find a straight bar, roughly the same diameter as a handlebar and longer than the width of your hand. Hold out your arm in front of you and grip the bar with one hand. You'll see that it doesn't rest comfortably at 90° to your arm as its natural resting position is at an angle to the rest of your body. That's the kind of angle you want the bars to be swept back to so that they drop neatly into your palm.

▲ Straight bars give you precise control for nipping through traffic and make you that bit more aerodynamic

Straight bars

If you're looking for a position that's perhaps a bit more aerodynamic and sporty, you tend to lean further forward over the bars with your arms a bit bent to absorb the shock. This shifts the angle so your palms sit inwards a little and a straighter bar is a more comfortable option. Even then a slight sweep to the bars – between 3° and 6° – will make a big difference. And the angle that this points in can be critical. There was a fashion for a time of angling the sweep so that the bars pointed downwards. It may or may not have looked cool, but it was gruesomely uncomfortable. With relatively straight bars, look carefully at the angle of the sweep. The bars should point up and back, so that the angle of the grips sits neatly into the angle of your palms.

City bars

For pottering around town aerodynamics is one of the least of your concerns and comes some way behind being able to see where you're going and giving other people the best chance to see you. For this a curved, swept-back bar is ideal, bringing the grips upwards and backwards so that you sit more upright. This makes it much easier to turn your head and look behind you. It also makes you tall, so drivers can see your head clearly above traffic when you're busy weaving between lanes.

▼ City bars provide a comfortable, upright position

Drop bars

Being stretched-out and low-down has its advantages too. It makes you less of a target for the wind, saving your energy. In terms of comfort, it also spreads your weight out much more evenly since, instead of being concentrated on your bottom, it's divided between handlebars, saddle and pedals.

Getting the position right takes some fiddling, since the position of the brake-levers is crucial. Many people fit the bars, but leave the bar tape off for a few rides until they've had a good chance to adjust the angle and level of the levers perfectly.

**Drop bars make you aerodynamic with a range of hand positions
They also make you less of a target for the wind ▶**

Different kinds of lock

Because security is so important, your main lock should be a substantial, heavy-duty lock. You've got a basic choice between the more common U-locks and chunky motorcycle-style chains. In any price bracket, both styles offer a similar level of security and have advantages and disadvantages.

Chain-style locks are easier to pass around odd-shaped bits of street furniture. U-locks are easier to fit onto your frame and will usually come complete with a bracket that you can use to attach them. Some people prefer U-locks because it seems a bit mad to carry a heavy lock yourself when you have a bicycle that will do the job without complaining. Cyclists worry about carrying big chains around their waist because of the danger of landing on them if they fall off their bike. But it's all down to preference.

Your best bet with a U-lock is to go for one of the big brands – Kryptonite, Abus, Trelock, or Squire. Each manufacturer has its own testing regime, but there isn't a universally accepted test that can be used to compare locks of different brands. If you're insured, check that your insurer doesn't stipulate particular locks before you buy something – a lock may be perfectly good and strong, but if it wasn't on their approved list, they may refuse to make a payout. If they do insist on particular locks, keep the receipt when you buy one to prove that you had one of the acceptable kind. All decent locks are heavy by comparision with your light bike, which is a fairly depressing fact of cycling life.

Your main lock – whatever shape it is – should be used to lock your frame and one of your wheels. This leaves your other wheel vulnerable to theft, so a second lock is a good idea. Quick-release wheels are the easiest to steal, while old-fashioned wheels with nuts mean that the thief needs a spanner. But spanners aren't difficult to get hold of, so in some ways quick-release wheels are an advantage because they stop you from being complacent about locking your wheels up properly. A simple cable is usually sufficient for your second lock. The easiest to use are the extension cables with a loop at either end. Your main lock locks the frame and a wheel with the extension cable looped around the other wheel, slipping the extension cable loops onto your U-lock before closing it. If the extension cable is slightly longer, you can use it to secure your saddle as well. Thread the extension cable through your saddle rails and then pop one end of the extension cable through the loop at the other end. Pull all the way through. When you come to lock up, pass the free end through your back wheel and then stretch it forwards. Thread your U-lock through the frame, the front wheel and some substantial street furniture. Then slip the free end of the extension cable onto the U-lock and close it. When you're unlocking, disentangle the extension from the back wheel, but leave it wrapped around the saddle rails – use a toestrap or a Velcro strip to keep it from hanging into the back wheel as you ride along, or wrap it around your seat post. An alternative to using an extender lock is to use a coil lock as your secondary security. If the thought of having two separate keys is too confusing, the coil lock could be a combination lock.

▲ **A U-lock is easy to fit round your frame and stops opportunist thieves**

There are, obviously, myriad little gadgets you can buy to make your bike more secure. The most common of these are security skewers for your wheels. These can only be released with an Allen key. The more sophisticated systems use custom shapes and sizes of Allen key, so you can only release your wheels if you have the special key that comes with your skewer set. These are a great idea, but do make sure they're tightened securely as far too many people cycle around with loosely attached security skewers.

Many new bikes come with a quick-release lever that you use to adjust the seat height. These are especially common on mountain bikes when you often find yourself in situations where it would help to be able to change the seat height quickly. For instance, you might want to lower your seat before riding down a steep slope or jumping off a ledge. Riding around town, there are very few occasions when you need to change your seat height. If you're buying a new bike and it has a quick-release seat post, get it swapped for one that requires an Allen key.

It won't completely stop your seat and seat post being stolen, but it does make it a little more difficult.

Combination locks are quick and easy to use and don't require a key ▶

Locking your bike securely: where and how

You can buy all the locking and security devices in the world, but it's not worth as much as taking a little bit of care about where and when you lock up your bike. A lock won't do any good unless you use it every time. Otherwise, you're providing the light-fingered with a swift means of escape and depriving yourself of the means to chase them down. Even if you can run fast enough to keep up with somebody sprinting off on your bike, it's unclear what you would do if you actually caught them.

▲ Safety in numbers: park your bike in busy places

You've got to lock to something solid as well. A bicycle that's locked to itself is impossible to ride and fairly difficult to carry, but it's the work of a second to sling into the back of a van, where it disappears instantly. Signposts need a little care as it's easy enough to lift a locked bike up and over the top of shorter ones. Choose something tall with a big sign on the top.

Thefts that happen when your bike is locked to itself or not locked at all are usually the work of opportunists, who can't resist an easy lift. If you're leaving your bike for longer, you need to think about the more professional approach to depriving you of your bicycle. If you're commuting to work every day and you always work in the same place, it's worth investing in a second lock. Two locks are too heavy to carry around all the time as they'll make your bike feel sluggish and unexciting, but you can leave the heavier one locked up at work and just use it when you get there. Even better is if you can negotiate getting your bike into your work – perhaps there's a few of you that all cycle to work and you could get together and ask for somewhere safe to leave your bike during the day.

If you're on the street, crowded places are better than back streets, where somebody can fiddle about with your bike undisturbed.

The recent explosion in CCTV everywhere doesn't seem to help much in the fight against bicycle theft, but it might help psychologically to park somewhere that's obviously in full view of a camera.

If you're locking your bike to railings in the street, it pays to spend a while considering the best spot. On a busy road, the outside of railings is often a good bet. Anyone attempting to fiddle with your lock or your bike will have to contend with the risk of being run over. Even better are central reservations. They're very exposed, in full view of both passing pedestrians and car drivers. Avoid narrow pavements, where your locked-up bike will impede pedestrians pushing buggies or carrying lots of shopping. You'll annoy people, which is bad, and your bike may get damaged as people push past.

Finally, if you're forced to lock up somewhere that looks dodgy, lock your bike near someone else's that looks flashier in the hope that thieves will ignore yours and go for the eye candy.

Luggage: pannier options

The existence of panniers makes bicycles about twice as useful as they would otherwise be. Suddenly, they're not just great for carrying you around – they take care of all your goods and chattels as well. Backpacks and shoulder bags are all very well, but they're not ideal on a bicycle. They leave you with sore backs and shoulders and big sweaty patches wherever they sit on your body.

Panniers, however, swallow all your stuff and sit securely on your bike. Good ones will hardly alter the handling and, unlike plastic bags slung from your bars, they won't get caught in the spokes as you pedal.

There is, of course, a vast price range. Your choice will depend on how far you travel and how much you carry. Simple, cheap, nylon panniers are fine for short trips and are cheap enough to replace if they give up the ghost after a particularly enthusiastic shopping trip. The weather will have an effect on your decision too as, if you ride in the rain and carry papers, documents or a laptop, you'll need a waterproof pannier – wrapping things in plastic bags should work but it never does. A secure fitting also gets more important if the contents of your bag are valuable. More sophisticated bags have a locking clip, rather then a simple hook that clips under, as well as over, the tubes of the rack.

If you have to lug the bags around at either end of your journey, it's worth searching for something with a shoulder strap. Panniers work best on the bike in pairs, but once you've left your bike, you've got one in each hand, which doesn't leave room for you to carry anything else or to use your front door keys to open the door. Look also for reflective strips on the backs and sides of the bags as these are remarkably effective in car headlights. If you're intending going camping, the more traditional type of bags with a smattering of differently sized and shaped pockets make it easy to organise your possessions. Bright, cheerful colours help you stand out against the traffic and a light-coloured fabric inside the bag makes it very much easier to see what you've got in there.

One of the shortcomings of panniers is their well-established dislike of neat, flat A4 paper. They have an amazing capacity for making a sheet of it look like a piece of teenage homework finished on the school bus. If this kind of thing doesn't enhance your status at work, consider swapping one of your panniers for a briefcase/office-style bag. These are stiffened to keep the contents looking as they should and double up as a respectable executive-type bag. A combination of a normal pannier on one side – for your clothes, lunch or whatever – and a briefcase on the other balances the load on your bike and keeps smart things away from potentially wet and messy things. Padded inserts mean they'll carry a laptop, too.

1) Secure pannier hooks have an extra tab that locks under the tubing of your rack.

2) Reflective stripes or patches stand out well as they present a broad face to traffic coming up behind you.

3) Handles are essential as full bags are unwieldy otherwise.

4) Hooks at the base of the pannier allow you to compress your load with the shoulder strap, keeping the contents from flopping about and throwing you off balance.

5) Rugged, water-resistant fabric. These panniers have waterproof fabric with welded seams.

6) Watertight closure. Waterproof fabric won't do you any good if the rain can leak in through the openings. In this case, a roll-type fitting means that you can throw the bag in the sea without getting the contents soggy.

7) Wide, square shapes give plenty of capacity.

8) D-loops for a shoulder strap – essential when you have two panniers.

Racks

Racks are an essential first step before you can fit panniers and are also dead handy for strapping random bits of stuff to. For cheap theft-proofing use zipties to strap a second-hand shopping basket or fruit box to the top. It's perfect for slinging shopping into and makes your bike look instantly less appealing to the light-fingered.

There are myriad different rack styles, but luckily most work in the same sort of way. A leg on either side bolts onto the back of your frame, just above the rear wheel axle, and a pair of 'stays' – metal arms – reach forward from the front of your rack and bolt onto the top of the seatstays.

Almost all modern bicycles have special lugs or eyelets to attach racks and mudguards to. They take two forms: a hole may be drilled in the frame and then threaded so that you can screw a bolt into it or a small extra piece of metal may be attached to the frame with a threaded hole already in it. These lugs make rack fitting easier and more secure. In some circumstances, your bike may not have the correct lugs for fitting a rack to. It may be quite old, or it may be a road bike that's designed for racing, when the manufacturer will not be expecting you to fit a rack. All is not lost as you can get special rack brackets from your local bike shop that wrap around the frame and replace the lugs. These are fine if you're going to be carrying shopping or panniers but are not secure enough if you're intending to fit a child seat to the rack. You'll have to think again and either buy a child seat where the bracket bolts directly to the frame or carry your child around on a different bicycle.

Rack (and mudguard) bolts have a tendency to work loose over time. Check them regularly and especially before you set out on a long trip. If you find they have a habit of working loose, apply a small drop of threadlock to the threads before you fit them. Don't overdo it – the screws are very small so a tiny drop will do the trick. If you don't have any threadlock, nail varnish makes a fine substitute. Also, always fit a washer directly under each bolt head since, without one, the bolts will work loose much more quickly. Since racks are mostly made of soft aluminium, tightening the bolts down too hard without a washer will damage the rack around the bolt hole.

Racks will come supplied with a selection of hardware for fitting to your bike. Since nuts and bolts have such a well-known tendency to rattle loose, they're supplied with shake-proof nuts. These look like ordinary nuts, but have a thin plastic ring tucked in above the threads. The inside of the ring is slightly smaller than the bolt diameter, so that, as you tighten the bolt, the nylon ring grips it. It's confusing when you try to fit the nuts since, when you thread the bolt through the shake-proof nut, it moves easily at first and then gets stiff, which makes you think it's the wrong size. Don't worry, it's meant to be like that, but you'll have to hold the nut with a spanner while threading it onto the bolt.

If you're going to be carrying panniers, choose the type of rack that has a dog-leg. This means that the rear leg of the rack is bent backwards and stops the bottom corner of the pannier from getting caught in the back wheel as you ride along. You'll also need to set the rack up so that the top is flat and so that it's set far enough back to ensure the backs of your heels don't hit the front of the pannier as you pedal.

Occasionally, you'll find that the threads that the rack bolts screw into have become clogged with paint and you won't be able to get the bolts in. You'll need to clean the threads out with a small tool called a tap. It's like a bolt, but with sharp threads. You may want to take this to your bike shop to get done. Don't be tempted to just force the bolt into the threads as the chances are that it will snap off in the clogged thread and be a nightmare to remove without damaging your frame.

▲ The 'dog-leg' of the rack stays stop your panniers from getting caught in your back wheel

Shoulder bags and backpacks

For short journeys, where you're stopping and starting constantly and have to rustle about in your bag for keys, the A–Z, packages or whatever, a shoulder bag is perfect. You can swing the bag around your body and get into it really easily. This makes a shoulder bag perfect for messengers.

For the rest of us there is a big limitation as carrying a heavy bag slung over one shoulder tires your back out. Messenger bags are handy as the subdivided pockets and various flaps, clips and tabs make it easy to keep things organised, but you're still putting unnecessary stress on your body. If you insist on a shoulder bag, make sure it has a comfortable, padded strap and don't overfill it.

The ideal solution is always panniers – why buy a bike then go to the trouble of carrying stuff yourself? But for lighter loads a rucksack is a lot more convenient, since it gets off the bike when you do and needs no extra hands to carry. A well-designed rucksack will spread the weight evenly between your shoulders and the better ones have raised padded areas down either side. These keep the weight off your spine and allow air to circulate between the bag and your back, to prevent that sticky, sweaty feeling.

If you're going to use a rucksack on your bike a lot, choose something that's been specifically designed for cycling. Camelbak, Karrimor and Deuter (shown here) all make a range of cycling rucksacks. These usually have a waist strap, which are more important for cycling than for walking. When you're stretched out over the bike, a waist strap will reduce the tendency for your bag to roll across your back as you ride. It also spreads the weight more evenly between your shoulders and your waist.

Other useful features round town are loops of webbing that you can clip an extra back light onto. These always appear to be too low down when you try the bag on, but lower is better when you're on the bike, leaning forwards, since they point the light right backwards.

▲ Messenger bags are convenient for short trips

Waterproof covers, especially if they're in bright colours or have reflective strips, are great for bad weather as even if the rucksack fabric itself is waterproof, rain can leak into the bag through seams and zips. Good rucksacks often have a special little pocket for the rain cover separate from the rest of the bag, so that, when you arrive at your destination, you can tuck the wet rain cover away without soaking the rest of your belongings.

Most cycling backpacks are designed so that they can be used off-road. The idea of designing rucksacks specifically for cycling is another result of the influence of mountain biking. Rucksacks were pressed into service for carrying flexible plastic bags of water with a tube coming out the bottom that you can attach to the rucksack strap near your mouth. The bags quickly and inevitably came to be called bladders and the idea turned out to be very popular. On longer rides, they allow you to sip water frequently without having to stop riding and therefore encourage you to drink more water, instead of getting dehydrated.

This is a great idea for whole days in the saddle, but perhaps excessive for a simple commute where, if you suddenly realise you're thirsty, you can pop into a shop and buy something to drink. Rucksacks often come with a bladder and, if they don't, there will be a compartment at the back which you can use to slip a bladder into.

Round town, the bladder compartment should be the perfect size and shape to pop a newspaper into.

Rucksacks spread the weight across your back ▶

Trailers

Panniers, rucksacks and the like are all very well for the normal day-to-day loads that you're going to have to carry about with you. But some days you'll find yourself needing to move about something that's particularly large, heavy or even just an awkward shape – basically, unsuitable for either pannier or rucksack.

It's a bad idea to use your back for transporting heavy loads – that's what you have a bicycle for. Some loads are not particularly heavy – they're just a bit larger than pannier-sized. Fruit and vegetables are an obvious example as they don't weight much, but the stuff at the bottom will suffer if you stack it into a pair of panniers and then bounce down the road on your bike.

Trailers are a great option for these loads. When it comes to heavy stuff, they spread the weight out over more wheels. Lugging too much stuff about in your panniers will prematurely age your back wheel and tyre. Trailers have smaller wheels, which can take more weight without buckling. A larger, stiff base area allows you to stack your produce in a thinner layer so you don't squash soft or fragile items. The lower centre of gravity also means that the load doesn't sway about alarmingly if you stand up off the saddle to climb a hill.

People often worry that they will jackknife a trailer going round corners. Provided the trailer isn't overloaded and the load is secure, this is actually quite difficult to do. The real problem is forgetting that the trailer is there since, once you've got used to having it tagging along behind you, you won't notice it unless it's very heavy. This is fine until you try to slip between some bollards, whereupon you'll get brought to a halt quite abruptly. If the pavements are busy with pedestrians, watch out for people waiting to cross by the side of the road. They'll let you and your bike go by and then step out into your trailer. Fit a bell to your bars and use it often when it's busy as it seems to shake pedestrians out of whatever dream they're having and encourage them to actually look at you.

Trailers at night need a bit of thought as they're much lower than drivers expect, so fit as many lights to them as you can. Many come with a flag on a thin pole – at night, fix a light to the flagpole because the flag itself won't be visible.

Single-wheel trailers are the simplest and the best-known are made by BOB. These come with a special replacement quick-release skewer for your rear wheel. The trailer has an arm on either side at the front, which hooks over the slots on the special skewer and locks into place. It's very quick to attach or remove. The single wheel makes it very manoeuvrable and the narrow width means you can slip through the gaps in traffic. It's no wider than an average set of handlebars, so the trailer follows you through any gap. A single-wheel trailer is the only option if you want to go off road as two wheels are always too wide.

Two-wheeler trailers are more stable when riding along and also when parked as they're easier to load and unload. But they do take up more space, which can be an issue if your home isn't vast. Folding versions take care of this and the best will pack flat in seconds. Burley makes a great cargo trailer that unhooks from your bike and folds flat in a couple of minutes. Trailers have a downside in that decent ones will set you back a lot more money than a pair of panniers and, unless you're delivering heavy stuff on a regular basis, you won't need them that often. But if you can find a group of people to share one between, they're great fun.

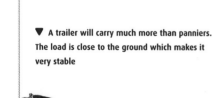
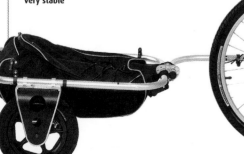

▼ A trailer will carry much more than panniers. The load is close to the ground which makes it very stable

Baskets, bar bags and toolbags

Panniers, briefcases and rucksacks are all very well and solve most simple transport problems, but sometimes something a little more specialized is called for in the luggage department.

Baskets are right up alongside an expensive U-lock on the list of effective theft-proofing devices. They seem to work as camouflage, blinding others to the value of your steed. The wicker versions are particularly good at this, but the wire mesh versions aren't bad either.

They're also great for short-hop shopping trips, when they'll swallow all sorts of odd-shaped packages without you needing to worry about clipping and unclipping your luggage every other step. Bigger baskets – deeper than about 35cm – need to be supported from underneath to stop them drooping onto the front wheel. A front rack does the job perfectly, but you can also get specific basket supports that clamp on either side of your front wheel. Smaller baskets, where there isn't as much potential for overloading, can clip onto the bars. The Busch & Muller one in the picture has a quick-release fitting, so will snap on and off the bike very easily.

Tool packs

An emergency tool pack and a tube make you self-sufficient in an emergency, but the rest of the time they're just heavy and clutter up your bag. The tools also tend to be grubby, so need to be kept separate from the other contents of your bag, like paperwork and sandwiches.

If you're lucky enough to be able to leave your bike somewhere secure, rather than having to lock it up all the time, the best option is a seat pack that sits under your saddle since it keeps everything in one place and means it's always all there, rather than you having to remember to pack it every time you leave the house. A tool pack keeps the extra weight off your back and on your bike and, if you have the misfortune to come off your bike, tucking all the hard sharp tools away under your saddle makes you less likely to land on them. They're just the right size for tools and a tube and will keep everything together neatly even if you end up having to take it off your bike and stuff the whole thing in your bag occasionally.

▲ Baskets make shopping trips easy and keep everything where you can see it!

Barbags

Barbags are traditionally the preserve of those highly organised and intrepid bands of long-distance cycle tourists, but need to be rehabilitated for town use. Smaller than a pannier, they're the perfect receptacle for all those urban essentials, like phones and front door keys.

The bag sits right in front of you where you can see it and they always have a clear map case on the top, which works just as well for your A–Z as it does for Outer Mongolian route maps.

Modern versions have simple one-handed quick-release brackets, rather than stiff leather straps and a shoulder strap leaves you hands-free off the bike.

Despite their association with drop handlebar road bikes, the bracket will clamp perfectly neatly onto more common flat or curved bars. They're also a handy box shape, so the stiff sides stop your cakes from getting squashed.

◄ Seat packs are perfect for carrying tools as well as a spare tube

Front racks

A rack at the back is plenty for normal amounts of luggage. You can fit a good big pair of panniers to it and unless you need to lug an unusual amount of stuff around with you, they will carry more on your bike than you can manage on foot. But some circumstances require a slightly different approach.

You either need a front rack because a back rack on its own isn't enough or because you haven't got room for a back rack. If you regularly drop your child off at school on your way to work, your child seat fills the space that your panniers would otherwise fit into. You can't easily sling a rucksack or shoulder bag on your back, because it'll sit in the tiny gap between you and them at their head level. A front rack may be your only option for stowage and will help to counterbalance the weight of your child at the back of the bike.

If you're touring by bicycle – rather than simply getting to work and back – you may find that your rear panniers won't hold enough gear as tents, sleeping bags, warm clothes and food take up a fair amount of space if you're off for more than a couple of days. Front panniers spread the weight evenly over the whole bike, which makes it feel more stable and corner more easily.

In either case, best results are achieved if the centre of gravity of the panniers is as close as possible to the front-wheel axle. This is much more important for the front wheel than for the back wheel, because the front wheel of the bike has to be able to move easily from side to side. The big movements – for example when you steer around something – are the most noticeable, but you're also rocking the front of the bike constantly from side to side as you pedal. If the weight of the panniers hangs much higher than the wheel axle, the wheel will tend to flop from side to side. Once it starts moving in one direction, it will tend to carry on over and needs to be wrestled upright, rather than self-correcting back towards the centreline.

This means that good front racks have a slightly different design to rear ones. Instead of having a platform on the top, there's a much simpler frame that holds the pannier away from the wheel on either side. The hooks on the pannier fit over the top of the frame and are prevented from sliding off the front or back by small lugs. This type of rack is called a 'low rider'.

Since they're lower to the ground, front panniers need to be quite a lot smaller than rear ones. This is a good thing, since it prevents you from overloading them, which will make steering hard work however well you've balanced the loads. But smaller panniers can be great when you're camping – separating out some of the essentials you need to be able to access quickly without rummaging through all your various pieces of luggage.

Front panniers come in two different types. The most solid type is called 'custom'. These bolt directly to each fork leg, but can only be used if the fork legs have the right rack fitting –

a threaded hole about halfway up the leg and an eyelet before and behind the bottom of the fork leg beside the dropout. There's a square loop frame on either side with a separate stiffening hoop that connects the fronts of the two frames over the top of your tyre.

If you don't have these threaded fittings, all is not lost – as long as you have an eyelet near each dropout, you can use a slightly clunkier version of the same thing, which uses a threaded U-bolt around each fork leg to attach the frames to the fork legs.

Once you've fitted the racks, adjust the positions of the pannier hooks, so that the bag fits as evenly as possible on the rack and the hooks can't slide from side to side. Tuck up any loose trailing straps since the last thing you want is for these to get caught in the front wheel.

You can take everything but the kitchen sink with you ▶

Front lights

Lights tend to be thought of as an added extra, but I can't see the point of having a bicycle if you're only going to use it in daylight. Front lights have two purposes which are equally important when the sun has gone down. They allow you to see along an unlit road and they also allow other road-users to pick you out in the dark.

On busy urban streets, the latter is much more of an issue. Generally, streetlights allow you to pick out enough detail around you to see where you're going, but those same streets also contain so many distracted drivers that a bright light is essential to attract any scraps of their attention. Flashing lights have a chequered legal history, but can help pick you out in busy traffic as drivers have seen enough of them by now to begin to know what they mean. It's difficult to be sure whether a flashing light is better than a steady light, but if in doubt, go for both – you can't have too many lights and one of each gives you a backup in case the other fails.

Your local bike shop will be full of front light options. Basic battery lights are best for occasional use, being relatively cheap. They usually come supplied with their own quick-release bracket, which is essential since there are as many different types of brackets as there are makes of lighting. If you've got more than one bike, pick up a spare bracket at the same time. Sadly, you can't necessarily assume they'll still be available as spares later.

If you're using the bike more than occasionally at night, it makes sense to think about rechargeable batteries. Using endless disposable ones is expensive. The best come with their own charger, so you just have to plug the lights in, rather than worry about taking the batteries out. This may not seem much of a problem, but generally lights have to go on charge just as you get home, while you still remember. In the winter it can just end up being one mission too many when you come in out of the cold, so you forget and then go out again with half-charged lights and get caught out.

For really serious commuting and long rides on unlit roads, look to the night lights that have been inspired by mountain bikers riding off road. Although much more expensive than standard bike lights – three or four times the price – these have a separate battery pack that straps on your frame or under your stem with a cord that leads to a small neat light unit on the bars. The separate parts mean that they're much more time-consuming to take on and off your bike and heavier to carry around, but you get enough light out of them to make oncoming drivers sit up and take notice as well as enough battery life to get you home. Once you're out of range of streetlights, the extra brightness means you can pick out potholes and loose road surfaces before you're upon them. The faster you travel, the brighter your light needs to be to keep up.

Rechargeable batteries are made in different ways – some need to be run down completely before they can be recharged, others should be switched off as soon as they dim. A new light will come with battery care instructions which will extend battery life considerably. If your usual commute is in busy traffic, think about a helmet light. Your head is **usually hi**gh up enough above cars to allow a light to be seen. This is particularly useful when you need to ensure you're visible to drivers pulling out of side turnings. If you're negotiating gloomy sidestreets, a helmet light means you can illuminate dark corners before you get there. LED versions are powerful enough to show you where you're going, without eating up batteries or giving you a headache from the weight.

Be seen at night ▶

Lights and computers

Your rear-facing red light has a much simpler task than the front light – it's just there so nobody runs you over. As with the front light, the best answer as to whether you should have flashing or steady lights is that you really should go for both as you really can't have too many rear lights.

The other advantage of having two separate lights is that you can't see them when you're riding along, so an extra set is insurance against one of them running out of batteries, bouncing off or switching off.

Carrying panniers with rear lights is often a bit of a tricky combination as one tends to obscure the other. Get somebody to stand behind you and tell you whether you can be seen from behind or not – if the tops of the panniers obscure the light, it will have to be moved upwards or backwards. Sometimes this can take a little ingenuity, so ask your bike shop for help as they'll probably have a little drawer of odd brackets that could be adapted to extend your normal light fitting. Panniers sometimes come with light pockets that face backwards and have a clear plastic panel your light shines through. They're a great idea for eliminating bracket hassles.

Lights on your rucksack or shoulder bag can be a mixed blessing. They have the advantage of always being there and don't have to be taken off your bike every time you leave it. But the positioning is tricky – far too many people cycle merrily around with a bright red light pointing directly up at the sky, which is useless unless you need to make emergency signals to aircraft. If you go down this route, get somebody to stand behind you and check which way you're pointing. Bags and rucksacks often have a webbing loop that lights can be clipped onto, which often but not always point in the desired direction.

Check and replace batteries on rear lights regularly as a subtle red glow under your saddle is not enough to wake up dozy drivers approaching from the rear. Dirty lenses don't help either – give them a wipe sometimes.

Your bike shop will probably have a daunting array of different back lights, all looking very similar but carrying different price tags. A more expensive light will contain more LEDs, and so be more visible from further away, which is worth paying a little bit extra for. You'll also get a more robust construction and bettter weatherproofing.

▲ **A good bright light gives motorists plenty of time to see you**

Computers

Computers are exactly the kind of thing many people ride bikes to get away from, but if it's important to know how fast you're going or how far you've gone, they're a handy little gadget. They're most useful if you're claiming mileage as work expenses and are also handy for navigating on longer trips. If you're reading the map and know that your next turnoff is in five miles, it helps to know when to start looking.

They calculate how far you've travelled by counting the number of times a little magnet fitted to your spokes passes a sensor fitted to your forks and multiplying that by the distance around your wheel. This means the computer needs to know how big your wheel is, so you usually have to spend a bit of time with a new computer setting it up and calibrating it. Once you've done that the first time, you shouldn't have to fiddle again.

Some computers have amazing features such as altitude measuring, heart rate monitoring and the like. Don't get so carried away when you're riding along that you forget to look where you're going. Normally, the fitting is relatively painless, although the initial calibrating can be confusing. Keep and follow the instructions – each model needs to be calibrated in a particular way. Wireless models use a radio signal from the sensor to the computer. They're more expensive, but easier to fit, neater and you don't have to worry about wires getting caught up and torn.

Dynamos

Dynamos are a seriously underrated piece of kit. Far too many people have a memory of really ancient versions, fitted to dodgy Seventies shopping bikes that barely cast the faintest of flickers on the road while adding enough resistance to your tyre to slow you down to a crawl.

It doesn't have to be like this! Decent, modern dynamos use very little of your power – some versions quote 0.5 per cent of your output – and are efficient enough to light up the road ahead of you as well as or better than a good set of battery lights. They have other advantages too: dynamos are always fixed to your bike, so you never get stuck without lights because you've stayed out later than you expected to. You never realise that you've left your dynamo behind on a pub table. If you're concerned about your effect on the environment, anything that reduces the number of batteries you use has to be a good thing, so rechargeable ones are better than disposables but no batteries is better still. Finally, the little hum they give off is kind of reassuring when you're rolling along quiet streets on your own late at night.

There are two basic types. Sidewall dynamos are bolted onto your bike, either onto the frame at the back or onto the forks at the front. They can be fitted to almost any bike, although folding bikes and suspension bikes often require a little inventiveness. Their advantage is they're simple and can be swapped from bike to bike. You do need to keep an eye on the sidewall of the tyre as the head of the dynamo will wear away at it slowly. Swap tyres over front to back or just reverse them every few months.

A second, slightly more complex, option is available. Several manufacturers, including Schmidt and Shimano, make hub dynamos. These replace your front hub with a generator so that electricity is produced continuously as you ride along. This may seem like a waste, creating drag during the day when you don't need light, but in fact they draw so little power that you'd be pushed to notice the dynamo is there. The drawback is that the hub is integral to your front wheel – you can't just bolt the unit onto your bike. The best time to convert to a hub dynamo is when you need a new front wheel as it makes the extra cost of the dynamo unit a bit less painful.

Either way, once you've got a generator attached to your bike, you've got to think about the actual lamp units and then connect it all together. If you're going to be riding a lot at night, it's worth considering the type of light where the lamp unit collects a little extra store of energy and keeps on shining for a couple of minutes after you've stopped moving. This is useful when you're waiting at traffic lights or turn across the traffic in the middle of the road.

It's well worth having a spare bulb for your dynamo lights. The front and back are usually different voltages and there are also a couple of different fittings, so keep one of each in hand and replace blown bulbs straight away. If you don't, all the power that was meant for both lights goes through the remaining bulb and will blow that as well.

Earthing

This is a bit of a diversion in a book about mechanics, but if we're talking about dynamos, we have to spend a moment on wiring. The whole dynamo wiring thing is made out to be a bit of a complex matter, requiring at least a degree in physics. It's actually remarkably simple. The electricity is generated in the generator. It must flow out to the bulb, then back to the generator. The part where it flows back is essential – if there isn't a complete circuit, the electricity will not flow. The section of the circuit from the generator to the bulb is called the 'live'. The section back from the bulb to the generator is called the 'earth'. The live section is always a wire. In many cases, instead of having a separate 'earth' wire, people use the frame of the bicycle instead because, if it's made of

metal, it will conduct electricity. The back of the bulb is connected to the frame or the metal stay of the mudguards and so is the generator. This works perfectly well in theory, but doesn't tend to be as reliable as a wire. A separate earth wire means a little bit more wiring on your frame, but as long as you're tidy about it, it takes up no extra room. If you're running both a front and a back light, they will each need a separate circuit from the generator to the bulb and back. For details on how to fit a dynamo to your bike, see Chapter 9.

Front light, generator and rear light – self-sufficiency in the darkness ▶

Mudguards

Countries with a long history of cycling as a means of transport and a healthy amount of rain, don't seem to be affected by the aesthetics of mudguards. There are, however, many places in the world where the humble, hardworking mudguard is regarded with something approaching scorn.

However, if you have to look smart when you arrive at your destination and there's a chance of rain, fit full mudguards. Once they're fitted, you don't have to think about them again, they don't need adjusting and they will last for years without wearing out. If you think they look ugly, there's a chance that the person thinking about stealing your bike thinks so too, so that's a bonus.

Don't be tempted to leave off the front mudguard. In wet weather, your front tyre picks up water as it rotates. Once you pick up speed, this is scooped up by the tyre tread and sprayed off backwards, where it's neatly aimed at your shoes. A front mudguard will keep your toes drier and make your shoes last a little longer.

Mudguard bolts do have a habit of rattling loose and leaving their stays – the thin rods that connect the mudguard to the frame – flapping in the wind where they're in danger of becoming entangled in your spokes. Deal with loose stays straight away. Make sure there's a washer under the head of all stay bolts and drip a drop of threadlock onto the threads before you fit them. If you don't have threadlock in your toolbox, nail polish makes a very effective substitute, irrespective of shade.

If you really can't bear the thought of proper mudguards, but still want to ride your bike in wet seasons, plastic clip-on ones will do the job better than nothing as a last resort. They're not as long or as close-fitting as proper ones, but can be popped on and off according to the weather forecast. Of course, if you take them off, chances are you'll lose them before it next rains. If you're using your mountain bike for commuting and you need to be able to strip it down for off-road use at a moment's notice, clip-ons suddenly become the sensible choice. Mountain bikes may also be missing the threaded eyelets you need to bolt mudguard stays onto, which reduces your options to clip ons. In which case choose something that follows the profile of the wheel as closely as possible.

Narrow versions are available that are specially made for road bikes where there may not be enough room between frame and fork for anything to fit through. Here, the mudguard is attached to the stays via two plastic blocks, one on either side. These can be secured with small rubber straps for maximum speed of removal. For a slightly more permanent temporary fit, they can be ziptied onto the stay, which reduces irritating rattling.

▲ **Mudguards should fit close to the wheel**

Front mudguards need to be taken particular care with. It's all too easy to treat them casually as, after all, there's no getting away from the fact that they're a cheap piece of plastic. But they live out their lives perilously close to your front wheel. If they're allowed to flap about, they'll get caught in the gap between your tyre and your fork, bringing you to an unscheduled halt and probably bringing you off your bike in the process. However little your front mudguard cost and however ugly it makes your bike look, it must be secure. Take hold of it and wobble it about – if you can get the tail end of it to touch your tyre, there's a possibility it will get caught. If it can be secured, do so before you ride. If it can't, take it off altogether.

◀ **Quick-release fitting**

Storing your bicycle inside

If you're not in the habit of using your bike regularly, you have to find ways to make it as easy as possible to just pop out on it. When you find the journey turning into a mission, the chances are you'll find some other means of transport. Give yourself as much chance as possible by making your bike as ready as it can be.

Living on the ground floor with a big hallway makes life easy as you can park inside the door and just wheel out whenever the urge takes you. But if you live up several flights of stairs or don't have a hallway big enough for your bike, it can take a bit of planning and investment.

Lifts are generally easy to deal with as all but the oldest are designed for wheelchair access and you can get a bicycle into any space you can get a wheelchair into. You'll have to roll the bike up onto its back wheel, so that it's balanced vertically – this sounds unwieldy, but once it's there, use your back brake to control it.

If you live in an older block, look around and see if there are any unused rooms that could be converted to bike storage on the ground floor. This often requires some negotiation. Most success seems to come from approaching other cyclists in your block and making a joint case to your landlord – perhaps you can get a new lock fitted to an old boiler room, with security keys given out in exchange for a deposit.

Storage in shared narrow halls can be a bit of an issue as bicycles fill places very quickly. As well as problems with fire exits, your pedals and handlebars always end up sticking out sideways, ready to bite the unwary non-cyclists who share your entranceway. It's best if you can get the bike up off the ground, where it won't snag anyone's ankles or fall over. A simple hook in the wall might be the solution but this will depend on the exact shape of your hall. Here are some starting points.

If there's an out-of-the-way corner, hang your bicycle vertically in it. A simple hook coming out of the wall at shoulder height is about right as it should point sideways, so that you lift your front wheel up and slide it in under the end of the hook. Your bike will hang there happily, pointing straight upwards as if you were cycling directly up the wall. You can get these from bike shops or hardware stores and you're looking for a hook that's big enough to fit easily around your front tyre.

Wall racks that lift your bike right up and out of the way keep hallways clear. Success depends mainly on what your wall is made of and whether it has the strength to support your bike. Storage racks and hooks usually come supplied with fixing bolts or screws, but this is no guarantee that they'll be suitable, or big enough, for your wall material. If your walls aren't particularly sturdy, swap the screws supplied for longer ones or for the appropriate type of fixture for the fabric of your building.

For narrow hallways even lifting your bike upwards doesn't necessarily help since, if it hangs parallel to the wall, the width of your bars will mean that it may well stick out inconveniently across the hall. A device that hangs the bike off the pedal, like a Mountain Ledge, can be just the right thing – keeping the pedal close in to the wall means that the bike hangs against the wall at an angle. With the wheels tucked in close against the wall, the bars stick outwards, but as long as you get the whole bike high enough the wide bits will be above head height.

Whichever type of indoor storage you use, think about security. Shared hallways seem to provide an abundant harvest for opportunist bicycle thieves. Lock your bike to something solid so that it doesn't get 'liberated'.

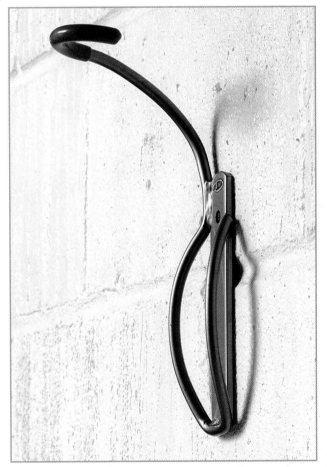

Hanging your bike on a bike hook can solve storage problems ▶

3 – Basic tools and repairs

One great thing about modern bicycles is that a large proportion of the fitting, adjusting and replacing of components can be done with a fairly small selection of tools. You don't need to spend a fortune to go a long way towards being self-sufficient. The ability to carry out basic repairs will also go a long way towards the same aim. This chapter takes you through some of the more common tools, explaining what they're for, when you need them and what the basic repairs you should get to know are.

The language of bicycle parts

People who talk about bikes can sometimes sound like they're speaking a language all of their own. Some of the words they keep using are completely unfathomable and bizarre, and some sound familiar but often mean something completely different than expected. The language of bikes isn't just a way of keeping in the clique though – it's vital to be able to identify specific parts.

Disc brake callipers: (aka disc brake units) These are bolted to mounts on your frame and fork. Pulling the brake lever at the handlebar clamps the disc rotor between thin, metal-backed brake pads. Powerful and resilient, they can seem daunting to service thanks to the hydraulic system but they're actually very straightforward. Mechanical versions use cables and V-brake levers rather than an oil-filled hose.

Cables and hoses: Connecting brake levers to callipers or V-brake units, these need to be kept in good condition to transmit an accurate signal. Speed control, as well as raw braking power, is vital. Steel cables run through lengths of outer casing from brake levers to V-brakes. Hoses are the stiff plastic tubes that transfer hydraulic brake fluid from hydraulic brake levers to callipers.

Rear derailleur: This moves the chain step by step across the cassette sprockets. Different-sized sprockets give you different gear ratios, so that you can pedal at a constant rate over a range of different speeds. The movement of the rear derailleur is controlled by a cable on the shifter on the right-hand side of the handlebar. Correct adjustment gives you slick shifting and ensures maximum life for your chain, chainset and cassette.

Chainset: This consists of two or three chainrings bolted together. Like the cassette sprockets, choosing a different-sized chainring gives you a different gear ratio. Larger chainrings give you a higher gear that is harder to push but propels you further on each pedal stroke. Smaller chainrings give you a lower gear, allowing you to climb steep hills. Chainrings will wear out over time, the teeth being worn away or hooked until the chain starts to slip and suck under pressure.

Cassette and freehub: Your cassette consists of a set of different-sized sprockets bolted together. Currently nine-speed cassettes are most common and combine with the three chainrings on your chainset to give you 27 gears. Smaller cassette sprockets give you a higher (harder) gear for maximum speed, and larger sprockets give you a lower (easier) gear for climbing hills. The cassette is fitted to a freehub on your rear wheel.

Chain: The chain connects your chainset to your cassette, turning the rear wheel to provide drive when you pedal. It needs to be strong so it doesn't snap when you stamp on the pedals but it also needs to be flexible enough to shift from side to side across the cassette sprockets and chainrings. Your chain's width needs to match your cassette: for example, nine-speed sprockets are narrower and more closely spaced than eight speed, so you need a narrower nine-speed chain.

Headset: The main bearing at the front of your bike, the headset connects your forks to your frame. This part is often ignored because it's mostly hidden in the frame. This bearing must be adjusted so it turns smoothly without – any play or binding will affect your bike's handling. There are two types of headset: the threadless, or Aheadset, which is found on the vast majority of bikes, and the old-fashioned threaded headset. Regular servicing of the bearings keeps them running smoothly and last longer.

Bottom bracket: Bottom brackets are another 'out of sight, out of mind' component. The bottom bracket axle connects your two cranks together through the frame. If worn and loose, the bottom bracket can lead to front gear-shifting problems and cause your chain to wear out. Worn bottom brackets can be spotted by checking for side to side play in your cranks. Usually supplied as a sealed unit, this part must be replaced when worn or stiff. This repair needs a couple of specific but inexpensive tools.

Wheels: Building wheels can seem daunting, but it is very satisfying to ride around on a pair you have built yourself. Building a wheel consists of two steps: weaving the spokes together to connect hub and rim, and tensioning each spoke so that the rim is flat and perfectly round. A wheel jig is essential for this task. It holds the wheel steady and has indicators that help you decide which spokes need to be adjusted and by how much.

Hubs: There are two types of hub bearing: cup and cone, and sealed cartridge. Sealed cartridge bearings are a sealed unit that includes the bearing race as well as the balls and are designed to be used until they wear out, when they should be replaced. Cup and cone systems can be serviced and should get an occasional clean and re-grease to keep them running smoothly and maximize their life.

Suspension: Suspension makes your ride smoother. Almost all new mountain bikes come with front suspension forks and full suspension bikes (with a rear shock unit as well) are available in a wide variety of flavours, from 4" short travel XC bikes to 10" downhill machines. Suspension forks absorb trail shock, making your ride more comfortable and increasing your control. They let you go faster than you would on a rigid bike, and they need setting up for your weight and riding style to get the most out of them.

Pedals: Introduced from road bikes, clipless pedals have replaced clips and straps. The cleats, small metal parts that are bolted to the bottom of your shoes, clip into a sprung platform on the pedals. They are intially daunting and everyone falls off when they're learning to use them, but once you're used to the release mechanism and have an idea of the force required, you'll appreciate the additional security. Alternatively, you may choose to use flat pedals; these usually have sharp pins to grip the soles of your shoes and you should make sure you use flat, flexible footwear rather than stiff, slippery shoes designed for use with clipless pedals.

Gear shifters

Seat post

Saddle

Rear derailleur hanger

Cassette

Disc brake calliper

Rotor

Valve

Tyre

Rim

Stem

Stem top cap

Headset

Suspension forks

Front hubs

Quick release

Pedals/cleats

Chainset

Chain

Dropout

Rear derailleur

Spokes

Tools and equipment

Of course, everyone starts off with very basic equipment. Then gradually, as you get more confident fixing your bike, you find you need various other pieces of kit. Your toolkit grows and grows, until it reaches the happy point where you can tackle complicated tasks without investing in any more tools.

The evolving toolkit

Some tools are universal, like screwdrivers. Others are highly specific and only do one task, or even just one task on one particular make and model of component. When I was 18, I bought a socket to change the oil on my VW Beetle car. I sold the car a couple of years later, but the socket hung out in my toolbox until I didn't notice it any more. One day I cleared out my toolbox and realized I hadn't used it in 15 years – now it makes a nice candlestick on my bath. You can always find a new task for old tools, so hang on to them.

The tools on the first list are good for starters and should allow you to carry out all the simple repairs. Tools for the specialist jobs appear under the comprehensive toolkit, pages 47–49 – buy these as you tackle the job. Same goes for your stock of oils and cleaning fluids – start with the essential list, and add to it over time as you take on major repairs.

As your toolkit grows, a clear separation will develop between your trail tools and your workshop tools. Trail tools need to be small and light and, preferably, foldable so they don't stab you from inside a pocket when you fall off your bike. With workshop tools, the bigger and chunkier the better, first for proper leverage, and second so they last longer without wearing out. Neat and lightweight gadget tools will wear out quickly if they get used frequently in the workshop.

Manuals and instructions are tools too

All new bikes and parts come with manuals or instructions. For some reason, it's traditional to throw them away without reading them. I don't know why. Don't do it. Keep all instructions and manuals together, they're part of your toolkit. It is particularly important to keep the original manual for suspension parts as fitting and setting-up instructions vary between make, model and years.

Once you find yourself using the manuals, feel free to scribble your own notes and diagrams on them as your knowledge grows.

The simple toolkit

When I started working on this section, I wrote and rewrote for the best part of a morning, adding and deleting items until, finally, I was happy with the result. Then a friend came round, and together we calculated that the total cost of all the tools came out to more than her bike. I started again. The result is two lists: one of indispensable tools and a second for when you get more confident.

The second list is broken down to match the chapters of the book, so you can buy items as you go along. Some tools are bike-specific. Some are obtainable from hardware or tool shops. Good tools last for years, and are an investment. Cheap tools let you down when you least need it and can damage the component you're trying to fix. A plastic toolbox costs very little, and both keeps tools together and protects them from damage.

Don't lend your tools to anyone. This sounds harsh, but if you like someone enough to lend them a spanner, fix their bike for them instead. For some specialist tools it may be worth clubbing together with friends to start a "tool library". There are some items, like headset presses, specific bottom bracket tools and bearing replacement sets, which are prohibitively expensive for a home mechanic's infrequent use but are nonetheless invaluable. Spreading the cost between you means that you can all benefit although you'll all be reliant on the members' honesty to make sure that the tools from the library don't vanish indefinitely into someone's shed.

◀ Bikes, components and even tools come with manuals. Keep them – they're a vital resource

◆ **Allen keys**. The best starter packs are fold-up sets of metric wrenches (keys) that include 2, 2.5, 3, 4, 5, and 6mm sizes. You can use the body of the tool as a handle and bear down hard on it without bruising your hand. I'd rather choose a set with a wider range of keys than you get with screwdrivers, which are intended for trail use. Later, you will want separate Allen keys as they are actually easier to use. Those with a ball at one end allow you to get into awkward spaces.

◆ **Torx keys**. The star-shaped version of Allen keys. The most common sizes are TX25, for disc rotor bolts, and TX30, for chainring bolts.

◆ **A long-handled 8mm Allen key** is essential for all square taper, ISIS and Octalink crank bolts. You will need the dedicated tool for external bottom brackets. A long-handled 10mm Allen key is necessary if you're going to be removing and re-fitting your freehub.

◆ **Screwdrivers**. You'll need one flathead and one crosshead No.2 Phillips.

◆ **Metric spanners. The 6, 8, 9, 10, 15 and 17mm sizes** are most useful but a metric spanner set that's got all the sizes from 6mm upwards is ideal.

◆ **A big adjustable spanner**, also called a crescent wrench, with a 200mm long handle is a good size for starters. The jaws must open to at least 32mm (1¼ inches). Always tighten the jaws firmly on to the flats of the nut before applying pressure to the handle to avoid damaging the nut and the jaws.

◆ **Good quality, bike-specific wire cutters** – not just pliers – can be purchased from your local bike shop. This tool can seem expensive, but both inner cable and outer casing must be cut neatly and cleanly.

◆ **Chain tool**. Again, quality really makes the difference. It's easy to damage an expensive chain with a cheap chain tool.

◆ **Chain-wear measuring tool**. An essential, this tool shows when your chain has stretched enough to damage other parts of the drivetrain.

◆ **A sharp knife with a retractable blade**, so you don't cut yourself scrabbling in your toolbox for a spanner, is useful for cutting open packaging, releasing zipties (cable or electrical ties), etc.

◆ **A pair of pliers**.

◆ **A rubber or plastic mallet.** You can get these from hardware shops. A metal hammer is not a suitable alternative!

◆ **Puncture kit**, for standard and/or UST tubeless tyres.

◆ **Track pump**. Mini pumps are designed to be carried either on a frame-mounted bracket or in your backpack whilst out riding. A track pump is a much quicker and easier way of inflating your tyres at home, particularly if you're running tubeless tyres. Buy one with its own pressure gauge, or get a separate digital gauge.

◆ **Pen and notebook**. Useful for drawing pictures and making notes as you take things apart to help you reassemble them later. This is also a good place to record your shock and tyre pressures if you care about such things.

Long-nosed pliers

Wire cutters

Allen keys

Pliers

Screwdrivers

Tyre levers

Plastic mallet

Adjustable spanners

Metric spanners

Spares box

You need a box of spares as well. It's worth keeping bits and pieces in your house so you don't have to rush off in the middle of a job to pick them up.

◆ **Two tubes**: the right size, with the correct valve for your wheels.

◆ **Brake blocks or pads**.

Brake pads

Puncture kit

Grips

Inner tube

Griplocks

Chain links

Cleats

Self-adhesive patches

Brake pads

◆ **Two brake cables** and a length of brake outer casing.

◆ **Two gear cables** and a length of gear outer casing.

◆ **Ferrules** (the end caps on casing) and end caps (the end caps on cables).

◆ **Powerlinks** to repair standard chains.

◆ **Shimano chain-joining pins** for Shimano chains.

◆ **Zipties** (aka cable or electrical ties). These hold the fabric of the universe together. Before them we had string. Mountain biking couldn't exist until the ziptie was invented. Whoever invented it deserves a major international prize. No toolbox should be without a few of them.

◆ **Electrical tape**

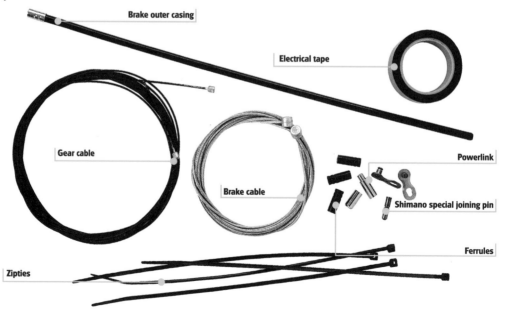

Brake outer casing

Electrical tape

Gear cable

Powerlink

Brake cable

Shimano special joining pin

Ferrules

Zipties

The comprehensive toolkit

As you start to tackle the major jobs, you have to add to your basic toolkit. (These items are broken down to match the chapters.)

Brakes

If you run disc brakes, you need a bleed kit. You can either improvise one from tubes and bottles, or buy a specific one for your brakes. If you've not bled brakes before, a kit makes everything a lot easier. You should be able to tackle everything else with the basic toolkit.

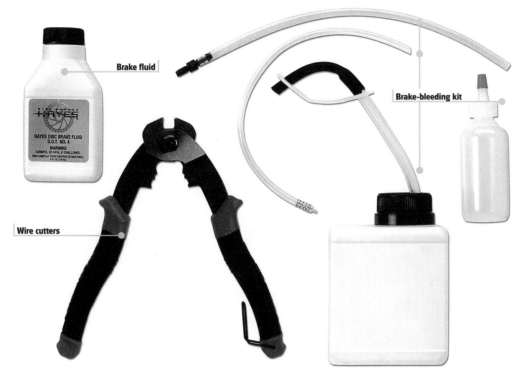

Brake fluid

Brake-bleeding kit

Wire cutters

Bottom bracket and headset spanners

You only need these for older, threaded headsets, which come in three sizes: 32mm (formerly standard), 36mm (called 'oversize' but actually standard now) and 40mm (Evolution size). Threadless headsets are adjusted with Allen keys and don't require spanners.

Bottom bracket tools

The most common style is the Shimano splined remover. This takes either a large adjustable spanner or a 32mm headset spanner. Remember, the right-hand side of the frame has a reverse thread. Facing the right-hand side of the bike, the right-hand cup is removed clockwise. Facing the left-hand side, the left-hand cup is removed anticlockwise. Splined designs are wider than the older square taper ones; if you have an older version of the tool, the hole in the middle may not be big enough to fit over the splined axle and you will need to buy a new tool. External bottom brackets require two specific tools: something to remove the preload nut, and a splined ring spanner to remove and refit the cups. The Park tool shown here combines both in one tool.

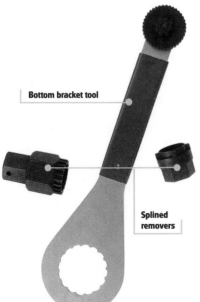

Bottom bracket tool

Splined removers

Transmission

◆ **Chain-cleaning box**.

◆ **Brush for chain cleaning**.

◆ **Crank extractor(s)**. Essential for removing square taper, ISIS and Octalink cranks and accessing the bottom bracket. You will need a spanner to drive the inner part of the extractor once the body is firmly screwed into the crank. The cranks are refitted using just the crank bolts – you don't need the extractor for this. There are two types of extractor: one for the newer splined axles, the other for the older square taper axles. An adapter allows you to use a square-type tool with splined axles, but splined tools will not fit square taper axles.

◆ **Cassette-remover and chain whip**. The cassette-remover fits into the splines at the centre of the cassette. You then need a big adjustable spanner to turn the tool. The chain whip fits around a sprocket and prevents the cassette turning as you undo its lockring. You don't need the chain whip for refitting the lockring; the ratchet in the middle of the cassette stops the cassette turning.

◆ **For freewheels** (how rear cogs were fitted on your wheel before cassettes were invented), you need the appropriate freewheel tool.

Chain splitter

Cassette remover

Chainset tool

Chain-cleaning box

Chain whip

Long-handle Allen key

Spoke wrench

Wheels

◆ **Cone spanners**. These are for cup-and-cone bearings. Cone spanners are very thin, so they can slot onto the narrow flats on the cones. Common sizes are 13, 15 and 17mm and 22mm but you'd best take your wheels to the bike shop and check the size before you buy.

◆ **Spoke wrench**, to fit your spokes. Take your wheels to the bike shop to check the size. Too small won't fit, too big will round off the nipple, which is really annoying.

◆ **Wheel jig**. This makes the job of truing wheels much easier and is essential for wheel building.

Cone spanner

Suspension
Shock tools.

◆ These depend on the make and model of the shock. Check the owner's manual (which you have neatly filed) for the tool list. If you have lost the manual, most are available on the internet. Check the list of resources at the back of this book.

◆ **Air-sprung forks need a shock pump**. These have narrow barrels and accurate gauges to allow a precise volume of air into your shocks. If you buy a new air fork, it may include a shock pump. You can also get tiny trail versions to fit in your pocket when you're out riding.

◆ **A small plastic measuring jug** for shock oil or a **plastic syringe**. They sell these in chemists for measuring out babies' medicine.

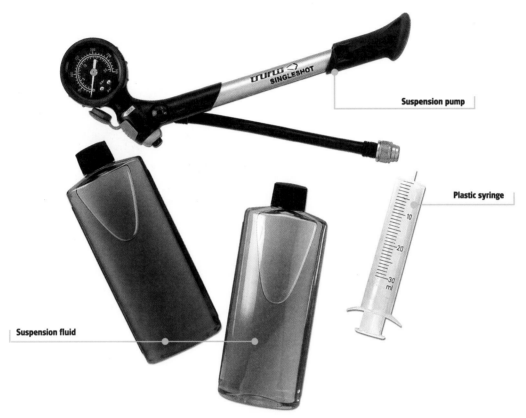

Suspension pump

Plastic syringe

Suspension fluid

Components
Pedal spanners

Most pedal models can be fitted and removed with a 15mm pedal spanner. Pedal spanners are narrower than normal spanners, so that they can fit between the pedal body and the crank without interference. They're longer for additional leverage and a thick, well-padded handle makes the sometimes significant amounts of pressure required to shift a pedal more tolerable. Some pedal models have no spanner flats on the axle and so must be fitted and removed using an 8mm or 6mm Allen key in the back of the axle. A good-quality, long-handled version is essential, as is a breaker or extender bar to increase your leverage.

Pedal spanner

Potions and lotions

A supply of cleaning and lubricating products is essential for routine maintenance. Your bike shop will usually have a choice. Ask for their recommendations, since they'll know what works well for your local environment. As you tackle more advanced jobs, you'll need some more specialized items.

Cleaning products

Always start with the least aggressive cleaning products, then gradually intensify.

◆ **A cleaning fluid**, such as Finish Line Bike Wash or Hope's ShitShifter, makes washing much quicker. Spray it on, give everything a good scrub with your brush kit, then rinse with warm water.

◆ **Degreaser**. This is great for deep-cleaning your bike's really filthy drivechain. Spray it on, leave it to soak for as long as the manufacturer recommends, then rinse with hot water. Do check the instructions, though, as some can be damaging to paintwork. Avoid getting degreaser anywhere near seals and bearings, too, as you don't actually want these to be stripped of their lubrication until its time for a service. A dedicated chain-cleaning tool helps to keep the powerful chemicals contained.

◆ **Hand cleaner**. Essential! Most jobs start with a dirty procedure and end with a clean one. Trying to assemble parts with new grease and dirty hands is a waste of time, so you need to be able to wash your hands in the middle of a job as well as at the end. Most hardware and motor spares shops sell cleaner that's specially designed for oily hands.

◆ **Cotton rag** is a workshop essential. You can buy rolls of window cleaner's scrim or hit up your local charity shops for a bunch of cheap T-shirts. Don't try and reuse your rags by washing them; once they're filthy, bin them and start afresh.

◆ **Brush kit**. Invest in a bike-specific brush kit to make cleaning easier. This should include a very stiff brush for removing mud from tyres, a soft frame brush and a narrow brush for cleaning cassettes and chainrings, amongst others. Try not to get them mixed up, though, as the stiffer bristles designed for removing oil from the drivechain will make a mess of your paintwork.

Lubricant and grease

◆ **Chain lubricant**. This is an absolute essential. Everybody has a favourite type: with me it's Finish Line Cross-Country. Ask the mechanics in your local bike shop what they use. Different lubes work in different climates. If you ride in a very wet and muddy place, you'll need a different lube from someone that rides in hot, dry climates. A dry climate requires a dry lubricant, to keep the drivetrain running smoothly while attracting minimal muck. In muddy, wet conditions you need a wet lube. These are stickier so they stay on in extreme conditions, but attract more dirt so you must be conscientious in your cleaning routine.

The important thing about chain lubes is that they should be applied to clean chains. Putting oil on a dirty chain is the first step towards creating a sticky paste that eats expensive drivetrain components for breakfast. If you haven't got time to

clean your chain first, you haven't got time to oil it. Whatever you use for oiling the chain will also do as a more general-purpose lubricant for cables, brake pivots and derailleur pivots – anywhere two bits of metal need to move smoothly over each other.

I always use drip oil rather than spray oil. Spray is messy and wasteful, and it's too easy to get it on rims and disc rotors by mistake, which makes your brakes slippery rather than sticky.

◆ **Grease**. Confusion surrounds the difference between grease and oil. Essentially, they're both lubricants, but grease is solid and oil is liquid. Grease is stickier and can't be used on exposed parts of the bike; dirt sticks to the grease, forms a grinding paste and wears out the bike rather than making it run more smoothly. Grease is used inside sealed components, like hubs. You don't get in there often so the stuff is required to last longer and remain cleaner. In an emergency almost any grease will do, but as you don't need much, get the good stuff from your local bike shop.

As your confidence grows, invest in a grease gun. This will keep your hands and grease stock clean. For a clean and simple system, I like the ones that screw on to the top of a tube of grease. To get the last bit out, though, you usually abandon the gun and cut open the tube.

Specific lotions

As with your toolkit, start with a stock of essential consumables and build up as you tackle specialist jobs.

◆ **Disc brake fluid**. Use only the fluid specified for your brake system. DOT fluid, an autoparts trade standard, deteriorates once the bottle has been opened so buy in small amounts and open as you need it.

◆ **Suspension oil** is formulated to have damping properties. Its 'weight' is critical and depends on the make and model of your fork or rear shock. Damping occurs by oil being forced through small holes. Lighter, thinner oil (e.g. 5wt) passes through more quickly. Heavier, thicker oil (e.g. 15wt) takes longer. Your fork or shock only works properly with the correct weight of oil: check the manual.

◆ **Carbon Grease**. Carbon components should never, ever see regular bicycle grease. As well as making them slipperier than they were to begin with, it can also damage the structure of the carbon, making the part fit only for the bin. Instead, arm yourself with a carbon 'grease' designed specifically for the purpose.

◆ **Antiseize** (also called Ti-prep or, if you buy from a hardware shop rather than a bike shop, Copperslip). This prevents reactive metals from sticking together and is especially important for titanium components, which react with and seize whatever they touch. This allows the use of lower torque, preventing parts seizing. Both Ritchey and First Line make great resins. Avoid skin contact with antiseize; this stuff is not good for you.

◆ **Plastic components**. These need their own lubricants. SRAM Twistshifter gear-changers and the Sachs equivalent, Twistgrips, have to be cleaned with a suitable degreaser (e.g. Finish Line Ecotech) or warm soapy water, and oiled with a special plastic lube (e.g. Jonnisnot).

◆ **Loctite compound**. The most common brand used is Loctite and it comes in a variety of strengths depending on what you're planning on locking. It's used to stop bolts rattling loose as well as inhibiting corrosion and the different colours indicate the different strengths. Loctite #222 is red and usually applicable up to M6 threads. Loctite #242 is blue and used for bolts with threads of M6 or above.

Suspension fluid

Brake fluid

Ti-prep

Plastic-specific grease

Your biscuit box

One of the most irritating parts of bike repair is being thwarted in a task because you need a simple but very specific part. Bike shop workshops always have racks of plastic drawers full of tiny little parts, many of which are essential for just one job.

Your biscuit box is essential but, like a good compost heap, it must grow over time and cannot be bought wholesale! Start one now. A biscuit box is any container into which you drop odd nuts and bolts left over from other bike repairs. Then, when you shear off an essential bolt after the shops have closed, your box of bits can save your bacon.

Useful items to keep in your biscuit box include M5 and M6 Allen key bolts in lengths from 10mm to 45mm, crank bolts, cable end caps and ferrules, threadless headset top caps with rude slogans on them, an assortment of odd washers and spacers, valve caps and valve lockrings, loose ball bearings and the scraps of chain that are left over every time you fit a new one.

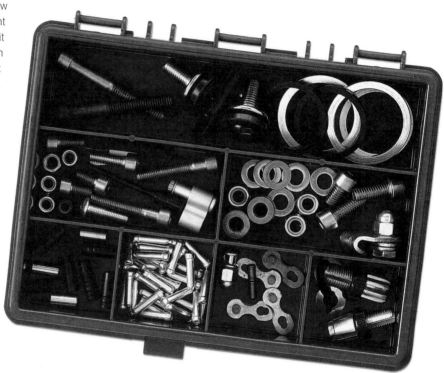

Your workshop

A proper workstand is probably your most expensive investment. Almost all the procedures listed in the main part of this book are easier if the bike is held steady with both wheels off the ground. Working standing up is easier than working crouched on the ground. A workstand also allows you to turn the pedals and wheels and observe everything working.

Take care where you clamp the bike into the stand. The best place is the seatpost. Try to avoid clamping onto the tubes – these are thin, and you can dent, or even bend, them too easily. Wipe the jaws of the stand before you clamp the bike into it, so you don't scuff the paintwork. If you're tight for storage space, look for a workstand that folds up when you're not using it.

The next level down from a full workstand is a propstand, which keeps the back wheel off the ground and holds the bike upright. These are relatively cheap compared to a workstand and a good compromise if you're not ready to commit to a workstand.

If you have nothing, then improvise. Avoid turning the bike upside down – bikes don't like it. Instead, find an obedient friend who will hold the bike upright and off the ground at appropriate moments.

You need enough light to see by, especially for close-up jobs such as truing wheels. Most repairs are messy too, so if you're working indoors, spread an old sheet on the floor before you start to catch things that drop and to protect the carpet.

Ventilation is important. Any time you use solvents or spray, you need enough air circulating to dilute chemical fumes to harmless levels. Anything powerful enough to sweeten your bike will probably damage your body.

The same goes for bodily contact with substances. Consider wearing latex or nitrile gloves. This saves loads of time cleaning your hands and reduces the quantity of chemicals absorbed through your skin. Lots of jobs involve removing something dirty, then either cleaning it or replacing it, and then fitting it. You must have clean hands for the last part of the job – there's no point fitting a clean component with dirty hands.

Torque

In order to measure how firmly we are tightening bolts, we use torque. There are two methods of doing this: the instinctive, common-sense version and the scientific version. Both have their advantages. Traditionally, the manufacturer of a part indicated to the mechanic how firmly things should be tightened by fitting an appropriate bolt.

Delicate parts, which just need holding in place, come equipped with small bolts. The spanners that fit these bolts are short so that you don't have enough leverage to overtighten the bolt. Parts that need to be clamped down firmly come with a big bolt that you can attach a nice hefty spanner to and lean on. This used to work well enough, but as riders we're demanding lighter equipment all the time, so manufacturers are designing components with less room for error. For example, replacing steel bolts with aluminium ones will save weight, but aluminium bolts are far less forgiving of overtightening; once stressed, they can snap without warning.

Overtightening bolts can also strip the thread that you're bolting into. This is a common problem with aluminium parts. For example, overtightening the bolts that hold the stem to the handlebars can damage the thread inside the stem, so that the bolt rotates uselessly rather than securing the bars.

The reverse problem, undertightening bolts, has a more obvious consequence; whatever you're trying to secure will rattle or work loose. Crank bolts often suffer from this – the left-hand one in particular needs to be tighter than people imagine. The first warning is usually a regular creaking noise as you pedal. If you ignore it, the crank bolt works loose, allowing the crank to shift about on the bottom bracket axle. This damages the mating surface between bottom bracket and crank so that even if you retighten the crank bolt, it works loose constantly.

As a consequence, it's becoming more vital to know exactly how much force you're putting on any specific bolt. This is especially true for suspension forks, where the bolts that hold the moving parts together are constantly being stressed by the cycling (moving up and down) of the fork. Most components now come with a tightening torque specified for every bolt.

Since torque specifications are a relatively recent obsession, most come quoted in Newton-metres (Nm). The imperial equivalent unit is the inch-pound (in-lb). To convert inch-pounds into Newton-metres, multiply by 0.113.

However, it's one thing to find out how tight a bolt is supposed to be and quite another to be able to tighten it to exactly that amount. There is a workshop tool that allows you to do this – a torque wrench. It looks like a ratcheting socket handle and works in a similar way. Standard socket heads fit onto the wrench, which can then be set to the specified torque by turning a knob at the base of the handle. The wrench is then used to tighten the bolt as normal. When you reach the correct level, the handle of the bolt gives slightly, and you hear a distinct click, telling you to stop.

These tools are simple and reliable to use and are becoming more and more common in bicycle workshops. A well-equipped workshop will have two torque wrenches. A small one, with a range from about 4 to 20 Nm (35 to 180 inch-pounds), covers delicate applications such as cable clamps and rotor-fixing bolts. A larger one, with a range from 20 to 50 Nm (180 to 450 inch-pounds), covers those that need more force, like crank bolts. The two sizes are necessary because the tools always work best in the middle of their range.

They used to be regarded as too expensive for home workshops but reliable versions are now available from around £60. The smaller size, (4 to 20 Nm), is a particularly good investment. If you don't own a torque wrench of your own, if you ever get a chance to borrow one use it to tighten a selection of the bolts on your bike to the specified torque setting, to get a feel for how tight they should be. Many mechanics use torque wrenches to set bolts to the correct level regularly to remind themselves what the correct torque feels like.

When working by feel, be aware of the size of the bolts you're tightening and use this as an indication of the amount of force you should be using. Small bolts take small spanners (or thin screwdrivers) and so should be tightened firmly but not excessively. If you're overenthusiastic with a delicate bolt, you'll strip the thread, snap the head off or round off the key faces. Large bolts or those that have to be tightened with chunky tools, like bottom bracket cups, should be wedged home with vigour.

The best place to find torque specifications are the instructions that came with the component, which will have the right torque for your specific make and model. New bikes come with a pack of booklets and leaflets, covering all the parts fitted to your bike. You may have to ask for it when you buy the bike. If you haven't got the instructions any more, use the Park Tools website to reference general torque specifications. Park Tools' website is www.parktool.com, and the page address is www.parktool.com/repair/howtos/torque.pdf.

All specified torques assume that the bolt you are using has been greased so that it turns easily in the threads, and that both parts of the thread are clean and in good condition. A dirty, damaged bolt will be harder to tighten than a clean one and so will give a false torque reading.

Rescue repairs: how to be self-sufficient on a bike

This section deals with the repairs you may need to make while out riding – and for these you need a toolkit. Do carry your own, even if you ride with other people who are well equipped. No one wants to be in a group standing around saying, 'But I thought you'd have your pump.' Also, ensure you can use everything in your toolkit, and immediately replace items that you run out of, like spare tubes.

If you've never tackled the following jobs before, practise: (1) getting the wheels on and off your bike; (2) removing and refitting tyres; and (3) splitting and rejoining chains in the comfort of your own home. None of these repairs are difficult, but they're all much harder if tackled for the first time in the cold and wet.

Considering what we expect them to do, bicycles rarely go wrong. If you keep your bicycle well maintained, it will be unusual to face a repair that is not on this list. However, you are occasionally faced with the unexpected. Once, miles from home with the night closing in, I had to make an emergency derailleur pivot. I succeeded using a spare pivot from the dismantled innards of an Allen key tool, held in place with a generous wad of electrical tape. The derailleur even changed gear quite effectively.

Keep your cool, be resourceful

Whenever you have to fix your bike by the side of the trail, think the task through carefully before you start.

If you're frustrated by a puncture or other repair, don't start fixing until you're less stressed. Do not, at any stage, throw your bicycle around, however petulant you feel. This improves nothing. You also look stupid.

Remember, everything you're carrying and wearing is a potential emergency spare. Shoelaces, watchstraps, almost anything can be useful in ways you'd never think of until you really need them.

If you have to release your brakes to fix the bike, remember to refit them.

Spread a jacket out on the ground to catch pieces before you start work. Any part that falls off your bike or drops through cold, wet fingers can make a break for freedom, lying still and quiet on the ground until you've given up and gone away.

Your bicycle is on your side and really wants to get better, but it needs encouragement, not abuse. Swear if you have to, but don't kick it.

Repairing your bike after a crash

The first priority after you've crashed is to assess yourself as safe to ride once the bike is fixed. I'm rubbish at this. I always stand up as soon as possible and say things like 'I'm fine', even if I can't remember who I am.

Don't believe it when anyone else puts on the act either. You may be shaken even if you're not injured. Stop and recover before you get back on the bike. Once you've decided you are all right, check over the bike. Don't get sidetracked by obvious damage because there can often be more than one problem. Decide if you can safely repair the bike, or whether it will be quicker to walk out than struggle vainly for ages with the repair before limping home anyway.

Tools for the trail

You can carry your tools in your backpack along with your water, packed lunch, waterproof and kitchen sink. If you don't use a backpack or are racing and only have your jersey pockets to stuff things into, then use a seatpack for your spare tube and toolkit as landing flat on your back with a large multitool in your pocket makes for interesting bruises. Use an old toe strap to stop the seatpack rattling against your saddle rails and seatpost as you ride – even the quick-release versions suffer this irritating characteristic that's as annoying to those around as it is to you. Lots of people carry their tools in a rucksack or bumbag, but they're heavy and painful to land on so I prefer to let the bike do the work. Seatpacks that clip on and off a clamp are best; it's fiddly messing about with muddy Velcro straps on the trail.

This selection of tools is a starting point rather than a definitive list. What you need depends on your bike and riding environment. For example, the bolts on most bikes are the Allen key type, but if yours has nuts, you need the corresponding spanners. If you often get punctures – for example, because you ride thorny trails – carry extra tubes and patches. Carry a patch kit even if you have a spare tube;

punctures can come in rashes. Ensure you know how to use what you're carrying! If you get desperate, you can stand by the side of the trail or road looking pathetic, hoping some kind soul who knows how to use your tools will ride past, but it's a risky strategy.

Rescue tool pack

◆ **Spare tube**, with the correct valve (thin Presta or fat car-type Schraeder) for your pump.

◆ **Pump**. Make sure it fits your inner-tube valves. Double-action pumps put air in as you both pull and push, refilling the tyre much more quickly. If you carry the pump on a bracket in your frame, use extra Velcro straps to ensure it doesn't rattle loose. After riding in muddy weather, clean the pump so the seals around the barrels stay airtight and won't leak. If you ride a lot in mud, carry the pump inside a backpack or bumbag to keep it clean. If the seals grit up and leak, the pump can't build up pressure.

◆ **Patch kit**. You can carry either a traditional puncture repair kit, with vulcanizing solution and rubber patches, or 'instant' ready-glued patches. The first creates a more permanent repair whilst the second is easier to use when you're crouched behind a drystone wall in a snowstorm, but whichever you choose make sure you've got a good bit of sandpaper in there too as the patches won't adhere to an unroughened tube.

◆ **Tyre levers**. If you're not confident about getting the tyre off the rim with two levers, then carry three – they don't weigh much. Plastic levers are far better than metal ones, which damage the rims.

◆ **Fold-up Allen key/screwdriver toolset**. I prefer the fold-up tools for outdoor use. They're easier to find if you drop them, and the body of the tool makes a comfortable handle for tightening and loosening bolts without hurting your hand. As a bare minimum, you need 4, 5, and 6mm Allen keys, a flat-head screwdriver and a Phillips screwdriver.

◆ **Chain tool**. For Shimano chains you also need to carry appropriate spare rivets. You can also buy spare Powerlinks (see Split Links later in this chapter), which are a quick and easy way to split and rejoin chains, and weigh almost nothing.

◆ **A couple of zipties**. These are essential for emergencies and come out top in the weight-to-usefulness chart.

◆ **A strip of duct tape**, wrapped around the barrel of your pump. Like zipties, it weighs almost nothing and can come in very handy in an emergency.

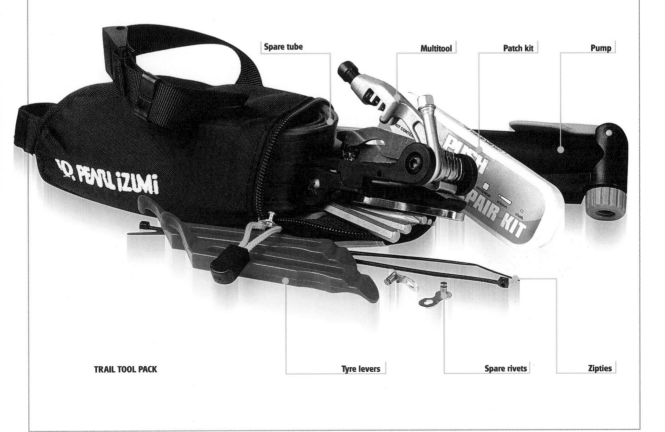

Spare tube   Multitool   Patch kit   Pump

TRAIL TOOL PACK   Tyre levers   Spare rivets   Zipties

Punctures

Punctures are inevitable. The pressure inside the tyre is higher than the pressure outside, and the world is full of sharp things. Don't worry if you've never fixed a flat before though; it's not as difficult as people make out. And, like learning to tie your shoelaces, it gets easier with practice.

There are ways to reduce the number of punctures you get. Occasionally you pick up a sharp object that cuts straight through tyre and tube and causes a flat, but often objects take a while to work their way through the casing of the tyre. Before you set out, check both tyres: raise each wheel off the ground in turn, spin each slowly and pick out foreign objects. Maximum and minimum pressures are printed or stamped on the tyre sidewall. Make sure the tyre is inflated to at least the minimum suggested pressure to reduce the chance of snakebite flats (caused when pressure from, say, a rock edge, squeezes two symmetrical holes in the tube against the sides of the rim). If you like running at very low pressure, choose a tyre designed to take it. These tyres have a thicker sidewall, which won't fold over itself and pinch the tube.

Problems with punctures at or around the valve can also be caused by low tyre pressures. If there isn't enough air in the tyre, it won't sit firmly against the inside of the rim. The tyre will creep gradually around the rim, dragging the tube with it. The valve is held in place in the valve hole, so the tube around it becomes stretched and tears easily, ripping the valve out of the tube. Check your tyres regularly for large cuts as well – under pressure, the tube will bulge out of these cuts and burst instantly.

Some people suffer from punctures more than others. If you feel unfairly blighted, consider investing in puncture-resistant tyres. These have an extra layer of tough material incorporated into the carcass of the tyre under the tread, which helps to stop sharp things working their way through. They do make the tyre a little heavier, but it's worth it if you find punctures irritating. Also, think twice before buying tyres that proudly proclaim their weight on the packet – there will always be a compromise between weight and puncture-resistance.

Fixing a puncture by fitting a new tube in a standard tyre

I always prefer to carry a spare tube as well as a puncture kit. It's much quicker than messing about waiting for the glue to dry or hoping that a glueless patch will hold. They don't weigh much or take up much room. Don't forget to check your tyre carefully before you fit the new tube and to remove whatever caused the flat in the first place. Take the punctured tube home with you, repair the puncture in the comfort of your own home and carry the tube around as your new spare. Once a tube has five or six patches, it's time to retire it.

If you're out and about, try to calculate how quickly your tyre is going down. Maybe, if you're on your way home, you could pump it up and get there. Doesn't work that way very often, though! More likely, you're going to have to fix it.

REMOVING THE TYRE

Step 1: If you have rim brakes, you need to release them to get the tyre out easily. For V-brakes, pull the black rubber boot off the end of the noodle, squeeze the brake units together and pull the noodle out and then up to release it from its nest. For cantilever brakes, squeeze the brake units together and push the cable nipple down and out of the slot in the unit. For calliper brakes, turn the release knob, then remove the wheel.

Step 2: Turn the bicycle upside down. Undo quick-release skewer. Unless you have a fancy skewer set, do this by folding (not turning) the handle over the axle. If you're unsure how to use quick-releases safely, read the section on them before you go any further (page 107). For the front wheel, undo the nut on the opposite side of the wheel several turns to get past the lawyer tabs (which stop the wheel falling out of the dropout slots if the skewer comes loose).

Step 3: The rear wheel is a little trickier to remove than the front. Stand behind the bike. With your left hand, pull the body of the derailleur backwards with your fingers and push the cage forwards with your thumb, as shown. This creates a clear path, so that you can lift the rear wheel up and forward, without getting tangled up in the chain.

Step 4: Inspect the outside of the tyre before you go any further to see if you can work out what caused the puncture. There may be nothing – you may have had a snakebite puncture or the escaping air may have ejected whatever caused the puncture. If you find something sharp, prise it out. (Later you also need to examine the inside of the tyre – see page 58.)

Step 5: If there's any air left in the tyre, expel it. Remove the valve cap. For Presta valves (long and thin), undo the little thumb nut on top of the valve and press it down. For Schraeder valves (car-tyre type), use something like a key, to push down the pin in the middle of the valve. Stand the wheel upright on the ground, push down and massage the tyre. The more air you get out now, the easier it is to get the tyre off.

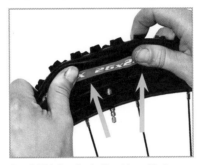

Step 6: Each side of the tyre is held on by an internal wire, or Kevlar hoop, called the bead. This is smaller than the outside of the rim so the tyre stays on when you pump it up. To remove the tyre, lift enough of the bead over the sidewall of the rim. With care, this can be done by hand. Hold the wheel upright facing you. Work around the tyre, pushing the side closest to you into the dip in the middle of the rim. This will give you enough slack to pull the bead off.

Step 7: With the wheel still upright and facing you, pinch a 10cm (4 inch) section of the side of the tyre nearest you with both hands. Lift this section up and over the rim, towards you. Hold it in place with one hand and work around the tyre with the other gradually, easing the bead over the rim. Once you've got about a third of the tyre off, the rest will come away easily.

Toolbox

Step 8: If you can't get the tyre off by hand, you need to use tyre levers. Starting opposite the valve, tuck one tyre-lever under the bead in line with the spokes. Fold it back and hook the tyre-lever under the spoke to hold it in place. Move along two spokes and repeat with a second tyre lever, then repeat with a third tyre lever. Remove the middle tyre lever, leapfrog one of the others and repeat, continuing until you can pull that side of the tyre off with your hands.

Step 9: If the valve has a little nut screwing it to the rim, undo it. Reach inside the tyre and pull out the tube. Leave the other side of the tyre in place.

- **Spare tube** – check that the valve matches the tubes on your bike
- **Puncture kit** – backup in case you get more than one puncture
- **Pump** – make sure it works on your valve type. A pressure gauge is useful
- **Tyre levers** – two is standard, take three if you're not confident
- **Spanners** – any spanners you need to remove your wheels
- **Tool pack** – carry these separately, so you can find them in a hurry
- **Warm clothes** – a hat to put on to keep you warm while you fix your bike – I get cold very quickly as soon as I stop riding

Refitting a new tube

It's vital to work out what caused the puncture before you fit a new tube. If the problem's still there when you fit a new tube, you'll puncture again straight away – which is even more irritating if you haven't got a second spare tube.

Your first step is to inspect the tyre carefully. Look around the outside for thorns, shards of glass or sharp stones. If you can't see anything from the outside, check the inside of the tyre too. The easiest way to locate the culprit is to feel around inside the tyre with your fingers, moving slowly and carefully to avoid cutting yourself. If you're still unsure what caused the flat, pump air into the tube and locate the hole. You may be able to hear it rushing out of a big hole. Smaller holes can be harder to find – pass the tube slowly through your hands so that you can feel the air on your skin. You can put the tube in a bowl of water and watch for bubbles, but I don't usually carry a bowl of water in my emergency toolkit. Sometimes you can use puddles as an alternative. Once you've found the hole in the tube, hold the tube up to the tyre to locate the area of the tyre where the puncture occurred, and inspect the tyre again carefully.

Remove anything that you find. It's often best to push objects out of the tyre from the inside, rather than forcing them through the tyre from the outside and making the hole bigger. You won't necessarily find something in the tyre because punctures happen in other ways too. Pinch punctures – also known as snakebite flats – happen when you don't have enough tyre pressure. If you hit a rock hard, the tyre squashes, trapping the tube between the rock and your rim. Pinch flats are usually easy to identify; you have two neat holes in your tyre, a rim width apart. Check the tyre sidewalls as well because a hole here will turn into a fresh puncture immediately. If you have rim brakes, the most likely cause of the puncture is the brake block sitting too high and rubbing on your rim. Either your brake block is set too high or the wheel has been refitted crookedly in its dropouts so that it sits off to one side rather than neatly in the centre of your frame.

Booting your tyre

Big tears or gashes in the tyre will need to be repaired before you fit a new tube; otherwise the new tube will bulge out of the split when you inflate it. The tube is much softer than the tyre, so any bubbles will either scrape on the ground and tear or get pinched in the tyre split as the wheel rotates. Both will cause another puncture immediately, which is irritating, especially if you don't have a second spare. Feel carefully around the inside of the tyre. Any holes big enough to push the end of your finger into will cause a problem. You can buy tyre boots – sticky-backed strips of plastic – but out on the trail, you'll have to improvise. The air pressure trying to force the tube out through the tyre is high, so you'll need something fairly stiff. Ideally, choose something sticky so that it stays in place as you refit the tube. Duct tape is ideal for smaller holes; it's worth sticking a strip of it to the underside of your saddle for occasions like this. Ordinary tube patches will also help. For bigger holes, you'll need something stiffer to bridge the tear in the tyre. This is a chance for you to use your imagination – try using food wrapping, cardboard, shoe insoles, whatever you have available.

FITTING THE NEW TUBE

Step 1: Now for the new tube. Remove the nut on the valve, if there is one. Pump a little air into the tube – just enough to give it shape. This will prevent the tube getting trapped under the bead as you refit the tyre. Pull back the section of tyre over the valve hole and pop the valve through the hole. Work around the tyre, tucking the tube up inside it.

Step 2: Returning to the opposite side of the valve, gently fold the tyre back over the rim. This gets tougher as you go. When there's just a short section left, you'll probably get stuck. Let a little air out of the tube again, and push the sections of tyre you've already fitted away from the sidewall of the rim and into the dip in the middle, like you did to get it off. You should then be able to ease the last section on with your thumbs, a bit at a time.

Step 3: If you can't hand-fit the last section, use tyre-levers. Work on short sections 5cm (2 inches) at a time, and take care not to trap the tube between the rim and the tyre lever as it's easy to pinch-puncture it. Once the tyre is reseated, push the valve up into the rim so that it almost disappears (to make sure the area of tube near the valve is not caught under the tyre bead).

Step 4: Pump up the tyre. If you had a snakebite flat last time, put in a little more air. Once the tyre is up, retighten the thumb nut on Presta valves, screw the stem nut back onto the valve stem and refit the dustcap. Don't fit the valve stem nut until the tube is inflated, as you risk trapping a bulge of the tube under the tyre bead.

Step 5: Refit the rear wheel. With the bike upside down, stand behind it and hold wheel in your right hand with sprockets on left-hand side. Put a left-hand finger in front of the guide jockey wheel and your thumb behind the tension jockey wheel. Pull finger back and push thumb forward, then place wheel so sprockets are within the loop of the chain. Guide the axle into the dropouts, and secure by doing up the quick-release.

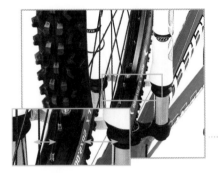

Step 6: Refit the front wheel. This is easier. Drop the wheel into the dropout slots; make sure there's an equal amount of space between the tyre and the fork legs, and tighten the quick-release lever securely. Again, if you're not sure about your skewers, read the quick-release skewer section on page 107.

Step 7: If you have disc brakes, wiggle the rotor **(A)** into place between the brake pads before settling the wheel into the dropout slots. You need to check that the rotor is sitting centrally between the brake pads inside the calliper. If it's hard to see, hold something light-coloured on the far side of the calliper as you look through. You may need to adjust the position of the wheel slightly so that the rotor is central.

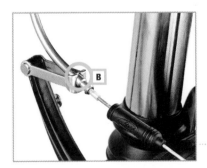

Step 8: For rim brakes, don't forget to refit the brakes – it's easy to overlook this vital stage in the excitement of fixing your puncture. Pull the brake units together and refit the cable. If you have V-brakes, take care to seat the end of the noodle **(B)** securely in the key-shaped nest.

Step 9: Turn the bike back over and check that the brakes work properly: pull the front brake on and push the bike forward. The front wheel should lock and the back one should lift off the ground. Pull the back brake on and push the bike forward. The back wheel should lock, sliding across the ground. Lift up the wheels and spin them. Check they spin freely, and that rim brakes don't rub on the tyre.

Checklist: what caused the puncture?

Check for:

- Sharp things (thorns, glass, flint) cutting through the tyre
- Cuts or gashes in the tyre that allow the tube to bulge out – check both the sidewall and the tread
- Snakebite punctures – when the tyre, without enough air, gets trapped between the rim and a rock
- Rim tape failure – when sharp spoke ends puncture the tube or when the tube gets trapped in rim holes
- Valve failure – when under-inflated tyres shift around on the rim
- Overheating from rim brakes – although rare, this can happen on long mountain descents
- Worn tyres – when tyres get old, the bead can stretch, allowing the tyre to creep out over the edge of the rim, where it will puncture
- Badly adjusted rim brakes – when blocks that are set too high rub on the tyre rather than the rim, cutting through the sidewall of the tyre in no time at all

Fixing a UST puncture by fitting a replacement tube

The simplest way of fixing a puncture in a mountain bike tubeless tyre while out on the trail is to use a standard tube. You can fix the tyre properly when you're home – the chances are that if the sealant hasn't managed to fix the hole on its own then you're going to need to get the patches out and fitting a tube is a much easier way to effect a temporary fix.

◆ Remove the punctured wheel. The first thing to do is locate the hole. If you're running sealant, it should be obvious as the fluid will have leaked from the hole. If you're not, then first look for any holes in the tread or rips in the tyre's sidewall. If this doesn't reveal the culprit, then pump the tyre up if it's lost all its air and pass it past your face – you should hear air hissing when the hole is closest to your ear, may see bubbles if the ground is wet or feel the air cooling your cheek. Once you've found the hole, mark it or make a note of where it is in relation to any labels on the tyre or rim.

◆ Remove one side of the tyre. Some combinations of UST rim and tyre can be exceptionally tight thanks to the extra-secure bead hook required to seal the join securely. Try pushing the tyre away from the sidewall using your hands, and if this doesn't work then gently stand on the tyre whilst lifting the rim away from it.

◆ Once you've released the seal, you'll be able to work the tyre away from the rim all the way around one side. Try not to disturb the seal on the other side so you don't have to reseat it later. Unscrew the lockring on the valve, then remove it and any washers, keeping them safe for when you ressurect your tubeless set-up at home.

◆ If there is sealant in the tyre, scoop as much of it out as possible.

◆ If you're using a UST rim, you won't need to worry about a rim tape as there are no spoke holes in the rim to puncture the tube you're about to fit. If you have a tubeless conversion kit fitted, however, you may find it easier to remove the conversion strip and fit a standard rim tape. A double thickness of electrical tape will do at a pinch.

◆ Put a little bit of air into the tube, just enough to make it hold its shape. Fit the valve through the valve hole in the rim and screw on the lockring loosely to stop it slipping out again. Tuck the tube into the tyre all the way around the rim.

◆ Start to work the loose tyre bead back onto the rim. An extra pair of hands can help here, by holding the bit you've already refitted in place whilst you work your way around the wheel, aiming to finish at the valve.

◆ Try not to use tyre levers on tubeless tyres if you can help it; the slight bends this causes in the stiffer tyre bead can make sealing very difficult in future. Tubeless tyres and rims can be very tight, so work your way around the rim a small amount at a time, lifting the bead into place and pulling both sides of the tyre down into the well in the centre of the rim to give yourself more slack to play with. The last section is usually the toughest; letting the air out of the tube can help but increases the risk of pinching the tube as you slide the last tight bit into place.

◆ Once you've got the tyre on, push the valve up into the rim to make sure the tube's not pinched between bead and hook, then pull it out, screw the lockring fully into place and inflate as normal. Screw on the valve cap, refit the wheel and re-hook the cable if you're running cantilevers or V-brakes.

The great grass myth

There's a long-standing story that if you puncture without a spare tube or patch kit, you can get home by stuffing the tyre with grass. This sounds feasible in theory, but in practice it's either rubbish or requires a special kind of grass that I've never come across. I've tried it and just ended up spending an enormous amount of time harvesting grass by hand and trying to force it into the tyre. This is trickier than you would imagine since the grass compacts as you pack it. Even if you can stuff enough in to give the tyre some kind of shape, the tyre rolls off the rim as soon as you cycle faster than walking pace anyway, shedding all your hard-won grass harvest instantly. If you try to cycle really slowly, the tyre is so soft that it squidges all over the place, making your bike feel like you're riding through treacle. You might as well leave the grass growing happily where it is and start walking anyway.

Patching UST tubeless tyres

Although flats are less likely with UST tyres, they do happen. If you're out riding, often the easiest thing to do is to stick an ordinary tube into the tyre (see opposite page) and fix it when you get home.

Once you get home, patch the tyre. Tyres are expensive, and patches work, so it's worth the effort. Finding the hole can be the tricky bit! Pump as much air as you can into the tyre and listen for hissing from the hole. Look carefully for a thorn or other spiky object sticking out of the carcass; you may also spot sealant bubbling out of the hole. Sometimes the hole is tiny and hard to locate, and you have to submerge the inflated wheel in water to look for the bubbles. This is much more awkward than doing the same process with a tube!

Once you've located the hole, mark it carefully or you will lose the place! I usually draw a circle in ballpoint around the hole, then draw an arrow pointing to it on the sidewall of the tyre where it's easy to see. Undo the thumbnut on the valve and let all the air out of the tyre.

It's important to do this next stage carefully. Both sides of the tyre have an airtight seal against the rim. It's much, much easier to refit the tyre if you only break one of the seals. If the hole is nearer one side of the tyre, start with that side. Push the sidewall of the tyre in and away from the rim. It will resist at first because the seal is tight, but once it's released the rest will pull off easily.

Sometimes the seal is very tight. If all else fails, lay the wheel on the ground and stand carefully on the sidewall of the tyre, as close to the rim as you can get. Don't stand on the rim – you'll bend it. Pull off the released side of the tyre all the way around and locate your hole from the inside. Pull out whatever it was that caused the puncture.

While you're in there, feel carefully around the inside of the tyre for anything else sharp – there may be more than one intruder. Use clean sandpaper to roughen up the area of the tyre around the hole. If you're used to patching tubes, don't underestimate this part – you need to make an area bigger than the patch much rougher than you would with a tube. Follow up by cleaning with solvent.

Spread the special UST glue around the hole. I start directly over the hole and work outward in a spiral, so that the patch ends up centred over the hole. Make the area of glue much bigger than the size of the patch. Then leave the glue to dry. Don't touch it or poke it, just leave it. It needs 5 to 10 minutes – if it's cold, give it the full 10 minutes.

The next stage

You'll find that your patch is now trapped between two layers of plastic, or a layer of plastic and a layer of foil. Peel off one layer, but don't touch the surface of the patch with your fingers at all or it won't stick. Use the other layer of packaging to hold it. Lay it carefully onto the glue. Don't move it about at all, just put it on. With the packaging still on there, press the patch firmly onto the tyre. A tyre lever is perfect for this, or the flat side of a spanner, or a spoon.

You can peel the backing off the patch now, but I usually leave it there – it doesn't weigh much, and you risk pulling off your carefully fitted patch if you try to remove it. Starting opposite the valve, refit the tyre onto the rim. The tyres are unwieldy, and it can feel like you need three hands, but once you've got most of the tyre on, it stays in place.

This last part is harder. Don't be tempted to use tyre-levers because if you do your tyre will leak forever. Fold the tyre onto the rim with your thumbs. Aim to finish at the valve. If it gets tough, return to the opposite side of the rim and massage the bead of the tyre into the well at the centre of the rim to gain enough slack to pop it on at the top. Once it's in, ensure that the bead of the tyre sits beside the valve, not on it, and pump it up. Be very vigorous at first to seal the tyre and keep pumping until it pops into place.

Sometimes, if the tyre is really tight, a bit of warm soapy water will help. Work in very small sections, lifting a 10–20mm (⅜–¾ inch) length of tyre at a time over the rim. The last bit will be a struggle and will pop into place just as you are about to give up.

Urban myths to ignore include pouring lighter fluid on the tyre and applying a match. Don't do this. Tyres are expensive, and this is not a time when setting something alight helps.

Big workshop track pumps are better at getting the initial volume of air in fast enough; very small mini-pumps can make hard work of this. Air canisters can be hit-and-miss. If the tyre seals straight away, they're quick enough; if it doesn't, you waste the canister.

It definitely helps when reinflating tyres if you can keep one side of the bead locked onto the rim. Fitting new tyres is particularly frustrating; they're usually packed folded up and the kinks that result from their being folded usually make for air gaps. Take new tyres out of the packet as soon as you buy them and store them unfolded until you come to fit them.

Even if you run very low pressures, it's worth pumping the tyre up really hard to seal it properly – check on the sidewall to see how high it will go, then pump it up to that pressure before letting it down again to however low you want to run it.

Sealant dilemmas

Sealants make the tyre very slightly heavier and do a fantastic job of plugging the small- and medium-sized cuts and tears. However, they'll make it very much more difficult to persuade a patch to stick to the tyre.

Try to take a spare inner tube with you out on your bike

It's always worth carrying a spare tube when you go out for a ride, because it's much easier to pop a spare tube in than to fix a puncture by the side of the trail or road. But it's definitely worth backing the spare up with a patch kit. Punctures often come in batches and carrying more than one spare tube gets bulky. So, hold onto your punctured tube and fix the puncture at your next opportunity. The repaired tube can become your new spare.

Schraeder inner tube/valve

Presta inner tube/valve

Fixing punctures

To repair a punctured tube, start by locating the hole. Pump up the tube to about twice the original diameter. You might be able to hear the air hissing out of the hole straight away, and locate the puncture that way. If not, lick the palm of your hand and move it along the tube, about a centimetre away; you'll feel the cold air from the puncture on your hand. Roughen the area with the sandpaper from the patch kit; this helps the patch stick – and means you don't lose the hole. Let all the air out of the tube again. Spread glue in a spiral out from the centre of the hole, making a glue patch that's generously bigger than the patch. This next step is the most important – let the glue dry completely. In average temperatures, this means five whole minutes. In the desert, you can wait two. If it's snowing, blow on the glue patch to keep it warm. Once the glue is dry, peel the foil off the back of the patch. Don't touch the rubber surface of the patch at all – use the clear plastic or paper to hold the patch. Drop it into place, then don't move it. Press it onto the tube with your hands. If it's very cold, clamp the patched part of the tube under your armpit to keep it warm enough for the glue to work, about another five minutes. You could peel the plastic or paper cover off next, but I normally leave it in place – it weighs nothing and saves you accidentally tearing off your neat patch. Refit the tube into the tyre before putting pressure into it because the newly stuck patch is vulnerable and won't stick properly until it's trapped between tube and tyre under pressure. Puncture glue doesn't last long once the seal on the tube has been broken – it dries out in six months, however tightly you screw on the cap, so replace it regularly.

Valves

There are two types of bicycle valve: Presta and Schraeder. Presta is the thin one that road bikes always have. Schraeder is the fat car-type valve. Cheaper mountain bikes sometimes come fitted with car valves because they can be pumped up at petrol stations. Presta valves are designed to work better at higher pressures and are more reliable – Schraeders leak if grit gets caught in them as you pump them up.

I always use Presta, but there is a bizarre law that says if you meet a stranger on the trail who's stuck because he can't fix his own puncture, he will always have Schraeder valves, so you can't help him with your Presta pump. Luckily, most pumps now convert to fit either type of valve; with newer ones, you simply push any valve into the pump head and flick a switch. Many older ones require you to take the cover off the pump head and remove a small rubber grommet and a small plastic thing. Turn both parts over and refit them into the pump in the same order they came out – plastic first, then rubber. Refit the cap, tighten it hand-tight and you're ready.

Crank and pedal repairs

It's easy to forget about the parts that connect you directly to the bike but every time you grind against a gradient or push a gear, it's your cranks and pedals that you're relying on. Most of the time they do the job just fine but occasionally they'll let you down.

The most common problem, which applies to all types of crank, is the crank bolts working loose so that the crank then begins to move on the axle. On a square taper, ISIS or Octalink crank, this can result in the crank bolt becoming so loose it actually falls out, allowing the crank to fall off completely. If you're using clipless pedals you'll find yourself with one foot attached to the bike and another with a useless crank and pedal dangling off the end! On a two-piece crank, you're less likely to lose the crank completely as the preload cap will hold it in place but you can damage the shallow splines inside the crank if you stamp down on the pedals whilst the pinch bolts are loose.

Both situations are likely to damage the cranks irreparably – a square taper, ISIS or Octalink crank will be deformed enough by the slight but persistent movement between axle and crank to never be properly tight again, whilst a stripped spline will never stay put. Keep your crank bolts tight to avoid having to solve the problem in the first place but if the worst happens, then there are a couple of things you can do to get yourself home.

If you have a square taper, ISIS or Octalink crank and have been lucky enough to notice the looseness before the bolt disappears, then tighten it as much as possible and make your escape, stopping to re-tighten the bolt every twenty minutes or when you feel the crank loosening again. If you don't have the necessary 8mm Allen key in your toolkit, then a stand-in made by using two 4mm, 5mm and 3mm, or 6mm and 2mm Allen keys wedged together in the bolt head is surprisingly effective. You can attempt the same fix with a two-piece crank, returning the left-hand crank to its correct position on the axle and tightening the two 5mm pinch bolts as much as possible.

If this course of action fails then your best bet is to remove the loose crank, stash it in your pack rather than hurling it into the near distance in frustration and heading for home prepared to push up descents, pedal one-legged on the flat (as long as it's not the driveside crank that's made its bid for freedom!) and coast the descents with one foot on the pedal and the other on the exposed end of the axle – it's surprisingly hard to balance on a bike one-legged.

Securing your crank

If you have a way to go to get home, a little bit of time spent securing your crank will pay off. Even if you can't find the original bolt, you still have a spare – it's holding your other crank on. Remove the right-hand crank bolt and use this to tighten your left-hand cranks as firmly as possible onto the axle. Remove it again and refit it back onto the right-hand crank. Chainsets are more expensive than cranks and so are not worth sacrificing.

An emergency crank bolt will help keep the crank in place. If you can carve a short stub out of a handy-sized branch, then screw it into the end of the axle. Cut off any wood that protrudes out of the crank though – it will be in just the right position to take chunks out of your ankle. Pedal gingerly!

Damaged pedals

Pedals can also seize, break or suffer crash damage. If the body of the pedal falls off leaving the axle in the crank, just use the axle as a pedal to get you home. It's not particularly comfortable but it will get you there, though you may have a hard time removing a redundant clipless pedal body from the bottom of your shoe without the leverage of the axle to remove it.

Occasionally, the whole pedal will tear out of the crank – usually as a result of failing to tighten the pedal up firmly in the first place. In which case, you have two choices: either jam the pedal back into the crank (the chances are the thread was stripped as the pedal worked its way out, so the crank will be going straight in the bin when you get home anyway), or fabricate an 'axle' from a handy stick. It only needs to be long enough to balance the ball of your foot onto and won't take much pressure but should be enough to enable you to balance successfully and help the pedal through the bottom of the downstroke. Stay in a low gear, spin as much as possible and don't expect the stick to hold your weight if you stand up on the pedals.

Mending a broken chain

After punctures, chain repairs are the most common task you'll carry out. Nine out of ten broken chains occur when undue pressure is applied to a chain that's in the process of shifting between gears.

The combination of angle and stress is too much for the fragile, put-upon chain and it gives way, leaving you suffering a sudden loss of drive and balance and possibly vaulting over the bars if you were stamping hard on the pedals at the time, too. Learn how to use your gears correctly and you'll avoid unnecessary problems; similarly, keep your drivechain in good condition, as old, worn and neglected chains are more likely to let you down under pressure. For most chain problems, you'll need a chain tool. These can be annoying to carry as they only do one job but it's extremely hard to botch a chain repair using anything else. Several manufacturers, like Park and Topeak, make good chain tools that also fold so invest in a version that you'll know you'll carry and then keep it with your toolkit at all times.

Your first step is to go back and retrieve your chain. It may have stayed with the bike but is more likely to have unravelled onto the trail. If you were moving at speed it may be some distance back up the path so retrace your steps and collect it. Then follow the steps below to repair it.

Checking the length of the repaired chain

When you've finished the steps below, it's important to check that the repaired chain is still long enough to reach all the way around your drivetrain. It will be slightly shorter, since you will have removed damaged links. It is essential that there is still enough slack in the chain even in the largest sprocket, so that the derailleur is not strained or twisted. Otherwise, you risk tearing the derailleur off, damaging both the derailleur and the part of the frame to which it attaches.

Get someone to lift up the back of the bike for you, then change into the smallest sprocket at the back and the largest chainring at the front – pedal with your left hand and change gears with your right. Then change gears click by click towards the largest sprocket at the back, while watching the derailleur. As you move into larger sprockets, the derailleur will get stretched forward. Check the tension of the lower section of the chain, where it passes from the bottom of the chainring to the rear derailleur. If this section becomes tight, stop shifting. If you force the chain into a larger sprocket once the chain is tight, you'll damage the derailleur.

If the derailleur is struggling to reach the largest sprocket at the back, it's important not to change into this gear as you ride along. Try to remember not to use this gear. Personally, I prefer to readjust the end-stop screw on the rear derailleur so that I cannot accidentally change into the largest sprocket, because it's all too easy to forget once you start riding. Shift click by click into larger gears until the chain becomes taut, then screw in the 'low' end-stop screw until you can feel resistance – it will touch the tab inside the derailleur that limits further movement. Once you get home, replace the chain with a new, longer one (you'll almost certainly need a new cassette too) and readjust your end-stop screw so that the chain reaches the largest sprocket. For more about end-stop screws, see pages 149 and 156.

MENDING A CHAIN

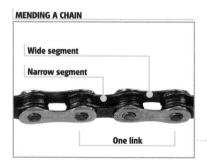

Wide segment

Narrow segment

One link

Step 1: Once you have the chain, find the break and look at both ends. One will end in a narrow segment and one will end in a wider segment. A complete link consists of one narrow and one wide segment. You may find that the plates that form the end of the wider segment are twisted and damaged, so this complete link (both the wider damaged plates and the narrow segment they're attached to) will have to be removed.

Step 2: Look carefully at the chain to choose the right place to break it. When you come to rejoin it, you need to match up a narrow and wide segment. Once you've selected the correct rivet, lay the chain over the chain tool as shown. If your tool has more than one set of supports, choose the ones furthest from the handle to support the chain.

Step 3: Turn the handle of the tool clockwise so that the pin approaches the chain's rivet. When you get close, line the pin up with the centre of the rivet very carefully; if the pin is on the edge of the rivet or the plate instead, it will bend and damage the tool, possibly irreparably, as well as further damaging the chain.

Step 4: Continue to screw. It will start to push out the rivet. You should feel some resistance but if you're having to turn very hard the pin probably isn't correctly lined up. If it's a Shimano chain and you have a spare replacement rivet, or if you're going to be rejoining the chain using a Powerlink, then push the rivet all the way through. For all other chains you need to stop before the rivet is loose of the rear plate, as you'll be using it to rejoin the chain.

Step 5: Once the rivet is sticking out of the back of the chain and is free of the inner plate but not the rear plate, remove the chain tool by backing off the handle and flex the two halves of the chain gently to slide them apart.

Step 6: You're taking out a complete link – one wide section and one narrow section – so repeat the process, two rivets along, on the other side of your twisted link. You should now have a broken link and a slightly shortened chain; one end should end in a wide segment, the other in a narrow segment. Turn it so that the rivet at the wide end faces towards you.

Step 7: Feed the end of the chain with the narrow segment between bottom tension jockey wheel and the tab at the bottom of the derailleur **(B)**, then between the tab and the top guide jockey wheel **(A)**. Don't go around the outside of the top tab; the shifting still works in a way, but things are noisy! If you have another bike, use it as a reference. Pass the chain around the front of the guide jockey, then over and back to the bottom of the cassette.

Step 8: Continue around behind the bottom of the cassette, up and forward over the top, and then forward toward the chainset. Pass the chain through the front derailleur. It will eventually have to sit on the chainrings but, for now, pass it around the front of the chainset, then drop it into the gap between the chainset and the frame to give yourself enough slack to rejoin the chain easily.

Step 9: If you're refitting a standard chain, ease the two ends together, flexing the chain so you can slide the inner segment of the chain past the stub of rivet sticking through to the inside of the outer plates. Once you've got it, though, the stub will make it easy to locate the rivet in the hole in the inner plates, lining the two ends of chain up. For Shimano chains, see page 67.

Step 10: Lay the chain over the furthest away chain supports on the chain tool. Turn the handle clockwise until the pin on the chain tool almost touches the rivet on the chain. Wiggle the chain to precisely line up the pin with the rivet.

Step 11: Keep turning the handle, while pushing the rivet into the chain, until there is an even amount of rivet showing on both sides of the chain. Remove the tool.

Step 12: Rejoining the chain usually squashes the plates together and makes the link stiff. See page 66 to free stiff links. Finally, reach around behind the chainset and lift the chain back onto a chainring. Stand up, lift the saddle up with your left hand and push the pedal around with your right foot so that the chain can find a gear.

Stiff links/split links

Often, the link you've just joined is stiff, although stiff links occur for other reasons: the chain may need lubricating, or you're riding in the wet. You feel a stiff link as you're riding – the pedals slip forward regularly, but at different places in the pedal revolution.

To find a stiff link, change into the smallest sprocket at the back and the largest chainring at the front. Lean the bike up against a wall, crouch beside it and pedal backwards slowly with your right hand. The chain heads backwards from the top of the front chainring, around the smallest sprocket, then around the front of the guide jockey and the back of the tension jockey. Then, it heads to the front chainring again. The chain is straight as it travels across the top, then bends around the sprocket. The links should be flexible enough to straighten out as they emerge from the bottom of the sprocket, then bend the other way to pass round the guide jockey. But a stiff link won't straighten out as it drops off the bottom of the cassette and then passes clumsily around the derailleur. Once you've spotted the area of the chain that's causing problems, slow your pedalling right down and check each link as it comes off the tension jockey.

REPLACING STIFF LINKS

Step 1: Once you've identified the problem link, get your chain tool out. You need to use the set of supports nearest the handle – the spreading supports. Look carefully at the problem rivet to identify whether one side of the rivet sticks further out one side of the chain than the other. If it is uneven, start with the sticking-out side. If it looks even, start with either side.

Step 2: Lay the chain over the supports nearest the handle of the tool, and turn the handle clockwise until the pin of the chain tool almost touches the rivet on the chain. Wiggle the chain to precisely line up the pin with the rivet. Turn until you can feel the pin touching the rivet, then just a third of a turn more. Back off the tool and wiggle it to see if the link is still stiff. If it is not yet as flexible as those around it, repeat from the other side of the chain. The rivet needs to end up as even as possible.

Step 3: If you don't have the chain tool with you, hold the chain as shown and flex it firmly backwards and forwards between your hands. Stop and check frequently to see if you've removed the stiff link. The last thing you want is to go too far and twist the chain plates.

Split links

A split link, also called Powerlink, is a quick and easy way to split and rejoin chains. It is particularly useful if you like to remove your chain to clean it, since repeatedly removing and replacing the rivets in chains can cause weak spots. It's also a great emergency fix. You still need your chain tool for removing the remains of twisted or broken links, but the split link will not be stiff when you refit it and does not shorten the chain.

There are a couple of different types of split links; the best is the Powerlink, which comes free with SRAM chains. All split links work in similar ways. The link comes in identical halves, each half with one rivet and one key-shaped hole. To fit, you pass a rivet through each end of the chain, linking the ends together through the wide part of the hole. When you put pressure on the chain, it pulls apart slightly and locks into place. They never release accidentally.

To split the chain, locate the split link and push the adjacent links towards each other. The Powerlink halves are pushed together, lining up the heads of the rivets with the exit holes. You can then push the two halves across each other to release them.

Powerlink – the quick and easy way to split and rejoin chains ▶

Shimano chains

Shimano chains need to be treated slightly differently from standard chains. The rivets that join each link are very tightly fitted together, so it will usually damage the chain plates if you try to reuse an original one.

When splitting and rejoining a Shimano chain, the rivet must be pushed all the way out, then replaced with a special Shimano joining link. The rivets are different lengths to match the different chain widths used by eight- and nine-speed systems, so make sure to choose the correct replacement: the longer eight-speed rivets are grey, the shorter nine-speed version is silver.

The replacement rivet is twice as long as the original rivets and has a groove in the middle. The first section is a guide to locate the rivet correctly in the chain and must be broken off once the second part of the rivet has been driven home with the chain tool. This means you need pliers to snap the guide off, as well as a replacement rivet. The rivets are different lengths to match the different chain widths used by eight-, nine- and ten-speed drivechains, so make sure to choose the correct rivet.

REFITTING A SHIMANO CHAIN

Step 1: Push the ends together until the holes line up, then push through the replacement rivet. The first half of the rivet goes through easily, holding things together while you use the chain tool. Lay the chain on the furthest supports of the chain tool, line up the chain tool pin with the rivet on the chain, and turn the handle of the tool clockwise. The groove in the centre of the new rivet appears from the other side of the chain. Turn until the second half of the rivet emerges.

Step 2: Snap off the section of rivet sticking out, ideally with pliers. If you don't have any, trap the end of the rivet between two Allen keys on a multitool and twist.

Step 3: Wriggle the new link. Often it is stiff because the plates get stuck together. Lay the chain back over the chain tool, with the stiff rivet in the set of supports nearest the handle. Wind the handle in until the pin touches the rivet, then a further third of a turn to loosen link. Reach in behind chainset and lift chain back onto a chainring. Stand up, lift the saddle with your left hand, and push the pedal around with your right foot so that the chain can find its own gear.

Successful chain-fixing – key points to remember

- Always use a good-quality chain tool. Cheap ones are fine for kids' bikes, but modern chains are manufactured so that the rivet is a very tight fit in the chain plate. This helps stop you from breaking them, but means that they will laugh at anything less than a proper chain tool.
- Big multitools sometimes include a chain tool. These are always better than nothing, but seldom as good as a proper separate one.
- Align the pin of the chain tool very carefully with the centre of the rivet, otherwise you risk damaging the chain plates and mangling the link.
- Always check links that you've just joined. They'll often be stiff because the chain plates get squashed together as you push the rivet through them. Use your chain tool to spread the chain plates back out again, or the chain will slip over your sprockets as you pedal (see page 66).

Twisted links

Twisted links are usually victims of clumsy gear shifts, although they may be caused by trailside objects hitting the chain, too. You feel twisted links first – a regular, slight chain slip but not on every pedal stroke – it's important to fix them quickly to avoid more serious damage to your chain and derailleur.

Twisted links

The gaps between the chain plates are only just big enough to fit a sprocket or chainring tooth into, so once a link is twisted it usually rides up over the tops of the teeth rather than dropping into the valley, causing your chain to slip under pressure. Alternatively, if the twisted link does mesh successfully onto a chainring tooth, it can get stuck and be sucked around the back of the chainring, getting jammed between the chainstay and the chainring. As well as being annoying, this damages the chainring and chainstay.

Even after you've worked out that you have a twisted link, it can be tricky to spot. The best place to see one from is behind the bike. Get someone else to hold the bike upright and pedal slowly backward. Get behind the bike and look along the chain from the same level as the cassette. You should see the chain stretching away from you, from the top of the cassette to the top of a chainring. The links should all be in the same line, with the two sides parallel. As your friend pedals, fresh chain is constantly fed up through the derailleur. Keep watching the top section of chain; the twisted link will make an obvious kink in the straight line of the chain.

You have two options for sorting out the twisted link. The easiest is to re-twist the link straight again. If it works, this solution is quick and simple, but leaves the repaired link weaker. You need an Allen key and a small screwdriver, or any other combination of two small pointy things. Insert one on either side of the twisted link and gently ease the chain back until it's straight. Try to straighten the link in one movement because working it backward and forward weakens the metal. If you have a chain tool, a better option is to remove the twisted link for a permanent repair. This will shorten your chain, so check first that your chain will still be long enough to go around the big sprocket at the back and the big chainring at the front. If you shorten it too much and then shift into this gear, you risk damaging the rear derailleur and the part of the frame that it bolts onto. Check that you have sufficient length to remove a link by shifting into the largest sprocket and chainring.

Looking at the bottom of your chainring, identify the last chain link that's meshed onto a chainring tooth. Holding the pedals still and making sure that the rest of the chain stays wrapped around the chainring, pull this last link downward so that it releases from the valley between the two teeth. Move it anti-clockwise around the chainring and fit it back into the next-but-one valley. As you do this, watch the rear derailleur. Shortening the chain like this will drag the lower (tension) jockey wheel forwards. Hold the chain in this position and push the bottom jockey wheel upwards. If there's still enough slack in the chain for you to push it up 10mm (½ inch), then you can safely remove the twisted link. As with rejoining broken chains on pages 64–66, if you have to reduce the length of the chain beyond what you need to reach around the big chainring and sprocket, adjust the "low" end-stop screw on the rear derailleur so that you cannot shift accidentally into this gear combination. Shift into the largest sprocket that the chain will comfortably reach, then screw the "L" end-stop screw in until you feel resistance. For more details on end-stop screws, see pages 149 and 156.

▲ **Twisted links (A) can cause the chain to kink**

Fitting chains

Find the twisted link, as above. You will need to remove a complete link – one wide section and one narrow section. Use the instructions on page 64 to split the chain twice, once on either side of the twist. The remaining ends of the chain should be different – one wide and one narrow end. For standard, non-Shimano chains, the wide section should still have the rivet sticking out of one side. Use this to rejoin the ends of the chain. For Shimano chains, use a special replacement rivet to rejoin the two ends of the chain. New chains are always supplied much longer than you will ever need them so that you can be sure to have enough. When fitting a new chain, I always like to make it long enough so that I can safely take a link out in an emergency.

Twisted link

Remove one complete link ▶

Shortening chain to singlespeed

If you destroy your rear derailleur or hanger in a crash, one way of getting home under your own steam is to convert your bike to an impromptu singlespeed. This is much simpler on a hardtail than it is on a full suspension bike, as the chain length on most suspension bikes changes throughout the shock stroke. If you have to shorten the chain on a full suspension bike, then make sure you take account of the chain growth by compressing the shock as much as you can and watching to see whether or not the chain length you've chosen is long enough to accomodate it.

The first task is choosing a suitable gear. This is dependent on chainline as well as your fitness, and the best chance for success lies in choosing the middle chainring and the middle cassette sprocket (usually the third or fourth). Choose a random place in the chain and use the chain tool to seperate the chain, as shown on page 64. Remember to leave the rivet sticking out of the back of the chain if you're going to be using it to rejoin the chain.

Unthread the chain from the rear derailleur and re-route it to pass through the front derailleur, around the chainring of choice and then around the cassette sprocket of choice, bypassing the broken rear derailleur altogether if it's still on the frame. Match up the ends of the chain and work out how many links you need to remove to make the chain short enough. Finding the perfect spot can be tricky but it's better to have the chain slightly too slack than too tight, as an overly tight chain is more likely to snap again.

Rejoin the chain, using the instructions on page 65. You will have to ride carefully to keep the chain in place without the tension provided by the rear derailleur. Be as smooth as you can, keep up an even pressure on the pedals and don't be tempted to stand up and pedal as the jerky motion this entails is more likely to unseat the chain. Remember to save the section of chain you removed - you'll need to refit it to the chain once you've replaced the broken derailleur. Chains and cassettes wear together, with the chain stretching at the same rate as it erodes the teeth on the sprockets, which usually means you have to replace both cassette and chain at the same time unless they're both reasonably new.

◀ **Route the chain around a suitable sprocket, bypassing the rear derailleur**

Magic moment

I can't remember seeing many emergency bicycle repairs in movies, but I can recommend the ziptie repair from *Two Seconds*. The film is about a woman downhiller who quits racing. She packs her bike up and sets up to build a new life, but when she tries to put her bike back together, she finds she's lost the smallest sprocket from her cassette. I'm not sure why she had to take her cassette off the wheel to ship it, but after some pondering she replaces the missing sprocket with a ziptie. The ziptie neatly holds the other sprockets in place, allowing her to refit the lockring. In a short scene that must have been highly appreciated by a small section of the audience, she carefully readjusts the high end-stop screw to prevent the chain from shifting onto the missing sprocket. Top movie, and full marks for imaginative use of zipties.

Emergency wheel repairs

Wheels are excellent at resisting forces that are in line with them, like supporting your weight, riding or jumping. However, they buckle easily under forces from the side, the kind of forces that are common when you crash. A common disaster is crashing and folding either wheel so badly it won't turn between the brake blocks. The temptation is to release the offending brake and carry on riding, but clearly this is a bad idea – you're careful for 10 minutes, then you forget you only have one brake and pick up speed. And suddenly you've crashed again.

Use these pages to straighten your wheel by adjusting the tension in your spokes.

Your rim is supported all the way around by the tension in your spokes. The tension in each spoke can be increased or reduced by tightening (anticlockwise) **(A)** or loosening (clockwise) **(C)** the spoke nipple, effecting the short section of the rim to which the spoke is attached. Alternate spokes are attached to opposite sides of the hub. Tightening a spoke that leads towards the right-hand side of the hub will move the rim toward the right **(B)**; loosening this spoke will allow the rim to move toward the left. Truing wheels is about adjusting the tension in each spoke, so that the rim runs straight with no side-to-side wobble. This process is not the magic art that it's often made out to be – as long as you're careful about three things:

1) Spend a little time choosing the right spokes to adjust. Spin the wheel and watch the rim. Identify the section of the rim that is most bent – you may be lucky and have one single bent zone that you can concentrate on, but if the wheel is really buckled, you'll have to estimate where the centreline should be.

2) Working out which direction to turn each spoke nipple is really tricky at first. Use the photo (left) as a guide. Watch the rim as you turn the nipple. If the bulge gets worse rather than better, you're turning the nipple the wrong way.

3) Adjust the tension in each spoke in tiny steps. It's much better to work a quarter of a turn of the nipple at a time. Cranking the spoke key around in whole turns is a recipe for disaster. Adjust a quarter-turn, check the effect that you've had on the rim, go back and repeat if necessary.

When to beat your wheel

There is an urban myth that you can straighten bent wheels by banging them on the ground, hard, at the point where they're bent. This myth is responsible for generations of gullible cyclists taking a slightly distorted wheel that could have been saved and beating it into a wreck.

The problem arises because there are, in fact, limited circumstances in which beating a wheel is worth a go. First, it must have a specific shape – it must look like a Pringle crisp, with exactly four evenly spaced bends, two in each direction. Second, the distortion must have been caused very recently. And third, the wheel must spring back into shape with exactly one firm tap. You will have a much higher chance of success (although, obviously, this takes all the fun out of it) laying the wheel flat on the ground and standing on the two high points. But don't try anything forceful at all. It usually doesn't work and is likely to make things worse – and more expensive to fix when you do get home.

Broken spokes

If you ride a wheel with a spoke missing and don't straighten it, you will bend the rim permanently. Yet, as only long-distance riders heading for the Himalayas ever seem to carry spare spokes, there's a limit to what you can do if one does break. Rear wheel spokes can't be replaced unless you have the tools to remove and refit the cassette, making an emergency fix unlikely. But you can adjust the surrounding spokes to make the wheel as straight as possible, getting your brakes to work better (if you have rim brakes), and making it more likely you will be able to fix the wheel properly later.

First, render the snapped spoke safe by preventing it from wrapping around anything else. If it's broken near the rim, wind it around an adjacent spoke to keep it from rattling around. If it's broken near the hub, bend it in the middle so that you can hold it still. Use a spoke key to unwind the nipple so that the spoke drops out of the end of the nipple. If it's broken in the middle, which is the least likely, do both.

Lift up the wheel and spin it gently to see how bent it is. There will usually be a single large bulge where the spoke is broken. Use a spoke key to loosen the spokes on either side of the missing one. It can be confusing working out which way to turn. Look at the spoke you want to turn and imagine you can see the top of the spoke nipple through the tyre. To loosen a spoke, turn it so that the top of the spoke head turns anticlockwise.

With rim brakes, check the clearance between brake blocks and tyre. You may find that the tyre rubs on the brake block in the broken spoke zone. If this is the case, loosen the Allen key bolt that holds the brake block in place, and move the block down slightly so that it clears the tyre.

Straightening a bent wheel

With a spoke key, you can sometimes get the wheel straight enough to ride safely. As a guideline, if the wheel has more than 2cm (1 inch) of sideways movement when you spin it, you are unlikely to be able to straighten it with a spoke key. One seldom appreciated advantage of disc brakes is that the brakes continue to work properly when the wheel is bent.

Turn the bike upside down. If it's the back wheel, get behind the bike; if it's the front, get in front so that you're in line with the wheel. Spin the wheel and look at the area where it passes between the brake blocks (or, if you have disc brakes, where brake blocks would be). If the wheel is too wobbly to pass between the brake blocks, release your brake units. If it's too wobbly to pass between the frame, pick your bike up and start walking home.

If you think you can straighten the wheel, spin it a couple more times and look at its shape. You need to identify the point where the wheel is most bent – the biggest bulge away from the centre line. If you have rim brakes, use one of the brake blocks as a guide. Hold the brake unit still and spin the wheel, watching how the gap between the brake block and the rim changes. If the wheel is badly buckled, you're going to have to make a rough judgment about where the centre of the wheel is, and work towards that. You won't get perfection in the field – just get it round enough to roll.

Adjustments of a quarter- or half-turn of the nipple are plenty. It's easy to start with a buckled but salvageable wheel and end up with a useless pretzel by going too fast. Much better to stick to small steps. Check the previous page if you're not sure which way to turn the nipple.

STRAIGHTENING A WHEEL

Step 1: If you don't have rim brakes, you will have to improvise a gauge to measure the wobble of the wheel against. Zipties are invaluable here – either ziptie a stick to the chainstay or fork so that it sits level with the rim, or zip a tie around the fork or stay, leaving a long tag hanging off. Use the tag as your gauge.

Step 2: Spin the wheel again and stop it when the middle of the biggest bulge is level with your gauge. Look at the spokes on the wheel. You'll see that alternate spokes lead to opposite sides of the wheel.

Step 3: Choose the spoke at the centre of the bulge. If it leads to the same side of the wheel as the bulge, loosen this spoke and tighten the spokes on either side. A quarter- or half-turn should be enough. If the central spoke leads to the opposite side of the hub, tighten this spoke and loosen the spokes on either side by a quarter- or half-turn. Spin the wheel again, and pick out the biggest bulge.

Gear cable failure

Gear cables are specifically designed to pull against the resistance of a spring inside the derailleur. When the cable is released, the derailleur springs back to its default position. This is usually the smallest sprocket or chainring, though Shimano briefly produced a type of rear derailleur known as Rapid-Rise, or low-normal, which defaulted to the largest sprocket. If you do snap a gear cable, one option is to allow the chain to return to its default position and ride home in that gear, which still gives you the flexibility to use the other derailleur normally.

If the cable is broken and trailing wires, get rid of them so they don't catch on anything. Either undo the pinchbolt that holds the cable on and remove it completely, or coil up the dangling wire and tape it to your frame. If you're removing the cable, coil it up and take it home – don't discard it on the trail.

Broken rear gear cables occur relatively frequently because the cable is long and passes through several angles, especially with dual suspension bikes. Occasionally the cable frays and breaks; more often the outer casing splits and gives way. Both breaks have the same effect: without the pull of the cable, the spring in the derailleur pulls standard derailleurs to the smallest sprocket, and rapid-rise ones to the largest. Broken front gear cables seem to happen less often, maybe because they don't work as hard as rear ones. The breakdown is still irritating because the spring in the derailleur will pull the chain to the smallest chainring, leaving your legs spinning furiously without making much progress.

Broken rear derailleur cable

Gear cables usually fray long before they break. It's worth getting into the habit of checking them whenever you clean your bike so that you can replace them at the first signs of wear and tear. But sometimes they catch you out and break unexpectedly. Without the balancing tension of the cable, the spring in your derailleur will pull the chain into its neutral position – the smallest sprocket (highest gear) for normal derailleurs, or the largest sprocket (lowest gear) for rapid-rise derailleurs. This may not be the most convenient gear for you to limp home in, so try these methods of temporarily locking your chain into a more useful sprocket.

If you'd like an easier gear than the smallest sprocket at the back, you can use the end-stop screws to reset the derailleur. Get someone to lift up the saddle to get the back wheel off the ground. Turn the pedals slowly with your right hand and use a Phillips screwdriver to screw in (clockwise) the high 'H' end-stop screw. As you turn the end-stop screw, the chain will gradually change gear from the smallest sprocket to the next one. It might even make it to the third sprocket. When the screw has gone in as far as possible, back it off (undo it, anticlockwise) so that the chain runs easily in the chosen gear, without clicking or trying to drop into another gear.

A spare scrap of cable can be used temporarily to set the chain to run in a lower gear. A spare brake cable will work if you have one; if not, remove the broken cable from the shifter and use the end with a nipple still attached. Feed the cable through the barrel-adjuster on the rear derailleur so the nipple sits in or over the barrel-adjuster. Next, push the rear derailleur across by hand so that it sits under a more convenient sprocket, and clamp the cable in the usual place under the pinch bolt. Use the barrel-adjuster to fine-tune the position of the derailleur so the chain sits directly under a sprocket without rattling. Coil up spare cable so it doesn't get caught in the chain or back wheel.

◀ **Using a scrap of cable to set the derailleur in a convenient sprocket**

Broken front derailleur cable

Your front derailleur cable pulls your front derailleur outwards when you operate the shifter, shunting the chain from the smallest chainring to the middle and then largest chainrings. When you release the cable tension by clicking the triggershifters or rolling the twistshifters back, the spring in the front derailleur pulls the cage back, shunting the chain back into the middle and then smallest sprocket.

▲ **Pull the derailleur outward, over the middle chainring**

If your front derailleur cable breaks, the derailleur spring will simply pull the cage back over the smallest sprocket, leaving you with only your lowest range of gears. Cycling home in the smallest front sprocket is likely to be annoying. You will probably want to try to set the front derailleur so that it runs in the middle sprocket, rather than the small one, unless your whole route home is up a steep hill.

If the low 'L' end-stop screw **(A)** will reach far enough, you can use it to set the derailleur position so that the chain runs in the middle ring. Reach in behind the chainset and lift the chain from the smallest chainring so that it sits on the middle chainring. Pull the front derailleur cage outward so that it is centred over the middle chainring. Holding it there, tighten the low 'L' adjustment screw (turning it clockwise) as far as it will go. Release the derailleur cage with your right hand and assess where it sits.

The front derailleur is ideally positioned when there is a 1mm (1⁄16 inch) gap between the outer plate of the front derailleur cage and the chain, with the chain in the smallest sprocket at the back. If the cage is too far out, so that the gap is bigger than this, undo the 'L' adjustment screw by turning it anticlockwise until the derailleur sits in the right place. You will now be able to use the rear gears normally.

You may find that even when it's screwed in as far as it will go, the 'L' end-stop screw will not push the derailleur out far enough – not surprising, since this is not really what the end-stop screw was designed to do. If you can persuade it to sit mostly over the middle ring, you may still be able to use the larger rear sprockets normally. Avoid shifting into the smaller sprockets as this will cause the chain to rub on the derailleur, pushing it over so that you drop back annoyingly into the smallest chainring.

Alternatively, if you can't make any progress with the end-stop screw, you may be able to wedge something behind the front derailleur to hold it out from the frame. Nature is packed with suitable devices – sticks are perfect. Pull out the derailleur and tuck something in to hold it in place. This is one of those occasions when it's handy to have a sharp knife in your toolkit, so that you can shape the wedge. The spring in your front derailleur may be enough to hold your wedge in place, but zipties can help to stop it rattling free. You may even be able to set the derailleur so that your chain runs on the largest chainring. If you come to a hill, stop at the bottom and pull your wedge out, climb the hill in your small chainring, and refit the wedge at the top. Again, you should still be able to use your rear derailleur, but don't shift into gears that mean that the chain rubs on the derailleur cage – it will slow you down and wear out the cage.

Coil up the broken derailleur cable and secure it out of the way so that it doesn't get tangled up in your wheel, brakes or suspension. The frayed broken ends are surprisingly sharp. Make sure they don't stick out and stab your legs. Undo the cable clamp bolt and remove the stray piece of cable. Retighten the cable clamp bolt so that it doesn't rattle loose.

Derailleurs that have been badly bent in a crash may not respond to this treatment. If the cage is too twisted to allow the chain to pass through it, you will have to remove the derailleur completely. Undo the cable clamp bolt and coil the cable out of the way. Undo and remove the front derailleur fixing bolt. Your chain will still be trapped in the derailleur cage. Avoid splitting and rejoining the chain, which can be fiddly and weakened. Instead, undo and remove the bolt at the back of the derailleur cage and slide the chain out from inside the cage. Sit the chain back onto one of the chainrings. You may not have this option on recent front derailleurs.

You would expect the chain to stay in whichever chainring you've chosen, but without the guidance of the front derailleur, it will usually jump off. Mostly, it will head for a smaller chainring. You can minimize unexpected changes by pedalling as smoothly as possible, and by staying in the larger sprockets at the back, which helps to keep the chain tension high.

Occasionally the bolt that holds the back of the derailleur cage together can rattle loose. This tends to make front shifting sluggish rather than hopeless, but you can secure the two halves together with a ziptie through the bolt hole to restore full function.

Twelve routine safety checks before you ride

Checking your bike every time you ride it can seem like a lot of effort, and it can also seem a little bit boring. It needn't take more than a few moments, however, and occasionally you'll appreciate the time it takes because you'll pick up a problem waiting to happen that is far easier to fix before you set off. Looking carefully at your bike on a regular basis also makes it easier to spot when something is wrong.

It's worth having a routine for checking your bike. Doing it in the same order every time means you're less likely to miss something. It's worth going through a mental checklist at the same time to ensure you have everything else you need for a ride. Your needs will depend on how far you intend to leave civilization behind, but normal items include plenty of water, emergency food, appropriate clothing, sunblock, map, tools and pump, as well as checking that somebody knows where you're going and when you are expected back. If you can rely on coverage, a mobile phone can be a fantastic asset in an emergency. It's not a substitute for careful preparation though.

1) **Quick-release skewer:** Check both wheels are securely attached. Quick-release levers must be firmly folded to line up with the fork blade or rear stay; otherwise they can snag on things and open accidentally. Most levers have 'open' and 'closed' printed on opposite sides. Fold the lever so the 'closed' side is visible. Bolt-thru axles should be checked for security too.

2) **Tyres:** Check tyres for bald patches, tears and sharp things. The glass and thorns, etc., which cause punctures often take time to work through the tyre casing. Inspect your tyres frequently and pick out foreign objects. It's tedious but quicker than fixing the punctures they cause!

3) **Spokes:** Check for broken spokes. Gently brush a hand over both sides of both wheels, with the ends of your fingers brushing the spokes. Even one broken spoke weakens a wheel considerably. A permanent repair is also much easier if the wheel hasn't been ridden on.

4) **Front wheel:** Lift front end of the bike off ground and spin the front wheel. Check it runs freely and doesn't wobble between the forks.

5) **Rim brakes:** Check the brake blocks don't touch the tyre or rim as the wheel turns. Rubbing blocks wear quickly and slow you down. Check position of the brake blocks. Each block should be parallel to the rim, low enough to avoid hitting the tyre but not so low that any part of the brake block hangs below the rim. (N.B. Photo opposite is of a disc-brake bike.)

6) **Disc-brake calliper:** Check disc pads. You should have at least 0.5mm of brake pad on each side of the rotor; if you don't, fit new pads before you ride.

7) **Brake levers:** Carry out a simple brake check every time you ride. Stand beside the bike, push it gently forward, then pull on the front brake. The front wheel should lock on and the back one should lift off the ground. If not, don't ride!

8) **Brake levers:** Use a similar test for the back brake. Push the bike forward, then pull on the back brake. The back wheel should lock and slide along the ground. If not, do not ride.

9) **Chain:** Check the drivetrain. The chain should be clean and should run smoothly through the gears without falling off either side of the sprocket or the chainset. Turn pedals backwards and watch the chain run through the derailleur. Stiff links flick the derailleur forward as they pass over the lower jockey wheel. It's worth sorting them out since they can cause your gears to slip under pressure.

10) **Cables and hoses:** Check all cables (brake and gear) for kinks in the outer casing or frays in the cable. Frayed cables should be replaced immediately. Clean and oil rusty or dirty cables. Check hydraulic hoses for links or leaks; inspect the joints between hose and calliper, and hose and brake lever. Run your finger down each hose while pumping the brake levers – you'll feel any leaks or weak spots.

11) **Stem:** Check that stem and bars are tight. Stand over the front wheel, gripping it between your knees. Try turning the bars. They shouldn't move independently. Try twisting the bars in the stem too. If you have bar ends, lean down on them. Tighten any loose steering components.

12) **Pedals:** Check the cleats in the pedals. Make sure you can clip into and out of both sides of both pedals easily.

Toolbox

Tools for three comfort zones

- 6mm Allen key to adjust saddle position
- 4 or 5mm Allen key to adjust saddle height (or quick release)
- 5 or 6mm Allen key to adjust bar and stem position
- 4mm Allen key to adjust cleat position

Tools for cleaning routine

- Muc-Off or bike wash
- Degreaser
- Stiff brush
- Sponge frame
- Chain oil to re-lubricate
- Plenty of warm water

Three comfort zones

You touch your bike in three places: at the handlebars with your hands, at the saddle with your butt and at the pedals with your feet. If these points on the bike are in the right place, and of the right shape, you will be comfortable. If they're not, you won't.

Bike size

A bike that is the wrong size will always be uncomfortable. Always test-ride before buying a new bike and get the shop to help you choose. Different bike manufacturers measure frames in different ways so you can't assume that if one 18-inch bike fits you they all will. As a guide, stand over the bike with your feet flat on the floor. Lift up the seat and handlebars as far as you can. You should have 7–14cm (2¾–5½ inches) clearance between the tyres and the ground. If you have to raise the seatpost above its safety mark to get enough leg extension, the frame is too small. When buying a new bike, don't just check for frame height. Try different models to find one that also feels a comfortable length, since this varies from bike to bike. You can make small changes to the reach by altering the saddle position and stem length, but it helps to start from a position close to the right one.

Bars & stem

Saddle

Pedals

The saddle

Get the height right first. Sit on your bike in the normal way with hands on the bars, leaning against a wall. Turn the pedals so the cranks are vertical, and put your heel on the lower pedal. Your knee should just lock straight in this position. Check the measurement with your other leg too; it's not unusual to have one leg shorter than the other. Set your seat height for the shorter leg. With this measurement, when you pedal normally – with the ball of your foot on the centre of the pedal — your leg will be almost, but not quite, straight at the bottom of its stroke. Next, set the saddle angle. For almost everybody, the most comfortable angle is with the top of the saddle exactly horizontal. If you find yourself tipping the nose of the saddle down more than a couple of degrees to be comfortable, think about swapping your saddle for a different one. Everybody has a different shape so you may have to try a selection of different models before finding the correct profile. See page 23 for help adjusting your saddle angle and position. Finally, set the fore-and-aft position. Start with the saddle in the centre of the rails. If you find yourself pushing over the back of the saddle when climbing, move the saddle backwards a little. Move the saddle forwards if you feel you need to be closer to the bars – this can be a good alternative to fitting a shorter stem if you feel too stretched out. A popular guideline is to sit on the saddle and use a plumbline to check that the front of your knee is directly over the centre of the pedal. I prefer to sit slightly further forward than this, but it's a matter of personal taste.

Don't fool yourself into suffering an uncomfortable saddle. There are so many different kinds; at least one will fit you. Equally, don't expect the saddle that comes on your new bike, or the first you try, to be perfect. If you have a saddle that suits you, transfer it to new bikes. Titanium rails are not only lighter but more flexible, giving a comfortable ride. Leather covers breathe better than plastic ones, which makes a big difference on hot days.

Women's saddles have become comfortable in the last five years; manufacturers have realized that women not only buy bicycles, they also expect riding them to be a pleasant experience. Again, there are different types so try before you buy. Holes and slots cut in the centre of saddles are good for relieving pressure but can be disconcertingly draughty on cold days.

Bars and stem

Reach (the distance between handlebars and saddle) and handlebar height affect how comfortable you are on the bike, as well as how effectively you can use your shoulder strength for control. Threadless headset systems give less opportunity to adjust the stem height than the older threaded version but new bikes should have had spacers fitted beneath or above the stem to give at least some choice. Height and reach can also be altered by changing your stem (see page 26). Shorter, higher stems give a comfortable riding position for beginners but be careful to avoid cramping your reach. They do encourage you to look where you're going, though, and the magic nature of bicycles means they go where you're looking (thus the common warning, "look at the trail, not at the view").

Short stems liven up the steering and give more control at speed, and in conjunction with wider bars are currently popular on everything but out-and-out race bikes. These tend to flaunt longer, lower stems, which stretch your body weight forwards. This helps to keep the front wheel on the ground whilst climbing steep trails and roads and transfers some of your body weight from the saddle to the front wheel. The aerodynamic advantage found in such a position is irrelevant for mountain bikers, though, as anyone who's watched the spectacle of a bunch of mountain bikers, with large backpacks and flapping baggy shorts, adopting aero-tucks in an attempt to beat each other to the bottom of the hill will testify. Riser bars give an extra 3cm (1¼ inches) or so of height and can be rolled around to match the sweep of the bars to the angle of your wrists, which can make all the difference to sore shoulders. Handlebar material is also important for comfort. More costly bars are usually made of thinner-walled tubing, or even carbon, both of which are better able to absorb the vibration that can leave you with tired wrists though the effect of this is all but completely overshadowed if you're running a suspension fork, rather than a rigid fork. Bar ends give extra leverage when climbing and provide an alternative hand position so you can shift about on the bars to ease fatigue through your wrists. The easiest way to find the optimum angle for bar ends is to loosen them off so they rotate on the handlebars, sit on the bike, close your eyes, and grip them. Then tighten them securely in that position. Take a bit of care when choosing grips. Your hand is going to spend a lot of time holding them. Match the grip diameter to your hand size. For hot weather, choose a pattern with ribs or grooves so they don't get too slippery when wet. If your hands get sore, choose a grip that supports the palm, to keep the blood flowing through your wrists.

Pedals

The third point of contact with the bike is through your feet, and, as with the other points of contact, a little care makes your machine more comfortable. Most SPD pedals are very small so they're light and don't snag on the ground. This can cause discomfort, with all the pedalling pressure concentrated on a small area of your foot. Use stiff-soled shoes so that the pressure is spread over the whole of the sole. Alternatively, consider using an SPD shoe with a cage, which can support your foot over a wider area.

Regular cleaning routine

Cleaning your bike is the best time to spot worn or broken parts that could otherwise fail and leave you stranded in the wilderness. Beware of jet washes though. The power hoses on garage forecourts can leave your bike looking very shiny without much effort, but, no matter how careful you are, they force water in through the bearing seals, flushing grease out. This shortens the lifespan of bearings, pivots and other components radically.

As a principle, start with the dirtiest bits and work up to the cleaner ones. That way, you minimize the amount of recleaning you may have to do.

If starting from scratch, here's a routine to transform your bike. Drop off the wheels and hang it up so you can reach everything.

1) Start with the drivetrain: the chain, sprockets, chainset and derailleurs. If the chain isn't too dirty, clean it with a rag.

2) If your chain is too oily and dirty to respond to this treatment, give it a thorough clean. You can do a very respectable job without removing the chain from the bike, which is a lot of trouble and can weaken the link you remove. For the best results with the least fuss, tip a little degreaser into a small pot. Use a toothbrush or washing-up brush dipped in degreaser to scrub the chain clean. A chain-cleaning box is a good investment, making this job cleaner and quicker. See page 48.

3) Sprockets and chainsets need regular cleaning too. They're close to the ground and exposed to whatever's going around. If they're oily and dirty, it's worth degreasing them. Oil is sticky and picks up dirt as you ride along, wearing out the drivetrain. As above, use a little degreaser and work it into the sprockets and chainset with a brush. It's very important to rinse things very carefully afterward to remove all traces of degreaser. Also, dry components carefully. Be careful not to get degreaser into bearings.

4) Once everything is clean and dry, re-lubricate the chain. I prefer drip oils to spray types because you can direct the oil more precisely, which ensures you can get it where it's needed without wastage. Drip a little onto the top links of the bottom stretch of chain all the way around. Don't use excessive amounts of oil. Leave the oil to soak in for five minutes, then carefully remove excess with a clean rag. Don't worry about re-lubing other drivetrain components as they need no more than is deposited by the chain onto the sprockets.

5) Next, clean the wheels. Muddy tyres are best cleaned by riding your bike along a tarmac road (with your mouth shut) once the mud is dry. Use a sponge and a bucket of warm soapy water, hold the wheels upright to keep water out of the hubs, and sponge the hubs and spokes clean.

6) Rim brakes work much better on clean rims. They pick up dirt from the ground and from the brake blocks, which stops the blocks from gripping the rim effectively, causing both rims and blocks to wear out prematurely. Green nylon Brillo pads are ideal for this job. Wire wool is too harsh but nylon gets detritus off the rims without damaging the braking surface. While you're there, check for bulges or cracks in the braking surface. These indicate that the rim is worn out and needs replacing urgently. If your rim has rim-wear indicators, check them now too. (N.B. Photo opposite is of a disc-brake bike.)

7) Disc rotors, the alternative braking surface, also work much better when clean. It's important not to contaminate them with oil. Use bicycle disc brake cleaner or isopropyl alcohol for disc rotors. If they have become oily, clean the rotors with isopropyl alcohol (from chemists), which doesn't leave a residue. Don't be tempted by car disc cleaner – this leaves a residue that cannot be scrubbed off by the brakes.

8) Brakes next. For rim brakes, remove the wheel and clean the block surfaces. Use a small screwdriver or knife (carefully) to pick out shards of metal. If the block surface has become shiny, use a strip of clean sandpaper to roughen it. When looking at the brake blocks, check they aren't excessively or unevenly worn. Most blocks have a wear-line embossed onto the rubber. If the blocks originally had slots, make sure the slots are still visible. Once they disappear, it's time for new brake blocks.

9) For disc brakes, wipe the calliper clean. Check hydraulic hoses for oil leaks. There should be no trace of oil at any of the connections. Also check for kinks in the hoses. Look into the rotor slot on the calliper, and check that the brake pad is at least 1mm thick.

10) Clean and oil the parts of your cables normally trapped inside casing.

11) For rear cable brakes, follow the black casing back from the brake lever to the frame. At the cable stop, pull the casing forward to release it from the cable stop and wiggle the brake cable out of the slot. Use the same method to release the other sections of casing. Run a clean rag over the part that's normally covered by outer casing. Relubricate each section with a drop of oil. Refit the outer casing.

12) Repeat with the gear casing. You need to click your rear shifter as if changing into the highest gear, then push the derailleur away again (see page 149 if you are unsure how to do this). This creates enough slack in the cable to pull a section of casing out of its cable stop. Repeat with all the other sections of casing, cleaning and oiling – especially the last loop of rear derailleur cable. This loop is nearest to the ground and tends to collect dirt. Refit the outer casing.

13) Pull the front derailleur out over the largest chainring, click the shifter as if to change into the smallest sprocket, then release the casing in the same way. Clean, oil and replace. A sticky gear cable causes sloppy shifting.

14) Pedals are often forgotten, even though they get more than their fair share of mud and abuse. Use a small screwdriver to clear all the mud from around the release mechanism. Make sure you do both sides of both pedals. Mud gets forced into the springs every time you clip in with your shoes, building up until you can no longer clip in and out properly. Lubricate the moving parts sparingly with a light oil, like GT85 or WD40.

Clean the frame and forks. You need a sponge and a bucket of warm water to rinse everything off afterwards. All components work better and last longer if they're not covered in grime. Finally, a quick polish. Wax-based polish helps stop dirt sticking to the frame, keeping it cleaner for next time. Refit the wheels, reconnect the brakes. This is a good time to pump up the tyres, just to finish the job off neatly.

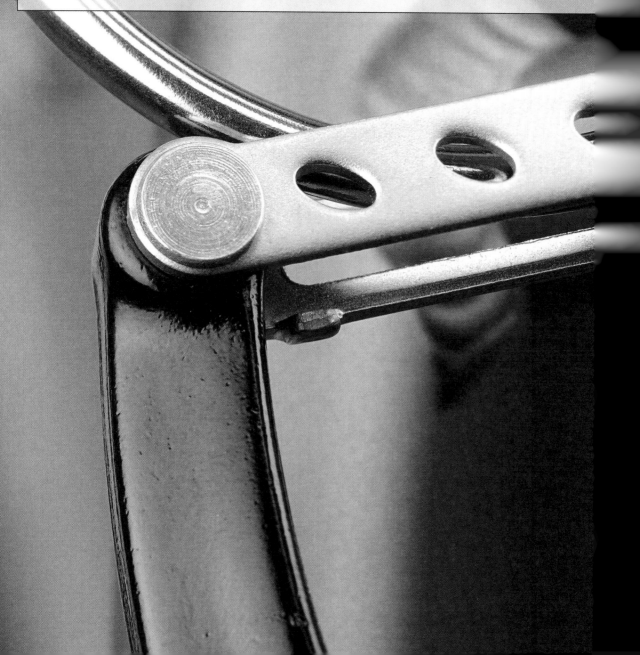

4 – Brakes

The brakes on your bike probably need more attention than all the other components put together. It's an inevitable part of cycling that you'll need to do lots of stopping and starting, and that some of this will need to be done in a very short distance at very short notice. Learning how your brakes work and how to adjust them, means you can ensure they're always giving you as much control as possible. Constant use will wear your brakes out, giving you plenty of opportunity to practise replacing them.

Brakes: build your stopping power

Well-tuned brakes make you go faster. This might seem like a contradiction, but it's true. In order to be able to go fast, you need to be able to control your speed safely. Crisp, reliable brakes will make you feel more confident and get you out of trouble when you push things too far.

Brakes are very satisfying to work on. Their performance tends to deteriorate slowly, with pads and cables getting slightly more worn and dirty with each ride, but not usually so suddenly that you notice them getting worse. The good thing about this is that when you come to fit fresh parts, or clean and service units and cables, your brakes will feel significantly better – always very satisfying!

Brakes are obviously a mission-critical safety component. Always check them very carefully after you've done any work on them so that you can be sure you're safe to ride away. Make sure both brakes are working properly, then go back over all your nuts and bolts and check that you've tightened them all up. Anything that's left a little bit loose will rattle free as soon as you ride hard, likely leaving you in trouble.

Rim brake pads have universal fittings, but disc brake pads haven't settled down to a standard yet. Consequently, there are about 30 different patterns, with slightly different shapes, sizes and fittings. This is really annoying as the pads won't fit unless you get exactly the right kind. It's worth making sure you always have a spare set so that you don't get caught out.

Cable brakes are simpler to deal with than hydraulic ones, but the extra braking power you get from the hydraulics makes them well worth learning about. Dealing with brake fluid can seem a bit of a leap into the unknown, even if you feel very confident working with other parts of your bike. But it's not really significantly more complicated than other tasks, just a bit different. Treat brake fluid – whether it's DOT or mineral oil – with respect: it's not good for your skin. Both fluids will contaminate brake pads, causing them to have trouble gripping the rotors properly. DOT will also strip the paint off your frame if you spill it. Wear gloves, and work slowly and patiently.

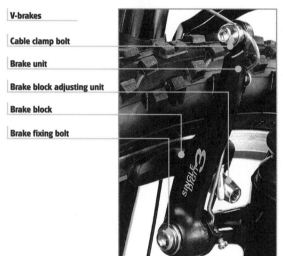

V-brakes

Cable clamp bolt

Brake unit

Brake block adjusting unit

Brake block

Brake fixing bolt

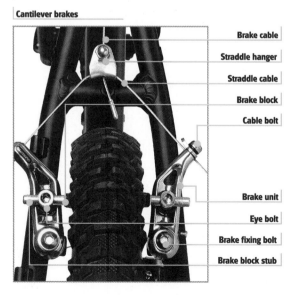

Cantilever brakes

Brake cable

Straddle hanger

Straddle cable

Brake block

Cable bolt

Brake unit

Eye bolt

Brake fixing bolt

Brake block stub

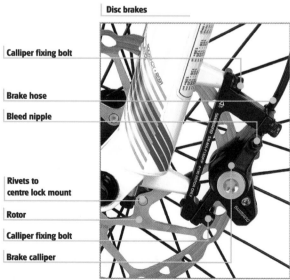

Disc brakes

Calliper fixing bolt

Brake hose

Bleed nipple

Rivets to centre lock mount

Rotor

Calliper fixing bolt

Brake calliper

V-brakes: a general introduction and how to manage wear and tear

V-brakes were standard issue on mountain bikes until disc brakes took over but are still a very useful braking system for hybrid town bikes. They are cheap and simple to maintain and provide a good amount of braking power. Here follows an outline of the advantages and disadvantages of this braking system.

V-brakes ousted cantilevers because they are more powerful, as well as being easier to adjust. However, there has always been a trade-off in terms of pad wear – cantilever pads last much longer. V-brakes stop you faster because the way they are designed pushes them onto the rim harder than cantilevers, wearing out both the rim and brake blocks faster. So, enjoy the powerful braking but remember that as a direct consequence you are going to have to learn to inspect brake blocks frequently for wear and replace them. Depending on where and how you ride, you can wear out brake blocks at the rate of a set per day, and through a rim in a matter of months.

Regular maintenance

Keeping blocks and rims clean will make a huge difference to how long they both last. Dirty rims will wear out brake blocks, while flakes of grit and metal caught in your brake blocks will scour the rim surface. It's easy to forget that the rims are an integral part of the braking system. Unless they're clean and flat, the brake blocks will struggle to grip them and stop you in your tracks.

This section takes you through the processes of checking that your V-brakes are set up and working correctly, fitting new brake blocks, fitting a new cable and servicing your brake units. Careful brake-block alignment and smooth cables will help you get the most power out of your brakes. You'll also get more feedback from them. Good set-up means that when your hands are on the brake levers, you will be able to feel what effect the brakes are having, increasing your control over the bike. Good brakes don't just lock the wheel up, they allow you to control your speed accurately.

One important thing to remember is that brake blocks and cables often just need cleaning rather than replacing. Cables can be cleaned rather than replaced as long as they're not frayed or kinked. Use the following procedure for replacing your cable. Keep to the instructions for removing the old cable, then clean it with a light oil like GT85. If necessary, soak congealed dirt off with degreaser. Cut the end of the cable off cleanly so that it can be neatly threaded through the outer casing. Clean the inside of the outer casing by squirting spray oil through it to flush out dirt. Replace any sections that are cracked, squashed or kinked. Replace bent ferrules. Then refit as a new cable.

Worn-out brake blocks

Brake blocks must be replaced if they're worn below the wear-indication lines stamped on the block. If there are no wear lines, replace the brake blocks when you've worn down to the base of any grooves moulded into the block. They're also due for replacement if any of the metal over which the rubber block is moulded is showing through. Otherwise, they can be cleaned and freshened up. Follow the instructions for removing the blocks. Use a sharp knife to cut off overhanging lips at the edge of the brake block, and use clean sandpaper to flatten the braking surface of the block. Pick out any flakes of metal or grit. Refit as new brake blocks.

V-brakes are bolted onto your frame or forks by studs called brake pivots. Newer, disc-only frames and forks, as well as road bike frames, don't have these pivots, and so cannot be fitted with V-brakes. Currently, many new hybrid bikes have both disc mounts and V-brake pivots, allowing you to upgrade from V-brakes to discs.

The brake units are designed to rotate around the pivots so the condition of the pivots is important. If the surface is rusty or corroded, your brakes won't pull smoothly onto the rim or spring back smartly. If your brakes are sluggish and fitting a fresh cable has no effect, see page 92 to service your brake units, and to clean and oil the pivots.

Crashing can also bend the brake pivots, preventing you from adjusting them properly. Look at the brakes from face on: the front brake from in front of the bike, the rear brake from behind it. You'll see the heads of the two brake-fixing units at the bottom of each unit. These should point straight out from the frame so that the bolts are parallel. Bent brake units don't just make it awkward to adjust the brake block position, they can also be a liability. Many fork pivots, and some frame pivots, can be replaced; check with the manufacturer for spares. Although, if you have disc mounts as well as V-brake pivots, this could be a good excuse for an upgrade.

V-brakes: a quick check-up to help ensure performance every ride

However casual you are about bike maintenance, you need to make sure that your brakes are working properly every time you set off on a ride. This doesn't need to be a lengthy procedure – just give your bike a careful visual check before you head off.

The steps below make up a quick and regular check to keep your brakes in good running order and they give you warning when it's time for a more serious overhaul.

Each of the steps below includes relevant page numbers, so that if any of the checks show a problem with your braking system, you can sort it out straight away. Whatever you do, don't set off on a ride with brakes that don't work properly.

Lift each wheel and spin it, to check the brakes don't rub on the rims or the tyre as the wheel turns. Look at the gap between the brake block and the rim on each side of each brake. See pages 85–87.

You'll need to disconnect the brake cable so that you can pull the brake blocks out from the rim. V-brakes are designed to make this easy. They also help when you want to remove and replace the wheels because you can get the tyre out past the brake blocks without letting the air out.

The brake cable

The brake cable arrives at the brake unit via a short curved metal tube called a 'noodle' or 'lead pipe' (pronounced as in 'leading in the right direction', not 'lead, the heavy metal'). The end of the lead pipe has a pointed head with a raised collar. The brake cable passes through the noodle and then clamps onto one of the brake units. The other brake unit has a hinged hanger with a key-shaped hole for the noodle. The collar stops the noodle pulling through the hanger, so when you pull on the cable, the two brake units are drawn together, pulling the brake blocks onto the rim. The section of cable between the hanger and the cable clamp bolt is often concealed inside a black rubber boot that helps keep the cable clean.

To release the brake units, draw back the rubber boot to reveal the head of the noodle where it emerges from the hanger. Squeeze the two brake units together to create slack in the cable. Pull the noodle back and out of the key-shaped hole, then pull up to release the cable from the slot in the key-shaped hole. Let go of the brake units – they will spring right back from the rim.

To reconnect the brakes, squeeze the brake units firmly onto the rim. Pull back the rubber boot so that it's out of the way of the noodle, and guide the head of the noodle into the hole in the hanger. Make sure it's seated securely: the raised collar must be butted firmly up against the hanger. Refit the rubber boot back over the head of the noodle. Pull the brake lever to confirm that everything is seated correctly.

CHECKING V-BRAKES

Step 1: Inspect the condition of the pads. Release the brakes (see above), pull each side away from the rim, and check that each braking surface is flat, has nothing stuck in it and isn't worn through. If they're worn, see pages 86–87 for replacement instructions. Otherwise, reconnect the brakes, checking that the brake noodle is firmly and securely located in its hanger.

Step 2: Check that each block hits the rim flat, square and level. Brake blocks that are too high will cut through the tyre, causing explosive punctures. Blocks that are too low hang under the rim, wasting brake potential and creating a lip that eventually starts to snag on the rim. See page 85 for brake block adjustment.

Step 3: Run your hand along each cable, from lever to brake unit, checking for corrosion, kinks, fraying or damage to the casing **(A)**. See pages 90–91 for tips on cable care. Pull the lever firmly towards the bars and check that each brake locks the wheel when the lever is halfway to the bars; if it doesn't see page 85.

Brake blocks: keeping your eyes open for regular wear and tear

Inspect your brake blocks frequently for wear, replacing them as they get thin and pick up grit and swarf. Worn blocks make for a useless braking surface and eat expensive rims for breakfast. Ignore this important task and your rims will wear right through the rubber of the block to the metal innards of the moulded pad. Brake blocks have a wear line indicating when they should be changed. If you can't see a wear line, change the pads when they've worn to the bottom of the grooves moulded into the pad.

Even if you don't wear out blocks very quickly, you should still change them periodically as they harden with time and don't work as well. Every couple of years should do.

In between full changes, check on the condition of the pad and improve it. This is easiest to do with the wheels removed.

Release the brakes and remove the wheel. Look at the condition of the pad. It should be flat and even, without visible contamination. If you can see flecks of metal, use a sharp knife and carefully pick them out. If the pad has been sitting too low or at an angle, it will wear unevenly, leaving a lip that gets caught under the rim and prevents the brakes from letting go properly. This is a waste of brake block and braking potential. Carefully cut the offending lip off with a sharp knife, then follow the instructions to reposition your brake block so that it contacts the rim more evenly. If the brake block sits too high, it will wear through the tyre – an expensive error.

Lightly sand the surface of the brake block with clean sandpaper. People often use a file for this, but shouldn't – it will hold metal flakes from whatever it was you last filed, and they will now embed themselves in the blocks. Clean your rims too. If they have sticky black streaks, use degreaser. Oil or tar on your rims will squeal alarmingly, allowing your wheels to slip through the blocks without slowing you down. A green nylon washing-up scourer works well for stubborn stains, and will scrub off contamination without damaging your rims.

Some brake blocks are designed with removable rubber blocks. The old, worn ones are removed by pulling out a retaining pin at the back of the metal cartridge and sliding the rubber part backwards. Replacement rubber blocks slide in in the same way and are held in place with the retaining pin. Always make sure the open end of the cartridge faces towards the back of the bike; otherwise heavy braking will rip the rubber out of the cartridge. The replacement blocks can be stiff to slide into the slots in the cartridge; it often helps to dip them in warm water.

ADJUSTING BRAKE BLOCKS

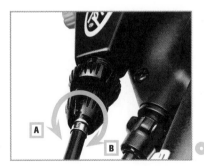

Step 1: Loosen the brake block fixing nut. Wiggle the block so that its top edge doesn't touch the tyre, and the bottom edge doesn't undercut the rim. The top and bottom of the block should be equal distances from the rim, with the front of the block 1mm closer than the back – 'toe-in'. Once it's right, tighten the fixing nut firmly – hold as shown so the block doesn't twist as you tighten.

Step 2: Adjust the cable tension: undo the cable clamp bolt, holding the cable as shown so you can use your other fingers to steady the brake unit. Pull or release cable so that the gap between brake blocks and rim is around 2mm. Retighten the cable clamp bolt firmly, then spin the wheel. The rims should pass freely between the brake blocks, then lock when the lever is pulled halfway to the bars.

Step 3: Fine-tune the brake using the barrel adjuster at the brake lever. It's normally prevented from working loose by a lockring – turn this anticlockwise several turns to release the barrel adjuster, then roll the barrel adjuster anticlockwise **(A)** to move the brake blocks closer to the rim, or clockwise **(B)** for more clearance. Spin the wheel, retest and readjust. When you're satisfied, roll the lockring clockwise to wedge it against the brake lever.

Replacing and adjusting brake blocks

One of the points used to sell V-brakes originally was that changing the brake blocks would be easier than with cantilever brakes. This is slightly misleading – changing blocks is not difficult, but it can be fiddly. I often find myself wishing I had smaller fingers – or more of them.

The key is to set up the brake units so that they're parallel and vertical before fitting the brake blocks into the units. Most new brake blocks come with a new set of curved washers but occasionally you'll have to reuse the old ones. It's a good idea to clean your rims at the same time so that the new brake surfaces can get maximum grip.

CHANGING BRAKE BLOCKS

Step 1: Undo and remove Allen key nut on the end of the old brake block stud, then wriggle out the old block and its curved washers. The new brake block comes with fresh washers, but keep old ones as spares. Now look at the position of the brake units. They should be parallel and vertical **(A)**. Get the position of the units right before you fit new brake blocks. If they're not parallel, undo cable pinch bolt and pull in or release cable. Retighten the pinch bolts.

Step 2: You may find the units are parallel but pointing off to one side. If so, use the balance screws **(A)** at the bottom of each unit to even out the spring tension. This screw is normally a slot head but might be an Allen key. Choose the side that sits closer to the wheel and move the screw half a turn clockwise. Pull and release the brake to settle the spring and repeat until brake arms are even. See page 88 for detailed explanation of the balance screw.

Step 3: Check whether the brake blocks are designed for fitting in a particular direction. Any arrows should point forwards, and the shape of the block should follow the curve of the rim. Each block comes with a collection of curved washers to space and angle the block. Their order of use varies from bike to bike and depends on the distance between the brake unit and the rim.

Step 4: There should be a domed washer on the inside of the brake unit with the flat side facing the brake unit, and a cup washer between the dome and the brake block. Choose either the thick one or the thin one so that the block sits close to the rim, but not touching. A gap of about 2–3mm (around 1/8 inch) is ideal.

Step 5: The adjustment does not need to be perfect at this stage, just approximate. With the stub of the brake block sticking out through the slot in the brake unit, fit the other domed washer, flat side against the brake unit. Then fit the remaining cup washer, followed by any flat washers. Finally, loosely fit the Allen key nut.

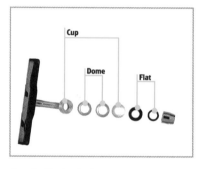

Step 6: You will find that with this arrangement you can alter the angle of the brake block, and also slide it up and down in the slot in the brake unit. Set the position of the brake block so that when you pull on the brakes, the block hits the rim with the fixing bolt at 90° to the surface of the rim. The block should be level, not higher at the front or back. None of the block should hang over the top or bottom of the rim.

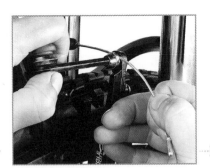

Step 7: 'Toeing-in': the front of the block **(B)** should be 1mm ($\frac{1}{16}$ inch) closer to the rim than the back, facing the same direction as the bike. Toeing-in helps stop your brakes squealing. Position the block and tighten the fixing bolt firmly. Check you cannot twist the block; the bolt must be firmly secured! Fit the other block the same way. The washer arrangement should be the same on either side, but may be different between front and back brakes.

Step 8: You will probably have to adjust the tension in the cable again to get the correct gap between brake blocks and the rim. For big changes, undo the cable pinch bolt again, pull through or let out cable, and tighten the pinch bolt. For a more subtle change, use the barrel-adjuster on the brake lever. Roll the lockring (if there is one) away from brake lever. Now roll barrel-adjuster anticlockwise to bring the brake blocks closer to the rim.

Step 9: Roll barrel-adjuster clockwise to move brake blocks away from the rim **(C)**. Turn lockring **(D)** so it wedges back up against the body of the brake lever. (Some barrel-adjusters don't have lockrings!) Pull the levers firmly to check the brake action. Brakes need to be fully locked when the lever is halfway to the bar. If you run out of barrel adjustment, reset the barrel centrally, make a rough adjustment with the cable pinch bolt and use the barrel-adjuster to fine-tune again.

Readjusting balance screws

Finally, you will probably need to readjust the balance screws. Turn the balance screw clockwise to pull that side brake block away from the rim, but remember that this also pulls in the opposing brake block towards the far side of the rim. Pull and release the brake levers frequently as you adjust the balance screw because they have to settle into place every time. For a more detailed explanation of how to adjust your balance screw, see page 88. Check every nut and bolt to make sure each one is tight. Pull on the brakes firmly, and check that the wheel locks up. Spin the wheel and watch the brake blocks – if the wheel isn't completely true, you might find that the tyre rubs on the brake block as the wheel spins. Readjust the brake block position if necessary.

Choosing new brake blocks

This V-brake block set-up, using a threaded stud with curved washers, is used almost universally, making V-brake blocks completely interchangeable between makes and models. This might seem unremarkable, but the situation with disc brake pads is completely different. Every make and model requires a specific pad – and nothing else will do. The interchangeability of V-brake blocks has helped to keep the price down, since each manufacturer knows you can go elsewhere for replacements. Good makes include Aztec, Fibrax and Shimano. Longer or fatter brake blocks won't give you more braking power but are more durable. Slots cut in the surface of the block can help channel water away, but they can also collect grit if not cleaned regularly. Ceramic-coated rims need matching ceramic-specific brake blocks, which are harder than standard ones. Normal ones will wear away very quickly, as will ordinary rims if you use them with ceramic blocks.

Toolbox

Tools for replacing or adjusting brake blocks
- Allen keys – almost always 5mm but occasionally 6mm
- New V-brake blocks

Tools for fitting new cable
- Allen key for cable clamp bolt – almost always 5mm but occasionally 10mm spanner
- New cable, casing and ferrules
- Oil for lubricating cable – chain oil is fine
- Good wire cutters

Tools for adjusting balance screws
- Usually crosshead screwdriver, occasionally 2.5mm Allen key

Tools for fitting or servicing brake units (see page 92)
- 5mm Allen key for brake-fixing bolts
- Oil to lubricate pivots
- Wet-and-dry sandpaper to clean pivots

The function of the balance screws

Each V-brake unit has a balance screw. You'll find it at the bottom of the unit, usually a crosshead bolt but occasionally a small Allen key. The end of each bolt rests on the end of the brake-return spring, so that the spring is forced against the bolt when you squeeze the brake unit towards the rim.

Turning the balance screw alters the preload on the spring, pushing its starting point further around the unit for a stronger spring action and releasing it for a weaker spring action. The confusing part is remembering which way to turn the screws for the effect you need.

▲ **Balance screws**

◆ Turning the balance screw clockwise **(A)** pushes it further into the unit, increasing the preload on the spring, making it springier and pulling the attached brake block away from the rim.

◆ Turning the balance screw anticlockwise **(B)** unscrews it from the unit, decreasing the preload, softening the spring and allowing the brake block to move nearer to the rim.

Since the two units are connected together by the cable across the top, adjusting one balance screw will affect both units: if one unit is pulled away from the rim, the other will be drawn towards it to compensate.

To adjust the balance screws, look first at each brake unit from face on – the front brake from directly in front of the bike, the rear brake from directly behind.

If the balance screws are badly adjusted, the units will point off to one side, rather than being parallel and vertical. There will be an uneven distance between brake blocks and rim, perhaps with one closer than the other, or even with one brake block dragging on the rim. To correct the problem, locate the balance screws. Start with the unit that's closer to the rim, and wind the balance screw in (clockwise) a couple of turns. You'll need to squeeze and release the brake lever every time you make a balance-screw adjustment to resettle the position of the spring. Look again at the angle of the two units. You should find that the adjustment has both pulled the closer brake block away from the rim and pulled the other block closer.

One confusing thing about the balance screws is that turning the screw has a different effect at different points – sometimes a couple of turns seems to make no difference at all, sometimes a quarter-turn makes a radical change. You'll have to experiment, adjusting the balance screws a quarter-turn at a time to find the central position.

Lever modulation

Modulation is just a fancy word for 'how much the cable travels when you pull the lever'. Adjusting the modulation means changing the distance between the point that the cable attaches to the lever blade and the pivot that the lever turns around. Increasing this distance means more power, but it also means more lever travel. Some levers have an adjustment for this, usually a thumb screw on the front of the lever. In the example (see picture on right), the red thumb nut situated on the front of the lever adjusts the position of the cable nest. Turning the thumbscrew clockwise moves the nest further away from the pivot of the brake lever, so that more cable is pulled through the lever when you move the lever blade. Turning the thumbscrew anticlockwise moves the nest nearer to the pivot of the brake lever, so that less cable is pulled through when you move the lever blade. Adjust the lever modulation so that it gives you a comfortable amount of lever swing. This will depend on the size of your hands.

Checking rim sidewalls for wear and tear

It's easy to forget that the rims are just as much a part of the braking system as the brake blocks. Every time you brake, you're forcing your brake blocks against your rims. Powerful, controllable braking depends upon the condition of both blocks and rims. Whenever you brake, you wear both surfaces.

Rim design is subject to two competing demands. When you're trying to go faster, it helps to have rims that are as light as possible. Your wheels are spinning around as well as along, so saving weight on them makes the bike feel substantially faster than saving the same weight on a static part of your bike like the handlebars. So ideally, the rims should be as thin as possible so that they don't weigh much. Light wheels mean it's much easier to make your bike accelerate, as well as to make it change direction when you're moving fast.

If this doesn't make sense to you, take a wheel off your bike. Hold each end of the axle and move the whole wheel up and down. Then spin the wheel and do exactly the same thing again. Even though the weight of the wheel hasn't changed, you'll find it harder to move it where you want it to go when it's spinning.

But when you're trying to slow down, you need the rim material to be thick because the action of braking wears it out – and you don't want the brake blocks to wear through the rim. The deal is that rim manufacturers make their rims light so you buy them, but they expect you to keep them clean so they wear as slowly as possible and to inspect them regularly so that you can replace worn rims before they blow on you.

Rim sidewalls

Having a rim sidewall blow suddenly is very alarming. People can think they've been shot – there's a loud bang and suddenly they're lying on the ground, like in the movies. Because of the pressure inside the tyre, the sidewalls don't give way gracefully. Over time, the sidewall gets thinner and thinner. One part of the sidewall gets too thin to hold in the tyre. Then you brake suddenly – the moment of reckoning! Once one section of the rim starts to give way, it cannot support the next section, so within a fraction of a second most of your sidewall is ripped off. This punctures your tube, the resulting mess usually jams on your brake and you fall off the bike.

Rims also give way when you're pumping your tyre up. The extra tyre pressure on the inside of the rim sidewall is all it takes for the rim to finally give way. This is just as alarming and may also shower you with rim shrapnel.

Some newer rims come with indicator marks that show when the rim is worn out. The rim will have a small hole drilled from the inside, but not all the way through. The position of the hole is marked by a sticker on the rim with an arrow pointing to where the hole will appear. As you wear away the sidewall, the bottom of the hole appears from the outside; you can see your tyre through it. Time to get a new rim. Another type of rim indicator consists of a groove milled all the way around the braking surface of the rim. When the rim is worn away to the base of the groove, it is worn out and should be replaced. To help you see it, the bottom of the groove will be a different colour than the sidewall of the rim; for example, a silver rim will have a black groove in it and a black rim will have a silver groove.

If you don't have a wear-indicator, check the condition of the sidewall by running your fingers over it. It should be flat and smooth, without deep scours and ridges. Check both sides because one sidewall may be far more worn than the other. Curvy, bulging or scarred rims are due for replacement. If they look suspect, ask your bike shop for an opinion (you know straight away once you've seen enough of them). If you find any cracks in the sidewall when you inspect, stop riding immediately.

It's also worth checking the join where the two ends of the rim meet. It's usually directly opposite the valve hole. Good-quality rims will have a milled sidewall. The wall is made slightly too thick and welded together in a loop. The surface is then ground off flat. Cheaper rims are simply pinned together, relying on the spoke tension in the built wheel to push the joined ends properly together.

Sometimes, the ends don't meet exactly, making a bump in the rim that knocks against the brake blocks. Small imperfections can be filed flat, but if the join protrudes by more than 0.5mm (1/50 inch), take the wheel back to your bike shop for inspection because overenthusiastic filing will just weaken the joint. Also check for cracks around the spoke holes and the valve hole. These are less dangerous but still mean the rim should be replaced.

Rim sidewalls can be made to last longer without increasing their weight by covering the brake surface with a hard ceramic coating. This is expensive, but it radically reduces the speed at which the brake blocks can wear the sidewalls. Since the rim is much harder than normal, it's necessary to use harder brake blocks too, specifically designed for ceramic rims.

Maintaining your cables to help keep your brakes in good shape

You should check your cables regularly for corrosion, kinks and damage to the outer casing. Over time, dirt and water creep into the cables. It happens slowly so you hardly notice the brakes are getting harder to pull on and are not releasing properly. Fitting new cables is easy and you will feel the difference instantly.

Cables generally come in either standard or fancy versions. The luxury versions tend to be either lined or protected by a sheath that runs from shifter to brake. Luxury cables can make a significant difference if you ride in very muddy environments, as they stop grit from creeping into the gap between cable and outer casing. However, they are generally much more expensive. All cables come with comprehensive instructions though, so we'll stick to standard cables here. You can either buy brake-cable sets in a pack, with cable, outer casing and ferrules – Shimano make a good value pack – or you can buy the parts separately. Ferrules are the metal caps that the end of your outer casing sits in. Either way, you'll need a decent pair of cable-cutters to cut the casing to length; every bike has a different configuration of top tube lengths and cable-stop positions so the casing needs to be cut for each one. The key thing to remember when cutting casing is to make a square cut across the tube so that the end of the casing sits firmly inside the ferrule. Look into the end of the cut casing and make sure there isn't a stray tang of metal across the hole. This will catch on the cable every time you pull and release the brakes, making your brakes feel sluggish. Use the sharp point of a knife to open out the end of the white lining that runs through the casing as it gets squashed shut as you cut the casing.

Occasionally, you come across cheap, unlined casing. Don't fit this to your bike – it will feel terrible. It's fine for lawnmowers, but the extra money you spend on proper lined casing will make your brakes feel at least twice as good.

You'll notice throughout this text that I'm obsessed with ferrules. They cost almost nothing, protect the ends of your casing from splaying out and make your brakes feel crisp. Yet they are often treated as an optional extravagance. The only place you won't usually need a ferrule is the end of the section of casing that fits into the V-brake noodle. The noodle has its own built-in ferrule.

Fitting new brake cable to a flatbar lever

Before you start taking things apart, have a good look at how the cable is currently set up because you need to recreate that later with the new cable. Snip the cable end off the old cable and undo the cable pinch bolt. Unthread the old cable from the brake noodle and outer casing, leaving the casing in place. When you get back to the lever, have a good look at how the cable fits into it. It helps to pull the lever back toward the bars, to look up at it from below.

FITTING BRAKE CABLE

Step 1: Turn the lockring on the barrel-adjuster, and then the barrel-adjuster itself, so that the slots on both the barrel and the lockring line up with the slot on the body of the brake lever. Then pull the cable gently outward, or down, to release it.

Step 2: The nest, where the cable nipple sits, normally has a key-shaped hole so the nipple cannot pop out when you're braking. The most common fitting has a pivoted nest riveted to the lever blade, with a slot in either the front or the underside of the lever. Wiggle the cable so the nipple lines up with part of the hole that it can pass through, and pop it out. You may have to twist the cable so the end of the barrel lines up with the key hole.

Step 3: Some Shimano levers use a variation where the nipple is trapped behind a lip halfway along the lever blade. Once again, line up the slots on the lockring and barrel-adjuster with the slot on the body of the cable. You will need to flick open the plastic cover on the back of the lever blade, then push the cable towards the outer end of the lever. Once there's a bit of slack, you should be able to wriggle the cable out from behind the lip.

Replacing outer casing

Clean out the brake lever; in particular, wipe dirt from the nipple nest. Remove each section of outer casing in turn. Measure and cut new sections to fit. Take care when cutting the sections of outer casing. It's important that the ends are cut square and that you don't leave a tang hanging across the opening. If the casing lining has been squashed where you cut it, use the point of a sharp knife to open it out again. Fit a ferrule on each end of each section, except the brake unit end of the final section because the noodle will usually have a built-in ferrule. Occasionally these are bigger than normal, so if the casing is floppy in the end of the noodle, try fitting a ferrule. If you can fit one in, you need one. The ferrules protect the end of the casing from splaying out and keep braking crisp.

If there is no old casing to measure up against, you have to decide how long each section of casing should be. Ideally, sections should be as short as possible without binding. Make sure the handlebars and suspension can go through their full range of movement without pulling on the cable. Sections of casing should approach cable stops so that they are already lined up with the cable stop. Sharp curves cause sluggish brake performance. Refit the nipple in the brake lever, using the reverse process you needed to get it out. Line up the barrel-adjuster slots and tuck the cable back into the barrel-adjuster, then give it a quarter-turn to trap the cable.

It's important not to let the new cable drag on the floor and pick up dirt as you fit it. Slide the cable through each section of outer casing in turn, with a drop of oil on portions of the cable that will end up inside casing.

Step 4: When you get to the final section, feel the cable through the casing, then through the noodle. Ensure the section of cable inside the noodle has a little drop of oil. Fit the noodle into the key-shaped hole in the brake unit. Make sure it's lodged securely, with the entire nose of the noodle sticking out of the hanger. Slide the black rubber boot over the cable and push it firmly onto the nose of the noodle. Pass the brake cable behind the pinch bolt.

Step 5: The cable normally clamps on above the bolt, but there will be a groove in the unit where you put the cable. Put it there. Pull cable through, so there is a gap of 2–3mm (around $\frac{1}{8}$ inch) between brake blocks and rim. Steadying the cable with one hand, tighten the clamp bolt with the other. Leave about 5cm (2 inches) of exposed cable, cut off the excess and crimp on a cable end; i.e. 'squash it with pliers'. Tuck the loose end behind the brake unit.

Step 6: Test the brake; pull the lever hard twice. The cable might give slightly. Ideally, the brake should lock on when the lever is halfway to the handlebar. Use the barrel-adjuster to fine-tune; undo the lockring and turn it twice, away from the brake lever body. If the lever pulls too far, turn the top of the adjuster toward the handlebars. Do a couple of turns and retest. If the blocks rub on the rim, turn the top of the adjuster away from the handlebar.

Final adjustments

If you run out of adjustment on the barrel-adjuster (either it's adjusted so it jams on the brake lever body, or it's at risk of falling off), go back to the cable clamp bolt, undo it, pull through or release a bit of cable and retighten. Then go back to the barrel-adjuster and make fine adjustments. Pull firmly on the brake lever again and check that it locks the wheel when it's halfway to the bar. Make sure that the brake blocks don't rub on the rims as the wheel turns. Check that every bolt is tight. You're done.

Barrel-adjusters

People are often confused by barrel-adjusters. They're a common feature of cable-operated brakes and are used to adjust the indexing on derailleurs as well so it's worth getting you head around how they work. The barrel-adjuster on your brake lever is easiest to deal with because you can see it all. The barrel-adjuster acts like a cable stop, holding the casing still, while allowing the cable to pass freely through a hole in the middle. Since the barrel-adjuster is threaded, whenever you turn it, it moves further in or out of the body of the brake lever. If you turn it so that it winds out of the brake lever, more of the barrel-adjuster thread is visible.

The cable inside has to travel this extra distance between the nipple, where it lodges in the lever, and the bolt that it's clamped to at the other end. This increases the tension in the cable, drawing the brake blocks closer to the rim. The lockring serves only to stop the barrel-adjuster rattling loose, so it is wound finger-tight against the body of the lever when you've finished adjusting.

Fitting new V-brake units

V-brake units get very tired if you use them hard. Every time you pull and release the brakes, the units rotate around the pivots, bending then releasing the spring. The pivots and springs won't last forever, particularly if you ride in muddy or dusty conditions. Simple, single-pivot types (like the Avid units in the pictures, or the Shimano Deore types) tend to last longer than those with a complex multi-pivot arrangement.

All V-brake units are made to fit the same size and shape of brake pivot, so you can swap between makes and models without running into compatibility problems. New brake units are supplied with a set of new brake blocks. Once you take the price of these into consideration, a new set of brake units is a good-value upgrade.

FITTING NEW V-BRAKE UNITS

Step 1: Undo and remove the Allen key bolt that holds the units onto the brake pivots. It may be stiff to turn because Loctite is often used on these bolts to stop them from rattling free. The bolt heads can be quite shallow, so scrape them clean with a screwdriver before you try turning them with the Allen key – you risk rounding off the bolts.

Step 2: Pull the old units off the brake pivots. Clean the brake pivots **(A)** carefully, removing all grease and dirt. If the surface is corroded, use wet-and-dry sandpaper to carefully smooth it. Put a drop of oil onto each brake pivot and spread it over the surface. This helps the brakes return smoothly after you've squeezed them against the rim.

Step 3: Slide the new units onto the brake pivots. Line up the stub of spring on the back of each unit with the hole beside the brake pivot. You may have to undo the Allen key bolt on the back of the brake blocks and twist the blocks out of the way to line up the spring properly. If you have three holes for the spring, use the middle one. Refit the brake fixing bolt and tighten firmly.

Servicing V-brake units

Old brake units that are a bit tired can be revived with servicing. You'll need to release the brakes, then disconnect the cable clamp bolt. Undo and remove the fixing bolts at the bottom of each unit, then pull the brake units off the brake pivots. You may need to wiggle and pull at the same time, especially if the brake pivots have become corroded. Use a small brush (old toothbrushes are ideal) and degreaser to scrub all the dirt out from the gaps between the moving parts. Hold the unit still and wiggle the spring – if there's dirt in there, flush it out. You may find that you can pull the spring off the back of the unit. This makes it easier to clean behind, but remember to note the position and orientation of any washers or spacers.

It's best to work on one brake unit at a time; that way, you always have the other unit for reference if you get confused when reassembling the parts. Rinse the unit to get rid of residue from the degreaser, and oil the gaps between the moving parts. Move the spring against the unit to work the oil into the gaps, then wipe off the excess. Remove the cable clamp bolt and clean off any trapped dirt under the bolt head or the washer. Oil the threads of the cable clamp bolt and replace it. Clean the brake pivots carefully, removing any corrosion with wet-and-dry paper. Oil the pivots, then refit the brake units as above.

Troubleshooting: V- and cantilever brakes

Symptom	Cause	Solution	Page
Brakes squeak	Brake blocks set flat to the rim or with the back of the block touching first	"Toe-in" brakes so that the fronts of the brake blocks touch the rims first	86, 87
	Rims dirty or contaminated	Clean rims with bike wash and nylon scouring pad	79
Brakes don't stop the bike or don't stop the bike quickly enough	Brake blocks are set too far from the rim	Set brake blocks closer	85
	Surfaces of brake blocks are contaminated or have picked up debris	Remove wheel, pick debris out of blocks with sharp knife, roughen surface with wet-and-dry sandpaper, replace wheel	85
	Rims are contaminated or dirty	Clean rims with degreaser	79
	Brake blocks are worn out	Check wear on brake blocks – replace if necessary	83, 84, 85, 95
	V-brakes – brake arms too close together, head of noodle jams on cable clamp when braking	Reset brake units to vertical, reorder brake block washers appropriately	86, 87, 92
	Cantilever brakes – link wires make unit angles too wide or too narrow	Reset straddle or link wire angle, readjust brakes appropriately	95, 98
Brakes pull on, but they don't spring back from the rim when you release the brake lever	Dirty or frayed brake cables, kinked brake outer casing	Clean and oil brake cable or replace it	83, 90, 96-97
	Brake blocks are set too low and have worn so that a lip of brake block gets trapped under the rim	Remove wheel, cut off offending lip with a sharp knife, replace wheel, reset brake block position	86-87, 94
	V-brake noodle is full of grit or squashed	Flush out noodle with light spray of oil or replace	83, 90
Brake blocks wear very quickly	Rim surface worn	Replace wheel or rim	89
Brake levers take excessive effort to pull, brakes don't release smoothly	Brake pivots worn, corroded or dirty	Remove brake units, clean and lubricate pivots	92, 99

Cantilever brakes

You really don't see many cantilever brakes on mountain bikes nowadays, though they're still popular on cyclocross bikes (where they're not expected to actually stop you, but simply slow you down). They were the forerunners of V-brakes and whilst they've both now been surpassed in terms of power and practicality by the disc brake, cantilevers are still to be found on the steeds of those who lovingly restore 'retro' builds to their former glory – or who just still ride an old bike.

Take care to use the correct brake levers for cantilever brakes because they are not compatible with V-brake levers. V-brake levers are designed with a greater distance between the lever pivot and the nest that the cable nipple sits in. This means that more cable is pulled through the lever with V-brakes than with a cantilever brake lever. You can see the difference if you compare a V-brake lever to a cantilever brake lever. For a cantilever brake to work properly, the distance between brake lever pivot and cable nest needs to be around 30mm (1⅛ inches).

Cantilever brake blocks usually last much longer than V-brake blocks, but they will wear through eventually. Change them every couple of years whether they're worn down or not; the rubber hardens and ceases to work well after a while. This seems to be especially true if your bike lives outside or in outbuildings that get cold in the winter.

Check for wear by looking on top of the block for a wear-indication line. Usually stamped in black writing on the black surface of the block, they can be hard to spot, and you may be able to feel the line with a fingernail more easily that you can see it. There may not be an indication line; in this case, replace blocks before they've worn down to the base of the grooves moulded into the blocks. Leave it too late and you risk wearing through to the metal bolt that the block is moulded around. The bolt will scrape the surface off your rims.

The brake block is held in place by an eye bolt. The stub of the brake block passes through a hole in the eye bolt, which in turn passes through a curved washer then through a slot in the brake unit. On the other side of the brake unit is another curved washer, then a nut. When you tighten the nut, it pulls the eye bolt through the brake unit, squashing the stub of the brake block against the first curved washer, and holding it securely.

This design means that when you loosen the nut on the end of the eye bolt, you can move the position of the brake block in different and useful ways. You can move the eye bolt up and down in the slot on the brake unit so that the brake block hits the rim higher or lower. You can push the stub through the eye bolt, moving the brake block towards or away from the rim. You can roll the stub in the eye bolt so that the block approaches the rim at an angle. You can also twist the eye bolt on the curved washers so that the front or the back of the brake block touches the rim first. We use this flexibility to get the block precisely positioned.

The vital adjustment for cantilever brakes is setting the position where the main cable splits into two, just above the brake units. The split can be made with a straddle hanger bolted onto the cable, with a straddle wire that passes from one brake unit to the other via the straddle hanger, or with a separate link wire, through which the main cable passes, then clamps to the brake unit. Either way, it's important that the two sections of straddle cable, or the two arms of the link wire, are set at 90 degrees to each other. The best time to get this right is when fitting new brake blocks.

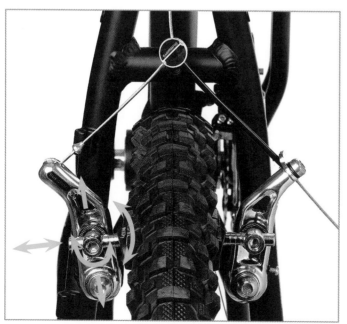

◀ **Four degrees of freedom**

Fitting and adjusting brake blocks

I find it easiest to work on one brake unit at a time, removing the old block then replacing it straight away with the new one. This way, you will keep the washers and eye bolt in the correct order. If you take both blocks off at once, the washers and eyebolt have a tendency to drop off one unit when you're working on the other.

Hold the eye bolt still using a 5mm Allen key in the head of the eye bolt, and undo the nut at the back of the unit – usually with a 10mm spanner. You don't need to take the nut off, just loosen it enough to pull the old brake block out of the hole in the eye bolt. Feed the stub of the new brake block back through the hole in the eye bolt so that the brake block faces the rim. Most brake blocks will fit either way around, but if there are any arrows printed on the block, point these forward. If one end of the brake block is shorter than the other, this goes at the front.

FITTING BRAKE BLOCKS

Step 1: Tighten the nut just enough so that the brake block doesn't fall out. Don't worry about adjustment at this stage, as long as the block is pointing vaguely towards the rim. Leave a generous gap between rim and brake block at this stage. Repeat with the other side. Now we're going to leave the brake blocks for a bit and set the units up at the right angle.

Step 2: For straddle wire types, adjust the height of the straddle hanger and the length of the straddle wire, so that the two halves of the straddle wire are at 90° to each other. Link wire types are much simpler – undo the cable clamp bolt, pull in or let out until the two arms are at 90° and reclamp. Most link wires are stamped or printed with a helpful guide line. See page 98 for more detail.

Step 3: Next, the balance screw. Cantilevers usually only have one. Pull brake lever and watch the units. If one sits closer to the rim, adjustment is needed. If the unit with balance screw is closer, turn screw clockwise to strengthen spring and move it out. If it is further away, turn balance screw anticlockwise. Start with half-turns, pulling the levers to ease things into place. At first there's no effect, then the spring gets sensitive to quarter-turns, so move slowly.

Step 4: Once everything else is set up, return to the brake blocks. Loosen the nut on the back of the unit so that you can manipulate the brake blocks. Push in each one until it's almost touching the rim. Each block should hit the rim at 90°, midway between the top and bottom of the rim.

Step 5: The front of the block should be about 1mm (¹⁄₁₆ inch) closer than the back. This is called 'toeing in' and helps to prevent the brakes from squealing. People often mess about with bits of cardboard stuck behind the back of the brake block. This is just making work for yourself – look at the brake block and the rim, and set the angle of the brake block so that it's closer to the rim at the front than at the back.

Step 6: Hold the block in place with your hand and tighten the 10mm nut gently. Once it is fairly secure, hold the eye bolt still with a 5mm Allen key and tighten the 10mm nut firmly. Try to waggle the brake block – if it moves, it's not tight enough. The cable will now need fine-tuning – see page 97, 'Adjusting the cable tension'.

Fitting a new brake cable

When you pull your brakes on, you can haul the brake cable through the casing with all the strength in your fingers. However, when you release the brake lever, you're relying on the strength of two small springs, one in each brake unit, to pull the units back out from the rim again.

If your cables are gritty, rusty or kinked, they won't release freely, leaving you with sluggish, dragging brakes.

When cutting new lengths of outer casing, check that each section is long enough; for example, the section that joins the handlebars to the frame should be long enough so that the bars can turn freely, without kinking the casing. The casing for the front brake should make a smooth, graceful curve. Cut new lengths, neatly and squarely with good, sharp cutters. Don't leave a ragged edge. If the lining gets squashed as you cut, prise it open with a sharp knife. Fit ferrules on each end of each section of casing.

The final section of cable – connecting the cantilever units to the cable – is set up in two ways: a link wire or straddle hanger. Both are shown below.

LINK WIRE

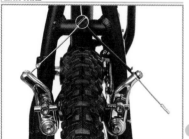

STRADDLE HANGER

Pull the quick-release nipple down and out of the slot on the brake unit. Cut off the cable end, and undo cable clamp bolt with a 5mm Allen key or a 10mm spanner. Pull cable out from under cable clamp bolt. Pull link wire gently. The V-shaped link wire should come away completely. Unless it is frayed or kinked, reuse it because they don't wear much. The section of outer casing may fall off. Don't worry, just reassemble it when you fit the new cable.

Step 1: One brake unit has a cable clamp bolt, the opposite unit has a slot for the straddle wire nipple. Hold this unit so the brake block is pushed against the rim and pull nipple down and out to release it from the slot. Straddle wire and brake cable now hang loosely. Unhook straddle wire from straddle hanger, cut off cable end, undo clamp bolt and pull the cable out. If it's frayed, replace it: cut off the cable end, undo the clamp bolt and pull it out of the unit.

Step 2: Cut off the cable end on the old cable. Undo the cable pinch bolt that holds the straddle hanger onto the brake wire. You have to check what size tools you need, common sizes are 9mm and 10mm spanners, and 5mm Allen keys. Irritatingly, they often use two 10mm spanners – which is fine for workshops, which are usually awash with 10mm spanners, but may ask too much of a home toolbox.

Replacing the brake cable

Pull the cable out of the outer casing a section at a time, leaving the casing in place for reference. Work out how the nipple on the end of the cable fits into the lever. As the nipple is attached to the lever blade, you usually need to pull the lever all the way in to see how it fits. Looking at the lever from below often helps. Undo the lockring on the brake lever barrel-adjuster until the slot on the adjuster lines up with the slot on the front of or underneath the lever body. Turn the adjuster to line up its slot.

Pull the old brake cable gently out of the slot, then pull the brake lever in toward the handlebar and wiggle the nipple out of its nest. You may have to pull the cable forward to line it up with an escape slot for the nipple. Remove each section of outer casing. The front brake has just a single section, but the rear may be in a couple of parts that are separated by an exposed section of cable across the top tube. Refit the sections on the frame or cable hanger.

Take your new cable and sit the nipple back in the nest on the lever, then back through the slots in the lever. Feed the cable back through each section of casing in turn. Drip a drop of oil onto parts of the cable that end up inside the outer casing.

◀ **The brake cable pulls out through the slot in the lever**

Cantilever brakes: refitting the cable to the brake unit

Once you've got the cable attached to the brake lever, and threaded through the outer casing, you'll need to reconnect the cable to the brake unit. The procedure differs depending on whether you have link wire or a straddle cable. However, once you've connected the units, the procedure for adjusting the cable tension is the same.

Link wire

Look at the disc in the middle of the two arms of the link wire. Of the two different slots the cable could go into, one makes it easy to push the cable through by lining up precisely with the section of outer casing. Once you've fed the cable through the link wire, push it across to sit in the other slot on the link wire disc and hang it at the right angle. Refit the nipple on the end of the link wire into the quick-release slot on the brake unit. Feed the brake cable under the cable clamp bolt and pull through until the blocks sit close to the rim without touching. Tighten the cable clamp bolt firmly, cut off any excess and fit a cable end. Pull the brakes firmly several times to settle things in place.

Straddle wire

Back at the brake, push the cable through the hole in the pinch bolt. With a standard hanger, the assembly order is straddle hanger, cable, washer, nut. The height of the straddle hanger is crucial to the effectiveness of the brake. Push up the brake units so the blocks touch the rim and look carefully to estimate the correct hanger height. Clamp on the straddle hanger with the straddle wire arms at 90 degrees to each other. Firmly tighten the pinch bolt. This is critical, otherwise the straddle wire can slip down the brake cable and lock up the wheel.

Fit the straddle wire nipple into the slot on the brake unit, over the straddle hanger, and under the cable clamp bolt on the opposite side. Pull the straddle cable through so that the brakes are drawn in towards the rim. Ideally there should be about 2mm (⅛ inch) clearance on each side between the brake blocks and the rim. Hold the cable in place and tighten the cable clamp bolt firmly. Cut off any excess, leaving 5cm (2 inches) of spare cable, and then fit an end cap. Pull the brakes firmly several times to settle everything into place.

Adjusting the cable tension

Use the barrel-adjuster on the brake lever to fine-tune the adjustment. When you spin the wheel, it should spin freely without dragging, and it should lock when the brake lever is pulled halfway in toward the handlebars. If the blocks rub on the rim, you need to release tension in the cable. Roll the lockring away from the lever body and turn the barrel so it screws into the lever body **(A)** – clockwise, looking from the direction that the cable enters the lever. Test, repeat if necessary, then roll the lockring to wedge it against the lever body.

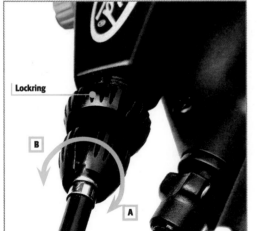

Lockring

B

A

If the lever moves more than halfway to the handlebars before the brakes lock the wheel, you will need to increase the tension in the cable. Undo the lockring a couple of turns, then roll the barrel-adjuster out of the lever body **(B)** – anticlockwise as you look from the direction that the cable enters the lever. Test by squeezing the brake lever again, repeat as necessary, then roll the lockring back so that it wedges against the lever body.

You may find that you run out of barrel-adjuster – either it's screwed completely into the body of the brake lever or it's screwed so far out that it threatens to fall off. Set the barrel-adjuster so that about half the thread shows. Make a crude adjustment by going back to the cable clamp bolt on the brake unit, pulling cable through or letting cable out. Then go back and repeat the fine adjustment with the barrel-adjuster.

◄ **Roll lockring away from lever before turning barrel-adjuster**

Cantilever brakes: adjusting straddle or link wire angle

The angle at which the cable connects the two brake units is critical since it determines how powerfully the brake blocks are forced onto the rim when the brake cable is pulled.

Readjusting your cable angle will help you stop more quickly, but you may have to readjust your brake block positions. If you're fitting new cables and blocks, adjust the cable angle first, then fit the brake blocks to match.

The brake unit is attached to the frame by a single fixing bolt so that the brake unit can rotate around the bolt. The cable attachment points on the tops of the brake units move in a circle around the fixing bolts. This means the cable must be set up to pull the brake units around this circle – there's no point in pulling them in any other direction. This brake cable angle is best estimated by setting the sections of cable that connect the brake units so that they're at 90 degrees to each other – a right angle or square corner.

There are two different styles of cable fitting: link wire and straddle wire. Adjusting the cable angle is slightly different for each; adjusting brake blocks and cable tension is identical. To work out which you've got, check the last section of cable, where the single cable comes from the brake lever and splits into two cables, which each serve one brake unit.

The older method was to bolt a straddle-hanger onto the cable, then run a short piece of separate cable from one side of the brake unit over the hanger, bolting it onto the other brake unit. The straddle-hanger is usually a metal triangle with a pinch bolt, but there was a fashion for purple anodizing and wacky shapes. Luckily, V-brakes put a stop to all that. I like this style because it is easy to adjust the height at which the cable splits in two. The downside is that if the brake cable breaks, the spring in each unit pulls down the straddle wire onto your tyre, where it can get trapped, lock your wheel and throw you high over the bars.

The link wire style was designed by Shimano to prevent this from happening. In this design, the straddle-hanger and straddle wire are replaced by a link wire. This is a V-shape set-up, with one arm of the 'V' a short section of cable with a nipple at the end, and the other a short section of outer casing. The brake cable from the lever runs down to the link wire, through the section of outer casing, then bolting onto one brake unit. The other arm of the link wire hooks onto the other brake unit.

Both types of fitting tend to suffer from fraying just beside the cable clamp bolt. This part of the cable always gets squashed by the clamp bolt, and is then kinked and released every time you operate the brakes. Over time, the separate strands of the cable snap, reducing the number of strands carrying the load, therefore increasing the stress on each one. Replace cables as soon as they start to fray and inspect the clamped area regularly. Use these steps to set your straddle or link wire angle to 90 degrees, maximizing your mechanical advantage for powerful braking.

ADJUSTING STRADDLE OR LINK WIRE ANGLE

Step 1: Too low – with the link wire at this angle, your brakes feel spongy. Loosen the nut on the back of each brake unit and pull the brake blocks back from the rim. Undo the cable clamp bolt and pull through enough cable so that the link wires are at 90°. Retighten the cable clamp bolt and reset the brake blocks just clear of the rim.

Step 2: Too high – with the link wire at this angle, your brakes won't be particularly powerful. Undo the cable clamp bolt, release the cable until the angle between the link wires is 90°, retighten the cable clamp bolt and readjust your brake blocks so that they sit closer to the rim.

Step 3: Just right! The pictures show a link wire type, but the principle is the same for straddle wire types. Play with the position of the straddle-hanger until the two sides are at 90°. Ideally, the brake block studs should be central on the eye bolt, with an equal amount showing on either side.

Fitting new brake units

Brake units usually last for years without complaint. Generally, the first thing to go will be the cover that protects and contains the spring. Spares for these are not generally available, but without the cover, the spring splays open under pressure rather than snapping the units briskly away from the rim. Replace units with broken spring covers; they cost barely more than a new set of brake blocks, which come supplied with the new units.

There is not as much choice available in cantilever brakes as there used to be once upon a time, although some very good-quality models are still made for cyclocross bikes; for example, Avid Shorties are light, strong and powerful, though some people say they squeal too much.

FITTING NEW UNITS

Step 1: Pull the quick-release on your brake unit down and out to release it from the slot on the unit. If the slot in the brake unit has become squashed, use a thin screwdriver to carefully ease the slot apart so that the cable slides out without damage.

Step 2: Cut off the cable end, undo the cable clamp bolt and release the cable from the units. Use this opportunity to check the condition of the cable, particularly where it gets clamped under the cable clamp bolt.

Step 3: Remove the bolts at the bottom of each unit and pull them off the frame. You may need to twist and pull at the same time; dirt that works its way into the gap between the brake and pivot can stick the two parts solidly together. For stubborn cases, try spraying a light oil into the gap, then work the brake back and forth.

Cleaning the pivots

Clean the pivots on the frame. If they're lumpy, uneven or gritted, use a scrap of wet-and-dry sandpaper. Oil the pivots and slide the new units on to them. Line up the spring that protrudes from the back of each with the middle of the three holes on the frame beside the pivot bolts. The new bolts may come with a stripe of Blue Loctite 242, but if not, it's worth adding one since the last thing you need is your brakes rattling loose. A thin stripe will do, 2mm (⅛ inch) wide or so, for most of the length of the bolt.

Refit the cable, setting it up so that the two sections of link wire or straddle wire are at 90 degrees to each other. You may need to loosen the eye bolts that hold the brake block in place and push the brake blocks back away from the rim to give yourself enough space. Once you have set up the cable, follow the instructions for fitting new brake blocks on page 95.

Servicing units

If your brake pivots are dirty and corroded, your brakes will feel sluggish. Clean and oil pivots regularly for crisp braking.

Undo the quick-release and the cable clamp bolt and pull the cable out completely. Undo the fixing bolts and remove them completely. Pull the units off the frame and clean them. Use wet-and-dry sandpaper to clean the pivots. Undo one of the eye bolt nuts, remove the eye bolts and clean all the curved washers. Put a drop of oil on each of the mating surfaces and reassemble. Just do one at a time so that you can refer to the others to put the unit back together in the right order. Oil the brake pivots and slide the brake over the pivot, lining up the spring on the unit with the middle of the three holes beside the pivot on the frame. Refit the bolts that hold the units on, then follow the instructions for fitting new brake blocks.

Calliper brakes: adjustment

Calliper brakes are found on road bikes. For best performance, these brakes must be adjusted so that your wheel will run cleanly between the blocks without touching either block.

However, the blocks must be close enough so that when you pull the lever the blocks bring the wheel to a stop when the brake lever is somewhere near the middle of its travel. You shouldn't be able to pull the brake-lever back far enough to touch the handlebars. This means you haven't got enough power to bring the bike safely to a stop. Some prefer a little bit of movement of the levers before the brake blocks bite as it means they can get a proper grip on the lever.

This adjustment will only work if the wheels are aligned centrally in the frame. Check that the gap between the tyre and the frame or fork is the same on either side of the wheel and realign the wheel if necessary.

CALLIPER BRAKE ADJUSTMENT

Step 1: Before you adjust anything, make sure the brake cable isn't seized or sticky. Undo the cable pinch bolt so that it's not gripping the cable at all. Pull down gently on the cable and squeeze the brake-lever at the same time. You should feel the cable pulling upwards. When you release the brake-lever, a gentle tug should pull the cable smoothly back through again. If the cable feels rough or gritty, then change it. (See page 102.)

Step 2: Check where the cable lies as it clamps under the pinch bolt. There will always be a groove marking the correct place and there will always be a washer – often a specially shaped one – between the cable and the pinch bolt. Squeeze the brake blocks onto the rim with one hand while pulling through any slack cable with the other. Let go the cable, but keep hold of the block and tighten the pinch bolt firmly.

Step 3: Squeeze the brake-lever firmly several times to settle slack out of the cable. You may now find that you can pull the brake-lever all the way to the bars. If so, you need to pull through slack cable at the calliper again. Hold the cable just where it emerges from under the cable clamp bolt, undo the cable clamp bolt a couple of turns, pull through any slack cable and retighten the cable clamp bolt firmly.

Step 4: Check the gap between the brake blocks and rim. Spin the wheel gently. The blocks shouldn't touch the rim. Squeeze the brake-lever – you should be able to get about halfway to the bars. Make minor adjustments with the barrel-adjuster. Turning the barrel-adjuster out of the calliper will bring the blocks closer to the rim, turning it into the calliper moves the blocks further away. Experiment to find the best position.

Step 5: You may find that the brake block on one side touches the rim, while the other block doesn't. Newer callipers have a balance screw that allows you to readjust the angle of the whole calliper. Try to remember which way the balance screw turns; just experiment as different mechanisms have opposite effects. Turn the screw gently – quarter of a turn at a time – until the rim runs centrally between the blocks.

Step 6: You may find the blocks are way off to one side, further than the balance screw can correct, or you may have a calliper without a balance screw. If so, you'll have to adjust the position of the whole calliper. Hold it as shown and undo the calliper fixing bolt until the calliper swings freely. Correct its position and retighten the calliper bolt firmly. If you've got a balance screw, use it now to make final adjustments.

Calliper brakes: fitting blocks

Calliper brake blocks don't wear out as quickly as V-brake blocks, but they'll still need occasional attention.

The calliper mechanism means you can't apply as much force to the block to stop you as you can with a V-brake, so it's worth investing in good-quality brake blocks and replacing them when they're worn. Good makes include Aztec, Shimano and Kool-Stop. Of the three types of rim brake, calliper blocks are the easiest to change. Give your rims a good clean at the same time, and check them for wear. There are only two types of fitting for brake pads – most common are 4 or 5mm Allen keys, but some need a 10mm Allen key. You may decide when you've got the old brake block off that it will survive a little longer – if so, clean it up carefully. Use a sharp knife to pick out any bits of metal or glass, then flatten the surface with sandpaper. Refit in the same way as a new block.

FITTING BRAKE BLOCKS

Step 1: Start by removing the old brake block. Undo the bolt at the back and slide the block downwards and outwards. Inspect the surface of the block. You may decide that it will survive a little longer, in which case follow the instructions above to clean it up and then refit as below.

Step 2: If you've got the kind of brake blocks that have replaceable pads, undo the screw on the back of the pad. The old pad should then slide backwards out of the brake shoe. Clean up the shoes then slide the new pad in and replace the screw. It is very important to replace the brake blocks the right way round: the opening on the block must face towards the back of the bike.

Step 3: Check for marks indicating the direction the new blocks must face. The block may be marked 'left' and 'right' or be curved, in which case the shape of the curve must match the shape of the rim. The block may come supplied with shaped washers. If so, fit the cup-shaped washer so that the flat side rests against the brake flock. Fit the domed washer so that the curve of the dome faces into the cup of the washer you just fitted.

Step 4: Wriggle the brake block into place. It should be parallel with the rim, but not so high that it will touch the tyre nor so low that any part of it would hang down below the rim. The curvature of the fitting washers will allow you to make minor corrections to the angle. Once you've got it in place, hold the block still with one hand while you tighten it with the Allen key, or spanner.

Step 5: Next, check the toe-in. Pull the brakes and watch the gap between the rim and the brake block. The front of the block should touch the rim just before the back – the difference should be about 1mm $\frac{1}{25}$ in). If it's not correct, loosen the fixing bolt slightly, adjust the angle of approach and tighten the fixing bolt firmly. Check that the brake block is at the right height as you pull and release the brake-lever.

Step 6: The new brake blocks will probably be a different thickness to the old ones, so you will need to adjust the clearance between the brake block and the rim. It should only be a minor adjustment, so use the barrel-adjuster on the calliper. Loosen the lockring slightly to get it out of the way, then adjust the clearance using the main part of the barrel-adjuster (see page 100 for details). Retighten the lockring.

Calliper brakes: fitting cables

Road bike brake blocks won't be as sharp as V-brakes or disc brakes even when new, so make sure your cables are in good condition for the best possible braking.

The back brake in particular has a long cable, and both cables are routed under the bar tape, so they're forced around tight turns. Once the cables start to deteriorate, you'll find that the levers become steadily harder to pull, and the brake blocks don't spring easily back from the rims once you release the levers. Replacing the cable makes a massive difference.

If the outer casing is kinked or damaged, it should be replaced at the same time as the cable. Use the old sections to measure out new sections, taking care to cut the ends clean and square. New bits of casing need a ferrule at each end of each section. The exception is the last one, where the casing enters the calliper. There may not be room for a ferrule, in which case it doesn't need one.

FITTING BRAKE CABLES

Step 1: Make sure you have the right kind of brake cable before you start – road bikes use a different type from the ubiquitous mountain bike with a pear-shaped nipple on the end rather than a barrel-shaped nipple. Once armed with the correct type, cut the cable end off your old brake cable. You'll need a decent pair of cable cutters – a pair of pliers isn't good enough as you'll just end up fraying the cable.

Step 2: Feed the brake cable back up through the outer casing. You can leave this in place, but check each piece as you pass it through since sections that are kinked or crushed, or have patches of the protective plastic coating missing, will need to be replaced. If the cable feels gritty as you remove it, it's also worth replacing the casing.

Step 3: When you get up to the handlebars, you'll have to pull the lever back to expose its innards. Push the cable through the casing from the other end. You should see it emerging gently from the lever. Keep pushing though until a handful has emerged, then pull the whole lot out. Watch as you extract the last bit of cable so that you can clearly see the nest where the new cable has to go into.

Step 4: Now the tricky bit: getting the new cable back into the lever. Success depends on having a neat, non-frayed end on your new cable. Keep the brake-lever pulled back against the bars and feed the cable back into the nest in the brake-lever. Once it's through the nest, feel for the hole in the back of the brake-lever. You should be able to see the brake casing under the bar tape, which will give you an idea what you're aiming for. Feed through.

Step 5: Once the cable emerges from the outer casing, pull it through until only the last 10cm (4 in) of cable sticks out of the lever. Keeping the brake-lever against the bars, drip a drop of oil onto this last bit and pull through completely. For the front brake, the cable goes directly into the front brake. Ensure as you route the back brake that there is enough slack in the outer casing for the handlebars to turn freely. Oil the cable as it passes through the outer casing.

Step 6: On the brake calliper, pass the cable through the barrel-adjuster. Set this so it's about halfway through its travel. Check the cable pinch bolt – there will be a clear groove where the cable rests. Sit the cable in place and squeeze the brake blocks against the rim. Pull through the cable to take up slack. Release the cable, keeping the blocks against the rim, and tighten the cable pinch bolt. See page 100 for final adjustment.

New outer casing and bar tape

You may find when you're replacing the brake inner cable that it feels gritty as you feed it through the first section of outer casing – this runs from the brake-lever under the bar tape to the frame, in the case of the back brake, or directly to the front brake unit. If this is the case, you will need to peel back the bar tape and replace the outer casing as well as the inner cable. It's an irritating job, but will make your brakes feel much crisper and more responsive.

There are other circumstances in which you might want to replace the first section of outer casing. You may want to raise the bars and find that the casing isn't long enough to do so without forcing it around tight bends. You may also have found damaged or kinked spots in the casing.

Either way you'll need to get some fresh bar tape before you start. It is possible to reuse the old stuff, but it's sticky-backed so doesn't often come off without tearing and tends to refuse to lie flat when you wind it back on again. Treat yourself to new tape – it makes your bike look much smarter too.

Best results come from changing the whole lot at once. Peel off the old stuff gently. You're trying to lift off as much of the sticky glue as you can as you go along. Remove the bar-end plugs. Clean up the bars as best you can, but take care not to scratch the bars as small scratches can form the roots of cracks in the material.

Now you're free to work on the brake cable and casing. You'll have to tug the old brake casing out from inside the back of the brake levers. Look carefully to see if the cable finishes in a ferrule – if it does you'll need to remember to refit the new casing with a ferrule.

Measure up the new casing and then cut it carefully to length, making sure that the cut end is a clean cut and that there isn't a tag of metal cutting across the hole through the middle of the casing. Replace any other sections if necessary and feed the inner cable through the middle. Pull through any slack in the cable, clamp it under the cable pinch bolt and pull the lever firmly to settle the new outer casing into place. You may find after this that you have a fair bit of slack. Loosen the calliper cable pinch bolt again, pull through more slack and tighten the bolt firmly.

It may be a little bit of a struggle to get the new outer casing to sit properly into the brake lever. It can help to loosen the bolt that clamps the brake lever onto the handlebars in order to give the casing a little bit of space. The bolt may be in one of two places. Pull the lever towards the bars and look into it from in front. You may see the head of an Allen key bolt at the back – often a 5mm. You should be able to wiggle an Allen key in there.

If the fixing bolt isn't inside the lever, it will probably be on the side of the lever, under the rubber lever cover. Again, it will usually be a 5mm Allen key and will be on the outer side of the lever (the right-hand side of the right lever and the left-hand side of the left lever). Loosen the fixing bolt, wiggle the brake casing home and then retighten the fixing bolt firmly.

Tape the brake casing onto the front of the bars with three strips of electrical tape to hold it neatly in place. Three strips of tape on either side should do the job.

Once you've got everything taped together it's time to refit bar tape. Start by filling in behind the brake levers. This is always too wide a gap for the bar tape to cross without leaving gaps. Your new pack of bar tape may have come with a couple of extra short strips. If not, cut two strips about 7cm (23/4 in) long off the end of the bar tape. Fold back the rubber brake lever hoods so they're out of the way and wrap a horizontal strip around the bar from one side to the other. Leave the brake hoods out of the way. Start at the bottom end of the handlebar. Start with a strip of tape facing down on the inside of the bar with about half the width of the tape overlapping the end of the bar. Wrap so that each new layer overlaps a third of the last layer. When you get to the brake lever, wrap up to the short strip you already put there and then head diagonally upwards in one layer. Don't be tempted to weave the tape back down again as you'll just make the bar feel really bulky behind the brake lever. Once you get above the brake lever, carry right on up towards the middle of the bar – you'll need to finish about 5cm (2 in) from the stem. Cut off the tape so that it finishes underneath the bar and then tape neatly in place with black electrical tape. Bar tape sometimes comes with little plastic grip ties, but they're more fiddly than they're worth and a layer of tape does the job better.

If you've been careful with wrapping the tape around the bottom section of the bars, you may find there's enough to increase the overlap on the top section. This makes the bars more comfortable when you're sitting in a more upright position. Fold the end of the tape into the ends of the bars, and refit the barend plugs. As well as keeping the ends of the bars neat, the plugs protect you from cutting yourself on the end of the bar in case of a spill.

Servicing calliper brakes

Without mudguards, calliper brakes are right in the line of fire for anything your tyre picks up off the road. Dirt ends up on the pivots that hold your callipers together and stops them moving freely. This is one of those satisfying jobs that looks much harder than it is and makes your bike feel much better as soon as you've done it.

Like your gears, your brakes are operated by a combination of a cable and a spring. Cables are great for transmitting a signal through all the curves from your handlebars to your brakes and they're light and strong, but they can only pull, not push. Once you've used the cable to pull your brake blocks onto the rim, you release the brake-lever and rely on a spring in the calliper to push the blocks back off the rim so that you can ride and the blocks are back in their original position. However, your hands are generally much stronger than the little coil of wire that does the springing-back job. The effect of this is that, once your calliper pivots start to get all clogged up and sticky, you will still be able to pull your brakes on, but they'll be more reluctant to spring back away again. Leave it longer still and it will start to be hard work pulling the brake levers on. Luckily, it's not difficult to clear away the muck and apply a little oil, but the sooner you do it, the more effective it will be. Dirt that's left long enough will start to corrode the pivots, the washers and the calliper. Once the surfaces that rub against each other become rough and damaged, there's a limit to how much improvement you can make.

It's possible to give the callipers a quick wipe over without removing them from the bike, but it's not difficult to take them off completely and it means that you can really get in properly behind the calliper. An old toothbrush is the perfect size. You can try using plain water if your brakes aren't too bad, but if you've been riding in wet conditions or around town, you'll probably need something a little stronger. Bike washes like Muc-Off or Finish Line Bike Wash should do the trick. For really stubborn, caked-on dirt – a sign that you really need to invest in mudguards! – try some degreaser. Pour some in a jar then dip the toothbrush in and scrub. Spray-on degreaser is much too messy and wasteful for this kind of job, where you need precise application. Don't forget to rinse off carefully afterwards.

As with the degreaser, when you come to lubricate the pivots, drip oil is much better than spray. Take particular care not to get any oil at all on your brake blocks as it will spread all over your rims in no time and you'll lose most of your stopping power. The gaps that need lubricating are easiest to see with the calliper off the bike. Squeeze the blocks together as if you were squashing them onto the rim and watch how the brake mechanism moves. Anywhere where two sections of calliper move against each other needs the gap between lubricating. After you've dripped oil into the gap, squeeze and release the brake unit a few times to work oil into the space and then wipe off excess.

You may find, once you've got the calliper off and you've started cleaning it, that it's too corroded to be worth servicing. If this is the case, replace it. You'll need to get the right size – measure the distance between the middle of the hole that the calliper bolts into and the middle of one of the braking surfaces on the rim. This distance is called the 'drop'.

◀ **Front calliper brake – Brompton folding bicycle**

Servicing calliper brake units

Follow these instructions if your calliper brakes clog with road dirt, if the brake-levers stick or if the brake doesn't return smartly when you release the brake-lever.

Always do one brake at a time – that way, you've always got a complete one to refer back to if you get stuck in the middle of reassembly. Take particular care to clean road grime away from around the return spring. There isn't much of a gap between the spring and the calliper arms, so it doesn't take much of a build-up of detritus to make everything feel sluggish.

For the full spring clean effect on tired brakes, combine this service with a new pair of blocks and a new brake cable. Once you've got all your tools out, it doesn't take much longer to do the whole lot at once, and you'll feel the difference in increased braking control straight away. Fresh brake blocks are easier on your rims, minimising wear so that they last longer.

SERVICING CALLIPER BRAKE UNITS

Step 1: Start by cutting off the cable end on the brake cable, undoing the cable pinch bolt and pulling the brake cable and casing out of the barrel-adjuster. If you're thinking of fitting a new cable or cable and casing, do this now by following instructions on pages 102, 103.

Step 2: Undo the bolt that attaches the calliper to the frame/fork. It's either a 5mm Allen key or a 10mm nut. If you're doing both brakes at once, don't get the front and back mixed up – the pivot bolt that sticks out of the back of the front calliper and through the fork is slightly longer. Clean and inspect the fixing bolt – the 5mm Allen key type is called a sleeve nut – for cracks. Clean and inspect the bolt hole.

Step 3: Turn the calliper over and have a look at the back surface. You don't usually get to see this side of it and it tends to collect grit. Clean it thoroughly with degreaser or bike wash and a scrubbing brush. You can see the return spring clearly from here. Get right in close and clean up all around it so it can move freely. Squeeze the brake blocks together a few times to work out stray bits and pieces of dirt or grit.

Step 4: Turn the calliper so you can see the top and give this a good scrub, too. Again, squeeze and release the calliper and clean all the bits that squeezing it reveals. Once the whole calliper is clean, rinse off all the degreaser. Drip a little drop of oil down into the gaps between each part of the mechanism and squeeze the calliper to work the oil in. Wipe off excess – it will only collect dirt. The calliper should feel much smoother.

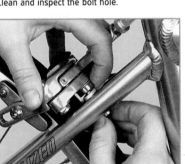

Step 5: Pop a drop of oil on the calliper fixing bolt and slide the bolt back through the frame/fork. Make sure you replace any washers that sat between the calliper and the frame. These are there to stop the back of the calliper getting jammed on the frame/fork. Refit the fixing bolt.

Step 6: Hold the calliper as shown so the wheel runs centrally between the blocks and tighten the fixing bolt firmly. Wiggle the calliper to check the fixing bolt is secure – otherwise it will work itself loose. Feed the brake cable back through the barrel-adjuster then under the pinch bolt washer. Hold the blocks against the rim, pull through any excess cable and tighten the pinch bolt firmly. For final cable adjustments, see page 102.

Disc brakes: powerful and reliable braking on demand

Along with suspension systems, disc brakes have been the major source of innovation in bicycles over the last decade. They are now fitted as standard on mountain bikes, some hybrid bikes and, increasingly, cyclocross bikes.

There are two parts to a disc brake: the calliper, which bolts onto specific mounts on your frame or fork and the rotor (or disc), which fits directly onto the hub of your wheel.

Disc brakes have two distinct advantages over rim brakes. Firstly, they don't wear out your wheel by abrading the rim every time you brake. Secondly, the harder, cleaner surface of the rotor makes for powerful braking. Mechanical disc brakes are easier to work on because they use standard V-brake levers and cables. Hydraulic brakes are more powerful and more resilient to wet, muddy conditions. Disc brakes are available to suit every purpose and budget, from super lightweight XC bling to workhorse heavyweights.

Braking power

Braking power is dependent on two things: the rotor size you choose to use and the piston arrangement within your brake's calliper. Large rotors with diameters of 180–200mm (7–8 inches) give powerful braking with more modulation but are heavier than smaller cross-country rotors, which are typically 160mm (6 inches) or even 140mm (5.5 inches) across.

Callipers may have one, two or three pairs of slave cylinders (pistons); turin piston systems are typically found on cross-country bikes whilst four- and six- or three piston systems appear on downhill or all mountain bikes, where more speed needs to be scrubbed off quickly. The current crop of disc brakes are now significantly more powerful than their predecessors, though, with one-finger braking now possible across the spectrum.

Disc brake callipers are relatively simple to fit and need little maintenance as long as they, their pads and the rotors are all kept clean and free from lubricating substances. This includes road grime, which contains a high proportion of oily fuel residue and the grease from your fingertips, as well as the ubiquitous overspray from over enthusiastic chain lubing and system leaks from a damaged hose or piston seal.

The callipers themselves aren't subject to the same barrage of dirt flung up by your tyres as rim brakes, so they will work better for longer in most conditions. Maintenance is usually limited to regular checks of the pads and rotors, plus an occasional bleed or fluid change. Bleeding is straightforward, if a little on the fiddly side, but do handle brake fluid, particularly DOT, with care as it's corrosive to both paint and skin.

Calliper adjustment

Calliper adjustment is the same whether the brake is mechanical or hydraulic. It's worth investing the time to get this right, as whilst it's a fiddly task there is a marked performance difference between brakes with pads which aren't hitting the rotor square and brakes where both pads are working exactly as they should. Most hydraulic brakes work by pushing both pads onto the rim at the same time, and function best if there is an equal gap between each pad and the rotor. Most mechanical brakes and some basic hydraulic brakes work by pushing the outer pad onto the rotor, which then flexes until it hits the opposite pad. This is more effective than it sounds but works best if the gap between the stationary pad and the rotor is as small as possible to minimize the distance the rotor has to bend.

Calliper mounting

The concept of standardized component manufacture was invented for gun making by Guillaume Deschamps for the French army. It encouraged the interchangeability of individual parts rather than the making of each gun as an individual mechanism. However, artisan gun makers were so resistant to a process they believed would damage their trade that they prevented the idea from being realized for more than fifty years. Bicycles are the same. Each manufacturer has its own preferred way of doing things and it takes time for any one way to be accepted by a majority. This turned out to be exactly the situation when disc brakes were introduced to the bicycle market – a few different standards fought for dominance, with International Standard and Post Mount as front runners.

Post Mount fixings use two threaded lugs in the frame or fork, with bolts that point roughly forward. International Standard mounts have a pair of unthreaded holes in the frame. Bolts pass through the holes, and thread directly into the calliper. The Post Mounts seem to have become the prevailing standard, as it's generally considered easier to adjust the position of the brake callipers relative to the brake rotor. In either case, there are a range of converters available to fit one kind of calliper to the other kind of frame, and also to remount brake callipers to accommodate different rotor sizes, so don't panic if your callipers don't appear to match the fittings on your bike – your bike shop should be able to identify a suitable converter.

Disc brakes: the ins and outs of axles

Disc brakes are much more powerful than rim brakes and exert their forces in a different way. The braking force can remove any wheel that is not securely clamped within the frame or fork, with potentially lethal consequences. This is obviously something to be avoided at all costs!

▲ Shimano disc brake

There are now several different axle standards, each with their own benefits. Quick-release hubs are still very common despite evidence that they lack the clamping power to resist the forces created by powerful brakes with large rotors and at the speeds which longer travel bikes allow riders to attain. If you're running quick-release skewers with disc brakes, use robust, good-quality skewers. Shimano and Mavic are both excellent – and ensure that the mechanism is clean and well lubricated. 'Lawyer tabs' are now standard on quick release forks, and though the little protruding lips below the drop-out mean you have to undo your quick release that much further to get the wheel in and out, they make it harder for the wheel to be accidentally removed if the quick release is not secure, for whatever reason. They are not a substitute for ensuring that your quick releases are in good working order and done up correctly. If you're not sure how to do them up, then refer to page 188 for instructions, and if in doubt please ask your friendly local bike shop for advice as this is not the time to experiment yourself.

The alternative to the quick release is the bolt-through hub (or through-axle). There are several different standards currently in use but the most common are the 20mm and 15mm versions. Bolt-through used to be the domain of the downhill bike only but they are becoming more popular on lighter, shorter travel forks now, too. As well as offering significantly improved security for disc brake users, they also make the front end of the bike much stiffer, improving steering on demanding terrain. A few manufacturers are also starting to experiment with bolt-through rear ends in search of the same benefits, and it's likely that this too will become more common as technology progresses.

You will need to make sure that your hub matches your axle, as both standards require specific diameter axles. However, if you want to switch forks to a model that uses a different-sized axle you won't necessarily need to buy a whole new wheel. Several hub manufacturers offer conversion kits that allow you to use one hub with different fork standards, which can be useful if you're running several bikes and need to swap parts between them too. One drawback of bolt-through hubs used to be that you needed tools to remove them, making fixing punctures or loading onto car racks even slower and more fiddly tasks. Thankfully those same designers who are now looking at bolt-through rear ends have already lavished plenty of attention on the forks and have come up with a variety of devices that make the bolt-through axle easier to use. Essentially Rock Shox's Maxle, Fox's QR15 and similar systems are just overblown quick releases that fit through one fork leg and the hollow hub shell before screwing into the opposite fork leg and tightening into place with a cam lever. Check the instructions for your particular model if in doubt, though – you should be able to find these in the fork manual or on the manufacturer's website if you don't have the manual to hand.

Whatever system you're running, you should check that your wheels are fitted securely before each and every ride, and even during a ride if you're ever in doubt about their status (being careful not to touch the disc rotor, which will be very warm indeed if you've just been braking hard!). If a strange knocking noise or rattly feeling occurs halfway through a technical descent, stop and make sure that your bike is safe to ride. It's a task that takes moments but it could save you from serious injury.

Disc brakes: fitting International Standard callipers to your bike

International Standard, or IS callipers are bolted to the bike using bolts which pass through the mounts on the frame or fork and then screw into the calliper, which is threaded. The horizontal alignment is adjusted with shims (thin washers) between the frame and the calliper.

The instructions that follow are to fit IS callipers to an IS mount fork, but if you're fitting them to a frame then just substitute the word 'frame' for 'fork'. It's wise to make sure that your fork has been correctly faced before fitting an IS mount calliper. Facing involves shaving off the inner face of the mounts **(A)** to make sure that they are exactly parallel. It's a job that requires a specific and very expensive cutting tool, so is one for the bike shop only, but it is worth doing as even a brand new fork may not be straight.

'Shim' is a fancy name for an accurately sized washer. Shims have to be of a precise thickness because the spacing between the calliper and the frame must be the same for each bolt. If the washer stacks are of different thicknesses, the calliper sits crookedly over the rotor and the pads will drag as you ride, rubbing noisily as well as making the brake feel mushy and soft. You'll need a variety of different shim widths: the thicker ones sort out the general alignment and get the rotor to pass through the centre of the slot in the calliper, whilst the wafer-thin ones fine tune the position. Front and rear callipers are fitted in the same way: the bolts pass through the mounting tabs and thread into the calliper, whichever end of the bike you're fitting them to. If you're reusing calliper bolts, make sure you use threadlock (new bolts will have threadlock already applied). Braking forces will twist and vibrate the bolts, so they need extra care to stop them rattling loose.

To fit the calliper

With the rotor fitted securely to the wheel (see page 111), slide the calliper into place over the rotor. Fit a single washer to each bolt and pass it through the mount into the calliper. Watch the relative positions of the calliper and the rotor as you tighten both bolts in turn, a little at a time. Look along the rotor, in through the slot in the calliper – it helps to hold a sheet of paper behind the slot.

◀ **(A) Rear International Standard disc mounts**

INTERNATIONAL STANDARD CALLIPER FITTING

Step 1: As you tighten the bolts, the calliper will draw closer to the frame. If the inside pad starts to touch the rotor before the bolts are snug, you'll need to add shims. Make sure you have shims in a variety of thicknesses. You will have to remove the bolts to fit the shims. Add an equal thickness of washers to each bolt and refit the bolts, repeating the process and watching the gap between pads and rotor again.

Step 2: Use the thicker washers at first, then use the thinner ones for fine-tuning **(A)**. The gap between both pads and the rotor should be the same on callipers where both pads move. For a calliper where only one pad moves, the rotor should be as close to the stationary pad as possible, to avoid unnecessary bending of the rotor. Squinting at gaps through callipers can be confusing so holding a piece of white paper up behind the slot really will help you to see what you're doing.

Step 3: The process of fine-tuning an IS calliper like this is made significantly simpler if you've been lucky enough to get hold of some of Shimano's 'tuning fork' shims, which look like open-ended tuning forks and can be inserted with the bolts still in situ **(B)**.

Disc brakes: fitting Post Mount callipers to your bike

The Post Mount system was developed by Hayes and is now used widely across the industry. Adaptors are available that will allow you to fit a post mount brake to an IS mount fork or vice versa, so don't despair if what you have doesn't seem like it will fit.

Calliper position is easy to adjust with the Post Mount system but it's important to ensure that the pads are parallel with the rotor before tightening the bolts that hold the calliper in place. It's remarkably easy to bolt the calliper on at a slight angle, so that one pad touches the rotor at the top and the other at the bottom. Even if this doesn't make the brake noisy and draggy, it will make it feel mushy rather than sharp and is to be avoided.

POST MOUNT CALLIPERS

Step 1: If you are reusing the calliper bolts, place a spot of thread-locking compound on the thread. New bolts should come with this already applied. Fit a washer to each bolt if one's not already on there, then push the bolts through the holes in the calliper. Line the bolts up carefully with the threaded holes in the Post Mounts.

Step 2: Screw the bolts in until they're almost tight; you should be able to wiggle the calliper about from side to side but you shouldn't be able to rock it backwards and forwards. Pull the brake lever so that the pads both contact the rotor and keep pulling it as you nip up the bolts. If you tighten one bolt fully before tightening the other, you will find that the rotation of the bolt pulls the calliper over to one side and you will never get the pads to hit the rotor straight. Instead, tighten each bolt alternately a quarter-turn at a time until they are tight.

Step 3: You will usually find that this has spaced the calliper perfectly. If it doesn't work first time, try again, and if the pads are still hitting the rotors unevenly you will need to look at the gap between pads and rotor, work out which pad is too close, loosen the bolts and move the calliper over by hand before tightening the bolts up again. This is a more fiddly way of setting the alignment but it's not difficult, it just requires patience.

Sizing of disc brake mounts

IS mounts are almost always 51mm apart. An additional standard was briefly used with 21.5mm spacing. The holes in an IS mount are not threaded – the fixing bolts pass through the mount and thread into the calliper.

Post Mounts are now more common, though some quirky variations in size appear every now and again: standard Post Mounts are 74mm but 68.8mm and 70mm have been used.

All calliper fixing bolts are M6 thread, regardless of mount standard.

If you have Post Mount discs and an IS mount frame/fork or vice versa, don't despair – you can buy adapters to convert from one standard to the other. They may seem expensive for a small lump of machined aluminium but without them your mismatched brakes simply won't work – there are no bodges that can be done here. Bolt the adaptor firmly to the IS component, whether that's the frame/fork or the calliper, then follow the Post Mount adjustment instructions to set up your brake.

Don't panic if you have an older bike with a non-standard mount, either. Contact the manufacturer who should be able to supply an adapter that allows you to use a more regular standard.

If you have a frame without disc mounts but would like to use discs, you may be considering using one of the conversion kits that are available. These place additional stresses on a frame in areas where it was not originally designed or tested to take them, and may be damaging to the tubes. Their success also depends on the precise shape of your frame, so get advice from your bike shop before pursuing this option.

Disc brakes: introduction to rotors

The rotor is the proper name for the disc that gives the disc brake its essential raison d'être. As with calliper mounts, it has taken time for the industry to decide on a standard – four- and five-bolt hubs have been and gone (and in the case of Hope Technology, four and three bolt hubs have come around again) but the six-bolt hub is now the most commonly used.

Shimano's alternative to the six-bolt mount, the Centrelock, has been adopted by other manufacturers including DT Swiss. It uses a rotor with a splined ring which mates with a splined ring on the hub shell and is locked into place with a modified cassette lockring. It's quicker and easier to swap discs with this system, as you only need to loosen and tighten one 'bolt', but that bolt can only be tightened with the dedicated lockring tool and a large spanner, rather than the easy-to-carry Torx/Allen key that a six- bolt mount requires. If you have Centrelock hubs and want to run six-bolt rotors, you can buy adapters that allow you to switch between the two.

As well as the choice of size and mount, you will also have to decide whether you would like regular, one-piece rotors or floating and vented versions. The former are lighter and slightly easier to coax back into shape should you manage to bend them, whilst the latter have appeared as a crossover from the motorbike industry. Floating rotors consist of an inner spider and outer braking surface which are only loosely joined, whilst vented rotors are two very thin braking surfaces with a gap in the middle that allows air flow. Both allow the faster dissipation of heat than a standard rotor, but both types usually carry a weight penalty. If you're interested in shaving grammes from your bike, you can even upgrade your rotors to featherweight versions.

Your disc brake rotors can get very hot, particularly on extended descents. Don't touch them they've it's had long enough to cool down or you really will burn yourself and end up with a nice scar. Rotors are also razor-sharp and quite capable of slicing right through a finger when spinning – blood will contaminate your rotors and pads just as effectively as oil, so keep your hands well clear of the brakes when the wheel is turning.

Each model of calliper is designed to work with a specific rotor – the diameter and thickness are crucial. If you are attempting to mix and match, make sure that the rotors aren't rubbing on the calliper body and that the full face of the pad is hitting the rotor rather than overhanging the inner edge. It really is best to use the dedicated rotor for your brakes, though.

Rotors do wear out eventually, though it takes a while and they last much, much longer than rims do under V-brakes. To check the wear, you can either measure the rotor with a pair of vernier callipers or simply take a close look at the surface. If there's a noticeable difference in thickness between the rotor face and arms, then it needs to be replaced.

The braking surface also needs to be smooth and shiny – torn, pitted or corroded surfaces mean inconsistent braking and accelerated pad wear. This can be caused by the pad compound wearing out, leaving you braking on the metal backing plate – so if you're out riding and the scraping noise of a muddy disc suddenly turns into an excruciatingly loud banshee wail, it's well worth checking whether or not you've worn your pads out and, if so, replacing them with the spares you've (of course) got in your toolkit to avoid damaging the rotor irreparably.

It's vital that the bolts securing the rotor are fitted securely, otherwise they will rattle loose. Many manufacturers supply their rotors with Torx bolts, which require a tool that's a little like a star-shaped Allen key. The Torx bolt is no stronger than a standard Allen key and is actually easier to damage if tackled without care. Don't attempt to bodge the tool, as a standard Allen key or screwdriver simply will not work. Park make several excellent Torx key sets and many multitools now include them as standard, too.

If you ride frequently in muddy conditions, you may find that a wavy or sawtooth-edged rotor like those manufactured by Hope and Avid will stop the calliper from clogging. Curved cut-outs on the rim of rotors allows hot rotors to expand uniformly, reducing cracking.

Braking efficiency

Your rotors are your braking surface. Your brake system's efficiency will depend as much on their condition as on the condition of your brake pads. Cleaning the rotors and replacing your pads should be the first priority if your brakes aren't behaving as they should be. The majority of problems here are due to contaminated pads, or worn or dirty rotors, rather than more glamorous bleeding issues.

Cleaning rotors

Disc brake pads willingly absorb grease or oil from any nearby source, with an immediate effect on your braking power. Keep the rotor clean; it's best to avoid even touching the rotor with your bare hands if you can as they leave grease behind. Some people dab grease or copper slip onto the back of the pads to try to stop any squealing. This is a bad idea, as the copper slip will soften under the heat of sustained braking and inevitably find its way onto the rotor.

Clean your rotors with either dedicated mountain bike disc cleaning spray or isopropyl alcohol, which doesn't leave an oily residue behind.

You can get the former from bike shops and the latter from chemists and electrical wholesalers. Don't be tempted to use a car disc brake spray. Car brakes run much, much hotter than a mountain bike disc brake and can burn off the residue the spray leaves behind, whereas you'll find yourself needing to start anew with the cleaning and a fresh set of brake pads.

Bikes that get a lot of use on the road will need their rotors cleaning more often, too. The roads are covered with an oily residue that contains the remnants of fumes as well as leaks; this finds its way onto rotors very quickly and can cause reduced braking power. You may also find it helpful to change or sand down your brake pads more often. The absence of abrasive mud means that the pads become glazed (shiny to look at) and noisy; you can minimize this problem by using softer resin brake pads rather than sintered.

Replacing a rotor

Some rotors – primarily Shimano – are supplied with tightening plates. These are thin metal plates which sit behind the bolts, which you bend up and around the head of each bolt once it's tight. If you wish to fit them then a flat-blade screwdriver will help you form them around the bolt but they serve no real purpose once the bike is out of the factory.

To replace your rotor, first arm yourself with the correct tool and some thread-locking compound. Never try to bodge the tool – an Allen key or screwdriver will not substitute effectively for a Torx key, and vice versa. If you do find yourself in the sticky position of rounding off the bolts, enlist the help of either a Dremel with a fine cutting disc or your friendly bike shop of choice, depending on how confident you're feeling, because once you've destroyed the heads on rotor bolts they are extremely difficult to remove.

Rotor bolts tend to be fitted tight and abandoned to the ravages of salt and grit, so they will often let go with a sharp bang. Wrap a rag around the tool to protect your hand if you find the percussive crack uncomfortable, and if you've managed to undo five of the six bolts but the other is sticking, try tightening the rest again to relieve the pressure on the stuck one – chances are it will come free with ease.

Once all six bolts are free, remove them, clean up the hub and threads, then work out which way your new rotor needs to be fitted. Most will have direction arrows etched into them but if not, the offset of each arm of the rotor usually needs to point forwards at the top.

If you're reusing the old bolts, clean them and apply a small dab of thread-locking compound. New bolts will have this already applied. Fit each bolt through the rotor and thread them loosely into the holes in the hub. Once the bolts are snug but not tight and you can still waggle the rotor slightly, rotate the rotor clockwise as far as you can, then tighten the bolts in the correct order, shown below.

Once you've followed the star-shaped sequence below and the bolts are tight, go round a final time – you'll probably find that the first bolts in the sequence are not actually tight and need further work. Use a torque wrench if you're worried about over-tightening. The correct torque is 2–4 Nm.

Once you've been out on your first ride, check the bolts are still tight, and then check them again every 500 miles.

▼ **Tighten rotor bolts alternately across the centre to hold tightening plates (A) in position**

Mechanical disc brakes

Mechanical discs are often thought of as a halfway-house between V-brakes and hydraulic discs. They're not as powerful as hydraulic brakes, but they're much cheaper. The simplicity of cables may also be appealing, though hydraulics aren't any more complicated to maintain.

The advantages of not using the rim as the braking surface apply equally to mechanical and hydraulic discs, though hydraulics escape the drag issues that affect V-brakes and mechanical discs equally once the cables start to get wet and dirty.

Since mechanical disc callipers all work in slightly different ways, there isn't space here to show you how to strip and service each and every one but the general method is the same. Refer to your neatly filed manual for full instructions.

There are two designs of mechanical disc brake. The first, and most common, consists of one moving and one stationary pad. The moving pad, mounted on a piston mechanism, pushes against the rotor when the brake lever is operated at the bar. This bends the rotor slightly so that it's pushed against the static pad and trapped between the two, stopping the rotor from turning and slowing the wheel. When you release the brake lever, a spring acting on the moving pad returns it to the calliper body so the rotor and the wheel are free to move again.

Mud, dust and salt can work through the seals, getting trapped inside the mechanism. This makes the piston action sluggish, so it's well worth taking the time to learn how to strip them down. Mechanical disc brakes respond well to being stripped, cleaned and reassembled.

Although all callipers work in slightly different ways, they're so similar that it's possible to generalize. Most brakes have a selection of small washers separating the internal components. It's vital that these all go back in the same order. By laying everything you remove out in a line, you can avoid the classic moment of discovering a stray washer after reassembling the calliper. For jobs like this, I like to set the parts out on a clean sheet of paper – you can draw diagrams on it as you go along to remind yourself which way round the parts went.

It's worth disconnecting the cable and removing the calliper completely from the bike, so that you can lay the brake on a flat surface and see properly what you're doing. If you can remove the pads by wiggling them out of the calliper slots, do so now. The stationary pad, the one nearest the wheel, may be held in place with a little steel washer. The teeth on the inside of the washer grip the post on the back of the pad. Use a small screwdriver to lever off the washer. Take care not to damage it.

Disassembly from here will vary, so make diagrams of what you're doing as you go along. Remember to make a note of which direction parts like seals face. Remove the actuation lever by undoing the bolt in its centre. Take out any seals. Remove the innards of the brake carefully, there's a spring inside pulling the pad away from the rotor. You'll find a spiral groove inside the body of the calliper – this is what pushes the piston against the rotor when you rotate the actuation lever and is normally the part that gets gummed up with mud. Clean the groove carefully. Cotton buds are perfect. Wipe the inside of the calliper body and the other internal components clean, and reassemble according to your diagram. Don't regrease the piston head – the grease melts when the calliper body heats up, creeping onto the brake pads and contaminating them.

The actuation lever bolt needs a strip of Loctite to stop it from vibrating loose. Retighten firmly, then test the action of the brake. Squeeze the actuation lever, pinching the barrel-adjuster and cable stop together while looking into the calliper slot. The brake pad should move smoothly across the slot, springing immediately back when you release the actuation lever. If the actuation lever won't rotate easily, check that you've not left out a washer on reassembly. If the pad doesn't spring back smartly, your spring is misaligned or there's still dirt in the spiral groove.

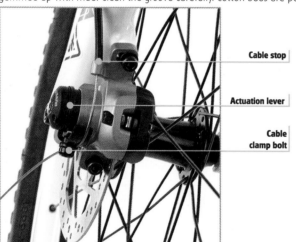

Cable stop

Actuation lever

Cable clamp bolt

◀ **Shimano mechanical disc brake calliper**

Changing and adjusting cables

Mechanical discs seem to suffer from dirt ingress slightly less than V-brakes. Corrosion in the cables will still make the brakes feel sluggish, though, and frayed or kinked cables will need replacing.

Cut the cable end off the old cable. Undo the cable clamp bolt and free the end of the cable. Unthread the cable from inside the casing, leaving the casing in place. Keep any rubber boots. Once back at the lever, look to work out how the nipple is seated (it's usually in a pivoted nest attached to the lever blade). Pull in the lever and look at the exposed section from underneath. Most are variants on the type shown in the picture. Undo the lockring on the barrel-adjuster until its slot lines up with that on the front of the lever body, then undo the barrel to line up its slot too. (Shimano XT and XTR levers don't have lockrings anymore.)

Pull the cable forward, so it slips out of the lined-up slots, then pull the lever towards the bars. The nest that the nipple sits in has a key-shaped hole so the cable cannot pull out under pressure. Wiggle the cable to line it up with the slot in the nest and pull it out gently. Remove each section of outer casing and cut a fresh piece to length. Cut the end of each section squarely, making sure you don't leave a ragged tang of metal across the hole. If the cable lining has got squashed where you cut it, use the point of a sharp knife to open it out. Each end of each section will need a ferrule. The cable stops on disc brake bikes are often larger than usual to accommodate hydraulic hoses. If this is the case, reuse the ferrules from the old casing. The far end of the last section may not need a ferrule, but fit one if there is room.

Reverse the procedure you used for removing the old cable to fit the new cable back into the lever: line the nipple up with the key-shaped hole in the nest, wiggle it into place, line the slots on the barrel-adjuster and lockring up with the slots on the lever body, guide the cable into the lever body and barrel-adjuster through the slots, then turn the barrel-adjuster a quarter-turn to trap the cable in place. Feed the cable

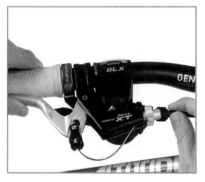

through each section of outer casing in turn. Fit a ferrule on each end of each section. Make sure you don't allow the cable to drop onto the ground and pick up dirt. Drip a drop of oil onto any section of cable that will end up inside the outer casing. Feed the cable through the last section, then through the barrel-adjuster or cable stop on the disc brake. Finally, pass the cable under the cable clamp bolt, pull through until the brake pads almost touch the rotor and tighten the cable clamp bolt firmly – see below. Lift the wheel and turn it. It should spin freely. A slight rub is fine, but the wheel shouldn't drag. The brakes should lock on when you pull the brake lever without the lever touching the handlebar. If either of these situations does happen, go to the adjustment section on page 116.

◀ **Line up slots in barrel-adjuster and lockring, then pull cable forwards**

REFITTING THE NEW CABLE

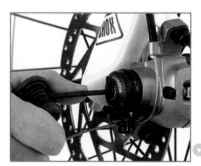

Step 1: Refit any rubber boots – give them a clean first if they're grubby – and slide the cable in under the cable clamp bolt. It is clear where it should fit – make sure it lies in the groove under the clamp bolt. Leave about 5cm (2 inches) of spare cable, cut the rest off and fit a cable end.

Step 2: Pull the cable through the clamp bolt to take up any slack, and hold it with one hand while you tighten the cable clamp bolt up with the other. Then pull the lever firmly several times to settle the casing and ferrules into place. You will probably find that the cable is so slack that you can pull the lever all the way to the bars without locking the wheel. If this is the case, undo the cable clamp bolt and pull more cable through. Retighten the cable clamp and retest.

Step 3: Usually, the stationary pad (on the inside, nearest the wheel) is adjustable. Most adjust by turning a 3 or 5mm Allen key on the back of the pad clockwise to move the pad closer, and anticlockwise to move it farther away. Get it as close as possible without touching the rotor.

Changing disc brake pads

Disc brake pads usually last much longer than V-brake pads. The material in the disc rotor is much harder than the material in the rim, allowing the disc brake pad to be much harder as well. Were you to use the material in the disc brake pad as a rim brake, the rim would wear away in next to no time. The harder material also means that the pad can touch the rotor as the wheel spins without slowing down significantly – so you don't have to worry about a slight rubbing noise when you spin a wheel with a disc brake.

Make sure you get the right pad for the brake; the fittings and shapes vary between makes, and between models from the same make. Take the old ones along to your bike shop for comparison if you're not sure. Even if you know the make, the shape will vary from model to model and from year to year. After fitting, new pads need to be bedded in – they don't work properly until you've braked a few times. Once you've got the new pads in, find somewhere you can ride the bike safely with limited braking power. Ride along slowly, haul on the brakes and bring the bike to a halt. Repeat at increasing speeds, until you're satisfied. This may take 10 or 20 repetitions.

The pads on mechanical brakes sometimes wear unevenly. The most common design has the cable from the brake lever pull an actuation lever (mechanic's term for 'lever that does something'), which pushes the outer brake pad onto the rotor. The rotor flexes under the pressure, gets pushed against the other disc pad, then ends up firmly trapped between two pads. This can cause uneven wear, but you must still change both pads at the same time even if one looks more worn than the other. They should be replaced when either of the pads has less than 0.5mm (1/16 inch) of thickness left from any direction. You may need to take them out to check how they're surviving. If in doubt, follow the procedure for removing them below, and refit them if they have life left. Clean your rotors whenever you fit new pads.

Changing brake pads

Drop the wheel out of the frame. Look at the brake calliper. You'll see that it has a slot into which the rotor fits. Most often, the pads will pull out in the same direction that you pulled the rotor out of the slot – towards the centre of the wheel. Some will pull out of the top of the brake calliper, away from the centre of the wheel. Have a good look at the calliper before you start and draw a picture if necessary to help you put everything back together. There will be a pad on each side of the rotor, and it will often have little ears or tabs to pull it out. Use these to manipulate the pads, rather than touching the pad surfaces.

CHANGING BRAKE PADS

Step 1: Often the pads will not pull straight out; they will have some kind of device that stops them from getting rattled out as you ride. This will normally be a pin that goes through the opposite side of the pad, so look on the other side of the calliper for a retaining pin or split pin. (If necessary, use pliers to bend the ends of the split pins straight.)

Step 2: Pull out split pins, retaining pins or P-clips – keep them safe because you need to fit them back at the end. There may be one or two retaining pins. Split pins need to be bent gently straight with pliers before you can pull them out.

Step 3: Gently pull the pads out, either by grabbing the little ears that poke out of the slot, or by pulling on the corners of the pads. If you're not sure of the correct replacement pads, take the old ones to your bike shop to match them up.

Step 4: The pads may have a retaining spring; make a note of its position and orientation, and refit it with the new pads. Take care when fitting the new pads that the arms of the spring sit beside the pads, not over the braking surface. It's easiest to squash the spring between the pads, then fit both into the slot together, rather than trying to get the pads into the slot one at a time.

Step 5: Slide the new pads back into the calliper, pushing them in until the holes in the pad line up with the retaining pin holes in the calliper. Refit the retaining pin or pins, bending over their ends, so that they don't rattle out. Then pull the pads firmly to make sure they are held securely in place.

Step 6: Refit the wheel, wiggling the rotor back into the gap between pads. You may need to readjust the cable because new pads will be thicker than the old ones. Pick up the bike and spin the wheel. It should spin freely, without binding. However, it's fine if you can hear the pad rubbing slightly on the rim – this won't slow you down. If the rotor drags or the brake lever pulls back to the bar without braking, go to the adjustment section on page 116.

Brake-fitting tips

◆ Ensure you have the correct replacement brake pads before you start – they vary between make, model and year of manufacture.

◆ Most pad set-ups rely on a return spring that sits between the two pads to help them release when you're finished braking. If you don't get a new one with the new pads, clean the old one before reusing. Ensure that the side arms of the spring sit beside, not over, the brake pad surface.

◆ Pads will need replacing when there's less than 0.5mm ($^1/_{16}$ inch) of brake pad left. Don't leave it too late – once you wear through to the metal backing, it will tear up the surface of your rotors.

◆ If there is life left in the old pads, wrap them up and put aside for emergencies.

◆ You can freshen up the surfaces of dirty pads by cross-hatching them with a clean sanding block. However, once the pads become contaminated with oil, they will need replacing.

◆ Resin pads are cheaper than sintered, but wear out more quickly. They're more suitable for commuting than off-road use – on long descents they may overheat, diminishing your braking power. Sintered pads are recommended for off-road use.

◆ Titanium-backed brake pads are lighter, but also disperse heat buildup more effectively that standard pads.

Keeping pads and rotors clean

Cleaning rotors

Your rotors should be a routine step in your regular bike cleaning-routine – they'll last longer and stop you better with a bit of care on the braking surfaces. Indications that attention is overdue include squealing when you apply the brakes and deterioration in your braking performance.

The most common contaminant is stray oil from overzealous chain lubrication – one of the many good arguments for drip application! They'll also pick up oil from your fingers, from any leaky seals in the brake calliper or from diesel spills on the road. If you suspect anything's found its way onto your rotors, act swiftly – rotors can be cleaned, but if the contamination spreads to your brake pads, you're more likely to be looking at replacement.

Recommended cleaning fluids include isopropyl alcohol and dedicated bike brake cleaner. Muc-Off make a good-value, effective version. Just don't be tempted to use car or motorbike disc cleaners, they'll leave a residue on your rotors. Use a clean cloth or fresh kitchen towel to wipe the rotors.

If you're still getting a squeal after cleaning the rotors, check they're securely bolted onto your wheels – loose rotors will vibrate noisily as you brake. In particular, for six-bolt rotors, loosen off all the fixing bolts so you can wiggle the rotor from side to side. You'll be able to feel that the bolt holes are slightly larger than the bolts, so you can rotate the disc just slightly back and forth as well. To minimize brake squeal, roll the rotor backwards as far as you can (clockwise as you look at the face of the rotor) before tightening the six fixing bolts in sequence to torque (2-6Nm) (see page 111). This helps reduce the potential for vibration under heavy braking.

Mechanical disc brakes: adjusting brake pads for controlled stopping

The pad position will need adjusting after changing a brake cable, after fitting new pads or as the pads become worn. Ideally, the pad position should be set so that you can lock up the wheel by pulling the brake lever halfway to the handle bar. This gives you enough lever movement for precise speed control, without the risk of trapping fingers between lever and bar during emergency stops.

Mechanical disc brakes can be fiddly to adjust. The clearance between pads and rim must be small, without allowing the pads to rub on the rotor. A common source of confusion is that only the outer brake pad gets moved by the action of the cable, pushing the rotor against a stationary inner pad. This means that the two pads have to be adjusted in different ways.

You will really benefit from a workstand for this task. If that's not possible, press-gang a mate into lifting the wheel off the ground at opportune moments. Before you start adjusting, spin the wheel, look into the calliper slot and check how much clearance there is between rotor and pads. If the brake binds as you ride, one or both pads are rubbing on the rotor and need to be moved away. If you're finding that you can pull the rotor all the way back before the wheel locks, one or both of the pads needs to be moved towards the rotor.

The calliper slot is quite narrow, and it can be tricky to see what's going on. Clean the calliper before you start trying to make adjustments. Then hold something white on the far side of the slot to make it easier to see the gap. Spin the wheel while watching the slot. Unless they're brand new, rotors will often have a slight wobble. Make sure you adjust for an estimated central position.

Adjusting pad position

Before you start adjusting the pad position, ensure that the rotors are not dragging on the side of the rotor slot — this will damage the rotors and slow you down. Adjust the calliper position (see the calliper fitting section, page 117), so that the rotor runs centrally before you adjust the pad position. Check that the wheel is properly and securely located in the dropout too — the rotor position will be affected if the wheel's not straight in the frame or forks.

It's worth keeping a spare set of brake pads. There is no standard size and shape (unlike V-brake blocks), so it can be tricky to find the right one. Spares are light and easy to carry for emergency replacement, but it's far easier to adjust pads at home than out in the open because the job involves too many small fiddly bits aching to start a life of freedom in the long grass beside your favourite trail.

Toolbox

Tools to fit new callipers
- Allen keys — 5mm or 6mm, to fit heads of fixing bolts
- For IS mount callipers — a selection of shims. Useful sizes are 1mm, 0.5mm and 0.25mm

Tools to change brake pads, and adjust pad position
- Depending on model, pliers to extract and refit split pins
- Fresh pads of correct make and model
- Allen keys for stationary pad adjustment bolt — usually 3mm, 5mm, or Torx TX25
- Allen key for cable clamp adjustment — usually 5mm

Mechanical disc brakes: adjusting Shimano callipers

The most common arrangement for mechanical disc brakes is that used by the Shimano callipers shown in the pictures.

The position of the outer pad is controlled by the cable tension, while the inner pad remains stationary. When you pull the brake lever, the outer pad is pushed onto the rotor, which flexes sideways against the stationary pad and becomes trapped between the two.

The distance between the rotor and the pads is adjusted separately on each side. The brake lever barrel-adjuster is used to set the gap between the outer pad and the outer surface of the rotor, while a bolt on the back of the brake calliper allows you to fine-tune the gap between the stationary pad and the inner rotor surface.

The gap on either side is critical – too much space, and you'll have to pull the brake lever all the way back to the bars before the brakes bite. Too close and the pads will rub as you ride, slowing you down.

ADJUSTING SHIMANO PADS

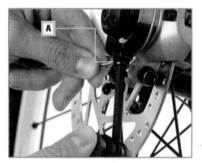

Step 1: If the outer pad rubs on the rotor, use the barrel-adjuster to release cable tension. If the barrel adjuster has a lockring (the XT lever in the picture doesn't), roll it a couple of turns anticlockwise. Turn the barrel adjuster into the lever (clockwise as you look along the brake cable) to loosen the cable, increasing pad clearance. Turn clockwise to move the pads closer to the rotor.

Step 2: You may run out of barrel-adjuster range, so that the barrel falls out of the lever or won't screw any further in. If this happens, reset the barrel to the centre of its range, then undo the cable clamp bolt **[A]** at the brake calliper and make a course adjustment. Reclamp the cable firmly, then return to step 1. Test. Once you're satisfied, reseat any lockrings clockwise back against the lever body.

Step 3: If it's the inside pad that's rubbing on the rotor, the stationary (inside) pad will need adjusting. This usually requires a 3mm or 5mm Allen key, or a Torx T25, which will have to be threaded in through the spokes. Normally, clockwise moves the pad closer, anticlockwise increases the gap, but there are exceptions – watch the pad as you adjust to confirm the effect. Quarter-turns are enough to make a difference.

Alternative methods

Alternative arrangements for centring the pads over the calliper do exist, although the above method is now becoming standard since it's the easiest and most accurate way to set the clearance between pads and rotor.

Some older callipers have an integral adjuster, allowing you to wind the whole calliper sideways to adjust the gap between the pads. Turn the thumbscrew slowly. Once you get close, small adjustments make a big difference. Pull the brakes on hard between each adjustment to settle everything into place.

If the stationary pad is not adjustable, you will have to move the whole calliper sideways to set the gap between stationary pad and rotor. Then use the cable to adjust the clearance on the outside of the rotor. For Post Mount callipers, undo the two calliper mounting bolts just a little — just enough so you can move them. Ease the calliper sideways, checking the gap beside the inside of the rotor nearest the wheel. This needs to be approximately 1mm (¹⁄₁₆ inch). Hold a piece of white card on the far side of the calliper to make it easier to see the gap. Retighten the bolts firmly. You may need to readjust the outer-pad spacing after this.

International Standard (IS) mounts are trickier. Estimate how much more gap you need for the pad to clear the rotor. Undo the calliper fixing bolts and add an equal number of shims between each bolt and the calliper. With normal washer-shaped shims, you need to remove the bolts completely. Shimano tunning fork-shaped shims can be slipped between calliper and frame without removing the bolt.

Add shims until the inside pad clears the rotor, then retighten the calliper fixing bolts firmly. You may need to adjust the outer pad spacing after this.

Hydraulic disc brakes

Hydraulic brakes are much more powerful than cable operated ones. The principle is simple: pulling the lever towards the bars activates the master cylinder, pushing fluid down a narrow tube to the calliper, acitvating the slave cylinder which pushes the pistons outwards. The pistons push against the brake pads, moving them inwards until they contact and grip the rotor attached to your wheel. The brake fluid is incompressible – any movement of the lever is transferred directly to the brake pads via the two cylinders and the pistons – and a hydraulic brake can be very powerful indeed. The idea of dealing with hydraulic fluid can be daunting, but as long as you're calm and careful, it's not difficult at all.

There are two types of fluid that are commonly used in mountain bike disc brakes and you MUST use the right one for your brake – using the wrong one will damage seals throughout the system irreparably. DOT fluid has a higher boiling point and expands less at high temperatures, whilst mineral oil is easier to work with, less corrosive and less environmentally damaging. There isn't a significant performance difference between the two when used in mountain bike brakes, just don't confuse them. Both types will eventually absorb moisture from the air and become less effective, so buy small amounts and keep them sealed, disposing of leftover half-bottles responsibly if they're been hanging around for a while. Wear rubber gloves to protect yourself when using both types of fluid, as they are damaging to the skin.

One of the indicators of an upcoming brake bleed is a spongy feel to the lever, indicating that air has managed to get into the system. This could happen when you cut a hose to shorten it, or if you crash and manage to rip one of the hoses from the lever or nick it elsewhere. Air is more compressible than the incompressible brake fluid, so when you pull the brake lever all the air bubbles will be squashed before the fluid starts to go anywhere. Thankfully air is lighter than brake fluid, so if you open the system at the top the bubbles will rise to the top and escape.

The process of opening the brake, letting the air out and topping up the fluid level before closing the brake again is known as bleeding. Bleeding is often regarded as a mysterious and complicated process only to be carried out by druids. Actually, it's quite simple but people do tend to treat it as a universal cure for anything wrong with the brakes, whereas it should actually be one of the last things you consider unless you have good evidence that there's air in the system.

You should also take care not to get hydraulic fluid of either variety anywhere near your rotors or pads. If you're working with fluid, then remove the wheels and pads to get them well out of the way of any possible contamination. Do not refit them until you've finished the bleeding process, cleaned up and packed away. If the worst happens and you manage to contaminate the rotors, then you can try cleaning them with isopropyl alcohol but if the pads are contaminated, then they need to be replaced.

Open and closed system brakes

The vast majority of brakes currently on the market are open systems, rather than closed. Both types of brake operate in the same way, with a master cylinder at the lever operating a slave cylinder at the calliper. Under heavy braking, the fluid heats up and expands, increasing the volume of fluid in the system which would cause the pads to drag on the rotors if unregulated. This happens to both open and closed systems, but they differ in the way in which they deal with the heat build-up.

Open systems have a flexible rubber diaphragm inside the reservoir (usually at the top). As your brake fluid heats up and expands, the diaphragm deforms to accommodate the additional volume. The piston inside the lever is designed to close off the reservoir from the brake hose as soon as it's operated. This is vital – if the hose and reservoir remained connected then the force of the lever would simply crush the diaphragm, rather than acting on the pistons. With a basic open system, you can't adjust the pad position independently of the calliper, though some open brakes (like Hope's X2 and Avid's Elixir series) now include bite point adjustment.

Closed system brakes lack the diaphragm of open system brakes, so cannot auto-adjust for fluid expansion. They do however have an adjusting knob on the reservoir which allows you to dial the bite point of the brake in and out by changing the volume of fluid the reservoir can hold. Making the reservoir smaller by screwing the adjuster in forces fluid down the brake hose, pushing the pistons and pads towards the rotors. Making it larger, by screwing out the adjuster, causes the pistons and the pads to retract from the rotor. This means that under heavy braking, for example on a long alpine descent, you can back the pads right off to accommodate the fluid expansion and eliminate brake rub – the process which the closed system does automatically.

Adjusting hydraulic brakes

Every model of brake works a little differently, making it impossible to cover each and every one comprehensively here. Always keep the instructions which came with your own particular brake and refer to it for detailed instructions relevant to your brake.

The basic principle is the same for all hydraulic brakes, though: the pads need to sit close enough to the rotors to be able to bite swiftly and firmly onto the rotor's surface when you brake, but they need enough clearance to allow the rotors to pass freely between the pads without slowing the wheel down unnecessarily.

It's fine for rotors to rub a little on the pads. Disc brake pads are much harder than rim brake pads, so a little bit of contact isn't going to slow you down and light 'scuffing' at one or two points on the rotor's rotation isn't a problem. However, a badly bent rotor or poorly adjusted calliper will cause the pads to rub on the rotor permanently, which will slow you down and cause unnecessary heat build-up in the fluid as well as pad wear. Slightly bent rotors can be straightened by hand but warped rotors must be replaced.

The most common design for mountain bike hydraulic disc brakes uses two pistons, one on each side of the rotor. This is more than powerful enough for the majority of riders, but if you decide you want to go faster and need to look at brakes which are up to the task, then you could look at the more powerful variation which uses a pair of pistons on each side of the rotor (four in total). These are designed to fine-tune the action of the brake by making two of the four pistons slightly smaller; the pair of smaller pistons moves first, followed by the larger, pushing a larger brake pad. The greater surface area of the pad is less forgiving of maladjustment but helps dissipate heat effectively on long descents or under hard braking as well as giving more power. If this four-pot system is still not enough, then you could take the final step and fit a six-pot system; but if that's the case you're probably well beyond any advice this book can offer!

Adjusting pad clearance

Whilst older and more basic open hydraulic systems don't allow you to adjust the pad placement in the same way as a closed system does, many now come with a bite point adjustment in some form or another. The simplest of these are the tool-free versions found on Hope's Tech Levers or Shimano XT and Saint. Look into the gap between pad and rotor whilst adjusting the dial to work out which way the pads move; then turn the adjusting dial so that the pads hit the rotor when the lever is approximately halfway to the bar. This gives you enough lever travel for precise control over your speed but avoids any risk of trapping your fingers between bar and lever when braking in a hurry. Another useful adjustment is the lever reach. On a few levers this is also tool-free but the majority require you to use a tiny, 2.5mm or 2mm Allen key to turn an awkwardly placed screw that's usually located on the inside of the lever blade. Don't be tempted to try and hurry things along by using a long, ball-ended Allen key for this unless it's a proper T-bar version – a basic one will round off quickly as the short end of a regular Allen key doesn't give you enough leverage to turn the screw effectively.

To figure out where you should set the lever reach, sit on the saddle and place your fingers on the bars as if you were about to brake. If you have to stretch at all or find yourself rotating your hand around the bar in order to get your fingertips on the lever, then you need to move them inwards. Ideally your fingers should rest with the leverblade sitting between your first and second knuckles.

It's important to remember that the majority of disc brake systems are self-adjusting and so you'll need to pump the brakes frequently when making adjustments, to let them settle into place. This applies if you've fitted new pads, bled the system or are adjusting the bite point, as well as any other maintenance task. If you pump the brake lever and the lever comes all the way back to the bar before the pads bite, you're short of oil volume and probably also have air trapped in the system. Follow the instructions for bleeding your brakes on page 124–5. On the other hand, if the brake pads bind on the rotor no matter now many times you pump the lever, you may have too much fluid in the system. With care, you can drain a little of this excess away. Fit a length of clear hose to the brake calliper's bleed nipple to prevent air being sucked in, then open the bleed nipple a quarter-turn with the correct spanner. Squeeze the brake lever gently so that 3–4mm of oil creeps up the hose – no more. Close the bleed nipple, remove the hose and test operation, before repeating if necessary.

◀ **Brake pads can be removed easily for inspection or replacement**

Disc brakes: changing brake pads

Brake pads must be changed if they've worn down to less than a third of their original thickness, so replace them if you only have 0.5mm or less of compound left on the backing pad. You will also need to replace them if they have become contaminated. This could be the result of brake fluid leak, careless lubrication of the drivechain or other environmental factors.

Bedding in brand new brake pads is vital. If you skip this task you'll find that you suffer both poor braking and vanishing disc pads. New pads need to be 'cooked' to remove chemical residues left over from manufacture and harden the braking surface.

You do this by braking to heat up the pad, then allowing it to cool, and repeating until the braking performance improves, so find yourself somewhere that you can ride safely without having particularly sharp brakes (i.e. not a busy A-road or a steep descent). Then ride along slowly, before braking until you've nearly come to halt. Repeat this process until the braking performance improves; it's not unusual for it to take ten to twenty cycles. Be aware that the braking performance will improve suddenly so try not to go over the bars!

Once the pads are well bedded in, they usually last a long time. Exactly how long will depend on the trail conditions: gritty mud will wear them out faster than soft, sloppy mud, whilst dry trails could easily see you riding the same trails all summer long, though if you're running sintered pads you may find that they glaze and require a quick scuff with sandpaper to improve the bite and reduce the noise.

Pad fitting is similar enough from brake to brake for it to be possible to just give a general overview here. It's worth having a good look at your calliper before you start taking anything apart, even taking a picture or drawing a quick sketch if you're worried you might forget what it should look like.

Unfortunately almost every brake model from every manufacturer requires a different shape brake pad (there are exceptions - Shimano's newer systems all use the same pad shape). Take the old pad to the bike shop if you're unsure of the brand and model names of your brake to make sure you get the right replacements.

Removing the old pads

As a general rule, you need to remove the wheel to get at the pads and they fit into position via the central slot in the calliper, either from the same direction as the rotor or from the top. Each pad sits against its piston inside the calliper. When you pull the brake lever (or master cylinder), each piston (or slave cyinder) is pushed out, taking the pad with it until it contacts and slows the rotor.

Pads have a flat metal backing plate, onto which the compound is bonded. The backing plate will usually have a metal tab which allows you to handle it without needing to touch the braking compound. Pads can be left- or right- specific and though this information is sometimes stamped/etched on the backing plate, it's wise to make a note of which way round the old ones go.

CHANGING BRAKE PADS

Step 1: The pads will be held in place by a screw, a magnet, a spring clip on the back of the pad or simply a very precise fit in the calliper. There is often some sort of secondary security device to stop the pad falling out if the first fix should fail, so remove this first.

Step 2: Then remove the main retaining device, in this case a small Allen key bolt.

Step 3: Now the pads are free, you can remove them – simply pull gently on the tabs and they should come out with little more than a wiggle. If you're not planning on putting the same pads back into the calliper then use them to protect the pistons as you push them back into the calliper body, before you remove them.

Adjusting callipers

Disc brake callipers self-adjust as the pads wear out. The pistons will protrude slightly further as the overall pad width shrinks and this can make it very hard to fit the new pads with their full thickness compound. The vast majority of brakes are now open systems, so you will need to very gently push the pistons back into the calliper once you have removed the old pads.

You can use a tyre lever if you are worried about damaging the piston – they are relatively fragile, particularly those with a small locating pin that's easy to snap off. You may find that you need the leverage supplied by a longer tool though, so use a large, flat blade screwdriver wrapped in thick cardboard or a ring spanner which sits neatly on the face of each piston.

Push one piston gently back into the calliper body until it sits flush, then repeat with the opposite piston. You may find that as you push in one piston, the other moves out again; persevere with a few more cycles but if the pistons refuse to sit evenly and flush with the calliper, you will need to bleed them (page 124).

FITTING NEW PADS

Step 1: If dirt is allowed to lodge behind the pads, it can potentially damage the piston seals, contaminate the brake fluid and cause airleaks. Before fitting new pads give the calliper body a good clean. Use a clean rag or tissue, with plain soapy water – there should be no need to use a degreaser. Avoid solvents and brake fluid, too, as these can damage the silicon piston seals.

Step 2: Most pads use a spring to spread the two faces apart when not being pressed to the rotor. Fit this to the new pads, making sure you've got both left and right pads the right way round. Avoiding touching the braking compound, press the two pads together and make sure the spring is neatly fitted. Ensure that the spring arms sit beside, not over, the face of the brake pad.

Step 3: Push the pair of new pads into the slot in the calliper, reversing the action you took to remove the old pair. Push them in until they are firmly in the right place within the calliper and any retaining pin on the piston lines up with the pad's locating holes. Then fit the retaining pin, and finally the secondary retaining device, so that the brake looks exactly as it was when you started. Refit the wheel and pump the brake lever once or twice to settle the pistons into place. Finally, bed in your pads – see page 120.

A word about bite

Many modern brakes will have a bite point adjuster. This is usually a thumbwheel or a screw located by the lever. Screwing this in and out alters the internal geometry of the master piston in the brake lever, and consequently moves the pads in and out of the calliper. This allows you to control how far the lever moves before the pads hit the rim.

Sometimes this can also have an effect on the lever reach as well so you may need to reset your reach adjuster after you have finished. This feature is useful as it allows you to set the bite point of your brake to where you want it, something that was not previously possible on open system brakes.

When bleeding a brake that has a bite point adjuster it is important to set it all the way back before you start, so that the slave pistons in the calliper are retracted as far as possible. This will give you the full range of adjustment once you've finished bleeding the brake.

Hoses: shortening and clamping

Most new brake systems arrive in their boxes, fully assembled and ready bled. Whilst it's nice to be able to fit a brand new brake straight away without having to go through the rigmarole of cutting and bleeding, you will probably find that the hoses are too long for your bike and that you will need to cut them eventually.

Fit the new brakes to your bike first and go for a ride, though – tape the hoses to your frame if you have closed cable guides. This means that you will at least know how the brakes are supposed to feel before you tackle the task of shortening them, and so will be able to recognise whether or not any air has got into the system in the brief period that you have the hose loose from the lever.

All brake hoses can be cut to length, though braided ones require some care and effort. A little bit of a graceful curve is fine and you need to make sure that hoses are long enough to allow the bars to turn fully without being restricted by the hose. It's a good idea to allow a little extra, too, just in case you manage to have a bad enough crash to spin the bars round so far that you might manage to rip the hose from the lever. However, you want to avoid leaving the hoses so long that they snag on trailside hazards as you pass. If you're cutting your hoses down, then work out how much you need to remove before you dismantle the hose and mark it securely with tape - and remember the workshop truism: it's easy enough to take more off but you can't add more on once it's gone.

The most common connection between the hose and the lever is a soft brass ring called an olive. This fits around the hose and is tightened by the threaded shroud which covers it and joins it to the lever, making an airtight seal. The lever has a barbed fitting, which keeps the hole in the hose open so that the fluid can pass through. With patience and a bit of luck you can usually shorten hoses which use this system without needing to go for a full bleed, as they're less disposed towards dribbling oil everywhere.

Some other systems require you to fit the barbed lever to the hose, before connecting it to the lever. This type usually need bleeding as it's virtually impossible to fit the barbed fitting to the hose without displacing some of the brake's fluid as you go. Follow the steps for shortening the hose and don't forget to attach all the necessary fittings before connecting the hose.

If you're trying to reuse a barbed fitting from the end of a hose, hold the fitting carefully with pliers and slice away from you, down the hose, with a sharp knife. Point the knife upwards, so it cuts the hose without scoring the fitting. You can't simply pull the fitting out of the hose, no matter how hard you try; the more you pull, the tighter the barbs hold onto the inside of the hose.

You then have to fit the new or reclaimed fitting back into the new hose, which can be tricky as it's a tight fit. The correct method is to place the hose between two special guides and clamp it pointing upwards in a vice before tapping the fitting gently into the end. If you find yourself short of a guide or two and the bike shop can't oblige, then make your own by drilling a hole the same diameter as the hose through a 2cm (1 inch) deep scrap of wood. Cut the wood in half down the centre of the hole to leave two pieces of wood, each with a long semi-circular groove in which you can safely clamp your hose without fear of crushing.

Toolbox

Disc-brake tools: replacing brake pads
- Depending on pad securing system, pliers (for split pins) or screwdriver 2 or 2.5mm Allen keys for threaded retaining pins
- For Hayes – 10mm ring wrench to push pistons back into calliper

Disc-brake tools: bleeding brakes
- Tool to remove reservoir cover - 2 or 2.5mm Allen key or Torx key or Phillips screwdriver
- Plastic hose to fit over bleed nipple – available in a manufacturer-specific bleed kit from your bike shop, or from hardware shops or car spares shops – often in the brake and clutch bleeding section
- Bottle to route the hose into
- Plenty of duct or electrical tape to strap bottle and hose to your bike
- Spanner to turn bleed nipple – 7 or 8mm
- The correct brake fluid for your bike – DOT or mineral oil
- Cloth to mop up spillage and to protect your paintwork
- Rubber gloves

Tools to shorten brake hoses
- Tools as above, in case you need to bleed the brakes afterward
- Sharp knife
- Replacement olives
- Small screwdriver
- Spanner to remove shroud – usually 8mm

Shortening Hope Minis

Shortening brake hoses involves dealing with brake fluid so wear gloves. They look stupid and feel clumsy but then again so do brake fluid burns.

The brake hoses supplied with new brakes are almost always longer than you need, so that they can fit all sizes and types of bike on the market. Trimming them down keeps the bike looking tidy and also reduces the chance of the hose getting caught on trailside foliage, which can cause you to crash and possibly damage the hose, leaving you stranded and brakeless.

As with every cutting task, it's better to measure twice and cut once than vice versa but if in doubt err on the side of caution, as whilst it's easy to remove more from a hose, you won't be able to lengthen one you've already cut! It's best to use new olives every time you refit the hose – the old ones often become deformed when you remove them, so make sure you have all the fittings you need before you start the job.

Ideally, when doing this job you'll make a neat slice in the hose, then refit it without losing any fluid. In practice; this is easier said than done, so you may find you need to bleed the brake once you've refitted the hose.

REMOVING HOSE

Step 1: Undo the shroud and push it along the brake hose to reveal the hose fittings, including the olive and copper crush washer. Slide the shroud down the hose, beyond the point at which you're going to cut it so that you don't have to refit the shroud to the hose.

Step 2: The hose should come free of the lever easily, so avoid pulling it sharply and flicking brake fluid out of the hose. letting air in. Instead, ease it gently away from the lever.

Step 3: Cut the hose with a sharp knife at your chosen point, discarding the redundant fittings. Check that the cut is clean and the hose opening is tidy – you may need to remove any small pieces of outer sheath or inner weave to get a neat hole.

REFITTING HOSE

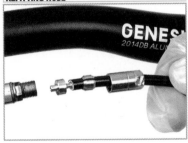

Step 1: Making sure that the shroud is still in place on the hose (it's surprisingly easy to drop it on the floor without noticing), fit the new olive and then the new barbed fitting into the end of the hose. Take care not to bend or damage it – it's relatively soft so don't hit it. Instead, gently work it into the hose until it's flush with the cut face. Fit the new copper crush washer to the end of the barbed fitting.

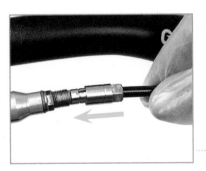

Step 2: Offer the new fittings up to the brake lever, then pull the shroud back into place over the whole assembly.

Step 3: Tighten the shroud, at first using your fingers to screw it back into place and then using a crescent wrench to tighten the last few turns. Make sure you don't overtighten it, as this is likely to damage the threads, but equally don't leave it loose as this can allow fluid to leak from the system. Test the brake by pulling the lever a few times – if it feels soft or mushy and the brake has lost its bite, then air has got into the system and you'll need to bleed the brake (page 124).

Bleeding hydraulic brakes: an overview with examples

Brake bleeding isn't a task you'll regularly need to carry out. The occasional service and fluid change is necessary but otherwise, as long as the system is kept free from air, you can forget about fettling and just go and ride. However, if air has managed to get into the system you'll need to get the tools out.

The bleeding procedure doesn't vary between the two fluid types – the aim is the same, though the method may differ from model to model. Both types of fluid will 'wear out' over time; DOT should last a year or so if you're doing a lot of heavy braking (i.e. riding or racing downhill) and up to four times that if you're just hitting the trails once a week. Mineral oil doesn't last as long and should be checked every six months or so; pop the cap off the reservoir and if the oil has lost its pinkish tinge or turned cloudy, it should be replaced.

Don't be tempted to treat brake bleeding as a regular task. Unless there's actually something wrong with the performance of your brake, fiddling with it isn't going to be of any benefit. If you frequently find yourself with real reason to bleed your brake, ie. the lever starts to feel spongy very quickly, then you need to track down the fault that's causing the problem. Disc brakes are very resilient and rarely 'just go wrong' – so take a close look at your hoses to see if there are any nicks or kinks along their length. Even if the outer surface of the hose doesn't appear to have a hole in it, it's possible for a kink to pierce the inner nylon pipe which holds the brake fluid, which will then seep along the fibrous sheath which protects the inner pipe. Baffling until you find the flaw, and then very obvious indeed.

Similarly, if your piston seals have been damaged by dirt ingress or one of the pistons has even been cracked or chipped, air will get into the system easily and hinder your stopping. Pull the pads out and check for visible damage or an oil leak; if you find a problem then the brake needs to go back to the bike shop for repair.

Regardless of model or brand specifics, the purpose of brake bleeding is to remove all air from the system, leaving only brake fluid within the hose, calliper and lever. It's a job which is made much easier if you have the correct bleed kit; in fact, you won't actually be able to bleed certain brakes without their dedicated bleed kit as they require a special screw-in bleed nipple. Other brakes use simpler tools, but the theory behind them all is the same.

Arm yourself with plenty of rags, a can of spray disc braker cleaner and mechanics' gloves before you start, too. Brake fluid, particularly DOT, is harmful to skin, paintwork and the kitchen floor so try not to splash it around and mop up any spillages immediately. If you manage to get fluid on your skin rinse it off immediately and, particularly in the case of DOT, consult the instructions on the bottle for any further action.

If your brake's bleed nipple is simply opened by a spanner, then you don't have to splash out on a dedicated bleed kit. Instead you can make one up yourself using plastic hose from a car repair or model shop that attaches snugly to the nipple and a plastic syringe from the chemist to top up the reservoir or force oil into the calliper, depending on how your system works. A small plastic bottle with a screwtop lid that you've punched a hose-size hole in is by far the easiest way to catch the surplus brake fluid, particularly if you're using DOT which will melt the thin plastic bags you sometimes find in mineral oil bleed kits. Make sure that the bottle is never used for food purposes, though, and tape it to the fork leg or frame to avoid it pulling the hose off the bleed nipple as the weight of the surplus oil increases.

Be careful when loosening and tightening bleed nipples. Avoid backing them off so far that they start to leak oil around the thread; this is a sure-fire way to find yourself puzzling over why you're still finding bubbles in the system after half an hour of work. Where oil can get out, air can get in.

Refer to the instruction manual for your own brake's particular quirks; the examples that follow are just that, but they should give you an idea of how the job you're trying to do should work.

Trapped air bubbles make your brakes feel spongy ▶

Bleeding Hope Minis

The first brake bleed that you do will probably feel horribly clumsy and fiddly. Don't panic – it gets easier every time. Once you've assembled your bleed kit, you'll know you have everything you need so it's a good idea to store it all in a dedicated plastic box with a tight fitting lid to avoid the inevitable dribbles of fluid escaping into the rest of the toolbox.

Hope Minis are my favourite brakes, and are likely to be around a while. They work very well, weigh very little, look pretty and are made by the same nice people from the north of England who answer the phone in a reassuring Lancashire accent to respond to your technical questions with useful, friendly answers. I didn't need to do anything to mine for years after fitting them except change the pads.

The Hope Minis use DOT 5.1 fluid, which you can buy in small bottles from car spares shops. Don't buy a large bottle because the fluid absorbs water and becomes ineffective once the seal has been broken.

BLEEDING HOPE MINIS

Step 1: Remove the wheel. The brake pads must be removed to avoid contamination – remove the spring clip on the brake pad retaining pin, remove the pad retaining pin and slide out the pads and spring. Wiggle a tyre lever into the calliper slot and push the slave pistons right back home inside the calliper. Squeeze a wedge of cardboard between the pistons to ensure they don't move during the bleed process.

Step 2: Remove the plastic cover from the bleed nipple on the calliper. Put an 8mm spanner over the flats on the nipple, then push-fit a short length of plastic hose over the nipple. Lubricate reluctant tubes with brake fluid. Tape the other end of the tube into a plastic bottle and secure to your frame or forks. Wrap a rag around the lever to catch overspill, because brake fluid is corrosive.

Step 3: Hope Tech levers are ambidextrous (the same lever can be used on either side) and so have a reservoir cap [A] on the top and the bottom of the lever. Loosen the brake lever clamp bolts and roll the lever so that the reservoir is level. Dial the bite adjuster as far out as possible, then remove the upper top cap and the black rubber diaphragm. Stash somewhere clean.

Step 4: Fill the master cylinder almost full. Open the bleed nipple one quarter-turn. Pull the brake lever gently, forcing fluid and air bubbles through the system and out of the bleed nipple. Hold the brake lever on, close the bleed nipple. Release the brake lever gently, drawing fluid into the hose from the master cylinder. Top up the master cylinder. Repeat until there are no more air bubbles. Close the bleed nipple.

Step 5: Refit diaphragm and reservoir cap and rotate the lever on the bars so it points directly downwards. Pump the lever, allowing any air trapped in the master cylinder bore to rise into the master cylinder. Rotate the lever so that the reservoir cover is level again, and remove the top cap and diaphragm. The fluid level will have dropped – top up the reservoir so it is completely full.

Step 6: Take a new diaphragm and roll it onto the reservoir (this ensures that no air gets trapped between the diaphragm and lever). Refit the top cap carefully so it sits in the correct groove of the diaphragm. Don't force it as you will damage the diaphragm. Realign and secure brake levers. Remove the bleed tube and replace the cover. Refit brake pads and wheel then pump lever to settle the pistons.

Disc brakes: bleeding Shimano hydraulic brakes

Shimano use mineral oil in their hydraulic brake systems. This is significantly less toxic than DOT fluid, so is not as damaging to your skin and your bike's paint but it's still a wise move to wear gloves. Make sure that you replace the fluid with the same mineral oil; filling it with DOT fluid will damage the seals irreparably and you'll end up with a very big repair bill. Shimano sell a dedicated bleed kit for their brakes which includes a single-use bottle of oil containing enough for one (careful) bleed. Conveniently, this means that there's no leftover oil to sit around absorbing moisture from the atmosphere.

    Mineral oil changes colour as it goes 'off', so if you haven't bled the brake for some months and are starting to suffer poor braking, remove the top cap of the brake lever and check the fluid – if it's lost its pink tint then you need to replace the oil.

    You'll be pouring the fresh oil straight into the master cylinder at the brake lever, which can be messy. Wrap a rag or paper around the lever before you begin as a pre-emptive mopping up exercise, and keep a wary eye out for oil running down the hose towards the front brake.

BLEEDING SHIMANO DISC BRAKES

Step 1: Start by removing the wheel and the brake pads from the brake you want to bleed, to prevent them becoming contaminated. Loosen the brake lever's clamp bolt, then swivel the lever around the bar so that the top cover is horizontal. Tighten the clamp bolts to keep the lever in place, then remove the top cover of the reservoir.

Step 2: Once the top cap is off, you'll see a rubber diaphragm. Remove it gently and place the top cover and diaphragm in a safe place, on a clean rag as they will be oily. Top up the reservoir with fresh oil.

Step 3: Push the pistons gently back into the calliper so that they're flush with the calliper body, then wedge them into place with either a fold of sturdy cardboard or the yellow plastic block supplied with all after-market Shimano brakes.

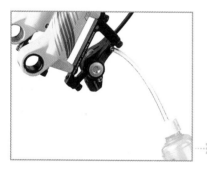

Step 4: As long as the brake lever is above the calliper and the hose is running in a vertical direction with no sharp bends, you shouldn't need to remove the calliper from the frame or fork mount. Fit the plastic hose supplied with the bleed kit to the bleed nipple, and then attach your chosen receptacle to the end of the hose. A plastic bag is supplied with Shimano's bleed kit but a small plastic bottle with a hole in the lid is a more practical receptacle to catch the oil.

Step 5: Using a crescent wrench, open the bleed nipple and pump the brake lever. You may see air bubbles appear in the reservoir and the oil level may drop. Keep topping up the reservoir and pumping the lever, until oil appears in the bleed hose at the calliper. Close the bleed nipple tightly, then pump the lever – it should firm up quickly. If not, then repeat the process, tapping the hose gently to encourage any air bubbles lodged in the hose to travel up to the lever.

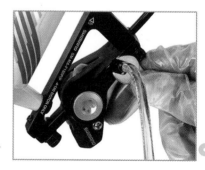

Step 6: Once the system is full of oil and free from air, close the bleed nipple, pull the lever back as far as it will go and quickly open and then close the bleed nipple. The bleed hose will fill with oil and there should be no bubbles in it – if there are, you will need to continue topping up the reservoir. Once the bleed is complete and the brake is firm, top up the reservoir, replace the diaphragm and top cap, return the lever to its usual position on the bar. Remove the bleed hose and replace the bleed nipple cover, clean up the calliper. Replace the pads and wheel before testing brake operation.

Troubleshooting disc brakes

Symptom	Cause	Solution	Page
Brake pads don't pull back smoothly after braking	Brake cable gritty, corroded or frayed inside casing	Clean and lubricate brake cable or replace it	113
	Piston heads dirty	Remove pads and clean, or replace	113–5, 116, 120
	Dirt has worked its way into the calliper body, jamming the mechanism	Strip and clean calliper body	112
	Pads have become contaminated with oil	Replace pads	113–5, 116, 120
	Rotors have become contaminated	Clean rotors with degreaser, isopropyl alcohol or warm soapy water	110
	Pads are too far from rotors	Adjust pad position	116, 120
Brakes rub constantly on rotors	Rotor is warped	Bend back or replace rotor	111
	Calliper body is touching rotor	Adjust calliper body position	121
	Pads set too close to rotor	Adjust pad positions independently – outer pad using cable tension, inner pad using adjustment screw	116, 121
Brakes not very effective – cannot lock wheels by pulling lever	Pads have become contaminated with oil	Replace pads	113–5, 116, 120
	Rotors have become contaminated	Clean rotors with degreaser, isopropyl alcohol or warm soapy water	110
	Pads are worn out	Check pad thickness – replace if less than 0.5mm ($\frac{1}{50}$ inch)	113–5, 116, 120
Brake pads rub on rotor	Calliper misaligned	Refit calliper, with rotor central between pads	108, 109
	Rotor warped	Bend back or replace rotor	111
Brake levers feel spongy, brakes ineffective	Air in system	Bleed brakes	124–6
	Leaking hose	Inspect hose carefully, especially at joints, tighten leaking joints, bleed brakes	124–6
Brakes squeal	Contaminated brake pads or rotor	Clean rotor, replace pads	113–5, 116, 120
	Worn or roughened rotor surface	Replace rotor	111
	Loose fixing bolts causing vibrations	Check and tighten brake-fixing bolts and rotor-fixing bolts	111

5 – Transmission

This chapter deals with your transmission – all the parts of your bike that transfer your pedalling power to your back wheel. It explains how to adjust your gears so they change smoothly and quickly, and how to replace parts that are worn out or damaged. The parts that make up your transmission are relatively simple but are exposed to the elements. They have to be lubricated to work efficiently. If you don't clean your tranmission, oil and dirt will form an abrasive grinding paste, which will quickly eat into your components.

Transmission: naming the parts

You need to know what all the parts of your transmisssion are called before you can start fixing them; it makes going into bike shops and asking for replacement components a whole lot easier. The appearance of each mechanism may vary from bike to bike, but don't worry too much about the detail for different components: all do the same jobs regardless of what they look like. All the parts here are dealt with in more detail later in this chapter.

1) **Shifters:** It's all very well having a million gears to choose from, but you need to be able to decide which one to be in, without taking your hands off the bars. Shifters put the controls where you need them – directly under your hands. The shifter unit might be integrated with the brake-levers, making a slightly lighter combination than two separates. However, there are a couple of advantages to having separate brake-levers and gear shifters as you can adjust them independently and also replace them independently if they wear out or break.

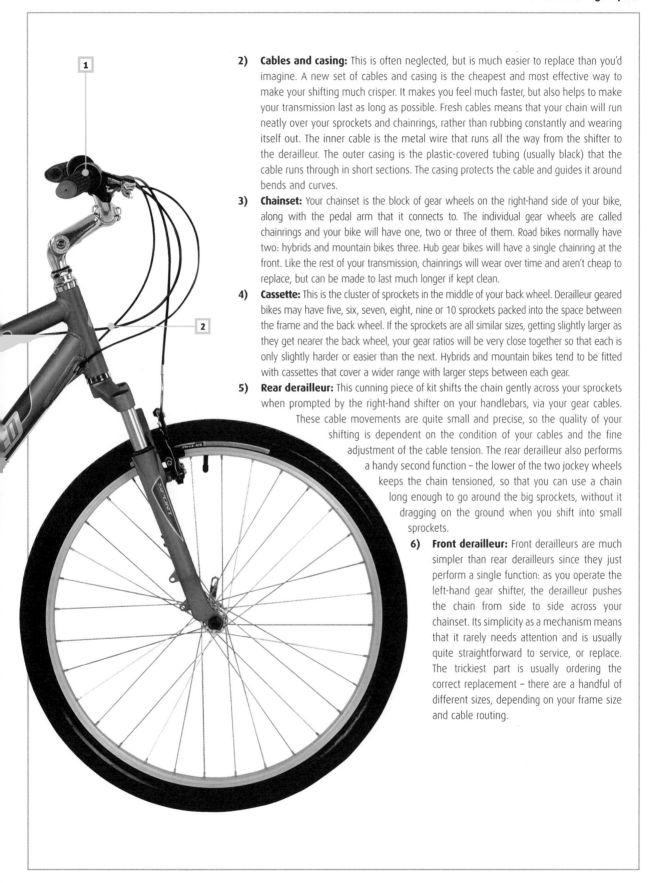

2) **Cables and casing:** This is often neglected, but is much easier to replace than you'd imagine. A new set of cables and casing is the cheapest and most effective way to make your shifting much crisper. It makes you feel much faster, but also helps to make your transmission last as long as possible. Fresh cables means that your chain will run neatly over your sprockets and chainrings, rather than rubbing constantly and wearing itself out. The inner cable is the metal wire that runs all the way from the shifter to the derailleur. The outer casing is the plastic-covered tubing (usually black) that the cable runs through in short sections. The casing protects the cable and guides it around bends and curves.

3) **Chainset:** Your chainset is the block of gear wheels on the right-hand side of your bike, along with the pedal arm that it connects to. The individual gear wheels are called chainrings and your bike will have one, two or three of them. Road bikes normally have two; hybrids and mountain bikes three. Hub gear bikes will have a single chainring at the front. Like the rest of your transmission, chainrings will wear over time and aren't cheap to replace, but can be made to last much longer if kept clean.

4) **Cassette:** This is the cluster of sprockets in the middle of your back wheel. Derailleur geared bikes may have five, six, seven, eight, nine or 10 sprockets packed into the space between the frame and the back wheel. If the sprockets are all similar sizes, getting slightly larger as they get nearer the back wheel, your gear ratios will be very close together so that each is only slightly harder or easier than the next. Hybrids and mountain bikes tend to be fitted with cassettes that cover a wider range with larger steps between each gear.

5) **Rear derailleur:** This cunning piece of kit shifts the chain gently across your sprockets when prompted by the right-hand shifter on your handlebars, via your gear cables. These cable movements are quite small and precise, so the quality of your shifting is dependent on the condition of your cables and the fine adjustment of the cable tension. The rear derailleur also performs a handy second function – the lower of the two jockey wheels keeps the chain tensioned, so that you can use a chain long enough to go around the big sprockets, without it dragging on the ground when you shift into small sprockets.

6) **Front derailleur:** Front derailleurs are much simpler than rear derailleurs since they just perform a single function: as you operate the left-hand gear shifter, the derailleur pushes the chain from side to side across your chainset. Its simplicity as a mechanism means that it rarely needs attention and is usually quite straightforward to service, or replace. The trickiest part is usually ordering the correct replacement – there are a handful of different sizes, depending on your frame size and cable routing.

Gearing up – or down – for the smoothest possible ride

Bicycles have gears because people are lazy. To make the bicycle move, you have to push on the pedals. If you only had one gear, you could set the bicycle up so you had to push very hard, but each pedal stroke would make the bicycle go a long way. This is called a high gear.

Alternatively, you could set it up so you didn't have to push the pedals hard, but one pedal stroke wouldn't take you far. You would have to do a lot of strokes to get anywhere. This is called a low gear.

Both extremes work in their own way, but your body is most efficient pedalling at a medium rate – pushing moderately hard and pedalling moderately fast – between 80 and 100 revolutions per minute. Gears were invented so that you can maintain a steady pedalling rate ('cadence' – roughly speaking, how fast your legs are going round) while the bicycle travels at different speeds.

Mountain bikes are designed to have a very wide range of gears so you can maintain an efficient cadence both when moving very slowly – for example, up a steep, rough hill at 2mph – as well as when moving very fast – for example, plummeting downhill at 40mph.

Small steps between the gears allow you to make subtle changes from one gear to the next, matching your pedalling speed precisely to the terrain you're cycling over. In recent years, manufacturers have steadily increased the number of gears on your cassette, giving you smaller, subtler gaps between gears, and making modern bikes more responsive than their old-fashioned counterparts.

Less haste, more speed

New cyclists – along with many who've been around long enough to know better – are seduced by the idea that in order to go faster, it's imperative to force the pedals around using as much strength as possible with every stroke. With experience, it becomes plain that this only gives an illusion of speed and, in fact, serves mainly to exhaust you in the short term and wear your knees out in the long term. Generally, you'll get where you want to go faster, feeling less exhausted, by using a lower gear: your legs spin around faster, but you don't have to press down so hard on each pedal stroke. It's worth watching the next person who overtakes you; chances are, their legs will be spinning faster than yours in a lower gear, and that's the main reason they're flying past you.

Turning on the power

There are some circumstances in which it makes sense to use a relatively high gear. For short bursts of speed, nothing beats standing up on the pedals in a high gear and hauling the bike forwards. It means you can use your shoulder muscles, pulling up on the bars as well as stamping down on the pedals – perfect for keeping up momentum while you power up short inclines. Sometimes ground surfaces

dictate gear choice as well. If you're approaching a sand trough or trying to cross a swathe of deep, sticky mud, the best approach can often be to shift into a high gear, keeping your cadence low so that your tyres have a chance to find the last scraps of traction without you getting bogged down.

By comparison, road-racing bikes have fewer gears, but they are very closely spaced. This reflects the fact that road-racing bikes are designed to be used at a much narrower range of speeds – fast, very fast and faster. Close ratios are vital to allow the rider to maintain a comfortable, efficient cadence while being able to ride at the speed of a tightly packed peloton.

◀ **Shifting to a higher gear**

How gears work

What's great about modern gear design is that it allows you to keep pedalling at the same speed, regardless of terrain, by varying the amount of energy needed to turn the back wheel. Here, I'll explain it with math. Please ignore this page if it seems too technical – it makes no difference to how much you enjoy your cycling.

Imagine you no longer have a spangly bike with dozens of gears. Instead, you have a model with only two chainrings at the front, which you turn by pedalling, and two sprockets on the back, which push the back wheel around when they are turned. This leaves you with a 10-tooth and 20-tooth sprocket at the back, and a 20-tooth and a 40-tooth sprocket at the front. These combinations aren't useful for cycling, but they make the math easier.

Start with your chain running between the 40 at the front and the 10 at the back. Begin with one pedal crank pointing upwards, in line with the seat-tube. Turn the cranks round exactly once. Each link of the chain gets picked up in the valley between two teeth. Since there are 40 teeth on the chainring, exactly 40 links of chain get pulled from the back of the bike to the front.

At the back of the bike, exactly the reverse happens. Since each link of the chain picks up one sprocket valley, pulling 40 chain links through will pull 40 sprocket valleys around. But the sprocket you're using has only 10 teeth, so it will get pulled round four times (4x10 = 40). The sprocket is connected directly to the wheel, so, in this instance, turning the chainring one turn means that the rear wheel will turn four complete turns. To measure how far this is, imagine cutting across an old tyre to make a strip instead of a hoop, then laying it out along the ground. Measure the distance and that's how far the bike goes if you turn the wheel once. Turn the wheel four times, and the bike goes four times as far.

For comparison, leave the chain on the 40-tooth chainring, but move it to the 20-tooth sprocket at the back. Turn the cranks once and the chainring will still pull the 40 links around, but, at the back, pulling 40 links around a 20-tooth sprocket will only pull the wheel around twice (2x20 = 40), so the bike goes half as far as in the previous example.

Finally, leave the chain on the 20-tooth at the back, and pop it on the 20-tooth at the front. Now, turning the cranks around once only pulls 20 links of chain through, which in turn pulls the 20-tooth sprocket and the wheel around exactly once. Thus, turning the pedals around once moves the bike forward one tyre length – a one-to-one ratio.

In the first example, the bike goes much further, but it is harder work to push the pedals around one turn. In the last example, it is very easy to push the pedals around, but you don't go far. Sometimes, you need to go as fast as possible and you don't care how hard you work, so you use a combination of big chainring and small sprocket. You might be charging downhill or trying to catch someone ahead of you or sprinting for the sake of it.

Other times, like when you climb a steep hill or start off from rest, it takes all your energy simply to keep the wheels going round, so you need the easiest gear possible. Then you choose something like the last combination – small chainring and big sprocket.

Going back to the original bike, you have up to 10 sprockets at the back and up to three chainrings at the front. These allow subtle variations in how far the bike goes and how easy it is when you turn the cranks. The aim is to maintain a constant cadence, at a level that is most efficient for your body over varying terrain.

The two derailleurs (gear mechs – short for mechanisms) are controlled by separate shifters at the handlebars, the front by your left hand and the back by your right. These evolved by mechanical necessity but have proved very convenient.

On the back wheel you have a selection of sprockets on the cassette, as mentioned above, with small gaps between the sizes. Moving up or down from one sprocket to the next might make a gear 10 per cent higher or lower, allowing very subtle changes in pedalling speed. You shift the sprockets (i.e. rear derailleur) most often, so it makes sense for the handlebar shifter to be on the right-hand side, since most people are right-handed.

Your left hand controls the front derailleur. You only have three chainrings on the front, but the differences between the number of teeth on the ring are far greater to allow a radical change to pedalling speed with a single shift. This is useful when the terrain changes unexpectedly – for example, if you turn a corner and the trail suddenly climbs. By moving the chain from the big to the little chainring, you can change into a much lower gear quickly enough to maintain momentum. Although it's possible to change into all the combinations of chainrings and sprockets, in practice, some should be avoided. Using the largest chainring and the largest sprocket means that the chain has to cut across from one to the other at a steep angle, which makes the chain wear faster and wastes pedalling energy. The same goes for the combination of the smallest sprocket and smallest chainring. Both these gears are duplicates – the same gear ratio can be found by switching into the middle chainring at the front and one of the middle sprockets at the back.

Chains: what are they made of?

Your chain is made up of a simple string of components, flexible enough to wrap itself around your sprockets but strong enough to pull your back wheel around when you stamp hard on the pedals. Each link is made up of a small selection of components – two sets of 8-shaped plates, a rivet that allows each set of plates to rotate relative to its neighbour and a doughnut-shaped roller encircling the middle section of the rivet.

Each link of the chain sits in turn in the valley between two of the teeth on your chainring, and so gets pulled forwards as the chainring rotates. The chain meshes in turn with the teeth on your sprocket, each link sitting in a valley and pulling against the back face of a sprocket tooth to drag your wheel forward.

The mating surface between tooth and chain link is very small, under high pressures and often dirty – a classic recipe for wear. But careful design means that chains last much longer than you'd expect them to in the circumstances. This longevity is down to a critical component – the roller shrouding each rivet. These can rotate freely around the rivet – give one a wiggle on your chain to see what I mean. This means that as each roller settles into the valley between two teeth, it can rotate into place, even under pressure, minimizing the kind of metal-on-metal sliding that promotes rapid wear.

As a result, the external surfaces of the chain require very little lubrication. This is a good thing, as oil is sticky and makes dirt stick to your transmission, which causes wear. However, there is an area where there is metal-on-metal contact – where the inside surface of the roller rotates about the rivet. This would wear if not lubricated. Luckily, because the roller is trapped between the chain plates, dirt finds it pretty difficult to work its way into this surface.

So, for minimum wear, the hidden, internal surfaces of your chain, which stay relatively clean, need lubrication. The external surfaces, that you can see, need only enough lubrication to limit corrosion – not a thick sticky layer that will pick up dirt. That's why the most effective maintenance routine is to clean your chain, oil it with good-quality oil, leave enough time for this to soak into the gaps between the plates and inside the roller, then wipe excess oil off the outside of the chain.

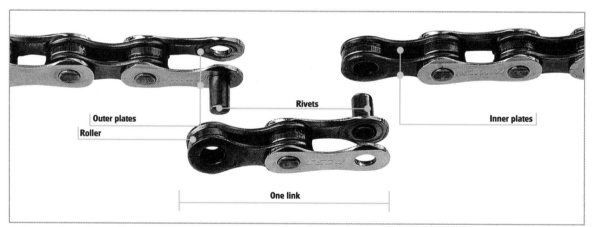

▲ Outer and inner plates, roller, rivets and link

Bike chains all have the same pitch, namely ½ in. However, they have different widths, determined according to the number of sprockets on the cassette at the back. Sprockets on, for example, nine-speed cassettes are narrower (both the sprocket plate and the gap) than eight-speed cassettes so that the extra sprocket can be packed into the same space. The narrower chains are also more flexible, so they change more slickly. By the same token, they need to be kept clean and well-lubricated or they will wear more quickly. A chain that is too narrow for the block will stick, whereas a chain that is too wide won't shift properly. Both will wear down the sprockets very quickly.

Compatibility between parts is an important issue. You can be as careful as you like with adjustments for your front and rear gears, but if the components aren't compatible, the adjustment won't make any difference. Shimano is the undisputed giant in the transmission department; other manufacturers make their components compatible with Shimano parts. The most sensitive combinations are chain, shifters and cassettes. For example, nine-speed chains are considerably narrower than eight-speed ones, and have matching narrow sprockets, so there is no compatibility between the two systems.

Chain hygiene: regular chain wipe-down

A clean chain shifts neatly, whereas a dirty one shifts sluggishly and wears expensive chunks out of the drivetrain. To find out how clean your chain needs to be, try reading the words stamped on the side plates. If they are legible, the chain is clean enough. If you can't read them, the chain needs your attention.

Ideally, clean your chain little and often – catching it frequently enough to only need a wipe-down. This is both the laziest and the best method – take advantage of this rare combination! Leave your chain dirty too long and you'll need to look at the deep-clean section on the next page.

After a ride, lean your bike up against a wall and hold a clean, dry cloth or piece of kitchen towel around the bottom stretch of chain. Slowly pedal backward for 20 seconds, dragging the chain through the cloth. If it makes a big dirty streak, move to a clean bit of cloth and repeat. Job done. Simply do that every single time you ride and you maximize the chain's life without ever undertaking a boring major clean.

You need to lubricate the chain occasionally as well, but note that you can do as much damage by overlubricating as underlubricating. Chains need a little oil, but no more than dressing for a salad. If the chain is squeaky, you've left it too long and the chain is gasping for lube. As a rough guide, oil the chain every 100 miles. If the chain collects greasy, black gunk as you ride, you are over-oiling.

As above, wipe the chain with a clean cloth. Drip a drop of oil carefully onto each roller on the top surface of the bottom stretch of chain. (Drip oil is much better than spray. It goes where you want with little waste.) The important thing is to allow five minutes for the oil to soak in (have a cup of tea), then wipe off any excess with a clean rag – drag the chain through it again. Oil is sticky. Leave it on the outside surface of the chain to pick up dirt and it makes a super grinding paste.

Cleaning your chain little and often like this ensures that it never builds up a thick layer of dirt, which means that you don't have to use harsh solvents on it. This is well worthwhile – cleaning agents, degreasers and detergent will all soak into the internals of the chain, stripping out lubrication from the vital interface between the insides of the roller. Each roller needs to be able to rotate freely on its rivet so that the roller can mesh neatly with the valleys between the teeth of sprockets and chainrings as you apply pressure.

Wax lubricants are an alternative to conventional oils. Several manufacturers make versions that work in similar ways. The wax sticks to your chain, protecting it from the elements but providing a layer of lubrication. The wax is not as sticky as oil, so it's less likely that dirt will adhere. But if it does, the surface of the wax will flake off, taking the dirt with it. New layers of wax can be laid over the top since the surface should stay clean, saving you from having to clean the chain. This system means that your chain stays dry too, avoiding oily streaks on your clothes and in your home.

However, the system only really works if you start with a very clean chain – preferably a new one. A word of warning: never mix wax-based lubricants with normal ones – you end up with a sticky, slippery mess that adheres to everything except your chain.

◀ **Laziest and best: a regular wipe-down**

Deep-cleaning your chain

If your chain doesn't respond to the wipe-down treatment, you must get serious. Dirty, oily chains need degreaser to clean them up. This is strong stuff, so take care not to let it seep into bearings, where it breaks down the grease that keeps things well lubricated and running smoothly.

I prefer liquid degreaser, which you can apply with a brush, to the spray cans. Spray is more wasteful and harder to direct accurately. But whether you use spray or liquid, you need a brush. Washing-up brushes work well; they're cheap and you can buy them in regular shops. Bike shops sell special sets of brushes, but my favourites are paint brushes. I cut off the bristles about halfway down, so what remains is firm but flexible. Keep the brushes you use for your drivetrain separate from those for frames, rims and disc rotors. Use rubber gloves to protect your hands from the degreaser.

Take your bike outside, as this business always gets messy. Keep the bike upright, with the chain in the largest chainring at the front. Dip the brush into the degreaser and work it into each link in the part of the chain that's wrapped around the front chainring. Do both sides, then turn the pedals around and work on the next section of chain. It takes a few minutes for the degreaser to work, so let it soak in, working around until you are back where you started.

Clean the chainrings next, front and back, picking out anything that's stuck between the chainrings or between the outer chainring and the crank arm. Clean up the derailleurs and the jockey wheels on the rear derailleur too, otherwise they dump dirt straight back onto the clean chain. Hold the back wheel upright and scrub the cassette clean. If there is compacted muck stuck between the sprockets, scrape it out with a stick or skewer. You can buy a special little brush if you want but remember: the world is full of sticks, which cost nothing. Be especially careful with the degreaser at this point: keep the wheel upright to prevent it from getting into the rear hub or into the freehub (the ratchet mechanism inside the cassette).

Using a clean brush, rinse off all the degreaser with warm water. Jet-washing may be tempting but don't – ever! The protective bearing seals cannot withstand jet-wash pressure and the grease that makes bearings run smoothly is soon displaced by water. If your drivetrain is really dirty, you may now decide to repeat the job. Once everything is as clean as possible, dry the chain by running it through a clean rag and re-lubricate. Sprockets and chainrings don't need lubrication. Pop a drop of oil on the derailleur pivots, front and back, and wipe off the excess, otherwise it just collects dirt.

Chain-cleaning box

A tidier option for regular cleaning is a chain-cleaning box. This is a case that fits over the chain, with little brushes inside that scrub the chain clean. Fill the reservoir with degreaser, then snap the box over the lower section of chain.

Pedal slowly backwards. Most boxes have a button that you press to release degreaser onto the chain. Don't pedal too quickly or you'll splash degreaser out of the back of the box. Keep going slowly until you've used up all the degreaser. Unclip the box and take a five-minute break to give the degreaser time to break down the dirt.

Rinse off with clean, warm water. If your chain was extremely dirty, you might repeat the process. Dry your chain with a clean rag and re-lubricate. It's worth cleaning the chain box with a little fresh degreaser straight away, so it is ready for next time.

A chain box helps keep you and your chain clean ▶

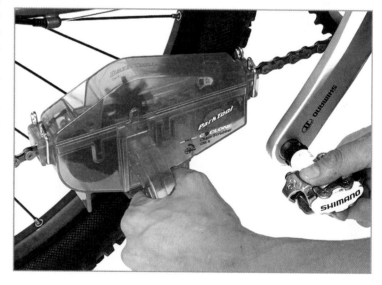

Measuring your chain for wear and tear

Your chain is under constant pressure as you pedal. A new chain arrives exactly the right size to mesh with the other components of your drivetrain.

Gradually, though, as time goes by and the miles rack up, the chain stretches. The gaps between each link grow and the chain inevitably elongates. Eventually, if you keep riding, the chain starts skipping over them instead of meshing with the teeth on the sprocket.

That's when you find yourself pushing hard on the pedals, expecting resistance. Instead of gripping, the chain slips and the pedal carrying all your weight gives way and spins like crazy, so you hurt yourself or even fall off. At this stage, your chain is already worn enough to damage other components.

Joining the chain gang

If you are disciplined about measuring your chain carefully and regularly with a chain-measuring device, you can replace just the chain before it has a chance to wear the other components of your drivetrain. This tool will tell you when you have reached this point. If you are attentive, you'll find it the cheapest option in the long term.

If you allow the chain to wear beyond this point, you will have to replace both the chain and the cassette at the same time. The old chain will have damaged the teeth on the cassette, so the new chain will be unable to mesh with it neatly. The consequence of changing the chain without changing the sprockets is that the new chain will slip over the old sprockets, and, even if you can make it catch, the old sprockets will wear the new chain into an old chain very quickly.

If you allow the chain to wear so that it starts to slip over the cassette as you pedal, you will definitely have to change the cassette and probably some or all of the chainrings as well. Look at the pictures on page 172 and compare them with your chainrings – if they are starting to look like the examples, change them at the same time as the chain.

Note that you cannot compensate for chain stretch by taking links out of the chain to make it shorter. The total length of the chain is not critical. It is the distance between each link that matters. If you take links out of a stretched chain, it is simply a shorter stretched chain.

MEASURING FOR WEAR

Step 1: A chain-measuring device is the quickest and easiest way of accurately measuring your chain. The best are from Park Tools and come complete with an easy-to-read dial. Buy one today – it saves you time and money.

Step 2: Alternatively, measure the length of 12 links. Twelve links of a new chain will measure exactly 12 inches. When it measures $12^{1}/_{8}$ inch or less, you can change the chain without changing the cassette. More than that, and you have to change the cassette as well.

Step 3: You can get an idea of stretch without using a chain-measuring device. Put the chain on the biggest ring at the front and the smallest sprocket at the back, then lean the bike left-handed against a wall. Hold the chain at three o'clock and pull it outwards. If the bottom jockey wheel of the rear derailleur moves, it's time for a new chain. If you can pull the chain off enough to see all or most of the tooth, you need a new cassette and probably new chainrings too.

Splitting and rejoining a chain

Every time you split and rejoin your chain, you risk making it weaker, so keep splitting to a minimum.

For example, if you're fitting a new rear derailleur, undo the bolts that hold on the jockey wheels, thread the chain around the jockey wheels, and reassemble them with the chain inside the derailleur, rather than splitting the chain.

Make sure you tighten both jockey wheel bolts securely – the top one, particularly, is prone to rattling loose. For the front derailleur, remove the bolt at the back of the cage, slide the chain into the cage and refit the bolt.

If you do have to split the chain, you'll need a chain tool. This is designed to support two adjacent chain plates while you push out the pin between them. It is important to do this carefully, as they may create a weak point and break later if you deform the chain plates. Shimano chains have to be treated differently from other chains – they need to be rejoined with a special rivet. See the separate section opposite.

SPLITTING A CHAIN

Step 1: Lay the chain onto the chain tool. If your tool has two sets of supports us the set of supports furthest away from the handle of the tool. Screw in the handle of the tool so that it approaches the chain. When it's close, line up the stud with the head of the chain pin. Screw in the handle to push the rivet.

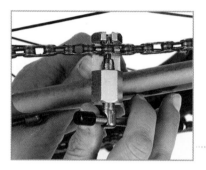

Step 2: It's important not to push it all the way out, otherwise it's difficult to get back in again. With the Park tool, keep turning until the handle jams on the body of the tool. With other tools, keep testing to check you haven't gone too far.

Step 3: Check you haven't gone too far by backing off the tool and trying to pull the chain apart. Ideally, you should have to flex it, as shown, to get the two halves of the chain apart. This is important because it means you have left a little stub of pin **(A)** inside the further chain plate, which you can then use to relocate the hole for the pin when you refit the chain.

REJOINING A CHAIN

Step 1: To re-rivet, hold the chain as shown. Flex both parts away from the rivet and slide together. The little bit of rivet showing through the outer plate should snap into place, then hold the two parts together with the rivet aligned in the hole.

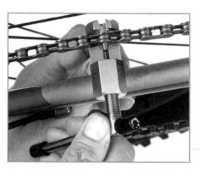

Step 2: Back the chain tool handle right off and place the chain back into the further supports.

Step 3: Turn the handle to push the rivet back through the chain so that an equal amount of rivet shows through each side. Here, you can see that one side of the rivet protrudes more than the other. Use the further chain supports to even up the amount that shows out of each side. The rejoined link will be stiffer than its neighbours – see page 100 to rectify.

Shimano chains

These chains need to be treated differently to others because the rivets cannot be pushed out of the plates and reused. The original rivets that hold the links in place are made exactly the same size as the holes in the chain plates, which means that they have to be installed with enormous force and accuracy. Consequently they are very strong once in place.

However, if you try to reuse the rivets, you'll find that they won't press back easily through the chain plates – often, instead of reseating itself neatly in the hole, the rivet will tear open the chain plate hole, mangling the link beyond repair.

Shimano make a special replacement rivet that can be pressed back through the chain to rejoin it. Whenever you split the chain, the original rivet must be pushed out completely and discarded. This can be irritating, but the payoff is that Shimano chains are strong and change very slickly.

One of the rivets on your chain is the original joining link that was fitted when the chain was put together. You mustn't split the chain again at this link. You can identify it easily – most of the links have words printed around the rivet, saying 'Shimano' and the code number of the chain. The original joining rivet has no words printed around it; avoid this one. Also avoid splitting the chain in the same place twice – any previously replaced rivets will have smoother heads. As long as you choose a different place every time, you can split and rejoin the chain as often as you need.

Shimano chains are not designed to be used with Powerlinks or other similar joining links, so if you have a Shimano chain, it's well worth making sure you always carry around a couple of replacement joining rivets. They weigh almost nothing, but if you need one, nothing else will do. Use gaffer tape to stick one under the bottom of your saddle so that it's always there in an emergency. Nine- and 10-speed chains are different widths, so they need different-length replacement pins – they're not interchangeable.

New chains come with a spare replacement rivet in a little plastic bag (it's easy to lose this when you open the packet because it's very small) as well as a semi-assembled rivet attached to the chain for initial assembly. You can also pick up spares separately from your bike shop.

Inevitably, you may find yourself in a situation where you have to rejoin a Shimano chain without the proper replacement rivet. If you are forced to try rejoining a chain by reusing a link, take as much care as you can when reinserting the rivet, so that it lines up with the hole in the chain plate. Be aware that the repaired link will be weaker, leaving the chain liable to break again. Therefore, you should always replace the repaired rivet or the entire chain as soon as possible.

SHIMANO CHAINS

Step 1: Line the chain up on the further set of supports. If you have a Shimano-specific chain tool, it may only have one set of supports. Push the rivet all the way out.

Step 2: To rejoin the chain, line up the holes in either end of the chain and push the new replacement rivet through them. It will go most of the way through by hand. Use the chain tool to push it through until the first half comes all the way out of the far side of the chain. There's a groove between the two halves of the replacement rivet – keep pushing until you can see all of the groove and a trace of the second half of the rivet.

Step 3: Use a pair of pliers to snap off the exposed part of the replacement rivet. You may not have a pair of pliers with you but if you have a fold-up multi-tool, you can improvise by trapping the protruding part of the rivet between two Allen keys, folding them down onto the body of the tool and twisting.

Stiff links

A newly fixed link will often be stiff because the process of pushing through the rivet has jammed the chain plates together. You may also find that stiff links develop while you're out riding. Heavy rain can do it, as can cycling through rivers. You can feel a stiff link when you pedal with moderate pressure – the chain regularly slips a little, enough to annoy you, but not always at the same point in the pedal stroke.

To locate the stiff link, lean your bike up against a wall with the chain in the big chainring at the front and the small sprocket at the back. Pedal slowly backward with your right hand and watch the chain as it feeds out of the bottom of the cassette, around the jockey wheels, and off the bottom of the bottom jockey. You see the bottom jockey wheel skip forward as the stiff link passes through the rear derailleur. Keep pedalling backward, and allow this section to pass through your fingers to pin down the stiff link.

LOOSENING STIFF LINKS

Step 1: Once you've found the stiff link, look at it carefully from above. You may find that one side of the rivet pokes out of the side of the chain more than the other. If this is the case, use the chain tool from the side that sticks out more to even it up.

Step 2: Lay the chain over the supports nearest the handle of the tool with the sticking-out end of the rivet nearest the handle. Wind in the handle until it lines up exactly with the centre of the stiff rivet and touches it. Carefully wind in the handle another third of a turn. If the link is still stiff, repeat from the other side of the chain.

Step 3: If you don't have a chain tool, hold the chain in both hands, with the stiff link in the middle. Put both thumbs on the stiff link and flex the chain gently backwards and forwards. You should feel the stiff link gradually loosen off. Don't overdo it though – you don't want to end up twisting the chain.

Powerlinks

An easier way of joining chains is with a Powerlink. Both ends of the chain must be narrow segments, so remove any wide segments with a chain tool. Drop the chain off the chainring into the gap between the chainset and the frame for slack. Fit half of the joining link onto each end of the chain, one facing toward you and one facing away from you. Each part of the joining link has a key-shaped hole. Push one half into the other, then pull the two sections of chain apart to lock them into place. Replace the chain on the chainring. To remove the Powerlink, push the links on either side of the joining link toward each other. You may also need to squeeze the plates of the link together – one of those tricky moves that would be easier if you had three hands. The Powerlink rivets should pop back into the inner part of the key-shaped hole, allowing you to separate the chain by pushing half away from you and half towards you. Powerlinks are not designed to be used with Shimano chains.

Pull apart Powerlink to lock ▶

Correct chain length and routing

It's critical to get your chain length right. If the chain is too long, it flaps about and the derailleur folds up on itself when it's in the smallest sprocket at the back and the small chainring at the front. Too short, and the chain jams when you shift into the big/big combination. These are not recommended gears, but everybody shifts into them sometimes. The right length of chain gives you the smoothest shifting and means your chain will last longer too.

The correct length chain is just long enough to wrap around the biggest sprocket at the back and the biggest chainring at the front, plus one link (a complete link is one narrow section and one wide section).

Fitting a new chain

To fit a new chain, first route it. Shift the two derailleurs so the rear one is under the biggest sprocket and the front one is over the biggest chainring. Start at the back at the lower jockey wheel and feed the end of the chain between the wheel and the lower tab. Next, feed the end between the top jockey wheel and the top tab. Route the chain around the front of the top jockey wheel and then around the back of the cassette, forward to the chainset, through the front derailleur, around a chainring and back to meet itself. Pull the chain as tight as it will go, as in the picture below – the rear derailleur will stretch forward to accommodate it. Add one link and calculate how many links you need to remove.

If you're rejoining the chain with a split link such as a Powerlink, remember to take this into account – you only need to add an extra half-link, because the Powerlink is half a link. Including the extra link, this means that, if you have to shorten the chain to remove a twisted link, you are still left with a working chain that can reach all the gears. Join or rejoin the chain and check through the gears. The chain should be long enough to reach around the big sprocket/big chainring combination with a little slack, but short enough so the rear derailleur doesn't fold up on itself in the small sprocket/small chainring combination.

Correct chain length

To check whether the chain you have is the right length, first make sure it's not too short. Step through the gears and check that the chain will stretch all the way around the big sprocket at the back and the big chainring at the front. It's fine for the cage of the derailleur to be stretched forward in this gear, but make sure the chain isn't too tight – there should be enough slack for you to lift the middle of the lower section of chain up at least 2cm (roughly ¾ inch). Then, check it's not too long. Change gear into the smallest sprocket at the back and the smallest chainring at the front. Look at the rear derailleur cage – the lower jockey wheel will be folded right back, taking up the maximum amount of slack. Make sure it's not folded so far back that any part of the chain touches any other part. The rear derailleur folds itself up in order to take up the extra slack created by shifting into the small sprockets and small chainring combination with the upper (guide) jockey wheel moving forward and the lower (tension) jockey wheel moving backwards and up. If the chain is too

long, the derailleur will fold itself up completely in the small/small combination. The lower section of chain can become entangled with the upper jockey wheel and the derailleur cage. As you pedal, putting pressure on the chain, the entangled chain will rip the rear derailleur off.

Similarly, if the chain is too short, shifting into the larger sprockets at the back while the chain is in the largest chainring will stretch the tension jockey wheel forwards. If there's not enough slack, the tension in the chain can cause the back wheel to jam, kicking you off the bike, or it can twist or tear off the derailleur hanger, the part where the rear derailleur bolts onto the frame.

◀ **Measuring the correct chain length**

Why chains break and what to do about it when they do

Some people never break chains, while others seem to break them every time they ride. Chains break for different reasons though, including bad luck, but sometimes it can be avoided. Sometimes small rocks or pebbles are kicked up by the tyres where they get trapped between chain and cassette. As you pedal, the chain breaks across the pebble. This is just bad luck and can happen to anyone.

Changing gears while stamping hard on the pedals puts a heavy strain on a few links. The links have to move sideways across your cassette to change gear, so they're at their most vulnerable because the pressure is applied at an angle. You do have to be turning the pedals to change gear, as this is what makes the chain derail, but your chain will shift across much quicker if you can slacken off the pressure as you change. Even when going uphill, try to anticipate gear changes so that you can build up enough momentum to lift off the pressure momentarily. A well-adjusted derailleur will change from one sprocket to the next in a quarter of a revolution of the pedals, as long as it's not under too much pressure.

Your chain will be even more likely to break if the extra pressure from shifting coincides with a weak spot. Weak spots include anywhere the chain is twisted and anywhere the chain has been split and rejoined, so split your chain as little as possible.

Treat your chain kindly

Habitually using a relatively high gear where you pedal slowly but with lots of force will wear and strain your chain (and your knees) much more than using a lower gear, where you spin the pedals around faster, but without stamping so hard on each pedal stroke.

A well-lubricated chain can cope with sudden loads better than a neglected one. Clean, oiled links will slide smoothly over one another, spreading peaks of force out over a number of links, so that none is taken beyond its breaking point. Excessive force will concentrate around stiff links. Over-oiling can be an enemy as well though – a sticky chain will pick up grit, wearing your chain faster and making it more likely to snap. Always clean excess oil off the outside of the chain once you've lubricated it. Only the thinnest layer of oil is necessary to stop the chain from rusting – all the friction that needs to be lubricated goes on inside the chain rollers.

As chains age, they collect more weak spots and become more likely to snap when you make sudden demands on them. Chains, cassettes and chainrings all wear each other out as you ride. Rather than spreading the load over a number of chain links, worn chainrings and cassettes support only the first few links that they mesh with. This concentrates force over a few links, which may mean that the chain's maximum load is exceeded. The links may not look visibly damaged, but once this point is reached, wear will accelerate rapidly, with the stretched chain then wearing out the sprockets and chainrings in turn.

Finally, some people are simply stronger or heavier than others. If this is the case, ask your bike shop to recommend a tougher chain. These will always be more expensive than standard versions but need not be heavier – for example, the SRAM PC99 has hollow rivets to save weight and is much stronger than a standard chain. Under the same levels of abuse, it will stretch less, making your cassette last longer and less likely to snap under pressure.

◀ **New chains fit the chainring snugly over the chainring teeth**

Cassettes

Replace your chain every time you replace your cassette. Worn cassettes allow the chain to slip over the sprocket teeth, rather than to mesh securely into the valleys.

The standard fitting for attaching sprockets to the back wheel is the cassette. The cassette fits over the ratcheting mechanism, the freehub. This is bolted onto the hub, with the bearing at the outboard end. The freehub allows the wheel to go round on its own without pushing the pedals, that is to freewheel. The freehub makes a clicking noise when you freewheel. Cassettes and freehubs are made by different manufacturers, but all adhere to the standard Shimano-fitting pattern. The outer shell of the freehub is splined, a fancy way of saying it has grooves in it. The cassette has a matching set of grooves to slide over the freehub. Everything is kept in place with a lockring, that screws into the outer end of the freehub. The first common cassettes were seven-speed. When eight-speeds were introduced, they needed a longer eight-speed freehub, but seven-speed cassettes and freehubs are not compatible with eight-speed ones. However, nine- and 10-speeds pack more sprockets into the same space, so nine-speed and eight-speed cassettes both fit onto the same freehub. The lockring makes a horrible noise when it starts to loosen. Don't worry! The lockring has a serrated surface that locks onto the serrated face of the cassette. These crunch when separated.

REMOVING THE CASSETTE

Step 1: Remove the back wheel from the frame. Remove the quick-release skewer or nut and fit the cassette-removing tool into the splines on the lockring. Make sure it fits snugly. Some tools have a hole through the middle so that you can refit the skewer or nut and hold everything in place, which is handy. Alternatively, for quick-release axles, use a tool with a central rod that slides into the axle and steadies the tool.

Step 2: Fit a chain whip around one of the sprockets on the cassette, in the direction seen in this picture. This will hold the cassette still while you undo the lockring. Fit a large adjustable spanner onto the tool – you need plenty of leverage so the handle will need to be about 30cm (12 inches) long.

Step 3: Place the wheel in front of you, with the cassette facing away. Hold the chain whip in your left hand and the adjustable spanner in your right, as shown. Pull the two tools apart to release the lockring. If you bolted the cassette lockring tool on, you need to loosen it once the tool starts to move, to make space into which the tool can undo. Remove the lockring, then slide the cassette off the freehub by pulling it straight out from the wheel.

Refitting the cassette

Wipe clean the splines of the freehub. (It is a mistake to use degreaser, as this drives grease from the axle bearings and freehub bearings.) Use the opportunity to check the wheel spokes, which are normally hidden behind the cassette – they get damaged if the chain comes off the biggest sprocket and catches behind the cassette, but you can't usually see the wear. If any are damaged, you have to deal with them – see page 204. Slide the new or cleaned cassette onto the freehub. One of the splines is fatter than the others and has to be lined up with the

corresponding spline on the cassette. Push the cassette all the way home. The outer rings are usually separate and must be correctly lined up. One of the separate rings may be narrower than the others and needs the supplied washer behind it. Grease the threads of the lockring, then screw it onto the centre of the cassette. Refit the cassette-removing tool and the adjustable spanner, and tighten the lockring firmly. You do not need the chainwhip for this since the ratchet in the freehub stops the cassette rotating in this direction. When the lockring is almost tight, it makes an alarming crunching noise. This is normal! The inner surface of the lockring has friction ridges that lock onto the cassette to stop it working loose; they will click as you tighten it down.

◀ **Sprockets ahoy!**

Freewheels

For years, freewheels were the standard way of fitting sprockets to a back wheel, but they have now been superseded by the cassette design. You only come across a freewheel type on an older bike or on a very basic new one. Axles on the freewheel type are more prone to bending and breaking, because the bearings that support the axle are much nearer to the centre of the wheel.

Notches, splines and dogs

The most difficult thing here is choosing the correct tool. When freewheels were standard, there were a plethora of different designs, involving splines and dogs. Luckily, there are now fewer designs, and the only ones you're likely to come across commonly are the Shimano splined freewheel and the SunTour 4dog freewheel. (A splined tool has ridges that fit into matching ridges in the component running along the tool. A dogged tool has pegs, called 'dogs', that fit into matching notches on the component.)

REMOVING FREEWHEELS

Step 1: To remove a freewheel, first choose the correct tool. If possible, take your wheel along to your local bike shop and ask them to help you identify the tool you need. Remove any nuts or the quick-release skewer, and locate the tool in the freewheel **(A)**. Splined tools hold themselves in place, but dogged tools need to be held in place with the nut or quick-release skewer. The tool in the picture is a 4dog freewheel remover **(B)**.

Step 2: Freewheels screw themselves into place as you cycle and are often very tight. You need a large adjustable spanner to turn the tool. Stand the wheel up, with the spanner horizontal in your right hand, hold the wheel steady and push down hard on the spanner. If you're using a dogged tool, you need to loosen the nut/quick-release a little when the freewheel starts to turn. Loosen the nut, unwind the freewheel a little and repeat as necessary.

Step 3: Refitting is much easier! Grease the threads thoroughly, to make removal next time as easy as possible. Carefully line up the freewheel on the wheel – the threads are very fine, so it's easy to cross them accidentally (which means the freewheel starts to go on crooked and gets stuck). Screw on firmly by hand.

Additional advice on freewheels

Fit the wheel back on the bike and change into the lowest gear (largest back sprocket, smallest front chainring). It's important to make sure that the freewheel is firmly screwed on. With the bike on the ground, turn the pedals round so that the cranks are horizontal, then hold on the back brake and push down hard on the front pedal. You should feel the pedal move down a little, then stop when the freewheel is screwed fully home. Finally, check the gear adjustment and tune if necessary.

Freewheels contain a ratcheting device. It's this which allows that rear wheel to continue spinning after you stop pedalling, to 'freewheel'. Pawls inside the freewheel are sprung so that they are pushed constantly outward against a toothed ring. The pawls point away from the direction of the wheel rotation, so that as you pedal they catch on the toothed ring and force the wheel around. When you stop pedalling, the teeth on the spring push the pawls inwards, so that they flap out of the way, springing back to be pushed out of the way again by the next tooth and creating a ticking noise as you pedal.

When the pawls become gummed up by mud or old oil, they fail to spring back and engage with the toothed wheel. If this happens when you pedal, the pawls won't catch, and your pedals will spin forwards uselessly. You can often revive freewheels without opening them up. Remove the freewheel from the bike and look at the back surface. The central part stays still while the outer part with the sprockets attached rotates. Hold the freewheel flat and squirt plenty of thin oil into the gap between the two parts – WD40, GT85 or similar. This will flush dirt out of the front of the freewheel. Re-lubricate with thicker oil – chain lubricant is exactly the right thickness. Hold the central part of the freewheel still and rotate the outer part to work the oil into the pawls. Replace the freewheel on the bike.

Derailleurs

Derailleurs are cunning bits of kit. The way they work is simple: they take advantage of your pedalling action to move the chain smoothly from one sprocket to another. The name comes from the French for 'derail' (pronounced simply 'de-railer' or 'de-rail-yer').

The rear derailleur hangs underneath the cassette and feeds the loose chain that's returning from the chainset back onto the cassette. This is the part of the chain that isn't under pressure – it's the top part that's doing the work as you pedal. The important part for changing gear is the guide jockey wheel, the one that sits closest to the cassette. It's also called the top jockey, even when the bicycle is upside down. The derailleur works by using the cable to move the guide jockey across the cassette. Because this part of the chain is not under pressure, the chain will follow the guide jockey and move onto a different size sprocket as it is fed onto the cassette.

The chain needs to be moving to mesh with a new sprocket, which is why you have to be pedalling to change gear. If you pedal too hard, the chain will not be able to engage properly on the new sprocket and will slip and crunch as you try to change gear.

The lower jockey wheel, also called the tension jockey, has a different function. It sits on the derailleur arm and is sprung so that it's always pushing backward. It is there because you need more chain to go around a combination of big chainring and big sprockets than for a combination of small chainring and small sprockets. The tension jockey is needed to take up the slack, otherwise the surplus chain would drag on the ground.

The next step is telling the derailleur what size sprocket you want to be in. In the pre-derailleur days of bicycle racing, road-racers had two different-sized sprockets, one on each side of the back wheel. When they came to a hill, they'd jump off their bikes, whip off the back wheel, turn it round in the frame, refit it with the larger-sized sprocket engaged, jump back on and ride up the hill. At the top, they'd reverse the process. Derailleurs were invented because anyone who could avoid this palaver saved enough time to win races.

In 1951, after experimenting with different styles, Tullio Campagnolo invented a derailleur called the Gran Sport, which looks pretty much like those we use now and works in a similar way. The derailleur is bolted on just below the rear axle. The top part stays still, but the knuckle, with the guide jockey attached, is hinged at an angle. This means that as the guide jockey moves across, it also moves down, tracking the shape of the cassette. There is a spring across the hinge, pulling the two halves of the derailleur together. Consequently, left to its own devices, the spring will pull the derailleur so that the guide jockey runs under the smallest sprocket.

Finally, here's where you tell the derailleur what you want. The shifter on the handlebars connects to a cable, which pulls the two parts of the derailleur apart. This moves the guide jockey across and down, and so pulls the chain onto a larger sprocket. Moving the shifter the other way releases cable, allowing the spring to pull the guide jockey and chain onto a smaller sprocket. This combination of cable and spring is common – V-brakes work the same way, with the cable pulling something into place and a spring returning it when the cable tension is released.

The two most important demands we place on our derailleurs are that they don't affect the transfer of power from the pedals to the back wheel and that they shift the chain from one sprocket to the next as quickly as possible so that the change from one gear to the next happens without breaking the rhythm of the pedal stroke.

In order to be able to deliver these objectives, the movement of the derailleur as controlled by the shifter needs to be very precise. Derailleurs are right down near the ground, in a prime position for picking up all kinds of grit, dirt and mud. All that gunk will wear the pivots around which the movement of your derailleur hinges. It's not surprising that derailleurs, especially rear ones, have a relatively short life. Keeping them clean and well lubricated helps, but if you ride hard, expect to replace them every year.

◀ **Slave to the rhythm: the derailleur**

Indexing: the delicate science of slipping from one gear to the next

In days gone by people used to be content just using the shifter to feel and listen for the right place under a particular sprocket when changing gear. Now indexed gears are universal. The shifter has notches instead of moving smoothly across its range and, if all the components are compatible and correctly adjusted, shifting one notch on the shifter pulls through enough cable to move the chain across exactly one sprocket on your cassette.

A few derailleurs are designed to work in reverse – the cable pulls the chain from the largest to the smallest sprockets and, when the cable tension is released, the spring in the rear derailleur can pull the cable back from the smallest to the largest sprocket. The Shimano Rapid rise (or low normal) derailleur is like this. Some people prefer it. I find it irritating.

The idea behind rapid-rise derailleurs is that the shift into a higher gear is controlled by cable action rather than spring action, so it's supposed to be better for split-second changes in races. If your transmission is working perfectly, there is a slight advantage – but this is offset by the design's inability to tolerate dirt or wear as well as the standard set-up.

Adjusting your gears

Well-adjusted gears should be invisible – one click of the shifter and you should move into whatever gear you need without thinking about it. You need to lavish care on your gears to keep everything running smoothly, though. Indeed, after keeping your chain clean, the next most important thing is to keep your gears well adjusted. They don't simply work better – your entire transmission lasts longer. Get used to adjusting your gears before you tackle any other gear work, as you have to make adjustments at the end of many procedures, especially fitting new cables or derailleurs. The rear indexing is the most important adjustment – proper tuning is not difficult, but practice makes perfect.

There are a couple of things to bear in mind as you learn to adjust your gears. The first is that your gear adjustment depends on transferring an accurate signal from your shifters to your derailleurs, so that when you take up or release a length of cable at the shifter, exactly the same amount of cable is pulled through at the derailleur. This will not happen if the cable is dirty or frayed or the casing is kinked. If you find that the adjusting instructions aren't working for you, check that cable and casing are in good condition.

All these adjustments require being able to turn the pedals to change gear, so you need to hold your bike up so that the back wheel is off the ground. Ideally, use a workstand. Otherwise bribe a friend to lift it up by the saddle at appropriate moments.

In the picture on the right, you can see the chain in the middle of a gear shift from a larger sprocket to a smaller one. The chain, dragged across to the right by the derailleur, has to climb up and over the teeth of the larger sprockets before dropping onto the next sprocket down. Careful design of both the sprocket profile and the chain links means that the chain will shift under pressure, transferring from one sprocket to the next without loss of power. Shimano chains have side links that bulge outwards, allowing them to engage quickly with the sprocket teeth. Look carefully at the faces of the sprockets on your cassette and you will see that these have also been cut away, making short ramps to help lift the chain up when shifting from smaller to larger sprockets. All these small design improvements, among others, help make your shifting instinctive and immediate.

Teeth that bite gently: shifting sprockets ▶

The best methods of adjusting the rear derailleur

Adjusting your rear derailleur can be tricky. The same problem could have one or more different – but similar – causes. Your derailleur is going to need adjusting if it's slow to shift up or down, if it changes gear all of its own accord when you're innocently cycling along or if it rattles and clatters whenever you change gear. This is how you do it.

Adjusting your indexing: derailleur types – standard and rapid rise

Before you start adjusting, use the following method to check whether you have a standard derailleur (by far the most common on all bikes) or a rapid-rise derailleur. Change into one of the middle cassette sprockets. Take hold of any exposed part of the derailleur cable where it passes along the top-tube or down-tube of your bike, and pull the cable gently away from the frame. Watch the derailleur:

◆ If it moves towards a lower gear (larger sprocket), you have a standard derailleur – follow the instructions on page 148.
◆ If the derailleur moves towards a higher gear (smaller sprocket) when you pull the cable, you have a rapid-rise derailleur (low-normal). These were introduced a few years ago, but never really caught on, so there aren't many of them about. They're just as easy to adjust as standard pull versions – use the same routine, but start from the largest sprocket instead of the smallest – see page 165 for more detail.

Shifter types

When you adjust gears, you shift repeatedly through them to test what happens. Although there are different makes and models of shifter, they all work in the same way – adjusting your indexing will be the same process whether your handlebar gear levers are twistshifters, triggershifters or STi shifters found on road bikes. Start by experimenting to see what happens to the cable when you shift. Find an exposed part of the cable, like you did for checking whether you had a standard or rapid-rise shifter, and pull the cable gently away from the frame with your left hand. Holding it away, use your right hand to change gear. You won't need to pedal at the same time, just operate the shifter. One movement makes the cable slacker, the other makes it tighter. Change up and down a few times so that you begin to remember which does what. For standard derailleurs, shifting so that the cable is tighter pulls the derailleur towards the wheel and onto a larger sprocket. Shifting to release the cable allows the derailleur spring to pull the derailleur away from the wheel, toward a smaller sprocket. Once you are familiar with the action of your shifters, you can start indexing your gears.

People often get confused with gear indexing, mixing it up with adjusting the end-stop screw. This is also important, but it's different. The end-stop screws set the limit of the range of movement of the derailleur, stopping it from falling off either end of the sprocket. Sometimes they are set wrong and accidentally stop the chain from moving onto the sprockets at either end of the cassette.

If this is the case, you cannot adjust your indexing properly – go to the section on end-stop screws on page 149, adjust them and then return here. Always check before you start adjusting the indexing that the chain reaches the smallest and largest sprockets, without dropping over the edge of either.

To tune the indexing, you have to adjust the tension in the cable so that one click of the shifter changes the cable tension precisely enough to move the chain across exactly one sprocket. Pulling the cable moves the chain toward lower gears, the larger sprockets near the wheel. Releasing tension in the cable allows the derailleur spring to pull the chain outwards, towards the small sprockets.

Key points to check if you have trouble adjusting your cable tension

◆ Compatability – have you got the same number of clicks in your shifter as sprockets on your cassette? This is a surprisingly common cause of intractable adjustment problems.
◆ Derailleur hanger angle – the derailleur will only follow the shape of the cassette if the jockey wheels hang vertically below the sprockets. Crashes often bend the derailleur or the derailleur hanger inward, so that the derailleur sits at an angle and will not respond to adjustment.
◆ Crusty cables – the cable must be in good condition so that the shifter can pull through precise amounts of cable. This makes the most difference when the shifter releases a length of cable. The spring in the derailleur will not be strong enough to pull through cable that's gummed up with mud or rust.

Adjusting the cable tension on standard rear derailleurs

This is possibly the single most important adjustment that you will learn to make on your bicycle, and it's not difficult. There are always clear signs when you need to adjust the tension of your rear derailleur cable. If the derailleur doesn't respond to your shifter, if it shifts more than one sprocket when you click the lever or if the chain rattles and clatters as you shift, it's time to look at your cable tension.

The important thing to remember during this procedure is always to start in the same place, with the cable tension at its slackest and the chain in the smallest sprocket. Otherwise, it's easy to confuse yourself, matching up the third shifter click with the fourth sprocket, or whatever. You will either need a workstand, to keep the back wheel off the ground, or the assistance of a friend, to lift the bike up for you at the appropriate moment.

Before you begin changing the cable tension, familiarize yourself with the action of your shifter. Follow the casing that emerges from the right-hand shifter to where it joins the top tube or down tube, emerging as bare cable. Hook your finger under the middle of this section of bare cable and operate your shifter up and down one gear. You'll feel the cable tension pull through, then release.

When the cable tension is exactly right, the chain sits exactly below each sprocket as you change gear. This maximizes chain life and stops the chain from clattering on the sprockets as you ride. Since the sprockets and shifter clicks are evenly spaced, once you have the adjustments for the two smallest sprockets, the others should work automatically.

Once you've worked out which action makes the cable tighter, and which makes it looser, shift so that the cable is as loose as possible.

Start by checking that the shifter is in the high gear position – turn the pedals and click the shifter so that the chain moves all the way into the smallest sprocket. Keep clicking, in case there's slack in the system, until you run out of gears. Keep turning the pedals and click the shifter exactly one click in the down direction, so that the derailleur moves towards the larger sprockets.

TAILORING THE TENSION

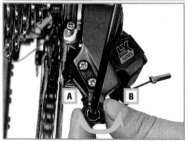

Step 1: The chain should move across to the next largest sprocket and sit directly underneath it. Use the barrel-adjuster to make fine adjustments. To get the barrel to move, hold it as shown with your thumb on the top of the barrel. Turning it one way tightens the cable and moves the chain away **(A)** from you onto larger sprockets. Turning the other way slackens the cable and allows the spring to pull the chain towards you **(B)**, onto smaller sprockets.

Step 2: If the derailleur doesn't move when you click the shifter, the cable is far too slack. Undo the pinch bolt, pull through a little more cable by hand, tighten the pinch bolt. This often happens when you fit a new cable. Start again in the smallest sprocket, clicking the shifter several times to make sure it is at the slackest position. Now increase the tension by half a turn of the barrel-adjuster and repeat until the chain lifts onto the second sprocket.

Step 3: Once you can move the chain from the smallest to the second sprocket, try shifting back from the second to the smallest. You may find you have to tune the position further – try a quarter-turn at a time. Once you've got the right tension, shift into the second-smallest gear and look at the chain from behind. The top jockey wheel, the one with the chain around it, should sit vertically below the second sprocket. Use the barrel-adjuster to finish off the tuning.

Adjusting the end-stop screw on your rear derailleur

The end-stop screws on your derailleur – also known as limit screws – prevent the derailleur from throwing the chain off either end of the cassette. This is a vital task: the end-stop prevents the chain from falling off both the largest sprocket into the gap between the cassette and the wheel, or the smallest sprocket so that it gets stuck between the cassette and the frame.

Either of these contingencies will damage your bike, cutting through the spokes where they join your rear hub or taking chunks out of your frame beside the cassette. The chain will get firmly wedged too, so the chances of you falling off and hurting yourself are quite high.

Only the heads of the end-stops screws are visible, the shafts of the screws are hidden inside the body of the derailleur. The derailleur is designed so that, at either end of it, the tips of the end-stop screws come into contact with tabs moulded into the pivoting part of the derailleur. Screwing the end-stop screws further into the body of the derailleur means that the ends of the screws hit the tabs sooner, limiting the movement of the derailleur and preventing the derailleur from pushing the chain off either end of the cassette. If you set the end-stop screws too far in, the derailleur won't be able to push the chain onto the largest or smallest sprockets.

It's easy to get confused when adjusting your rear derailleur because sometimes the same symptom can have more than one cause. For example, if you are having difficulty shifting onto the smallest sprocket, the cause could be that the 'high' end-stop screw, which controls how far out the derailleur can move, is screwed too far into the derailleur. However, too much tension in the rear derailleur cable can provoke the same response. For this reason, I find it easiest to adjust the end-stop screw when there is no tension in the rear derailleur cable. If you're fitting a new cable, use these instructions to adjust the end-stop screws before you fit the new cable.

In cases where the cable is already fitted, release it from the cable stops on the frame so that it hangs loosely. To do this, first turn the pedals and change into the largest sprocket on your cassette. Stop pedalling, and shift as if changing into the smallest sprocket. The chain won't be able to derail because you're not pedalling, but the derailleur cable will become slack. Follow the outer casing back from the shifter, to where the outer casing joins the frame at the first cable stop, and pull the casing forward toward the front of the bike. Wiggle the cable out of the slot in the cable guide. This will give you enough cable slack to adjust the end-stop screws without getting confused by cable tension issues.

Once you've finished adjusting the end-stop screws, replace the cable. To create enough slack in the cable, you'll need to push the rear derailleur toward the wheel so that it sits under the largest sprocket.

SETTING THE END-STOP SCREWS

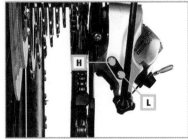

Step 1: Setting the high gear is easier, so we'll start there. Looking at the derailleur from behind, you see the two end-stop screws, marked 'H' and 'L', one above the other. Normally, the higher screw adjusts the high gear and the lower screw the low gear. But, annoyingly, some SRAM screws work the opposite way round. The writing is often small and difficult to make out. Turn the lower screw so that the chain hangs exactly under the smallest sprocket.

Step 2: The low end-stop screw is trickier. With the back wheel off the ground, turn the pedals with your right hand. Position your left hand with first finger hooked behind the cable entry tab at the back and thumb over the forward set of pivots. Push your thumb away from you **(A)** while turning the pedals. Push the derailleur across, so the chain runs to the largest sprocket but not so far that it falls into the gap between the largest sprocket and the spokes.

Step 3: If you can't move the derailleur across enough to shift easily into the largest sprocket, you need to unscrew (anticlockwise) the lower **(L)** of the two adjustment screws. Small adjustments make a big difference, so take it easy. If the chain threatens to fall too far, wind the upper screw clockwise. Once set, you should be able to push the derailleur far enough by turning the pedals to let the chain sit vertically under the large sprocket, and no further.

Rear derailleur varieties

There is a slightly bewildering array of derailleur options available, not all of which are intercompatible. Even when you've decided how much money you're going to spend, it can take some thinking to work out exactly what you need.

For example, in their XT and XTR mountain bike ranges, Shimano currently make three different versions (top normal, low normal and Shadow), with two different cage choices for each, making a total of six different options. Road bikes have fewer varieties.

Most bikes are fitted with a 'top-normal' rear derailleur. This simply means that increasing the cable tension makes the derailleur shift the chain onto a larger sprocket (lower gear), while releasing the cable tension allows the chain to drop back to a smaller sprocket (higher gear).

Less common are 'low normal' derailleurs, which used to be called 'Rapid Rise'. These work in reverse, so that increasing the cable tension makes the derailleur pull the chain onto a smaller sprocket, while releasing the cable tension means the chain climbs onto a larger sprocket. These were supposed to have all sorts of advantages, such as better shifting under pressure, but haven't really ever caught on. They take a bit of getting used to if you're used to conventional shifting responses.

Increasingly, more and more mountain bikes are coming with Shimano's latest rear derailleur design, the Shadow. This is 'top-normal' so works in the conventional way, but has a number of advantages. Firstly, the cable routing on the derailleur has changed, so that the final section of outer casing is much shorter and doesn't have to curve all the way around the back of the derailleur. This reduces cable friction. Secondly, the Shadow derailleurs have a dramatically reduced profile – they don't stick out so far from the side of the bike and so are less likely to get mangled in a crash.

Compatibility

Shimano have set the standards for compatibility – they are the stock derailleur for the overwhelming majority of new mountain bikes, so most other manufacturers make sure they're dancing to Shimano's tune.

The only significant exception is SRAM. The difference is the 'actuation ratio' – the amount the guide jockey wheel moves sideways in response to pulling or releasing cable with the gear shifter.

· The Shimano standard is for 1mm of cable movement to move the guide jockey 2mm sideways – a 2:1 ratio. SRAM Attack shifters are compatible with this standard.

· SRAM's x3, x5, x7, x9 and x0 mountain bike (and SRAM road bike) shifters and derailleurs all work on a 1:1 ratio, so every 1mm of cable pull moves the chain 1mm sideways. SRAM's XX derailleurs can only be used with SRAM XX shifters, as they use their own Exact Actuation ratio, migrated from SRAM's road groupsets.

Setting the derailleur angle with the B-screw

The B-screw sits at the back of your derailleur and adjusts the angle that the derailleur sits at relative to the frame, altering the gap between the top of the guide jockey wheel and the sprockets. If the chain sits too close to the sprockets, it will clatter on the cassette teeth as you ride. If the gap is too big, you'll get sluggish shifting because the chain will flex sideways when you try to change gear rather than meshing neatly with the next sprocket.

Use the B-screw to adjust the gap so that there are there is around 2.5cm (1 inch) of clear chain between the sprocket and the guide jockey. On Shadow derailleurs, the B-screw sits below the derailleur's main pivot (see left). On conventional derailleurs, the B-screw sits behind the derailleur's anchor bolt and abuts on a tab at the back of the frame. In either case, turn clockwise to increase the gap between cassette and guide jockey, anticlockwise to move them closer together.

▲ Shadow rear derailleur
◀ Conventional derailleur

Fitting a new rear derailleur

There are many reasons you might want or need to change your rear derailleur. First of all, it might have snapped in a crash. Alternatively, it might simply have worn out from hundreds of gear changes.

Derailleur pivots will wear over time, causing sluggish shifting as the guide jockey struggles to respond to changes in cable tension. Take hold of the bottom of the derailleur cage and rock it sideways, towards and away from the back wheel. A bit of flex is fine, but if you can feel the cage knocking, replace the derailleur.

This task is easiest when you have as much chain slack to play with as possible. That's why you should change into the smallest sprocket at the back, while at the same time dropping the chain off the smallest sprocket at the front and into the gap between the chainset and the frame. Clip the end-cap off the cable.

FITTING A REAR DERAILLEUR

Step 1: Undo the cable clamp bolt and unthread the cable from the barrel-adjuster. If you reuse the same cable, there is no need to unthread it further, although you may find that a new derailleur will have a different configuration and need a longer cable. It is best to split the derailleur to remove the chain from it, as splitting the chain takes longer and weakens the split link. First, undo the guide jockey bolt slightly.

Step 2: Remove the tension jockey bolt, which is the one in the middle of the lower of the two jockey wheels.

Step 3: Slide the tension jockey wheel forward. It has a washer on each side. Don't lose these; they tend to drop out as you pull the jockey wheel out.

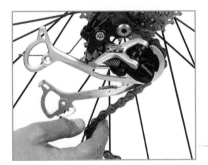

Step 4: Rotate the back of the cage slightly so that you can slide the chain out of the cage without splitting the chain. Undo the fixing bolt that attached the derailleur to the frame. Discard the old derailleur.

Step 5: Remove the tension jockey wheel on the new rear derailleur and loosen the guide jockey bolt. Hold the derailleur upside down, as shown. Fit the derailleur to the lower loop of chain, laying it over the guide jockey then trapping it in place with the tension jockey. Make sure it passes inside both tabs (**A**), so that the chain runs between the tab and the jockey wheel. Refit the tension jockey bolt. Tighten both jockey wheel bolts firmly.

Step 6: Turn the derailleur clockwise and pull it backwards, so the fitting bolt is aligned with the frame-hanger. Bolt the derailleur to the frame, ensuring the bolt does not cross-thread. It's important that the small B-tab behind the derailleur sits behind the matching tab on the lower part of the frame-hanger, stopping the derailleur from swinging too far forward.

Servicing the rear derailleur

The rear derailleur does all the shifting work and dangles down close to the ground getting caught on twigs and picking up debris. It's also the part that your bike lands on first if you crash on your right-hand side or drop the bike. If you have time to think when you're crashing, drop the bike on the left – it's far cheaper!

If your shifting is still sluggish after you've adjusted the end-stop screws and the cable tension, then it's time to treat your rear derailleur to a little clean and re-lubrication. The separate sections of the derailleur need to be able to move freely, so that your shifting is crisp. The pivots that connect the parts work best if they're not jammed up with dirt and have a little oil to lubricate them.

The first step is to clean your rear derailleur. This is easiest with the back wheel removed, so you can get to everything. Wipe down the outside, then use a little brush to get mud and dirt out from inside the mechanism. You don't need to carry that muck around with you. You need to move the derailleur through its range to get inside it. With your left hand, hook a finger behind the back of the derailleur and push the front part of the derailleur body away from you.

Once you've got the dirt out from the inside, clean off the jockey wheels. They collect oil and mud and grind them together into an excellent chain-eating paste. Scrape this off with the end of a screwdriver. Next, check how worn the derailleur is. The teeth on the jockey wheels should have flat tops, not points. Take hold of the bottom of the derailleur and wiggle it towards you. It should flex rather than knock or flap about freely. When these things happen, it's time for a new derailleur.

Next, oil the pivot points. There are at least four on the derailleur body. Drop a bit of oil into the jockey wheel bearings, the knuckle where the derailleur rotates on the frame, and the point where the derailleur body meets the arm to which the jockey wheels are attached. Once you've oiled all these parts, move them to work the oil into the gaps. Push the derailleur away, as if it was changing gear, then allow it to spring back several times. Wipe off excess oil. Refit the back wheel.

If you feel like giving your bike a Christmas present, remove the rear derailleur (see page 151) and give it a thorough scrub. Undo the bolts that hold on the jockey wheels, remove them and take the back of the cage off to clean properly between the cage and the jockey wheels. Push the bearings out of the middle of the jockey wheels, clean and oil them, then refit using Loctite 243 on the bolt threads. Don't be tempted to swap the top and bottom jockey wheels – they're usually a different shape because they do a different job. The top guide jockey wheel pushes the chain sideways, from one sprocket to the next. The bottom tension jockey wheel pulls the chain backward, taking up slack. In addition, guide jockeys like the one in the picture, from a Shimano XT derailleur, have a rotation direction. Set this up so that pedalling forward makes the jockey wheel roll in the direction of the arrows. This can be achieved by bolting the jockey wheel into the derailleur so that the writing faces outward.

Use a small brush to scrub dirt from inside the body of the derailleur and oil the pivot points. Refit the derailleur, again using instructions for fitting a new derailleur.

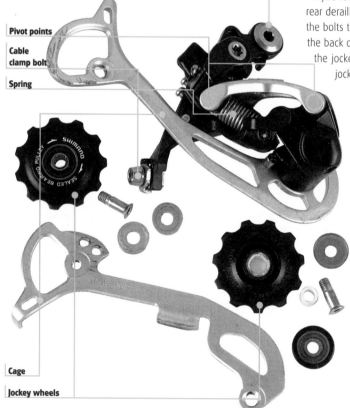

Fixing bolt

Pivot points

Cable clamp bolt

Spring

Cage

Jockey wheels

◀ **Shimano Shadow derailleur**

Rear hanger alignment

A lot is expected of your rear derailleur. You want it to be a precise, instant-shifting piece of kit even under pressure in a dirty environment. You need to be able to rely on it in all conditions and that's why it pays to nurture your poor toiling derailleur.

One of the most common problems to be routinely ignored is the alignment of the rear derailleur hanger (the part on the frame that the derailleur bolts onto). The gears are designed to work when the two jockey wheels hang vertically underneath the sprockets. This vertical alignment is the first casualty of a crash, but it's often overlooked – you get up and brush yourself off, look at your bike and, if everything looks okay, you ride away. Bad things can happen next. If you've crashed and bent your derailleur inwards, the gears may still work, but everything has shipped inboard a little.

Next time you stamp uphill in a low gear, you click the lever to find a bigger sprocket, but instead you dump the chain off the inside of the rear cassette, stuffing it into the back wheel just as you haul on the pedals. Likely results include falling off and hurting yourself – and expensive damage to your back wheel.

On a less drastic level, the shifting works best when the sprockets are aligned with the jockey wheels. The chain isn't being twisted as it runs off the sprocket; and the jockey wheels move in the direction they were designed to, rather than being forced up into the sprockets as they move across the cassette, which is what happens if the hanger is bent.

Look at the derailleur from behind. This way, you get the clearest view of whether or not the chain is running in one of the middle gears. The sprocket, chain and jockey wheel should make a vertical line. One of the most common problems is when the hanger is bent so that the bottom jockey wheel hangs nearer the wheel, as in the picture below.

It's not unusual for the hanger or the derailleur to be twisted rather than (or as well as!) bent, so that as you look straight at the sprocket, you can see the surface of the jockey wheels instead of just the edge. For precise shifting, the jockeys need to be flat and vertical to the sprockets. Because this is a common problem, all decent aluminium frames feature a replaceable hanger.

There are as many different types of hanger as there are makes of bike, and, even within a make and model, the hanger you need might depend on the year the bike was made. To make sure you get the right one, take the old one to your local bike shop for comparison. They are almost never interchangeable.

If you don't have a replaceable hanger, the frame will have to be bent back. You can do it yourself if you are careful, but if you are unsure, this is a job I recommend you take to your bike shop. You usually need to have snapped off a couple of hangers before you know how far you can go – an expensive experiment. If the bend is bad, it will be weaker after you have straightened it.

Leave the wheel in the dropout to support the frame. You have two options for bending back the hanger. The first is to clamp a large adjustable spanner onto the hanger – you need about 30cm (12 inches) of leverage to do the job – and to ease the hanger back into

place. It is very important to bend in one movement – the last thing you want to do is work the hanger backward and forward to find the perfect place. It will snap off.

The other option, which is trickier but safer, is to screw a rear wheel axle into the thread on the hanger. They are the same size, an M10 thread. I've had plenty of success bolting a whole wheel onto the thread, and using it for leverage. It's easy to see when you've got the angle right because the two wheels – your own, and the one bolted into the derailleur hanger – are parallel.

Some rear derailleurs come with a breakaway bolt. This means that the bolt that fixes the derailleur to the frame is designed to be slightly weaker than the hanger and the derailleur. In the event of a crash, instead of your hanger breaking or bending, your derailleur breaks off. Replacement bolts are still available, and are either push-fit or circlipped in, depending on the model.

◀ **Hangers need to be flat and vertical to sprockets**

Improving your shifting

It's often difficult to know where to start with gear adjustment. Sluggish shifting can result from a combination of factors, both constant and intermittent. The rear derailleur, in particular, relies on everything being set up perfectly so that all the components work together.

It's also tricky to adjust gears because they behave differently under pressure. Gears that feel perfect when you're trying them out in the garage can be disappointing when you try them out for real. Occasionally, the opposite situation occurs: you can't get the gears to shift properly at all in the shop, then you go for a ride anyway and unexpectedly they feel fine.

Adjust cable tension

If you're unhappy with the shifting, the most sensible place to start is with the cable tension adjustment. Click the shifters all the way into their neutral position (high gears for standard derailleurs, low for rapid rise) and then shift over into the neighbouring sprocket. If the chain doesn't sit vertically under the sprocket or doesn't shift crisply, you have an adjustment problem – see cable tension, page 108.

Check hanger alignment

Shift into the big sprocket and look at the chain from behind the bike. The chain should make a straight vertical line down the back of the sprocket and around the jockey wheels. If the jockey wheels are tucked in towards the back wheel, you have a hanger alignment problem – see page 153.

Replace or clean cables and casing

If your cable tension and alignment are correct, but your shifting is still sluggish, your gear cable may be dirty, kinked or corroded. In particular, check the section of outer casing that connects the rear derailleur to the frame as it is vulnerable to getting squashed or kinked.

Cables (the wires) are among the least expensive parts of the bike, so changing them doesn't break the bank. If you normally cycle in conditions where you need to clean your bike after a ride, think about changing cables at least four times a year. The rear derailleur cable is the bike part most susceptible to contamination because it transfers a very precise signal. Of all the repairs in this section, fitting and adjusting your rear derailleur cable is the best one to know. You can get all sorts of fancy cable sets that are designed to enclose the inner wire and keep it free from mud, but, in my experience, soil has an unrelenting urge to find its way into the piece of outer casing between my frame and derailleur where it lodges, specifically to make my gear changing feel like rubbish. Changing the cable is not a complicated job, and the reward is instant: an improved bike and ride. The first part of the procedure depends on what kind of shifter you have, so we'll go through each of those in turn – see page 161. Once you have the cable installed in the shifter, the procedure for adjusting the derailleur is identical. Start with the shifter that's most similar to yours, then hop to the adjustment section on page 148.

Before you fit any new cable, you need to remove the old one. Cut off the cable end and undo the pinch bolt that clamps the cable onto the derailleur. Thread the cable back through each section of outer casing in turn, leaving the casing on the bike. Make a note of the cable route because the new one will have to go back the same way. If you replace the outer casing as well (which is not a bad idea – especially the last section that leads to the rear derailleur), then go to the section on outer casing on page 159. Cut the cable so that about 15cm (6 inches) is left poking out of the shifter, then follow the instructions for your shifter to get the old cable out and the new cable in.

Clean or replace your rear derailleur

Your derailleur will work much better if it's clean and oiled. See page 152 for servicing instructions. Give it a good scrub and oil it. Hold the bottom of the cage, near the bottom jockey wheel, and rock it gently toward and away from the wheel. Knocking, clicking or moving more than 4mm (around ⅛ inch) sideways indicates that the pivots in your derailleur are worn out – see page 151 to replace the derailleur.

Replace shifter

If none of these works, check that your shifter is sending crisp signals. Shift into a large sprocket, then click the shifter as if changing into a small sprocket, but without turning the pedals. This creates slack in the cable. Pull the section of casing that joins the bars to the frame forward and out of its cable stop. Slide the casing toward the back of the bike. This exposes the cable as it enters the shifter. Take hold of the cable and pull gently away from the shifter. Operate the shifter, checking that, as you shift in either direction, the shifter pulls through little chunks of cable, and then releases them neatly, one at a time. If the shifter slips or misses clicks, service or replace it – see page 167.

Front derailleur

The front derailleur lies directly in the firing line of all the dirt and mud that get thrown up off your back wheel, so it occasionally deserves a bit of care and attention. Cheaper front derailleurs don't last that long. I find they are the components least resistant to winter, especially if you ride on salted roads.

They get covered in whatever the roads throw up, accumulating mud that is then forced into the shifting mechanism every time you change gear. Eventually, the spring that returns the chain to the smaller chainrings can no longer cope and the derailleur stops returning when you release the cable.

◀ Front derailleurs are less complex than rear derailleurs

Front derailleur: adjusting the indexing

Like the rear derailleur, adjusting the indexing on the front derailleur is the same whatever type of handlebar shifter you have. Check what your particular shifter does by taking hold of an exposed section of cable, pulling it gently away from the frame. Change gears in both directions and familiarize yourself with the effect that the shifters have on the cable. One of the directions or levers will loosen the cable, the other will tighten it.

Lift the back wheel off the ground for this procedure. Turn the pedals and move the front shifter so that the cable is in its slackest position. As you turn the pedals, the chain should shift into the smallest chainring at the front. If it doesn't, the cable tension is too high. The barrel-adjuster for the front derailleur is up on the shifter. To loosen the cable, turn the barrel-adjuster so that the top of the barrel moves towards the front of the bike. Try a half-turn at a time to start with.

As with the rear derailleur, it is possible to get muddled between a problem with the cable tension or the end-stop screw adjustment. If you continue to adjust the cable tension and the cable goes slack but the chain still doesn't drop into the smallest chainring when you change gear, you need to adjust the end-stop screws **(A)** – see page 156. Adjust the end-stops, then come back here.

Once you've got the chain into the smallest ring, keep pedalling and change gear at the shifter by one complete click. The chain should climb up into the middle ring. If it doesn't, or does so sluggishly, you need to increase the tension in the cable – turn the barrel-adjuster so that the top of the barrel moves towards the back of the bike. Once the chain moves onto the middle ring, adjust the barrel until there is 1mm (1/16 inch) of clearance between the outer plate of the derailleur cage and the chain, with the chain in the smallest sprocket at the back. The chain should now shift precisely between the three rings. If it won't reach the outer or inner ring easily, you have to adjust the limit screws. They are especially likely to need adjustment if you have changed the position of the derailleur on the frame.

You may run out of barrel-adjuster – you need to turn it further out, but, as you turn, it drops out of the shifter, or you need to move it further out, but it jams against the shifter. If so, you need to make a coarse adjustment with the pinch bolt, then restart the fine adjustment.

Roll the barrel most of the way back in, then undo the pinch bolt on the derailleur and pull a little cable through – start with about 3mm (around 1/8 inch). Try the gears again.

Front derailleur adjustment is particularly sensitive to the position of the derailleur – if it's too high, too low or twisted, you won't be able to make it shift neatly by adjusting the cable tension. If you try the adjustment above and the derailleur still won't shift neatly, try adjusting the derailleur – follow the instructions for fitting a new one on page 157. Similarly, a bent derailleur will not shift neatly. Once you've bent one, it is hard to persuade it back into the right shape. You are usually better off replacing it than trying to reshape it. It does work occasionally, but not very often.

Derailleur position is vital for crisp shifting ▶

Setting the end-stop screws

End-stop screws limit the movement of the front derailleur, so that it cannot drop the chain off the inside or the outside of the chainring.

There are two separate screws, each controlling one end of the derailleur range. The 'low' adjustment screw prevents the derailleur swinging too far towards the frame, dropping the chain into the gap between chainset and frame. The 'high' adjustment screw prevents the derailleur from throwing the chain off the outside of the chainring.

Before you start adjusting, work out which screw does what. They'll have H and L marked on them, or a long line next to the H screw (representing the big chainring) and a short line next to the L screw. These indicators will helpfully be printed in black on a black background.

Usually, on 'conventional' front derailleurs (where the band that clamps the derailleur to the frame is higher than the derailleur cage), the H screw is the one furthest from the frame. For 'topswing' derailleurs (where the band is lower than the cage, as shown below), this is reverse – the H screw is nearest the frame.

SETTING END-STOP SCREWS

Step 1: Start with the chain in the middle ring. Check the shifter is in the middle of the three positions. Turn the pedals and shift into high gear. The chain should lift onto the big chainring as you turn the pedals. If it won't go, you need to unwind the 'high' **(A)** end-stop screw (marked 'H' on the derailleur, or with a wider line that is often hard to see since it's usually printed in little letters). Unscrew the 'H' screw a couple of turns and retest.

Step 2: Once you've got the chain onto the big chainring, you need to make sure it won't go too far. With the chain still in the big chainring, gently roll in the 'H' screw until you feel it touching the body of the derailleur – it will roll in fairly easily, then you will encounter resistance. At this point, back it off half a turn and test again.

Step 3: Now try shifting into the smallest ring. Again, it should drop in first time. If not, you need to back off the low adjusting screw **(B)**. It will be marked with an 'L' or with a narrower line. Test, adjust, then test again. Once the chain is in the small chainring, you need to set the 'L' screw so it won't move too far. Wind it in, but watch the derailleur cage as you turn the screw and stop as soon as you see that turning the screw is moving the cage. Test again.

Choosing the right type of derailleur

There are three types of derailleur: 'conventional', 'topswing' and 'e-type'. The conventional type is the older design, where the clamp that attaches the front derailleur to the frame seat tube is higher than the derailleur cage.

Topswing derailleurs also bolt to the seat tube, but the clamp is lower than the derailleur cage. On many bikes, these two types are completely interchangeable, but some configurations of suspension frame will force you to use one or the other. If in doubt, replace like with like.

E-type derailleurs don't clamp onto the seat tube – they're usually mounted to the bottom bracket shell, via a separate plate which is sandwiched between the bottom bracket cup and the frame. On long travel full suspension bikes, there's been a movement towards mounting e-type front derailleurs directly to the swingarm. This means that the front derailleur moves with the suspension action.

Your frame will also dictate whether the front derailleur is 'top pull' or 'down pull'. As the name suggests, down-pull derailleurs are activated by a cable that runs down towards the bottom bracket, whereas with top-pull derailleurs the cable will head straight upwards then along the top tube. Most modern derailleurs are dual pull, so can be converted to accept either top- or down- pull routings.

The third piece of information you need to know for a band on derailleur is your frame diameter. The three sizes are 28.6mm 31.8mm and 34.9mm. (1 1/8", 1 1/4" and 1 3/8". Shimano derailleurs avoid this issue altogether, as they're supplied in a 34.9mm size with shims to convert them to either of the other diameters.

FITTING A FRONT DERAILLEUR

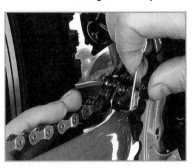

Step 1: Shift to the smallest chainring at the front, and the smallest sprocket at the back. Undo the cable clamp bolt and release the cable from the derailleur. Next, remove the bolt that fixes your derailleur onto your frame. Unfold the hinge that traps the band around the frame and pull the derailleur away from the frame.

Step 2: Check the back of the derailleur cage on both old and new derailleurs. If they've both got a little screw holding the derailleur together, you're in luck – undo and remove the screw and go to step 3. If either or both are a rivet, you'll have to split the chain, either using a chain tool or a Powerlink – see pages 98–100. Thread the chain back through the new derailleur and go to step 4.

Step 3: Spread the back of the derailleur cage and slide out the chain. Reverse the process with the new derailleur, ease the cage back into shape and refit the small bolt.

Step 4: Rest the back of the derailleur cage against the chainstay so you can tighten the bolt securely without deforming the derailleur cage. Now refit the derailleur back onto the frame and replace the fixing bolt. Don't reconnect the gear cable yet.

Step 5: The derailleur needs to be positioned so that the outer face of the derailleur cage is exactly parallel to the outer chainring. Pull the derailleur gently away from the frame with your hands, to check the alignment. If it needs rotating on the frame, release it so it springs back towards the seat tube, loosen the fixing bolt, rotate on the frame and retest.

Step 6: The height of the derailleur is also critical for smooth shifting. Pull the derailleur away from the frame, so the outer plate of the cage is exactly over the outer chainring and look from the side. The gap between teeth and cage should be 2–3mm (¹⁄₈ inch). If the height needs adjusting, let the derailleur drop back and adjust the height without rotating the derailleur. See below to refit the cable.

Adjusting a front derailleur

Turn the pedals and use the right-hand shifter to move the chain into the largest sprocket at the back. With the cable disconnected, the front derailleur should spring back towards the frame, pulling the chain onto the smallest chainring. If the chain doesn't drop onto the smallest chainring, you need to adjust the low limit screw (marked 'L' on the derailleur). Undo the screw a turn, then turn the pedals again. Repeat until the chain drops into the smallest chainring. With the chain in the largest sprocket at the back and the smallest chainring at the front, adjust the 'L' limit screw until there is 1–2mm (¹⁄₁₆–¹⁄₈ inch) clearance between the inside of the chain and the inner plate of the derailleur cage.

Pull the end of the still-disconnected gear cable gently and shift through the gears on the handlebars. You will feel the cable pull and release as you shift in either direction. Shift a few times to make sure the cable is in its most relaxed position. The chain should still be in the smallest chainring. Look carefully at the pinch bolt on the front derailleur and check for the position of the groove under the cable clamp bolt. Lay the cable in place and pull gently with one hand, just enough to take up any slack in the cable. Tighten the clamp bolt.

Now use the instructions for fitting a new derailleur cable to adjust the cable tension (see page 155).

Servicing the front derailleur

Front derailleur cable tension pulls the cage outwards, shifting your chain onto larger chainrings, but when you release the tension, the derailleur relies on a spring to pull the cage back toward the frame and to pull your chain onto smaller sprockets. If your pivots are dirty or worn, the spring won't be strong enough to pull back the change and shifts into lower gears will be slow.

Front derailleur: clean and oil

If your front derailleur is on strike, your first remedy is a good clean with a long soak in light oil (WD40, GT85, Superlube). Periodically work the derailleur back and forth as far as you can – gradually increasing until you work across the full range of movements. This is easiest with the chainset removed. Dirt will probably ooze from the pivot points as you go. Wipe it off.

Oil all the pivot points carefully. Use the shifter to slacken off the cable; shift it into the smallest chainring position. Take hold of the derailleur cage, pull it out from the frame as far as it will go, and push it back. Repeat a couple of times to work the oil into the pivots. Once the cage is moving smoothly, wipe off all the excess oil – don't leave any oil on the surface of the derailleur: it's sticky and picks up more dirt. For extra points, clean the derailleur cable – see page 160.

Front derailleur: reshaping

The shape and condition of your front derailleur are crucial for reliable shifting. Old-fashioned front derailleurs consisted of two very simple flat plates, one on either side of the chain, which pushed the chain from side to side under the control of the front derailleur cable. Modern derailleurs are shaped to lift the chain quickly into place, allowing you to shift accurately under pressure. When new, they work faultlessly, but wear, crashes and brutal gear changing will take their toll.

If you're having problems with your front shifting and adjusting the cable tension and end-stop doesn't cure it, it's worth inspecting the derailleur cage quite carefully. You can often identify the source of problems, and occasionally cure them, with some judicious bending. Check that the inside of the cage isn't worn out first though – the most usual problem area is the inside surface of the inner cage plate. This is the surface that pushes the chain from the middle chainring to the smallest one, and from middle to outer. It's tricky to get a good look, which is why wear in this area often goes unnoticed. Unless the derailleur is brand new, you'll see the marks where the chain has scraped across the cage. With time, these marks get deeper. If the marks are so deep that you can feel ridges with your fingers, the derailleur will need to be replaced – the chain will catch on these ridges as you change gear, twisting it rather than lifting it cleanly onto the next chainring. In extreme cases, the chain will wear all the way through the derailleur cage and it will snap. Long before this, the clumsy changes will have worn and damaged your chain, so it makes good sense to replace worn derailleurs sooner rather than later.

If the derailleur isn't worn out, check the shape. The curve of the cage should match the shape of the chainring. The front section of the outer plate should be parallel to the chainring. The top section of the cage, which links the front plate to the back, should be flat and horizontal. Clumsy shifting bends the derailleur cage, preventing it from following the contour of the chainset.

Use pliers to bend the cage gently back into shape. Ideally, you need to reshape the derailleur with one movement – using the pliers to lever the cage backwards and forwards will weaken the metal.

Check the condition of the derailleur pivots. Take hold of the back of the cage and wiggle it up and down. You will be able to feel the cage flex a little, but if you can rock it up and down, or you can feel it knocking, the pivots are worn out and the derailleur must be replaced.

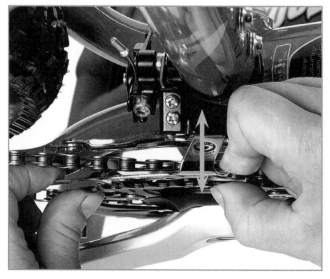

Work the derailleur back and forth ▶

Cable and outer casing

It's important to understand the differences between your gear and brake cables because they perform very different functions and require very different treatment. Here's the lowdown on these vital components.

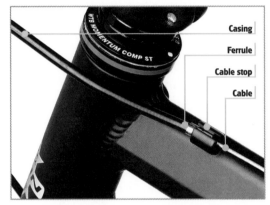

Cable: The wire that connects a shifter or lever to the component – it's usually silver.

Casing: The cover that supports and guides the cable.

Ferrule: A metal or plastic cap on the end of the casing that prevents the end of the casing from splaying out under pressure.

Cable stop: The part of your frame that the outer casing slots into – a slot in the cable stop allows you to slide the cable out of the cable stop for cleaning.

Cable end: A small metal cap that you squash over the end of the cable to prevent the cable fraying.

Nipple: The blob on the end of the cable that fits into the lever or shifter, stopping the cable from pulling through.

The outer casing used for gears is different to the casing used for brakes.
- Brake casing is made from tight spirals of square section wire.
- Gear casing is made from round section wire, formed into much longer spirals. It is covered in plastic (usually black), which protects the wire and keeps it in shape. It is lined with a Teflon tube (usually white) so that the inner cable moves smoothly inside.

The casings differ because they perform different functions. Brake casing must be very strong because it handles a lot of pressure. Gear casing must transmit a very accurate signal. When you shift from one gear to the next, you pull through mere millimetres of cable, so it is vital that the gear casing does not compress and influence the cable as you change gear or turn the handlebars. The long spirals prevent the gear casing from shortening under pressure, or as the sections of casing articulate with the bike.

The advantage of the tight spiral wind in brake casing is that while it is strong, when it fails, it does so gently. Gear casing cannot take so much pressure, but that's all right because gear levers are short, so you can't exert much pressure on them anyway. When the casing does fail, it tends to be catastrophic – the casing splits open and you get no shifting at all. Were this brake casing, this kind of failure would be bad news because the cable is likely to break under a strong braking force – that is, when you need it most.

Getting the cable and casing right is a cheap task that greatly improves your bike. It's worth changing the last section of outer casing (the piece that takes the cable into the rear derailleur) every time you change the inner cable, as it's nearest the ground. More expensive derailleurs have a boot (rubber gaiter) protecting the end of the cable and so they stay cleaner, but this piece of cable costs so little in relation to the importance of smooth changing that changing it is worthwhile. The casing is really tough, so you need proper wire-cutters to chop it to length – pliers won't do. It is important to cut the ends neatly and squarely – if you cut raggedly or at an angle the casing deforms as you change gear, making your shifting sloppy. Once you've cut the casing, check inside to ensure that the lining hasn't got squashed. If it has, open it out with the point of a sharp knife. Finish off the end of each length of casing with a ferrule. These protect the ends of the casing and stop them from splaying out. Getting exactly the right length can be tricky. If the casing is too long, it adds friction to the cable, which again means sloppy shifting – the spring in the derailleur has to pull the slack that is created when you release cable at the shifter all the way back to the derailleur, so the less friction here the better. If the casing is too short, the inner cable will be constricted as it goes around tight bends. Care needs to be taken with sections of casing that join parts that move in tandem with each other; for example, the section of casing that joins the handlebars to the frame or that join the frame to the derailleur. Dual suspension bikes need extra care with the sections that connect the main frame to the rear end. Make sure you have enough casing to allow suspension to move without stretching the casing. Ghost shifting is often caused by casing that is restricted or stretched. Replace these sections of casing every time you replace the inner cable. When the casing is the right length, it approaches the cable stops parallel to the frame and looks elegant. Check casing regularly for splits, cracks and kinks. Damaged casing should be replaced straight away – it has a habit of being fine for a while, lulling you into a false sense of security, then it goes suddenly just when you're farthest from home, leaving you to limp back in the smallest sprocket or chainring.

The importance of cleaning cables and searching out hidden grime

The most common cause of sluggish shifting is the bits of the nice trail or road you just rode concealing themselves between cable and casing. Cleaning the bike can sometimes serve only to solidify the mud or dust so you have to be careful. Full suspension bikes suffer particularly badly – the loops of casing necessary to connect rear brake and gear cables across the central hinge are often a magnet for unwanted grit. Luckily, the cable stops on frames are slotted, allowing you to remove the casing and clean the sections of cable normally hidden within.

▲ **Pull casing forward and out of cable stop**

Inspect cable and casing before you start – if either are kinked, frayed or corroded, it's time to replace them.

For gear cables, lift your back wheel off the ground. Shift into the largest sprocket front and rear, then stop pedalling. Click your shifters as if changing into the smallest sprocket and smallest chainring

For V-brake cables, squeeze the brake units together, slide back the rubber boot and release the noodle from its hanger. For mechanical disc brakes, push the actuation lever upwards, as if applying the brake. This creates slack in the cable. Follow the section of outer casing that emerges from the shifter or lever, to the cable stop on the frame. Pull the outer casing forwards and wiggle the cable out of the slot in the cable slot. Repeat at all the other cable stops. Slide the sections of casing along the cable and clean all the concealed sections (a light oil such as GT85 or WD40 works well). Re-lubricate the cable with a heavier oil – whatever you use for your chain is perfect. Slide the casings gently back into place, careful to avoid kinking the cable. Settle them back into the cable stops. For mechanical disc brakes, you need to pull the actuation lever up again to give yourself enough cable slack.

Reconnect the V-brake cable. For gear cables, lift up the back of the bike and turn the pedals around to allow the chain to find a gear. You may need to operate the brake or gear levers several times to pull the outer casing firmly back into the cable stops.

Upgrade cable kits
The standard cable set-up, with a steel cable running through a Teflon-lined casing, works well in most circumstances, as long as it's kept clean and lubricated. But a variety of upgrade cables are available that will last longer in messier environments. The simplest solution is to use a smooth inner wire that's been pre-coated with Teflon. These still need lubrication, but they will stay cleaner than standard cables and will reduce friction between cable and casing. They are slightly more expensive than standard cables but are no more difficult to fit.

Signed, sealed, delivered
A more extreme solution is to use a sealed cable kit – Gore-Tex cable kits are the most common example. These use a very smooth Gore-Tex coating (more commonly found as a waterproof, breathable jacket lining) on the cable. The kit comes with a plastic tube that protects the cable through its entire length. A rubber boot guards the end of the cable, stopping mud, grit or sand from creeping into the gap between cable and protective lining. The Gore-Tex coating has to be stripped off the end of the cable, so that it can be clamped securely. These sets are fiddly to set up, so follow the instructions that come with the pack carefully. Once fitted, though, the cables and casings are good quality and last much longer than standard cables. They're worth the extra money and effort.

The advantages and disadvantages of different types of shifters

Shifters come in different types, but they all do the same job. When you move them one way, they pull precise amounts of gear cable to move your chain across your cassette. When you move them the other way, they release a precise amount of cable, allowing the spring in the derailleur to move the chain the opposite way across your cassette.

There are three main types: twistshifters rotate around the handlebars, while triggershifters have two separate levers, one to pull cable and one to release. STi levers on road bikes combine the shifters with the brake levers.

Both twistshifters and triggershifters have loyal fans because, in practice, they both work fine. In situations where your grip is likely to get very slippery, triggershifters have a slight advantage, but twistshifters are less vulnerable to damage in a crash because they don't have any protruding levers. Twistshifters also have fewer moving parts, so they are a little more reliable and can be taken apart and serviced. The internals of triggershifters consist of lots of tiny parts, which were originally assembled by a huge triggershifter-making machine, and are too fiddly to fit by hand. STi shifters are common on almost all road bikes now.

Thumbshifters

Occasionally, you will still come across an old-style mountain bike thumbshifter – a single lever that sits on top of the bars; you push it forward to draw cable through and pull back to release cable. Some of these, like old XTII seven-speed thumbshifters, have a capacity to generate misty-eyed moments of tender memory in old and cynical bike mechanics. They also work really well, performing a simple task in a simple way, without needing exotic materials or computer-aided design. The levers were big and chunky so they could be easily operated with frozen hands . . . with so many advantages, they obviously had to go!

Combination units

Shifters are either separate from the brake lever or part of the same unit. They work the same whether or not they are connected. If you are fitting a combination unit, fit the shifter as if it was separate, then go to the brake chapter for the brake procedure.

Combination units are slightly lighter because brake and gear levers share a clamp, but the positions of the brake and gear levers obviously cannot be adjusted separately.

Having combined brake and gear units also forces you to use the brake system specific to that manufacturer: for example, a Shimano XT combined brake and gear lever will be compatible only with Shimano hydraulic brakes.

Whichever type you have, remember that you are constantly working the shifter back and forth.

The ratcheting mechanism inside, which holds the shifter in your chosen gear, will inevitably wear, so expect to have to replace your shifters every couple of years. The first signs are usually that your shifter fails to stay in your chosen gear, allowing the chain to slip back into the next smallest chainring or sprocket. You'll feel this start to happen first in the gears you use most often.

Whichever type of shifter you have, the derailleur adjustment works in the same way, so use this section to fit your cable or new shifter, clamp the new cable onto the relevant derailleur, then go to the derailleur adjustment section to tune your gears.

◄◄ **Triggershifters use two separate levers to change cable tension**

◄ **With twistshifters, rotating the grip changes the cable tension**

Fitting a new gear cable – triggershifters

Fitting a new gear cable is the easiest and cheapest way to upgrade your shifting. You'll need to arm yourself with a 5mm Allen key and a decent pair of cable cutters, as well as new cable, casing and ferrules for the ends of the sections of casing.

The procedure for changing cables is the same for front and rear shifters. Rear gear cables need changing more often because the section of cable near the back wheel gets filled with dust and mud easily, making your shifting sluggish. For either derailleur, cut off the cable end and undo the cable clamp bolt at the derailleur. Pull the cable gently out of each section of outer casing in turn. Work all the way to the shifter, so that you end up with bare cable hanging out of the end of the shifter.

Follow the three steps below to fit the new gear cable to the shifter, then route the new cable back through the outer casing to each derailleur. It's definitely worth changing the last section of outer casing on rear derailleurs every time, and on any other sections that are kinked, splayed or dirty inside. If in doubt, change it! Cut each new section to length, using the old sections as a guide. Cutting the casing often squashes the lining inside – use a sharp knife to reopen the end of the lining. Fit ferrules to either end of every section of casing.

As you feed the cable through the casing, check that it slides freely. If the inner cable doesn't run smoothly through the casing now, the gears won't work properly when you connect them. Replace any sections of casing that feel rough or sticky when you push cable through them. Take care not to allow the new cable to drag on the ground as you work, it will pick up dirt. Avoid kinks or sharp bends as you feed it through the outer casing. If you must use doughnuts (little protective rubber rings that stop the cable scratching the frame paint), use no more than two and make sure they're black. Feed the wire through the barrel-adjuster on the derailleur.

Check the action of the shifter by clicking through its range while pulling the cable gently away from the shifter – you should feel the shifter pulling cable through in steps. Release it in discrete jumps as you shift back. Replace any hatches that you removed from the shifter. Once you've got the cable fitted and movng freely, go to page 165 to connect the cable to your derailleur.

FITTING A NEW GEAR CABLE

Step 1: The head of the cable may be hidden under a hatch on the back of the shifter, between and above the triggers. Use a crosshead screwdriver to undo the screw and be ready to catch it as it falls out – it's quite short and will run away if you give it a chance. (Some Shimano pods – e.g. XT – have a hatch with two very small crosshead screws. These escape easily too.) Once you've removed the hatch, line up the slot on the barrel-adjuster with the slot on the shifter.

Step 2: Pull the old cable gently away from the shifter. Click the front trigger repeatedly. You'll feel the cable releasing a step at a time as you click. Repeat until you can't click any further – the cable will be in its slackest position. Push the loose end gently into the shifter. In this position, the head of the cable will emerge from the hatch. Pull it out. You may need to twist the cable slightly to free it. For shifters with a slotted barrel, pull the cable gently out of the slot.

Step 3: Without changing gear, look through the hatch from the end of the bar – you'll see the exit hole for the cable. Feed the cable through the shifter, pulling it firmly home so that the head of the cable sits snugly in its nest in the shifter. Next, feed the cable back through each section of outercasing in turn. Drip a drop of oil onto the cable as you feed it through each section, and push theferrule at the end of each section firmly into its cable stop on the frame (see page 165).

Fitting a new gear cable – twistshifters

SRAM GripShift cables have an undeserved reputation for being difficult to fit. The very first models were a bit of a three-dimensional jigsaw puzzle, but current designs are much easier. Check your old casing lengths as a guide to fitting new ones.

Remove old cable and casing, cutting off the old cable about 15cm (6 inches) before it enters the shifter. You'll need to shift into a particular gear to expose the head of the cable. When you look at your gear indicators, one may be a different colour than the others, or one of the numbers may have a circle drawn around it. If all the numbers look the same, shift into the highest number on the right-hand shifter (8 or 9) and into 1 on the left-hand side.

FITTING TWISTSHIFTERS

Step 1: Pull gently on the cable as it enters the shifter through the barrel-adjuster and shift into the correct gear. Remove the escape hatch or slide it to one side (sometimes this needs a little help from a screwdriver or pliers) and look into the shifter. You may see the head of the nipple, or the head of a 2.5mm Allen key grub screw, or a black plastic cover over half the nipple. If it's a grub screw, remove it completely. Careful not to lose the screw – they yearn for freedom.

Step 2: If it's a plastic cover, pry it gently back with a small screwdriver. Push the exposed cable into the shifter. The nipple will emerge through the hatch. Pull the cable out of the shifter.

Step 3: Without moving the shifter, slide the new inner cable in through the shifter. It will not feed in properly if the end of the cable is frayed, so cut off any untidiness. Pull it all the way through, make sure not to let the new cable dangle on the ground and pick up dirt. Replace the 2.5mm grub screw, if there was one, and tighten it firmly onto the nipple. Refit the escape hatch.

Other varieties of twistshifter

Some versions of twistshifters don't have a removable hatch – instead, the nipple is concealed under the edge of the rubber grip. Shift into the highest number on the right-hand shifter, or 1 on the left-hand shifter, and peel back the grip gently just below the row of numbers. You'll see the nipple – push the cable up through the barrel-adjuster and the nipple will emerge from the shifter. Feed the new cable back through without changing gear.

The end of the cable needs to be in good condition to pass freely through the shifter. It's easiest with new cables, which usually have a small blob of solder at the ends to stop them unravelling. Otherwise, use a good pair of cable cutters to make a clean square end on the cable. It can also help to make a slight bend in the cable about 2cm (¾ inch) from the end. Then twist the cable slightly as you feed it through the shifter. As you pull the cable through the shifter, lubricate the last section, which ends up inside the shifter. Jonnisnot, or other similar plastic-specific grease, is ideal.

Fitting drop bar shifter cables

STi shifters were a revelation for road bikes, allowing you to change gear without taking your hands off the bars and reaching for a downtube shifter.

There are two types of shifter. The first has two separate parts to each brake-lever. Swinging both parts inwards towards the centre of the bike pulls cable into the shifter; pushing just the part nearest the bars sideways releases cable from the shifter. Pushing this lever repeatedly inwards slackens the cable. The second kind has a single brake-lever. Swinging this sideways towards the centreline of the bike increases cable tension. There's also a thumb button on the side of the brake-lever body. Pushing this repeatedly releases cable until you reach the 'cable slack' position. The instructions on this page start after you've removed the old gear cable.

REMOVING CABLE FROM STI SHIFTERS

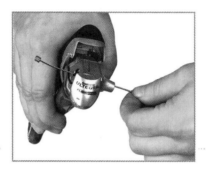
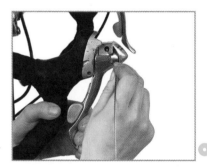

Step 1: Test the shifter action. Pull the gear cable gently towards the centreline of the bike. Operate the two levers in either direction – you should feel that one way pulls cable towards the shifter, the other way releases it in distinct chunks. If the cable skips about, or is reluctant to sit in some of the gear positions, the shifter is worn and will need replacing. Release it all the way by repeatedly operating the lever.

Step 2: Pull the brake-lever in towards the bars. This will reveal the exit hole for the cable. It's directly opposite the entry hole where the outer casing lodges into the shifter. There may be a black plastic cover. Pull it off. Push the exposed cable into the shifter and the nipple will emerge from the other side. Feed the new cable back through the shifter, but don't release the brake-lever until it's all the way through or it will kink the cable.

Step 3: Feed the cable back through each section of outer casing in turn and on into the derailleur. Thread it through the barrel-adjuster on the back of the derailleur. Fit the cable under the cable clamp bolt. There will be a groove on the derailleur or clamp bolt, indicating the correct cable route. Pull through any slack and tighten up the cable clamp bolt with your left. Crimp on a cable end. Now adjust cable tension, see page 148.

Derailleur angle of approach

Check the angle that the derailleur hangs at. The guide jockey needs to sit close under the sprockets, but not so close that the top of the jockey rubs on the bottom of the sprockets in any gear. There should be two clear links of chain between the bottom of the sprocket and the top of the jockey wheel. Turn the B-screw to adjust the gap. Turning clockwise increases the gap, turning anticlockwise will allow the guide jockey to move closer to the sprockets. Too close and the chain will rattle on the sprockets as you ride. Too far and shifting will be sluggish, because the chain will flex sideways when you try to change gear rather than meshing with the next sprocket.

Use the B-screw to sit the guide jockey close to the sprockets, then turn it to adjust the gap to the size you want ▶

Fitting a new cable to the front and rear derailleurs

Fit the new cable into your shifters first, using the instructions on page 162, then follow these steps to connect the cable to your front or rear derailleur. You'll need to adjust the cable tension once you've fitted the cables; see page 148 for rear derailleur, page 157 for front derailleur.

Conventional / top-normal derailleurs (including Shadow)

For the rear derailleur, push the cable through the barrel-adjuster on the back of the derailleur. Lift the back wheel off the ground and turn the pedals so that the chain returns to its neutral position – the smallest sprocket for most derailleurs, the largest for rapid-rise types. For rapid-rise, see below. Screw the barrel-adjuster all the way into the derailleur (turning it so the top of the barrel moves towards you), then back out a couple of complete turns. Look carefully at the cable-pinch bolt; there are often several possible ways to fit the cable under it, and only one of them makes your gears work properly. Look for a groove or a slot indicating the right place. The most common place is on the far side of the pinch bolt, pointing almost straight forward. Once you have the cable in the right place on the pinch bolt, pull it gently to the right, toward the front of the bike. Use the shifters to step all the way down and up through the gears. You should feel the cable pull your hand towards the derailleur as you shift down, then relax so your hand moves away as you shift up. Keeping a gentle pressure on the cable, change all the way up so that the cable is at its most relaxed and your hand is furthest from the derailleur. Guide the cable under the cable-clamp bolt and tighten up with a 9mm spanner or 5mm Allen key. Turn the pedals and shift all the way across the gears and back again. This will shake out any slack, so undo the pinch bolt again, gently pull through any slack cable and tighten the pinch bolt firmly. Cut off excess cable and fit a cable end. Now you have to adjust the indexing; see page 146.

Low-normal (rapid-rise) derailleurs

Push the cable through the barrel-adjuster on the back of the rear derailleur. Lift the back wheel off the ground and turn the pedals so that the chain returns to its neutral position – the largest sprocket. Screw the barrel-adjuster all the way into the derailleur (turning it so that the top of the barrel moves towards you), then back out a couple of complete turns. Pass the cable under the clamp bolt – a groove in the derailleur will indicate the correct place. Use the shifters to step all the way down and up through the gears. You should feel the cable pull your hand towards the derailleur as you shift up, then relax so your hand moves away as you shift down. Keeping a gentle pressure on the cable, change all the way down so that the cable is at its most relaxed and your hand is furthest from the derailleur. Guide the cable under the cable clamp bolt and tighten up with a 5mm Allen key. Turn the pedals and shift all the way across the gears and back again to the largest sprocket. This will shake out any slack in the cable, so undo the pinch bolt again, gently pull through any slack cable and tighten the pinch bolt firmly. Cut off excess cable and fit a cable end.

Front derailleur

Pull gently on the cable and shift back and forth to get familiar with the effect the shifter has on the cable. You need to start with the cable in its slackest position, which will correspond to the chain being in the smallest chainring. Before you fit the cable, check the derailleur is properly fitted on the frame. The derailleur is harder to adjust if it's not fitted correctly. Take hold of the cage and pull it out from the frame so that the outer plate of the cage is level with the outer chainring. You may have to manually lift the chain onto the middle chainring.

The front section of the outer plate of the derailleur cage should be exactly parallel with the chainring. There should be a gap between the top of the chainring teeth and the bottom of the derailleur cage of 1–3mm ($\frac{1}{16}$–$\frac{1}{8}$ inch). If either of these needs adjusting, let the cage spring back towards the frame. Loosen off the derailleur fixing bolt (usually with a 5mm Allen key), move the derailleur, retighten the fixing bolt, and check again. You may need to repeat this several times. Feed the cable under the cable clamp bolt. A very common error is to fit the cable the wrong way around the bolt. Check the derailleur carefully – it has a distinct slot or groove where you are supposed to put the cable. Generally, if the cable comes up from below, it sits behind the clamp bolt. If it comes down from above, it sits in front of the clamp bolt. Keep a gentle pressure on the cable and tighten the clamp bolt firmly, making sure that the entire diameter of the cable is trapped between the clap bolt and the derailleur. Turn the pedals and shift through the gears several times. Don't worry if the chain won't reach the largest chainring at this stage. Shift back into the smallest chainring. Undo the cable clamp bolt, pull through any slack cable by hand and retighten the cable clap bolt. Cut off any excess cable, bend it back so that it doesn't get caught in the chain, and squash on an end cap. Now you will have to adjust the indexing; see page 155.

New cables for STi shifters

Front gear cables on STi levers tend to last for years as they don't get forced around tight bends and aren't used as heavily as rear shifters.

The exit point for the cable is hidden beneath the cowl of the shifter. To access it, you need to pull the lever right back towards the handlebar. The exit hole will be on the outside of the lever blade, directly opposite the point where the outer casing enters the lever. The cable can only be extracted when the gear shifter is set so that the cable is slack.

There are two types of STi shifter. In the first, the brake-lever is in two parts. Swinging both inwards towards the centre of the bike makes the cable tighter; swinging just the back one towards the centreline loosens the cable. In the second, there is a single brake-lever, which you swing inwards to tighten the cable. A thumb button on the inner face of the hood loosens the cable.

FITTING A NEW FRONT DERAILLEUR

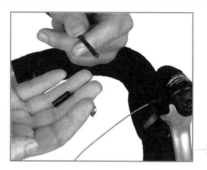

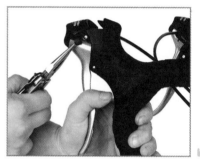

Step 1: Shift into the 'cable slack' position by flicking the inner lever (or thumb button) repeatedly while turning the pedals. Confirm this has got you to the right place by pulling up on the cable where it passes along the downtube or toptube, while changing gear in both directions. Cut the cable end off the old cable, undo the clamp bolt and ease the cable out from underneath it.

Step 2: Pull the end of the outer casing away from its seat in the lever, exposing the inner cable. Pull the cable out of the outer casing, drawing the whole cable through towards the lever. Watch its route as it comes out, so you can feed it back the same way later. Inspect the outer casing as you go along since any bits that are damaged or too short should be replaced. See page 159 for more information on outer casing.

Step 3: Pull the brake-lever towards the handlebars. You can see where the cable enters the lever – it comes out directly opposite and can only be removed when the lever is in its 'cable slack' position. There will either be a little exit hole or a little black plastic cover that will have to come off. You may need pliers.

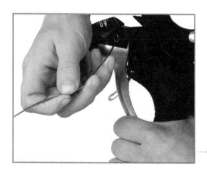

Step 4: Push the old cable through the lever until the nipple emerges from the outer side of the lever. When you can see it, take hold of it and pull it all the way out. If you can't get the cable to emerge, the most likely problem is that you're not in the correct gear. Check and shift again if necessary. If the cable has started to fray inside the shifter, it may help to turn it gently as you twist.

Step 5: Feed the new cable through the lever until the nipple is firmly bedded down. Refit any hatches etc. Check that the shifter is working properly. Take hold of the cable just as it emerges from the shifter and step through the gears with your other hand. If it doesn't index nicely now, it's not going to work with a derailleur attached to it. Shift back so that the cable tension is slack.

Step 6: Feed the cable back through the outer casing all the way back to the derailleur. Fit the cable under the cable clamp bolt. There will be a groove that indicates exactly where the cable should go. Pull up any slack with one hand and then tighten the cable clamp bolt with the other hand. Crimp on a cable end.

Fitting triggershifters

Shifters will wear out over time. The levers can be vulnerable in crashes. Occasionally they have a tendency to get tangled up when you pack your bike into cars, snapping off when you pull them out. It's surprising how crisp new ones feel – you don't notice the old ones getting sloppy and sluggish until you replace them.

New shifters almost always come supplied with a new cable, already fitted, which saves you from having to load the cable into the shifter. It's worth taking a bit of care when fitting the new shifter though – avoid bending the cable where it emerges from the barrel-adjuster. Kinks in the cable will make it difficult to adjust your cable tension accurately. The boxes in which new shifters are packaged are carefully constructed to protect the cable; if you take the shifters out of the box to have a look at them, make sure you repack them carefully until you're ready to fit them to your bike. Don't allow the cable to drag on the ground, where it will pick up dirt. Keep it coiled up until you're ready to fit it into the shifter.

Since you're fitting a new shifter with a new cable, it's worth replacing the outer casing at the same time. The old casing will have picked up dirt, which will quickly transfer itself to the new cable, making it sluggish. Make sure to fit ferrules on either end of each section of outer casing. Some shifters come supplied with outer casing – you'll need good-quality cutters to shorten these to the correct length. Use your old casing as a guide when you cut the new lengths.

Once you've fitted the new shifter, use the instructions on page 165 to attach the cables to your front or rear derailleurs. Left-hand shifters operate front derailleurs, right-hand shifters operate rear derailleurs.

Fitting triggershifters

Remove bar ends and grips. Even if you're replacing the grips at the same time, don't cut them off, because you risk scratching the surface of the handlebar, which can weaken it. The ideal tool is a chopstick – slide this between the grip and the bar, spray light lube under the grip, twist the grip and pull it off the handlebar. (Chopsticks are very useful. Keep any you get with takeout noodles in your toolbox. If

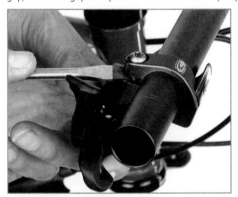

you don't ever get takeout noodles, live a little more.) Slide the grip off the end of the handlebars. Undo the Allen key that fixes the brake lever on, then undo the fixing bolt for your old shifters. Slide both off the ends of the bars. If they won't slide off easily, use a screwdriver to lever the fixing clamps open a little bit – just enough to get the levers and pods off without scratching the bars.

Slide the new shifters on, then slide on the brake levers, easing the clamps open in the same way if neccesary. Leave both fixing bolts loose, then refit grips and bar ends. Everyone swears by different stuff for this – degreaser, hairspray (my favourite), Photomount, Renthal Grip Glue from motorbike shops and more. If you don't have any such gear, pop the grips in a bowl of hot water for a few minutes, then slide them on, taking care not to burn yourself. Sit on your bike in your normal riding position, and roll brake and gear levers around to a comfortable position. If you're not sure, start with the brake levers at about 45 degrees to the ground, with the gear shifters tucked up close underneath them. If you have big hands, you might want to leave a gap between the ends of the grips and the brake levers. Once you've got the position right, tighten both brake levers and gear shifters firmly. Thread the cables through the outer casing, lubricating sections of cable that will end up inside casing with chain oil. Follow the instructions on pages 165 then 148 to attach cables to front and rear derailleurs and to adjust the cable tension.

Check that the grips have stuck firmly – don't ride away until you know they have!

▲ Ease the shifter clamp open to avoid scratching the bars
◀ Experiment with a comfortable angle for the shifters, then tighten the fixing bolt firmly

Fitting twistshifters

SRAM make three different types of shifter. Attack shifters are designed for a 1:2 actuation ratio, and so are compatible with Shimano rear derailleurs. Shifters whose name consists of an x and a number, like x3 and x9, have a 1:1 actuation ratio (so pulling 1mm of cable through the shifter results in the chain moving 1mm to the side) and are only compatible with SRAM rear derailleurs with the same naming scheme. SRAM XX shifters are only compatible with SRAM XX rear derailleurs and SRAM road rear derailleurs like the Rival, Red and Force models.

Fresh twistshifters aren't difficult to fit, especially as new ones come complete with a cable already installed. Keep this coiled up until you've installed the shifter on the handlebar and are ready to slide the cable into its outer casing. This stops it from dragging on the ground, picking up dirt.

As you're installing the shifters, avoid kinking the cable as it enters the barrel-adjuster. It's a vulnerable point until you've supported the cable by sliding it through the outer casing. Remove any bar ends and plugs. Then remove the short section of static grip – the section that stays still when you change gear. If you are replacing it, simply cut it off. Slide in a chopstick or similar instrument gently between the grip and the bar, without scratching the bar. Spray light lube under the grip and slide it off.

Find the clamp bolt for the twistshifters. These have come in a couple of different sizes over the years – usually small! Undo it enough to loosen the shifter – you don't need to remove the bolt completely. Then gently slide the shifter off. Slide the new shifter onto the bar and set its position so that the barrel-adjuster and gear cable run under the brake lever. I like to set the position so that the barrel-adjuster is as close as possible to the brake lever, but you have to leave enough room to turn the barrel-adjuster. Tighten the shifter clamp bolt.

Slide the plastic washer onto the bars so that it sits against the end of the shifter. Next, fit the static grip back on. These are shorter than standard grips, so you need to take extra care that they are firmly stuck. For extra grip, tighten a ziptie around the outboard end of the grip. If this doesn't do the job, your grips are worn out and should be replaced with new, tighter ones. Special short twistshift-compatible versions are available, but they're no cheaper than cutting a standard pair to length with a sharp knife or a pair of scissors.

Refit any bar ends and bar-end plugs

Next, the cable must be threaded through the outer casing. It's worth replacing this when you've got this far. It's only a little extra effort, and saves you transferring old dirt onto fresh cable. New shifters usually, although not always, come supplied with lengths of fresh outer casing. If they don't, pick some up from your bike shop, along with enough ferrules to fit on each end of each section of casing. Cut the

Barrel-adjuster

new sections of casing to length by comparing them with the old sections, fit the ferrules and slot the casing into the cable stops on your bike. Check the length of each section of casing – they should make graceful but not excessive curves. Extra length just adds friction, but if the sections of casing are too short, the casings will kink, squashing the cable inside. Check particularly sections between handlebars and frame, and sections where the casing runs from the main frame of the bicycle to rear suspension section – the cable should be long enough to allow these parts to move freely. Slide the cable carefully through each section, with a little oil on parts that will end up inside casing. Exposed parts of the cable don't need lubrication, excess oil will only serve to pick up dirt. Once you've routed the cable back to the derailleur, use the instructions on pages 165 and 148 to fit the cable to the derailleur and adjust the tension.

◀ **Set the position of the shifter easily, so that you can still turn the barrel-adjuster**

Servicing triggershifters and twistshifters

Crisp gear changes rely on your shifter pulling through and releasing precise lengths of cable every time you change gear. Over time, the teeth that hold the shifter in each individual gear position become worn, so that your shifting becomes vague.

Servicing triggershifters

There's little you can do with triggershifter pods once they are worn out; you can't get parts for them, and even if you could, your fingers need to be about half size if they are to have any hope of fitting them. This is particularly annoying if your shifter and brake lever are integral, as you will need to replace both levers and shifters. I prefer to fit separate brake levers and shifters – combined units are slightly lighter, but it's nice to be able to adjust the positioning of each independently and to replace them separately. Even if you can't service them, popping the cover off and giving them a blast of light oil, like G85, will often freshen them up.

Servicing twistshifters

Only lubricate the shifters with plastic-specific grease, for example, Finish Line GripShift grease. Other lubricants may contain petrochemical traces, which affect the plastic in the componentry. It's easiest to do this job after taking out the old cable and before fitting the new cable. Remove the shifters from the handlebars as described above. Different ones split apart in different ways. Commonly, there's a Phillips head bolt on the part of the shifter that curves down and has the cable coming out of it, which you remove along with the plastic cover through which it bolts. This releases the two halves. Gently pull them apart – you must see how the parts inside are assembled, especially the spring, which is a curved metal strip. This spring must go back in the same place, the same way round – draw a picture if you're not sure. Rocket shifters pull apart by squeezing the tabs at the outer end of the shifter – when fitted to your bike, the bars fit through the middle of the shifter and prevent the shifter from disassembling itself.

Clean the separated parts with soapy water, dry and lubricate with a little plastic grease (see above). Reassemble the parts, according to your drawing (if you have made one). Gently wiggle the two halves back together. This is usually easiest with the shifter set to the lowest position. Refit the plastic cover and bolt, and refit the shifter onto the bar. Fit the cable and proceed as on page 165.

Toolbox

Tools for adjusting your cable tension
- 5mm Allen key

Tools for fitting new cables
- 5mm Allen key, or 9mm spanner
- Good wire cutters

Tools to fit new rear derailleur
- 5 or 6mm Allen key for fixing bolt and cable clamp bolt
- Tools for fitting cables, as above

Tools to fit new front derailleur
- 5 or 6mm Allen key (see above)
- Tools for fitting cables, as above

Tools for fitting or repairing chains
- Good chain tool, e.g. Park or Shimano
- For Shimano–correct (eight- or nine-speed) special replacement rivet
- For SRAM chains – Powerlink

Tools for cassettes
- Chain whip
- Cassette tool
- Large adjustable spanner, to drive cassette tool

Tools for freewheels
- Correct freewheel tool – usually Shimano splined freewheel tool

- Large adjustable spanner, to drive freewheel tool

Tools to fit triggershifters
- 5mm Allen key
- Good wire cutters

Tools for chainrings
- 5mm Allen key for chainring bolts
- Shimano chainring bolt tool (TL-FL21)

Removing and refitting chainsets

Why do you need to remove your chainset? There are several reasons. Either to fit a new one, to fit a new bottom bracket, to tighten your current bottom bracket in the frame, to fit new chainrings or to clean properly behind the chainset. You might also need to access suspension bushings or bolts behind there.

Removing chainsets and cranks – square taper, ISIS and Octalink

◆ Remove both crank bolts. Most cranks are bolted on with an 8mm Allen key. Crank bolts must be snugly fitted, so you need a long Allen key for fitting and removal – use one that is at least 200mm (8 inches) long, otherwise you won't be able to free the bolt or refit it properly at the end. Both crank bolts have conventional threads that undo anticlockwise. Check inside the crank recess for any washers and remove them.

◆ Look into the hole that the bolt came out of. It is one of two types, an older square taper or a newer splined taper, which will look like a notched circle. If you have an older crank extractor designed for square taper axles and a splined taper you need a special plug to pop into the end of the axle, so that the crank extractor doesn't simply disappear down inside the axle without pushing it out. If you need to get one, Shimano makes one: a tl-fc15.

◆ The crank extractor consists of two parts, one threaded inside the other. The outer part bolts onto the threads in the crank, the inner part then gets wound in, pushing the axle out of the crank. Before you fit the tool onto the crank, wind the inner part out so that it disappears inside the body of the tool. Hold the body of the tool steady with one wrench and wind the shaft anticlockwise.

◆ Clean the threads inside the crank and grease them. They are cut into the soft alloy of the crank and must be treated with respect. It's very easy to accidentally strip them with the harder threads of the crank extractor, an expensive mistake to remedy. Start the crank extractor in the crank threads by hand, then tighten home with a spanner. Don't go mad.

◆ Wind in the extractor shaft using the correct size of spanner. It turns quite easily until the shaft touches the end of the axle, then gets harder as it starts to push the axle out of the chainset. Once it's moving through the crank, it should slide off easily. It helps to brace the crank against the spanner so they are as parallel as possible. Keep your arms straight and use your shoulder muscles to apply the force. On the chainring side, keep your knuckles well away from the chainrings – the spanner gives suddenly, and skinned knuckles are common.

◆ Once you've got the cranks off, look at them. Left-hand cranks are particularly prone to damage where they fit onto the bottom bracket axle. The thread is a normal right-hand thread, so if the crank gets a little loose, your pedalling action tends to loosen it further, until every pedal stroke deforms the mating surface between the crank and the bottom bracket axle. Square taper cranks are more prone to this than splined ones, but both need to be checked carefully. If the square taper or splines are damaged, the crank or chainset must be replaced – the taper splines will continue to work loose and will eventually damage the matching surface of your bottom bracket.

Refitting chainsets and cranks – square taper, ISIS and Octalink

Refitting is much easier than removing – the crank bolt acts as a refitting tool, so you won't need the crank extractor. Clean the ends of the axle and the hole in the crank or chainset. Some people like to grease the taper or splines, but I find this just makes the cranks creak as you pedal so I leave them dry. Titanium axles are the only exception to this – they need to be generously coated with Ti-prep or copperslip.

Slide the chainset onto the axle. Grease the threads of the crank bolt and grease under the head of the bolt. The crank bolts for splined bottom brackets use a fatter bolt with a separate washer, which needs a bit of grease on both sides. Older, 14mm spanner-type bolts have an integral washer. Fit the crank bolt and tighten firmly. You will not be able to get enough leverage with a standard length Allen key – use one with a handle that's at least 200mm (8 inches) long. Line the left-hand crank up so that it points in the opposite direction – this can be tricky with splined bottom brackets – and refit the crank bolt.

Retighten both cranks after your first ride.

If you have a torque wrench, this is one of the places where it's most useful – undertightened cranks will quickly work loose. Recommended torques for crank bolts are generally between 35–50Nm. See page 53 for more information on torque settings.

Removing and refitting chainsets compatible with external bottom brackets

External bottom brackets are much simpler to deal with – see pages 256–7 for instructions.

One-key release crank bolt

This part doubles as a crank extractor, so you can remove the cranks with just an 8mm Allen key. The crank cover is aluminium, rather than the standard plastic, and it is screwed into the cranks. The edge of the crank bolt head sits under the crank cover, so that as you undo the crank bolt it bears on the inside of the crank cover and pushes the axle off the crank.

With this, it's even more important to have a good, long Allen key; you won't be able to undo the bolt with an ordinary-length key. Use the Allen key to undo the crank bolt. It will be stiff at first, then will turn quite easily for a short way, and will become stiff again as the crank bolt begins to force the crank off. Keep turning, and the crank will be pushed off the axle. You should take the one-key release gadget off periodically and grease the parts. These tools will only work if the threads are well-lubricated and the parts are clean. There are two small holes in the crank cover that you turn to remove the cover. You can buy a pin spanner to do this job, although a pair of needle-nose circlip pliers also work fine. For fitting and removing details, see page 170.

Chainline

Your chain is at its most efficient when it's running in a straight line. Single-speed bikes are always set up so that the chainring and chain are directly in line with each other to waste as little energy as possible.

For everyone else, in order for gears to work, the chain has to be able to move from side to side across the sprockets and across the chainrings. It will be running at an angle for most gear combinations. The most extreme combinations, in which the chain is on the big chainring and big sprocket, or on the small chainring and small sprocket, should be avoided, as chain, chainrings and sprockets will wear quickly. Setting the position of the chainring so that the middle of the chainset lines up with the middle of the cassette will reduce the angle that the chain has to make to reach all the other positions to a minimum.

The chainset is bolted onto the bottom bracket axle, so changing the length of the bottom bracket will alter its position from side to side. A longer bottom bracket will move the chainset further out, so that it aligns with a smaller sprocket on the cassette, and vice versa. Bad chainline will cause unreliable shifting and accelerate chain wear.

To check your chainline, change gear so that you're in the middle chainring at the front and the middle sprocket at the back (or the fourth smallest for eight-speed sprockets). Look along the chain from behind the bike, so that you can see it pass over the cassette, forwards and then over the chainring. The sprockets and chainrings should be in a straight line. For double chainsets, use the notional mid-point between the two rings. A little bit of an angle is acceptable, but if the chain aligns better in the smallest or largest chainring, you will need to change the length of your bottom bracket to improve your chainline. Also look at the gap between your chainrings and your chainstay. There should be a clearance of at least 3mm ($^3/_{16}$ inch) **(A)** between the chainstay and any part of the chainring. The chainring will flex under pressure and it will eat the chainstay if it's too close.

The position of the chainset on the bottom bracket will vary from model to model, so you may find that changing your chainset alters your chainline, sitting it farther from or nearer to the bike. When swapping chainsets, be aware that you may also need to swap your bottom bracket. To make things a little easier, all chainsets have a recommended bottom bracket length, which you will find printed in the chainset instructions.

Don't let your chainring run too close – it will take chunks out of your frame ▶

Chainrings: removal, sizes, orientation, fitting and wear

All but the cheapest chainsets are made up of a spider and separate rings. The spider is the crank, with four or five arms onto which the chainrings bolt. There have been a number of different sizes and shapes of chainrings over the years, each with plausible reasons for existing, resulting in incompatibility between all the different versions. Whatever the science, it makes sense to take your bike or your old chainring to the shop when you buy a new one to make sure you get the right size.

Chainrings are machined to help the chain move across it when you change gear. The most difficult change for the chain to make is from the smallest to the middle ring, so good-quality middle chainrings are shaped to facilitate the change. They often have little ramps riveted onto the sides to lift the chain when it's halfway across. When the chain moves onto a bigger chainring, it has to lift itself up and over each tooth on the new chainring before it can settle in the valley between two teeth and do some work. Good chainrings are designed to make this shift as easy as possible.

Chainrings under pressure

The chain moves across the chainrings most easily when it's not under too much pressure, so chainrings are designed to encourage the chain to move across when the pedals are at the top or bottom of your pedal stroke, when you put least pressure on them. On many chainrings, these teeth are shorter than the ones on either side to make it easier for the chain to climb over them and drop into place.

It's all right for these teeth to be shorter. Because of their position on the chainring they don't get as much wear as those that are engaged when your pedals are level with the ground. It can be disconcerting though, to buy a new chainset and find that some teeth are shorter than you expect!

Chainsuck

Worn chainrings are a major source of chainsuck (for more on this, see page 174) – and a sign that you've been out riding having fun, so you're going to have to get used to replacing them. Worn chainrings also stretch your chain quickly, so changing them is a good investment.

You should be able to tell that your chainring is worn by looking at it and comparing it to these pictures. If you wait until a chainring is so badly worn that the chain slips across it, you're too late! You will usually find that one ring wears before the others, usually the one you use the most. It's fine to change rings one at a time, they don't have to be done all at once. When changing your cassette and chain, it's a good time to also change your most worn chainring.

Changing chainrings can be done with the chainset still on the bike, but the job is easiest if you remove it, saving yourself from bleeding knuckles too. Follow the instruction in the section on removing your chainset.

Once you've removed the chainset, turn it over to see what type it is. The chainrings are either bolted to the crank arm using an Allen key or in a few cases are attached with a lockring and a circlip.

New chainring

Old chainring

Worn teeth mean the chain slips over the chainring ▶

Replacing chainrings

Chainrings need to be replaced if they start to look like those on the previous page or if your chain skips across the teeth under pressure. The teeth that wear fastest are those under the most pressure – the ones at the top and bottom of the chainring when the cranks are horizontal. If your chainring teeth are worn sharp or the faces of the teeth are splayed outwards, replace the chainring.

Bent teeth will catch on your chain as you pedal, preventing the chain from dropping off the chainring at the bottom of each pedal stroke. This doesn't necessarily mean a new chainring though. Remove the chainring, as below, and clamp it flat in a vice. Support the chainring as near as possible to the bent tooth and ease it gently straight with pliers. Try to do this in one movement – sawing the bent tooth back and forward will weaken it.

REPLACING YOUR CHAINRING

Step 1: The smallest chainring must be removed first. Rest the chainset on a workbench or the floor, protecting the teeth of the largest sprocket with cardboard. Use an Allen key to undo all the bolts on the smallest chainring a half-turn, then go round removing them completely. Look at the orientation of the chainring. Note whether they face inward or outward. If any chainrings have spacing washers, note their location so you can refit them afterwards.

Step 2: Undo each of the Allen keys holding the middle and outer rings a half-turn each, and then go back around and remove them completely. Be careful undoing these bolts; they are hard to shift, then give suddenly, so mind your knuckles. Mostly, an Allen key does the job, but sometimes the nut on the back of the chainring moves around. A special tool, called a chainring bolt tool, is made for holding this and is available from your bike shop.

Step 3: As you remove the chainrings, note their orientation. There will often be a tab on the middle chainring and a peg on the outer chainring – both of these will have to line up with the crank when you refit the chainrings. Check which way the chainrings face – the middle chainring may have plates riveted to the inside face. Check also if there are any washers between the chainrings, as you will need to replace these correctly.

Step 4: Clean the chainrings and check them for wear. You put most force on your pedals when your cranks are horizontal, so the two areas of chainring at 90° to the crank will wear fastest. Hooked or pointed teeth, like the ones in this picture, will not mesh properly with your sprocket. This chainring will need replacing. Take worn chainrings with you when you go to buy new ones, so that you can match up the bolt pattern.

Step 5: Clean the crank, especially the arms that the chainrings bolt onto – clean out the bolt holes. Clean any of the old rings that you reuse. Check them carefully for bent teeth or teeth that have splayed under pressure. Bent teeth can be carefully bent back; the alignment is critical, so take your time about it. Splayed teeth are a sign that the ring needs to be replaced.

Step 6: Reassemble middle and outer chainrings. Be sure to get the orientation and position right – line up chainring tabs with your cranks. If your crank has a chainring bolt underneath it, orientate the chainring so the tab is directly opposite the crank. Refit any washers. Grease the bolt threads and refit them one at a time. Tighten each one firmly home, but don't go mad – the bolts have a fine thread and snap if you overtighten. Refit the smallest chainring.

Chainsuck: causes and remedies

You don't realize how annoying chainsuck is until your bike is infected. Then you can't stop talking about it until it's cured – which can take patience as chainsuck has several different causes and is sometimes caused by a combination of factors.

What is chainsuck?

Normally as you pedal, you push down on the cranks and the teeth on the chainrings mesh with the links on the chain, dragging it forward. The links on the chain also mesh with the teeth on the sprockets, dragging them around, which makes the wheel go around. As each section of chain is dragged around the chainring, it drops off the bottom and is pulled back around again.

Chainsuck happens when the chain fails to drop off the bottom of the chainset and, instead of heading backwards toward the cassette, it stays stuck to the chainring, getting dragged up and around it as you pedal. It rapidly gets jammed in the gap between chainring and frame, the entire drivetrain locks and you fall off your bike. To add insult to injury, the chain often takes chunks out of the chainstay.

The problem usually lies with the smallest chainring, but it can also happen in the middle chainring and sometimes even in the big one.

Worn chain, chainring, or both

When both the chain and chainring are new, the distance between each link in the chain is the same as the distance between each tooth on the chainring. When you put pressure on the pedals, dragging the chain around the chainring, the pressure is taken up by only the top few teeth. The pressure gradually reduces in each link as the teeth progress round the chainring, until at the bottom of the ring the links are released entirely and drop off freely, as intended. The pressure from the pedals is spread over just those few teeth at the top of the chainring, reducing the amount each chainring wears.

Once either chainring or chain is worn, nothing works so well. A worn chain on a fresh chainring engages only a single tooth at the top of the chainring, accelerating chainring wear. The chain links at the bottom of the chain get caught too far back in the valley of the bottom chainring tooth and are dragged upwards. As the chain wears and stretches, the distance between each link expands. As the chainring wears, the valleys between the teeth get wider and deeper, allowing the chain to slip back in each valley under pressure.

Chain and chainring damage

There is only enough room between the sprockets for a straight chain link. A twisted one always catches on the neighbouring sprocket and causes the gears to slip or catch. A twisted link is also a weak point, so sort it out before it busts and strands you in the middle of nowhere. With care, you can spot a twisted link by looking along the chain from behind while backpedalling gently. Check also for stiff links, which can easily cause your chain to slip under pressure, even when everything is adjusted correctly and none of the drivetrain is worn. To check for a stiff link in the chain, turn the pedals slowly backwards, while looking at the chain. Squat beside the bike and hold the lower part of the chain between two fingers. Roll your hand so that one finger is slightly higher than the other. Pedal backwards, so that the chain is dragged between your fingers. You feel stiff links as they pass between your fingertips. Use a good-quality chain tool to spread the outer plates that restrict movement and cause stiff links; see page 140.

To get a good look, remove the chainset from the bike and the rings from the chainset. Check particularly for bent or damaged teeth. You can pick out the areas on each ring where the chain is having problems, as the adjacent chainring will be scarred. Twisted teeth are irritating – they can be tricky to spot, but will hook onto the chain and lift it up and around, rather than releasing it as they should. Bent teeth can be eased back straight with care. File off any tooth or part of tooth that protrudes sideways. Each tooth has a pulling surface, at the front of the tooth at the top of the chainring. When the chain is under pressure, this area of tooth can get splayed so a lip forms on one or both sides. As a temporary fix, these can be filed off, but it's usually a sign that the chainring is worn and needs replacing.

Lubrication and cleaning

First, try cleaning everything – the cheapest option, but one that may make things worse if it proves you have at least one seriously worn component, held together only by its own dirt. Or try an ACSD (AntiChainSuckDevice). This is an ugly aluminium plate that bolts to the bottom of the chainstay tube behind the chainset. Steps on it are shaped to fit the steps around the three chainrings, but without quite touching. The chain gets sucked up behind the chainring and hits a step on the ACSD instead of carving chunks out of your chainstay. ACSDs are a mixed blessing. Sometimes they help, however, sometimes the chain jams in them, and makes everything worse. I recommend finding the source of the chainsuck and sorting it out, rather than hoping the ACSD will bail you out. The only exception is with carbon frames, which should be permanently fitted with protection under the chainstay; chains make grated cheese from expensive carbon chainstays in seconds.

Mountain bike singlespeeds: hubs, chainline, and appropriate gears

Like vegetables, gears are a good thing but sometimes I just want to throw my gears away and eat chocolate instead. And just as it is difficult to explain to someone who has never eaten chocolate what an excellent idea it is, so it is hard to make a convincing case for riding singlespeed (one sprocket, one chainring, no shifters, equals one gear and therefore just one speed). You have to take my word for it – or, better still, try it yourself.

The first amusing thing about riding singlespeed is you instantly lighten your bike without spending a fortune on Space Age materials handcarved by astronomically expensive robots. The second thing is you realize how much ride time you spend faffing around changing gear. Having no distracting gears, you just ride along. Sometimes you cannot speed up because you don't have a high enough gear, and sometimes you have to get off and push because you don't have a low enough gear. These things happen to me on my geared bike as well. The final thing you notice is that riding is much quieter than normal. Still not convinced? That's fine – someone has to read the 'adjusting gears' page to make writing it worthwhile.

There are two big issues. First, what gear to choose. In the end, your personal preference wins, but as a guideline, choose something around 65 inches. Gear size is equal to chainring size over sprocket size multiplied by wheel size in inches – so a 42-tooth chainring with a 17-tooth sprocket on a 26-inch wheel gives you 42/17 x 26 = 64 inch gear – which is as good a place as any to start.

The second big issue is chain tension. The chain mustn't slap or slip, nor can it be so tight that the pedals don't turn freely. Normally, the tension jockey on the rear derailleur does this job. On a dedicated singlespeed bike, the dropouts (where the wheel bolts to the frame) are horizontal, so you can adjust the chain tension by moving the wheel back in the frame. Almost all geared mountain bikes have vertical dropouts, so that the wheel cannot slip forward in the frame even if it isn't done up correctly. If you are converting your existing bike, you probably have to find a way to tension the chain. For initial experimentation, try using your old derailleur.

Fit the derailleur and run the chain through it as normal. If you can, wind in the high end-stop screw so that the top jockey wheel sits directly under the single sprocket. Often the end-stop screw won't go in far enough because it's not designed for this kind of use. Employ a little cunning, and use a piece of cable to hold the derailleur in place. Take a short section of gear cable, still with the nipple attached (it doesn't have to be in particularly good condition, since it's not going to move). Set the barrel-adjuster on the derailleur at the halfway position. Thread the cable through the barrel-adjuster so that the nipple sits in the barrel. Push the derailleur across so that the upper jockey wheel sits just under the single sprocket. Clamp the cable in place under the pinch bolt. Use the barrel-adjuster to set the position of the jockey wheel directly under the sprocket. Remove your chainset and take off the smallest and biggest rings. Refit the middle chainring and the chainset.

Dedicated chain tensioners, which look like half a rear derailleur, are available to buy as well. These will do the same job a bit more neatly.

Refit the chain

If you have vertical dropouts and are reusing the old derailleur to tension the chain, set the chain length quite short, so that the jockey wheels are at 45 degrees to the ground. If you're using a singlespeed chain-tensioner, the instructions in the packet explain how short to make the chain.

If you have horizontal dropouts, shorten the chain to take up all the slack, then adjust the position of the back wheel for at least 10mm (⅜ inch) of vertical movement in the middle of the top stretch of chain. The chain tension will change as you turn the pedals, so find the tightest spot and measure from there.

◀ **Singlespeed – simple and silent**

Singlespeed riding for getting about

Riding singlespeed means no complications with gears. You can't ride too quickly, because you run out of faster gears straight away and there's a limit to how fast your feet can spin around. If you have gears, you're tempted to shift up a gear and go faster. But with only one, you are forced to ride round calmly and arrive at places in your own good time, rather than hot and bothered, having just beaten your own personal best time for the journey for no apparent reason whatsoever.

▲ **Light, cheap and, above all, simple**

Once a niche part of cycling, you can now buy singlespeed bikes off the shelf in a bike shop – they are a common sight on the roads.

You can also make one out of your normal, geared bike. This has its advantages as a maintenance procedure – it mainly consists of taking parts off your bike and stashing them away to be recycled in a future project.

Shifters, cables, and derailleurs can all come off. Your chainset too. If it has removable chainrings, get rid of all but one of them. The chainring bolts that hold everything together will be too long to hold your now single chainring securely, but luckily they're available in a shorter size too. They're called single chainring bolts and you'll need as many as you have arms on your chainset. If your chainrings aren't removable, you can either just continue to use the chainring you have, ignoring the chainrings you're not using, or replace it with a single chainring.

Deciding on your gear ratio can be a bit tricky. It's a case of trial and error and working out what feels good to you. You need a gear that's low enough to get you up the steepest hill you normally climb without busting a gut. It depends on a combination of how fit you are and how flat the area you live in is. Once you've got rid of all the other kit, you need to concentrate on the back end of the bike. If you're converting from a geared bike, you have several potential solutions available to you.

- Simply leave the cassette on the bike, choose a gear that suits you and leave the chain running over that sprocket. With no shifters, the chain will stay put. This is the simplest solution and a good idea on a temporary basis, giving you a chance to experiment with gear ratios.
- Replace your cassette sprockets with a single sprocket and spacers to make up the gap. The DIY version is to use one of the sprockets you've already got and make up spacers from plastic plumbing pipe, cassette spacing washers or whatever else you can come up with. Make sure the washers take up all the available space and clamp it all on with your lockring. There are commercial versions of this such as the Gusset converter.
- If your wheel is on its last legs, replace it with one that has a purpose-built singlespeed hub – those made by Surly are great value, but for bling, check out Phil Wood singlespeed hubs.

The shape of your rear dropout determines what you do next. Look at the dropout and work out what direction the wheel moves in when you take it off the bike. If it moves downwards, you have a vertical dropout. If the wheel moves forwards (or even backwards), you're in luck as this is the easiest to deal with.

Vertical dropouts: these mean you need a gadget to take up the chain slack, a bit like a derailleur but without the guide jockey since you don't need to move the chain sideways. These are called chain tensioners or singulators – although you can use a normal rear derailleur if you're prepared to be a little bit inventive in getting it to hang exactly under your chosen sprocket.

Horizontal dropouts: these don't need to be precisely horizontal – sloping is fine as long as you can move the wheel back and forth in the frame. This allows you precise control over the chain tension. Pull the wheel back until the chain has about 1.5cm (½ in) of movement at its slackest point. Tighten wheel nuts firmly.

Fixed wheel

The step beyond singlespeed is fixed wheel. Fixed wheel bikes are for track and skilled road use only. They are similar to singlespeeds in that they only have one gear – a single sprocket at the back and a single chainring – but there is no freewheel in the back wheel. This is the ratchet that you can hear ticking along when you coast without pedalling on a normal bike. Riding fixed wheel means you have a really direct connection between the pedals and the back wheel and can control the speed of the bike very precisely.

You can slow the bike down just by pedalling more slowly. This feels odd at first. It's very much like pedalling forwards, but you have to put pressure on the pedal when it's at the back of its stroke, rather than the front. Riding fixed takes some practice to do safely as there are a few quirks that can catch you out.

It's often said that, once you learn to ride a bicycle, you never forget. Riding fixed, you have to deliberately unlearn some of the most basic lessons. The trickiest is that you cannot stop pedalling – the wheel will keep on spinning and the pedals are directly connected to it, so they'll keep moving. If you tell your feet to stop, the pedals will catch them and drag them forwards, jerking you with them. This is unsettling – a bit like thinking you've got to the bottom of a flight of stairs and then finding that there's another step. Cornering is another problem area. Cornering at speed usually means leaning into the corner. If you're on a normal bike which freewheels, you can stop pedalling and lift the inside foot up to stop the pedal scraping on the ground. On a fixed model, you can't stop pedalling so you have to judge corners very carefully, otherwise your pedals will slam onto the ground as you lean into the corner and flip you off the bike.

As well as going along and cornering, there's another potential problem as well – stopping. Fixed wheel bikes were inherited from track racing, where fit people on sparse track bikes hurtle round banked wooden tracks at unfeasible speed in the kind of tight bunches that means it's in everybody's interests to stay upright. Brakes in this situation are a liability – as long as everybody is moving at the same speed, there's hope of keeping your place in the pack. The last thing you want is for the person in front of you to panic and haul their brakes on. The gaps between each rider can be inches and there would be no time to take evasive action. Bikes that have been built for the track may not have brakes at all or, if they do, they've just been stuck on there to make the bike legal to sell.

Transferring the bike onto the streets involves different demands. Your biggest danger is a truck turning left in front of you, not the potential for inadvertently bringing down somebody riding right up your tail, so it's essential to fit some properly working brakes. Many people make do with just a front one, because you can use the pedals to slow the back wheel down. Some riders take it to the extreme and have no brakes at all, relying on controlling the speed of the back wheel alone to stop them. This is just stupid. It does make the bike look lean and mean, until you wrap it around something you should have been able to avoid. It may then still look pretty if it was a nice colour to begin with, but it won't work very well. Fit proper brakes.

You can buy singlespeed road bikes fitted with a fixed rear hub (or a 'flip-flop' hub, fixed on one side and with a freewheel on the other, simply take the wheel off and flip it around as necessary) off the shelf (or from several internet retailers) or make one by removing all unnecessary complications from a (usually old) geared bike. The one essential requirement for a conversion to fixed wheel riding is horizontal dropouts for the rear wheel. Since most modern frames are built with vertical dropouts, this restricts you to old road frames, and newer frames that have been specifically designed for singlespeed riding.

It's essential to use the right kind of hub with fixed wheel.

As well as a normal, right-hand thread for the fixed sprocket, it also has a slightly smaller reverse thread. This is for the lockring. The lockring must be tightened securely against the fixed sprocket, stopping it from unwinding when you put pressure on the pedals to slow down and stop.

It's essential that the threads on the fixed sprocket, the lockring and the hub are in good condition, so that there is no possibility of the sprocket working loose under the constantly reversing pressures from your pedal. Don't be tempted to make up a fixed hub out of a normal freewheel wheel and any likely-looking lockrings you may have lying around – the reverse thread on a fixed-specific hub is essential for holding everything safely together.

It may seem from this that riding fixed is anachronistic and more trouble than it's worth, but it does feel fantastically direct and makes any journey more exciting.

Hub gears

Hub gears have gone through all the highs and lows of fashion during the last few decades. There was a time when they were the only sensible choice for town bikes, propelling deliveries, shoppers and tourers alike. The unquestioned favourite choice was the Sturmey Archer three-speed hub, which could be relied upon to work fine for years under a regime of neglect and would last for decades if an occasional teaspoon of 3-in-1 was poured into the oil port on the hub.

Each one was stamped with the month and year of manufacture and it's not uncommon to come across hubs from the 1930s still happily chugging along. But with mountain bikes, emerged a desire for more and more gears and suddenly bikes with only three fell out of favour. Bikes with a plethora of close ratios made the big gaps between three seem clunky. Sturmey Archer, based in Nottingham, upped and sold all its machinery to the Far East and it seemed like hub gears were history.

But all was not lost. Some aspects of hub gears are just too attractive to ignore, especially for around town. Having a single chainring at the front makes it easy to fit an effective chainguard, reducing the amount of chain oil on your clothes. The city is also a particularly harsh environment for exposed gears, which tend to pick up all the nasty chemicals that get spat out of the back of cars in traffic and use them as a grinding paste, reducing expensive derailleur components to waste within a couple of thousand miles. Derailleurs also have plenty of delicate dangly bits, which don't respond well to being tangled up in big piles with other bicycles. So there are a lot of good arguments for tucking the complicated gear mechanism away inside the hub.

There is also a spectacularly bad argument for using hub gears, which is that they don't need any maintenance. While it may be true that they need a lot less attention than derailleur bikes, it's expensive to completely ignore them. Most damage is done when they get ridden around out of adjustment. The internal gear mechanism is made up of lots of tiny cogs and pawls. When these are all correctly aligned, they wear very slowly, but slight misalignments can cause rapid wear. This is where the problems start – as they wear, the cogs generate lots of tiny flakes of metal. Since the hub is enclosed, these have nowhere to escape to, and so travel around the internal mechanism, wearing away everything they come across. However, adjusting your hub to run smoothly has been made very simple and can usually be done with no tools at all. The most important thing is to be alert to possible problems. If your gears start to feel sluggish, don't change as quickly as you're used to or start changing randomly as you're riding along, check the adjustment straight away.

There are other simple procedures that can also be carried out without special tools. Changing the sprocket is not nearly as complicated as it looks. It's a good idea to change the sprocket every time you change the chain, since they wear together and putting a new chain on an old sprocket will wear your nice new chain very quickly.

Another good reason to change the sprocket on your hub is to change your range of gears. You can't change the gap between each gear as this is determined by the internal mechanism, but you can change where the range starts and finishes. Changing your sprocket for a slightly larger one will make all the gears slightly lower. The gaps will remain the same, but each one will be easier.

Changing the size of the sprockets also affects chain length. Minor changes – say one tooth more or less – can usually be accommodated by shifting the rear wheel backwards or forwards in its dropout (since you don't have a derailleur to take up the slack, this is the only way of ensuring the correct chain tension). If you're fitting a smaller sprocket, you can shorten your chain slightly. A larger sprocket will require a longer chain. It's usually more successful to fit a complete new chain than to try to add links from another chain as the uneven amount of wear in the links means the chain will be unlikely to mesh smoothly with the sprocket or chainrings. Luckily, decent chains for hub gear bikes are around half the price of a similar-quality derailleur chain and last twice as long. They don't have to move sideways across a cassette or chainset and always run in a straight line from sprocket to chainring.

Hub gears are also an excellent choice for folding bikes with small wheels because the absence of a derailleur means there's less to get caught up when you're collapsing or reassembling your machine. Keeping all the oily messy gear parts inside the hub makes you a more popular commuter too, being less likely to leave black stripes on other people's luggage in crowded train compartments. As well as the more traditional three-speeds, seven- and eight-speed versions have a wide enough range of gearing to get you up and down most hills. A 14-speed hub, by Rohloff, gives as wide a range as you'd get with a triple chainset, with smooth, close gaps between each gear.

Adjusting hub gears

Keeping hub gears adjusted correctly is the single most important piece of maintenance you can do to them. You'll most likely feel it if the adjustment starts to drift out and your bike may even take it upon itself to start shifting randomly when you least expect it. Be alert for any changes in the quality of your shifting and re-adjust sooner rather than later. Badly adjusted hubs will wear very quickly, requiring the replacement of expensive internals.

If these simple adjustments fail, it almost always indicates that some of the internal workings of the hub are already badly worn and will need to be replaced. This is the kind of fiddly job it's worth having your bike shop do – mainly because the range of different hubs has grown to such an extent that ordering exactly the right spare parts can be a bit trial and error.

These instructions are for the 2006 Shimano eight-speed hub, but the general principles apply across all their hubs. All Shimano hubs have one common method of adjustment. The cable starts at the shifter on the handlebar and ends at a cassette joint on the right-hand side of the hub. Shifting gear pulls the cassette joint around the hub in distinct steps, corresponding to the number of gears. One of the gears is always marked differently on the shifter. The number may be written in a different colour or have a circle around it. Set the shifter in this gear to adjust the cable tension.

The cable is the correct tension in this gear when the two halves of the cassette joint – the odd-shaped collection of plates that sits in the middle of the back wheel, between the sprockets and the frame – line up. They're made with coloured tabs, so that you can get the alignment right.

These tabs can sometimes take a little bit of finding as they're quite small and can be covered in road dirt. They may simply be short fingers of metal marked by a red stripe or they may be concealed beneath a tiny plastic window on the cassette joint. Once you've found the tabs, lining them up is simple. There will usually be a barrel-adjuster on the shifter – turn this and experiment to find out which way brings the tabs further apart and which way brings them closer. The alignment needs to be precise, with the two coloured tabs in as straight a line as possible, so you'll find yourself making quarter- and even eighth-of-a-turn adjustments to find the right place.

There are two possible locations for the barrel-adjuster. It may be on the shifter, where the cable emerges, or on the other end of the cable near the rear wheel. You may even have one at either end. It doesn't make any difference which one you use, but if you've got a choice, use the one near the rear wheel, since it's easier to see the adjustment tabs from there.

ADJUSTING SHIMANO 8-SPEED HUBS

Step 1: Here you can see the number 4 on the shifter is written in red. This indicates that the hub should be adjusted with the shifter set to this position. This is the most common way to pick out the right gear to do the adjustment in, but another possibility is that the chosen gear may have a circle around it. Twistshifters work in exactly the same way – just set the shifter so that it's lined up with the differentiated number.

Step 2: This view is looking down from above into the gap between the rear hub and the frame. In this case the tabs are underneath a clear plastic window – you'll have to wipe the window clean of road dirt before you can see the tabs clearly. Older hubs have two small exposed fingers of metal with a red stripe painted on each. You can see here that the two stripes are not in line – the right one is slightly lower.

Step 3: If you look at where the cable emerges from the shifter, you'll see the barrel-adjuster, which alters the tension in the cable. Turn the barrel-adjuster gently, while looking down into the gap and watching the tabs. You'll see them move relative to each other. It's not worth trying to remember which one has what effect – just turn so that they get closer, rather than further apart. When they're exactly lined up, stop.

Removing hub gear wheels

Hub gears often make people particularly nervous about the possibility of having a rear wheel puncture. Follow the instructions below and you needn't worry.

It's isn't always particularly obvious how to disentangle the gear cable enough to get the back wheel on, or how to reattach the gears once you've successfully repaired the puncture.

It's a little different to the procedure for derailleur gears, but luckily can be done with a minimum of tools. The main difference between hub gears and derailleur gears is that the gear cable is actually attached to the rear hub, so it has to be wriggled free before the wheel can be removed.

Be warned though, there's a slight added complication when refitting the wheel too – the position of the rear wheel in the frame needs to be set in such a way that the chain has the right amount of tension.

REMOVING THE REAR WHEEL – NEXUS HUB GEAR

Step 1: Take a moment to look into the gap between the rear wheel and the frame while you change gear. You'll be able to see the cassette joint stepping around the hub as you shift gear. Once you can see the effect that changing gear has on the cassette joint, set the shifter so that the cable is in its slackest position, where the indicator is pointing at gear 1.

Step 2: This is the most important step and the one that everybody misses out. It's essential that, when you come to refit the cable, it's correctly routed. However, once everything's come apart, it's not obvious how it goes back together. Take a moment to look at the cassette joint from behind and trace where the cable goes, so that you can put it back there later. If you haven't got a photographic memory, make a sketch.

Step 3: Look at the cassette joint from behind. You'll see a tiny hole, just below the cable clamp bolt. It's just the right size for a 2mm Allen key. Poke the key into the hole and use it as a lever, gently turning the cassette joint anticlockwise to create slack in the cable. It can be tempting to do this with your fingers, but don't as the spring inside the hub is strong and, if you slip, you'll definitely end up with sore fingers.

Step 4: Keep the Allen key in position, holding the cassette joint. This gives you enough slack in the cable to pull the gear outer casing gently to the right and out of the end of the cassette joint, as shown. There should now be enough slack to pull the inner cable out of the slot in the cassette joint. Release and remove the Allen key.

Step 5: You should now have enough slack in the cable to allow you to wriggle the cable pinch bolt completely free of the cassette joint. Note which way it sits before you release it so you can get it back into the same place afterwards. You'll have to use both hands to twist the cable, easing the pinch bolt out of its slot. Take care not to kink the cable.

Step 6: This leaves the gear cable completely free of the back wheel. With V-brakes and cantilevers, release the brake cable. If you have hub brakes, remove the bolt that holds the hub brake arm onto the frame/fork. It's essential to remember to refit these when you come to refit the wheel. Undo the wheel nuts on either side of the frame and slide the wheel forward and out of the dropouts.

Refitting the rear wheel

Refitting the back wheel simply means reversing the removal procedure. It's worth checking the gear alignment, as the cable may settle into a slightly different place.

It only takes a moment at the end of this process to reassure yourself that the adjustment is correct. In the unlikely event that the adjustment has slipped, it will save you the damage that riding on slipping gears does to them and to you.

The key to refitting the back wheel is to get the chain tension correct before you start messing around with the gears. Chain tension is automatically sorted out for you with derailleur gears as the rear derailleur takes up any excess slack in the chain.

With a single sprocket, you have to do this as you refit the wheel. It is for this reason that hub gear bikes (and single-speed bikes) have a horizontal dropout (see toolbox on page 182).

REFITTING THE REAR WHEEL

Step 1: Hold the wheel in the back end of the frame between the chainstays and loop the chain around behind the sprocket. Pull the back wheel back into the dropouts. If you removed any nuts and washers, replace them. On many Shimano hubs, these will be left- and right-specific with a tab that sits in the dropout to hold the axle at the correct angle. Locate the washers neatly in the dropouts. Tighten the wheel nuts by hand.

Step 2: Pull the wheel back in the frame to take up frame slack. It must be straight in the frame, with equal spacing between the tyre and the chainstay on either side. The chain needs to be almost tight. Pedal backwards to find the tightest point and make sure that you can still move the middle of the chain, halfway between the sprocket and the chainring, up and down 1.5cm ($^1/_2$ in). Tighten both wheel nuts securely. Refit brakes.

Step 3: Before you go any further, check the condition of the gear cable. The outer casing should be free from splits or kinks and should be long enough so that you can turn the bars in both directions without stretching it. Check that the cable pinch nut is tight on the cable. You'll need two spanners: one to hold the back still, the other to tighten the nut on the front.

Step 4: Before fitting the cable back into the cable stop, take the cable pinch nut and fit it back into the cassette joint. It will only fit into its nest at one particular angle and you'll have to roll it slightly further anticlockwise than you'd expect. Seat it securely and then route the cable back around the back of the cassette joint. There will be a groove for it to sit in. It should follow a straight path down and around.

Step 5: As and when you removed the cable, pop a thin Allen key into the hole in the cassette joint and roll it around anticlockwise. This should give you enough slack to refit the outer casing back neatly into its cable stop. Shift through the whole range of gears and check that the cassette joint moves around with each click.

Step 6: Finally, check the cable tension. In theory, the hub shouldn't need adjusting, but in practice the cable often settles back out of place. This has to be done in a specific gear. Look at the shifter – one of the gear indicator numbers will be a different colour to the others. Shift into this one. Check the gear alignment tabs are lined up exactly. If they're not, use the barrel-adjuster at the shifter, turning it until the tabs are aligned.

Replacing the hub sprocket

While hub gears can get along fine with far less attention than derailleur geared versions, it's a mistake to think that this means that they can be neglected.

Just as on a bike with derailleurs, hub gears mean that you're constantly putting pressure on the chain as you pedal and that inevitably means that the chain, sprockets and, to a lesser extent, the chainrings will wear out.

If left for too long, you will reach a point where the chain will slip over the sprockets under pressure. This is irritating at the best of times and dangerous in busy traffic. Chains are relatively easy to replace, but sprockets on the most common hubs are trapped behind a handful of hub-gear specific mystery components. These need a little care to remove and it helps a lot when you come to reassembly if you concentrate on the order and orientation of the parts that come off.

Sprockets are worn when the teeth start to get very sharp or when the two sides of the teeth don't look symmetrical. You may also find that the pressure of the chain on one face of each tooth has caused the surface of the tooth to splay outwards, making sharp lips at either side. It's not worth waiting until the chain links actually starts slipping over the sprocket before you replace them. By that time the worn sprocket will already have started to damage the rest of your transmission.

You'll need a tool that you don't often come across in bicycle repair toolboxes: circlip pliers. These are only useful for one job, which makes them a bit irritating to invest in, but it's difficult to do the job without them. People do improvise with screwdrivers, but it's far too easy to slip and stab your own fingers with the end of the screwdriver. Invest in the proper tool. These come in two variations: external and internal. External circlip pliers prise a circlip off the outside of a tube whereas internal ones lift them out of a groove on the inside of a tube. The kind you need here are external circlip pliers. You can get cheap versions that are supposed to be able to do both, but they're usually fairly wobbly at either end and so quite difficult to use and, if they slip in the middle of getting a circlip off, they'll most likely take a vindictive bite out of your fingers at the same time.

A completely different reason for changing a sprocket would be to alter your gear ratio. The steps between each gear can't be changed as they're determined by the design of the internal parts of the hub. But the entire range of gears can be shifted in either direction, since this is determined by the ratio of the chainring size to the sprocket size. You can change either of these – fitting a larger chainring has the same effect as fitting a smaller sprocket, both will make all your gears a little bit higher. You'll be able to ride faster on downhill sections, but will struggle a little more getting up steep ones.

All the pictures below right show Shimano hubs. They're the most common type, but there are others. SRAM have been making internal hubs for many years, which are reliable and last for many thousands of miles.

The same sprockets fit on both types of hub. SRAM ones are held on by a similar circlip arrangement, but it's easier to get to. The SRAM hubs don't use a cassette joint, so the circlip and sprocket are revealed as soon as you remove the back wheel.

DROPOUTS – vertical and horizontal – the merits and differences

This is one of those terms that sounds more complicated than it is. The dropout is the slot in the frame that the wheel bolts onto – it's the same word for the front and back wheels. Traditionally, the slots on the rear wheel dropout were almost horizontal, allowing you to slide the rear wheel back and forward in the frame. However, this is unnecessary for derailleur gears, since the derailleur takes up the slack in the chain and so vertical dropouts became more common. They provide a very secure fitting, since you cannot pull the rear wheel out of the dropout however hard you stamp on the pedals. This is a particular problem when the wheel nuts/quick-release levers aren't done up tightly enough or break, pulling the back wheel out of its slots and jamming it on the chainstays.

Swapping hub sprockets

Ideally, you should swap the sprocket every time you replace the chain. If you put a new chain on an old sprocket, you'll wear the new chain out fairly quickly.

Sprockets are available in a range of sizes and usually have a slight dish. This means they sit slightly off to one side when you fit them onto the hub. This allows you to line up the sprocket with the chainring so the chain makes as straight a line as possible between the two, reducing the amount it wears. Take note of which way the old sprocket faces when you remove it so you can get the new one back on correctly. There's only one common fitting for the sprockets, making them simple to interchange.

You'll have to remove the gear cable and then the wheel – as on page 180 – to get access to the sprocket. Remove the nut and all washers from the right-hand side of the axle, keeping a note of the order and orientation.

SWAPPING HUB SPROCKETS

Step 1: The cassette joint sits over the centre of the sprocket and so has to come off first. It's removed in layers. Correct removal and refitting depend on lining up a series of dots and arrows on the cassette joint. The first layer is a locking ring. It comes off anticlockwise. Steady the cassette joint by holding the cable stop and turn the lockring gently. It only moves about a quarter-turn and then lifts off.

Step 2: The next layer is of yellow dots. Look carefully at the next layer of the cassette joint and you'll see it's made up of two parts. Both parts have yellow dots printed on them. If there's lots of road dirt floating about, you may have to clean it off. Hold the back of the cassette joint steady with the cable stop and then turn the top layer of the cassette joint until all the yellow dots are aligned. It will now simply lift off.

Step 3: Repeat the procedure with the red dots that are now exposed, taking off the last layer of the cassette joint. Lay the parts out in the order they came off, all facing upwards so that you know how they need to be replaced. Wipe all the parts clean as it makes them easier to get back together if there isn't grit in between the layers.

Step 4: Next is the tricky bit where you'll need your circlip pliers. Locate the circlip – it's the ring of metal pressing onto the face of the sprocket. It may be a round section or a square section. It doesn't quite make a complete circle. Locate the gap, slip the noses of the pliers into the gap and squeeze the pliers to open out the circlip enough so that you can lift it up off the hub. Don't get in there with your fingers or it will bite you.

Step 5: Before you lift the sprocket off, check which way it faces – it's not usually flat. Now you can lift the old sprocket off and replace it with a new one, facing the same way as before. Line the three lugs on the sprocket up with the grooves on the hub and ease it into place. Lever the circlip back into place with a small screwdriver, keeping fingers well clear.

Step 6: Replace the first layer of the cassette joint, lining up the red dots and wriggling until it fits snugly. Repeat with the yellow dots. Finally, the lockring fits over the top and then twists to lock in place. It only needs a quarter of a turn or so to lock it, but if it won't move, don't force it. Instead, remove and recheck the previous layers fit snugly. Replace washers and nuts and replace the wheel (page 181).

Troubleshooting transmission

Symptom	Cause	Solution	Page
Chain slips, giving way suddenly under pressure	Worn cassette and chain	Measure chain for wear, replace if necessary, replace cassette at the same time	137, 141, 143
	Worn chainrings	Replace chainrings	172-3
	Damaged teeth on chainring	Realign bent teeth back	N/A
	Worn or damaged freehub body	Replace freehub body	199
	Twisted chain links	Straighten or remove twisted link	68
	Dirty or dry chain	Clean and lubricate chain	135-6
	Badly adjusted rear indexing	Adjust cable tension	148
	Incompatible chain, cassette or chainrings	Ensure compatability, especially between chain and cassette – don't mix eight- and nine-speed components	134
Rear derailleur doesn't index correctly	Incorrect cable tension	Tighten lockring and adjust gears	148
	Dirty cable	Clean and re-lubricate cable/ replace cable and casing	159, 160, 162, 165
	Split outer casing	Replace casing	159
	Bent derailleur	Replace derailleur	151
	Bent derailleur hanger	Replace or bend back hanger	153
	Shifter worn	Disconnect cable from derailleur and test operation of shifter while pulling on cable as it emerges from shifter – replace if necessary	148, 154, 166-9
	Cassette lockring loose, so that sprockets can move around on freehub body	Adjust cable tension	148
Rear derailleur usually indexes correctly but suffers ghost shifts when being ridden	Casing too short from handlebars to frame, or between sections of full suspension frame, so that movement of bars or frame tenses cable	Replace sections of outer casing with longer ones – you may also need to replace cable – ensure that casing cannot snag on parts of the frame	154, 159, 162, 165
	Chain worn	Measure chain wear, replace chain and cassette if necessary	137, 143
Chain won't shift into smallest or largest sprocket	End-stop screws are too far in	Undo end-stop screws so that chain can shift into the extremes of the cassette	149
	Incorrect cable tension	Adjust cable tension	148
	Guide jockey wheel too far from sprockets	Adjust B-tension screw	150

Symptom	Cause	Solution	Page
Rear gears index properly on smaller sprockets, but not on larger ones	Derailleur hanger bent	Replace or bend back hanger	153
	Chainline incorrect	Chainset too far out – fit shorter bottom bracket	170
Front derailleur doesn't index correctly	Incorrect cable tension	Adjust cable tension	155
	Incorrect front derailleur position	Adjust front derailleur so that the outer plate is parallel to the chainring, with 2–3mm of clearance between chainring and derailleur	155, 157, 158
	Bent derailleur	Bend back or replace derailleur	157, 158
	Dirty or corroded cable	Clean or replace cable	160, 162, 165
	Frayed cable	Replace cable	162, 165
	Split or kinked outer casing	Replace outer casing and cable	159, 162, 165
	Worn or broken shifter	Disconnect shifter from derailleur, pull gently on cable as it emerges from shifter, operate shifter to check for three distinct positions – replace if necessary	166-9
Shifting sluggish	Worn chain	Replace chain and cassette	141, 143
	Worn derailleur pivots	Clean and lubricate derailleur, replace derailleur	157, 158
	Ferrules missing from ends of sections of casing	Ensure that there's a ferrule at each end of each section of casing to help prevent the casing from shifting in the cable stops	159
	Cable in wrong position under clamp bolt	Remove cable and inspect area under clamp bolt – the correct position for the cable will be indicated by a groove in the derailleur	165
	Brake casing used instead of gear casing	Always use correct gear casing – brake casing is stronger but will compress slightly under load, causing erratic shifting	159
Front derailleur won't shift into largest sprocket	'High' end-stop screw too far in	Undo 'High' end-stop screw to allow chain to shift onto large chainring	156
	Chainset sits too far out from frame, so that derailleur cannot reach at full extension	Fit shorter bottom bracket or fit chainset that sits closer to frame	170
	Incorrect cable tension	Increase cable tension	165
Front derailleur won't shift into smallest sprocket	Incorrect cable tension	Reduce cable tension	155
	'Low' end-stop screw too far in	Undo 'Low' end-stop screw to allow chain to drop into smallest sprocket	156
Chain drops into middle or smaller ring randomly	Worn shifter	Replace shifter	166-9

6 – Wheels

The quality and condition of your wheels make more difference to your bike than any other single thing. After all, you only need your gears when you want to change how fast they spin and you only need your brakes to stop, but your wheels are going around all the time you're going along. Treat them right and they'll roll along without complaining. Neglect them and they'll make every climb feel like a vertical wall and every corner feel like you're riding on jelly. It's not as hard as you might think to build your own, either.

How to remove and refit wheels

Even if you do no maintenance on your wheels at all, it's important that you know how to take them off so that you can fix punctures and even more vital to be able to refit them securely. If you're not confident, ask your bike shop or an experienced rider to go through the procedure with you.

The standard quick-release lever was designed for road-racing bicycles. It's a great system, allowing you to lock your wheels in place without tools. But the original designers of the quick-release lever had no idea what we would be doing with bicycles now. Suspension for bicycles existed already, but was a feature of butchers' and postmen's bikes, and they seldom tended to use their machines for hurtling around off-road with 6 inches of suspension. The design has been modified along the way to make the fitting more secure – the 'lawyer tabs' at the bottoms of your fork dropouts force you to undo your quick-release lever nut a few turns before you can release the wheel. This gives you a little more time to notice that something is wrong before your front wheel jumps out and plants you face first in the dirt. Similarly, the move away from horizontal rear dropouts, which allowed you to adjust the chain tension to avoid dropout, was necessary to make wheels more secure. Once common on mountain bikes, these are now seen only on singlespeed-specific frames.

On mountain bikes, many suspension forks and the back of some suspension frames now come with a quick release 'through-axle'. This system is considerably stiffer and more secure, and is designed to resist the heavy forces that disc brakes are capable of applying.

The two most common systems are the RockShox Maxle and the Fox QR15. The Maxle system uses a 20mm through-axle on a 110mm wide front hub, while the QR15 system uses a 15mm axle on a 100mm wide front hub. Each type requires a matching fork and a dedicated hub to take the through-axle. Compatible hubs are available from Shimano and a range of other manufacturers. For Maxle rear ends, RockShox also make a 12mm rear Maxle. If you find that your skewers work loose, take your bike to your shop for a second opinion.

There is some disagreement about the best position for the lever. Traditionally, quick-release skewers were oriented so that the lever was on the left-hand side of the bicycle, and lay along one of the stays to prevent it getting caught. This is another legacy of road racing – the levers were always placed on the same side to save vital seconds after crashes – your mechanic could leap out of the team car and run with your wheel, already knowing which side your lever was on to reduce delay. Nestling the levers against the chainstay reduced the chances of your lever becoming entangled with someone else's bike and accidentally releasing your wheel.

On mountain bikes, it's important that the levers don't point straight forward, because they could get caught on a branch as you ride past and flip open. I prefer to fit them on the opposite side to disc rotors, as this reduces the chances of getting burned when fixing punctures. But the shape of your forks will often dictate where the skewer can fit, especially if there are adjusting knobs or fitting bolts behind the dropout. The most important thing is to ensure that the levers are firmly fitted. A ziptie around the skewer as an extra line of defence does no harm – I especially like Shimano XT skewers for this, as they already have a handy hole in them that's the perfect size.

FITTING QUICK-RELEASE LEVERS SECURELY

Step 1: Your skewer and locknut should have deep, sharp serrations to grip the frame. A spring sits on either end of the skewer, with the small end pointing inwards. To secure the skewer, fold out the handle until it points straight out from the frame. Hold the handle and tighten the locknut on the other end finger tight. Fold – don't twist – the skewer handle, so that the 'closed' label points outwards.

Step 2: The lever should resist being closed. If it closes easily, flip it open again, tighten the locknut, then fold the handle closed. If the handle won't close fully, flip it open, loosen the locknut and fold closed. Once you're satisfied, flip open the lever again and twist locknut and skewer the same amount, in the same direction, so that when you close the handle it lies beside the frame or fork.

Through Axles: Both the RockShox Maxle and Fox QR 15 systems work by threading the axle through the dropout and hub and screwing into the opposing dropout. The remaining slop is then taken up by firmly closing the quick-release lever. Each type will only work with dedicated fork and matching hub but the extra security and increased stiffness are well worthwhile.

Hubs: bearings

Bearings have been around since Roman times and appear in working drawings by Leonardo Da Vinci. His design for an early tank featured a device for enabling the gun turret to turn in different directions. He rested the upper part of the structure on a circle of wooden balls that allowed it to turn freely and support the weight (wood isn't the best bearing material, but is still used in cycle track racing rims). The modern ball bearing pioneer was Sven Wingquist, a visionary Swedish inventor who founded the SKF bearing company in 1907. The company still produces quality stainless steel bearings.

There are bearings in the centre of your wheels. They take different forms, ranging from handfuls of cheap steel balls to fancy sealed units, but they all do the same job – keep the wheel securely fixed onto your bike with no side-to-side movement, while allowing it to spin as freely as possible. Well-adjusted bearings run for years without complaint. Bearings that are too loose or too tight slow you down either way and wear out in no time, so it pays to check them regularly.

▲ Shimano Deore rear hub

Pick up each wheel and spin it gently. It should continue rolling a couple of times on its own, even after a really gentle spin. If it slows down quickly, first check that the brake blocks or pads are not rubbing on the rim or rotor, which can have the same effect as overtight bearings. If that's the problem, go to the brakes chapter and sort them out first, then come back to bearings. If the brakes aren't the problem, then your bearing is too tight and it's slowing you down. Put the wheel down again and crouch beside the bike. Hold the rim of the back wheel where it passes between the stays (seatstays or chainstays on a hardtail, otherwise whatever lies between the main frame and the back wheel). Just pinch the rim between your thumb and finger. Hold onto the nearest bit of frame with your other hand and rock your hands toward and away from each other, pulling the rim toward the frame then pushing it away.

The rim may flex slightly, but that's not what you're looking for. You need to check if there's a knocking feeling, or even a clicking noise, as you pull the rim back and forth. This indicates movement between the bearings and the surfaces supporting them, and means the bearings need adjustment.

Repeat with the front wheel, holding the rim where it passes through the fork and rocking gently across the bike. Again, the rim may flex slightly, but it shouldn't knock at all. The wheel should spin freely, gradually slowing down over a couple of revolutions.

Bicycle wheel bearings can be divided into two types:
- ◆ **Cup-and-cone:** Traditionally, bicycle bearings were of the cup-and-cone type – a cone-shaped nut on the axle traps a ring of bearings into a cup-shaped dip in the hub. The cone can be adjusted along the axle, making enough space for the bearings to spin but not enough for the wheel to move sideways. The cones are locked into place by wedging a locknut against each one, then tightening the cone against the locknut. The advantage here is that the parts can be serviced and adjusted with a minimum of tools.
- ◆ **Sealed bearing hub:** The modern type is called a sealed bearing hub, although the name is a bit misleading because the cup-and-cone type usually has seals too – anyway, you're liable to open up either kind and find your bearings in a mess. Instead of the cup shape, this type has a flat-bottomed round hole on each side of the hub. The bearings and the races they run on come as a unit, which is then pressed into the hole. They are trickier to fit because the bearings on each side of the wheel have to be prefectly parallel to run smoothly. The advantage here is that both the bearings and the bearing surface can be replaced when they wear. With the cup-and-cone type, the bearings and cones can be replaced, but the cup is integral to the hub and cannot be replaced cheaply.

Fitting and spacing hubs and sorting out hub seals

Before you start playing with spanners and ripping your hubs apart, check that they fit neatly into your frame – ill-fitting hubs won't clamp securely into your frame or forks and will wear quickly.

Hub spacing and fitting

Almost all mountain bike hubs come with the same spacing: the distance between the inside of the dropouts (technically called the 'over locknut dimension' – OLND). This is 100mm (4 inches) at the front and 135mm (5¼ inches) at the back. A 'dropout' is the part of the frame or fork with a slot for your axle. On forks, there's a dropout at the end of each fork leg; on frames, the right-hand dropout also has a hanger onto which your rear derailleur bolts. Road bikes use 100mm at the front and 130mm at the back.

It's important that the hubs fit snugly into the space between the dropouts. If the hub is more than a couple of millimetres wider or narrower than the frame or fork, the dropouts clamp it at an angle, rather than straight on. This puts uneven pressure on the hub bearings, wearing them out more quickly and, in extreme cases, bending or snapping the axle or the dropouts.

Each face of the dropout needs to be in good condition, so that the axle and skewer can clamp securely onto the surfaces. The locknuts on the outer end of the axle and the inner clamping face of your skewer are both knurled (notched) to increase grip. If you've ridden the bike with loose wheels, these notches will tear up the dropout surface, leaving the wheels less secure, even if you later tighten them correctly.

Care needs to be taken with your dropouts when you transport your bike too. They're very strong when the wheel is clamped in place, but are vulnerable when the wheel is removed. If you remove the wheels to put the bike on a plane, fit an axle support between the dropouts. You can usually pick one up at your bike shop – new bikes come packaged with them to protect the forks in transit.

Removing the front wheel and clamping the dropouts to transport your bike on a car roof rack can damage your suspension forks. Any movement between forks and clamp will twist the dropout, weakening it. Some fork manufacturers refuse to warranty forks with cracked dropouts if they've been carried in this way.

Hub seals

For me, getting dirty is a feature of biking. It might not happen every time we go out, but there's no point pretending (as, ahem, in the photos in this book do) that we always stay clean. Muddy tracks and roads aren't what designers working on bearings in clean studios consider as 'running conditions,' so your bearings definitely work best if you can keep the outside world out of them. Ideally, you create a completely watertight seal between your bearings and the world. Unfortunately, one of the features of bearing componentry is that one part needs to move smoothly against another. This means that at some point there's going to be a gap between the part of the wheel you want to move – the hub, rim and spokes – and the part you want to stay still attached to the bike – the axle.

But since we ride in grubby places, there's the issue of trying to stop detritus entering the gap between the hub and axle. Anything you put in the gap has to be carefully chosen to keep out dirt (so it has to touch both moving and stationary parts), but it cannot rub at all (so it's best if it doesn't touch either part). This is contradictory but true – a great deal of physics has gone into the problem. The practical upshot is that dirt gets into your hubs, and occasionally you have to get it out.

Different kinds of hubs

One major difference between cheap and expensive hubs is how well they're sealed. More expensive design and manufacture mean that the gap between moving parts can be made as small as possible, without the parts rubbing. Stronger, stiffer hubs also seal better – cheaper versions will flex under pressure, creating gaps around the seals. However, anything that completely keeps out the dirt won't spin around, so no seal is perfect, however much you spend on your parts. When you service your hubs, check the condition of the seals as you go along. Tears and cuts in the seals will allow rain and dirt into your bearings.

Many hubs have a large external seal protecting the exposed portion of hub and axle. It is often in the shape of a black cone and is usually found on the left-hand side of the rear hub and on both sides of the front hub. These help a lot, but if they get dry they squeak as they turn. To cure this problem, peel back the edge of the seal, clean it if it is dirty and drop a drip of oil onto the interface between seal and hub. As for the rest, learn how to strip and rebuild your hubs, so they turn round smoothly without ever letting in a mud-grinding paste.

Checking and adjusting cones

Wheel bearings last longest when they are properly adjusted. The purpose of your hub bearings is to allow your wheel to spin freely as you pedal, while preventing the wheel moving from side to side in the frame.

The first part is obvious – hubs that bind instead of spinning will obviously slow you down and sap your energy. But play in your bearings will slow you down as well – if your wheel can move from side to side in the frame, your braking surface (the brake rotor for disc brakes, or the rim for V-brakes) gets constantly dragged against the brake pads or blocks. Loose bearings will make themselves felt when you ride as well, with wheels rocking within the frame rather than tracking your movement neatly around tight twists and turns. Your bike will feel uncertain, with small unnerving pauses, before it follows your directions.

Checking for loose bearings is the same procedure for front and back wheels. Hold onto your rim, near where it passes between the forks or the frame. Pull the rim gently toward the frame. If the bearings are loose, the rim will rock toward you – you will feel, and maybe even hear, it shifting on its bearings. It's OK if the rim flexes a little, but it shouldn't knock at all. Loose bearings need to be adjusted straight away – as well as affecting your ride, they will wear quickly. If the bearings are allowed to bang onto the bearing surface, instead of rolling smoothly across it, they will create pits there. Check for tight bearings at the same time. Pick up each wheel in turn and spin it. The wheel should continue to rotate freely with just the gentlest encouragement. If it slows down prematurely, check the brakes first. If the brakes aren't the problem, your bearings are too tight. Use the steps below to adjust them. Front-wheel bearings are easier to adjust than rear-wheel bearings because both sides are accessible. With rear wheels, the right-hand cone and locknut are buried under the cassette.

Adjusting your bearings

Remove the wheel from the frame and remove your skewer – it just gets in the way. Spin the end of the axle between your fingers, then rock it from side to side across the wheel. If you found your bearings were too tight when you checked the wheel in your frame, the axle will feel gritty now – it may not move at all. If it felt loose in the frame, you will feel a slight rocking as you move the axle from side to side across the wheel. Since the axle runs through the centre of the wheel, you only need to work on one side of the axle to adjust both sides of the bearing. The right-hand cones on the rear wheel are concealed by the cassette, forcing you to adjust from the left side. The front can be adjusted from either side, so just follow the instructions for adjusting the back axle.

Check that the right-hand locknut is locked securely onto the axle before you start. If this side shifts about as you work on the other side, you'll not be able to set the critical distance between the two sides accurately. Hold the short stub of threaded axle that protrudes out from the middle of the locknut and try to turn the locknut. If it moves easily with your fingers, you really need to service rather than adjust the hub. Dirt and water will have been drawn into the hub as the loose cones shifted on the axle. The pictures below show the hub on its own, without spokes, so that you can see both sides at once. When you're doing this for real, the hub will be attached to the rest of your wheel.

ADJUSTING HUBS

Step 1: Turn the wheel so that the left-hand side of the hub faces you. Remove any black rubber seals, so that you can see the locknut nearest the end of the axle and the cone behind the locknut. There may be a washer, or washers, between the cone and locknut. Slide a thin cone spanner onto the cone and hold the cone still. Use a spanner to undo the locknut one turn anticlockwise.

Step 2: The locknut and cone on the right-hand side of the hub are locked together, clamped firmly onto the axle, so you can hold the axle still by transferring your locknut spanner onto the right locknut. Leave the cone spanner on the left-hand cone and turn to adjust the bearings – clockwise to tighten, anticlockwise to loosen.

Step 3: Holding the cone still, transfer the wrench back to the left-hand side of the hub and tighten firmly onto the cone in its new position. Check the bearing adjustment again – it can take several goes to get the cone position right. Refit seals, skewer and back wheel. Check the bearing adjustment once you've got the wheel back in the frame – it's annoying, but you can often feel only slightly loose bearings at this point.

Cup-and-cone hub service: front

The front hub service is a good place to start – it's less tricky than a rear service because you have no gear clutter on the hub. If you haven't serviced a hub before, start on the front for practice.

If you have disc brakes, take care not to get grease on the rotors during this procedure. I've seen people stick a plastic bag over the rotor, then cut a hole in the bag through which to work on the hub. However, this does seem excessive – simply keep sticky fingers and bearings off the rotor. You need to check what size spanners you need to adjust the cones. The cone itself needs a special flat cone spanner because its spanner flats are very narrow. The size you need is normally 13mm or 15mm. The locknut is usually turned with an ordinary spanner, often a 17mm, but sometimes you also need a cone spanner for that. Enough variations exist to merit taking your bike to the shop to buy the size you need. While you've got it there, ask them for the correct-size ball bearings for your hub. They're nearly always 5mm.

FRONT HUB SERVICE

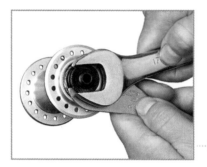

Step 1: Take the front wheel off and remove the skewer completely. Inspect each side of the hub. Seals may cover the cones, as in the picture. Peel them off by hand if you can to avoid damaging them, otherwise use a thin, flat screwdriver to peel back the edges. In order, you can see the threaded end of the axle, the locknut with wrench flats, spacers and the cone with wrench flats. Most of the cone is invisible, as it's inside the hub.

Step 2: Slide your narrow cone wrench onto the flats of one cone. Use the cone wrench to hold the axle still, then undo the locknut with the other wrench. Take it off completely. Remove any spacers. Lay them out in order on a clean rag so you can remember which order to put them back in. It's not difficult to work out the order for the front hub if they get jumbled, but it's good practice for when you come to the back one, which is harder.

Step 3: Switch the locknut spanner onto the other side of the wheel and use it to hold the locknut, and thus the axle, on that side still. Keeping your cone spanner on its original cone, undo that cone completely and take it off the axle. You should now be able to draw out the axle from inside the hub. Some bearings may drop out as you pull out the axle; be ready to catch them.

Step 4: Use a small flat-bladed screwdriver to extract all the bearings. Count them to be sure you replace the same number. Clean the axle and everything still attached to it. Wrap rag around the end of a screwdriver and use it to get grease off the bearing surface. For stubborn grime, you may need bikewash or degreaser. Rinse the bearing surface out and dry with a clean rag. Once all the old parts are clean, wash your hands to start fitting everything back.

Step 5: Inspect both the bearing surfaces on each side of the hub. A track will be worn in both cup and cone. Look for pits in the bearing surfaces. Any pitting prevents you adjusting the bearings nicely. Cones can sometimes be replaced individually, although you may have to buy a whole new axle. Pitted bearing surfaces in your hubs are more serious – you have to replace the hub, which means either buying a new wheel or rebuilding your rim around a new hub.

Step 6: Check the locknut is tightened against the cone. If the cone is pitted, note how much axle sticks out beyond the locknut, then hold the cone still with the cone spanner, and release the locknut. Wind all parts off axle. Fit the new cone and replace any spacers and the locknut. Wind the locknut onto the axle so the same amount of axle thread pokes out the end, then wind the cone back up to the locknut. Hold the locknut steady and tighten the cone against it firmly.

Refitting the axle

It's always worth making sure the cones and bearing surfaces are really clean and dry before you refit the bearings. Any dirt left inside the hub will shorten the hub lifespan and make the cones more difficult to adjust. A light oil, like GT85 or WD40, will help to dissolve the old grease and dirt that becomes compacted onto the bearing surface – squirt a little into each end of the hub, then roll the wheel around so that the oil has a chance to soak into the whole bearing surface. A toothbrush is just the right size and shape to shift stubborn dirt stains. Clean the central part of the hub between the two bearing surfaces – it's easiest if you use a screwdriver to poke a thin strip of cloth right through the hub, then twist and pull to clean. Dry the bearing surfaces, so that the grease sticks to it properly.

Once everything is clean, check again for pits in both bearing surfaces and both cones. Smooth worn tracks are fine – these just show where the bearings have been running. But any pitting at all – dents or rough patches on the bearing surface – means that the part must be replaced. Cones are slightly softer than the hub-bearing surface. This is so that they wear first, since they're easier and cheaper to replace. Take the old ones with you to the bike shop for replacement, since there are a number of variations in depth and diameter. Replace both cones at the same time – if one side is worn out, the other hasn't got much life left in it either. You may find that your hub cones are not available separately, so you may have to buy a whole new axle. If your hub surfaces are worn, you have no option but to replace the hub. If your rim is in good condition, you may wish to consider taking the wheel apart and rebuilding the rim onto a new hub.

Step 7: Grease the cups on both sides of the hub. There should be enough grease for each bearing to sit in grease up to its middle. With clean hands, pop as many bearings back into each side as you took out. If you push a bearing into place and another pops out, that's one too many bearings. The grease should hold them in place.

Step 8: Slide the axle assembly back through the hub. If you have a rotor, slide through from the rotor side, otherwise it doesn't matter. Wind the new or cleaned loose cone back onto the axle all the way, so that it touches the bearings and traps everything into place. Now replace any spacers and wind the locknut onto the axle so that it butts up against the spacer or cone.

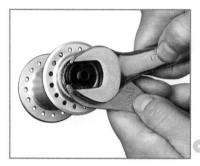

Step 9: All the adjustment must be done from the side of the axle to which you refitted the cone; we'll call this the 'adjustable' side. You tightened the locknut and cone onto the axle on the other side, the stationary side, before you refitted it, so you can use them to hold the axle still to adjust the cone on the other side. You don't adjust the cone on this side at all; it stays where it is.

Final adjustments

Now the tricky bit. Adjust the space between cones and cups so the wheel can turn smoothly, but keep it tight enough to eliminate side-to-side play. Hold the cone still, and tighten the locknut against the cone so the cone can't rattle out of place. The problem is that tightening down the locknut usually shifts the adjustment. Test by rocking the axle across the hub, and then rotating. If it rocks from side to side, the cones are too loose. If it won't turn freely, the cones are too tight. Tighten up the adjusting cone gently against the bearings, so it can still turn freely, but without side-to-side wobble. Hold the axle by sliding your cone spanner onto the stationary cone and holding it still, then use your locknut spanner to wind the adjustable locknut gently up to the adjusting cone. When they touch, transfer the cone spanner from the stationary side of the hub to the adjusting side and wedge the adjustable locknut firmly against the adjustable cone. Test the bearing adjustment – twirl the axle between your fingers. It should turn smoothly with little resistance. Turn the wheel to face you and wiggle the axle from side to side – there should be no play. Occasionally you adjust it perfectly first time but this is rare – normally you have to go back and try again.

If the axle doesn't turn smoothly, move the adjustable cone out a little. Using your two spanners, hold the adjustable cone still and undo the locknut one complete turn. Transfer the locknut over to the stationary side and use it on that locknut to hold the axle still. Undo the adjustable cone a little. Swap sides with both spanners, hold the axle still with the cone spanner on the stationary cone, and tighten the adjustable locknut so it touches the adjustable cone. Swap both spanners back onto the adjustable side and tighten them against each other so they lock together. Test again and repeat until satisfied. If there is play between the axle and hub, you need to undo the locknut; tighten the cone instead of loosening it and lock the locknut back down onto the cone. Replace any seals you took off and refit the wheel.

Cup-and-cone hub service: rear

The rear hub adjusts the same way as the front one, but the job is complicated by the cassette that is attached to the back wheel.

You must remove the cassette to service the rear hub; see page 199. One complication is that the right-hand cone is recessed into the freehub body, forcing you to make adjustments from the left-hand side. The most common spanner sizes are a 15mm cone spanner and a 17mm ordinary spanner, and 18 1/4 inch ball bearings. The rear hub needs servicing more often than the front: the rear wheel is forced around by the pedals and it carries more of your weight, so works harder. It's also too close to the drivetrain for comfort, lying first in line for debris flying from your chain. The right-hand side can be messy. Service it frequently for best results and always replace bearings when you service a hub. If the cups in the hub are badly pitted, think about replacing your hub. It's often best to take the wheel to your bike shop for an opinion. One option is to buy a new hub and spokes and rebuild your wheel around a new hub. See the wheelbuilding section (pages 209-16) for instructions. Once you've removed and cleaned the dirty stuff, wash your hands so you can fit things back together without contaminating the bearing surface.

REAR HUB SERVICE

Step 1: Remove the wheel and the skewer. Peel off any external seals covering the cone flats. It's best if you can do this by hand – pinch the seal between two fingers to release it, then pull. Otherwise, slide a screwdriver under the edge of the seal and twist. Check the condition of the seal and replace if the edges are cut or torn.

Step 2: Hold the left-hand cone still with your cone spanner, and loosen the left-hand locknut with your locknut spanner. Remove the locknut completely, then any spacers. Hold the spanners so that your hands move apart as the locknut releases – it often gives suddenly and will trap your fingers painfully between the spanners. Be careful.

Step 3: Swap the lockring spanner to the right-hand side of the wheel and use it to hold the axle still while you wind off the left-hand cone completely. Line up the parts as you go, so you can replace them in the right order, the right way around. Draw the axle out from the right-hand side of the wheel, catching any bearings that come out too.

Step 4: Clean axle with the right-hand parts attached, along with the parts removed from the left-hand side and the bearing surfaces inside hub. Wrap some rag round a screwdriver tip to get bearing surfaces clean. Use bike wash or degreaser for stubborn bits, but rinse and dry the hub afterward. Inspect the bearing surfaces. The bearings will have worn a track on both cups and cones, which is fine, but it should be smooth, with no pits. Replace pitted cones.

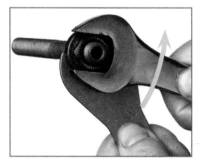

Step 5: If you're replacing a right-hand cone, note how much axle sticks out the end of the lump of cone, spacers and locknut. Hold cone steady on axle with cone spanner. Use the lockring spanner to remove the lockring. Wind old cone and any spacers off axle. Wipe axle clean and refit new cone. Refit spacers, then wind lockring onto axle to same position as before. Hold locknut still and firmly tighten cone and lockring against each other.

Step 6: Put enough grease into the cups on each side of the hub so the bearings sit in grease up to their middles. Pop into each side as many bearings as came out. There will always be the same number in each side, and it's usually nine. If you push a bearing into the cup and another one pops out, you don't need another bearing.

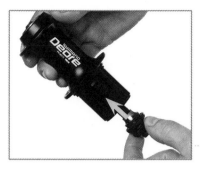

Step 7: Slide the axle, with the right-hand cone and lockring firmly tightened on to it, carefully into the hub from the right-hand side, making sure you don't dislodge any bearings. The cone will probably disappear completely into the hub.

Step 8: Thread the left-hand cone onto the end of the axle that's sticking out from the left-hand side, and tighten it down by hand so that it touches the bearings but can still spin freely.

Step 9: Refit spacers in order, followed by the locknut. Tighten the locknut down by hand so it wedges against the spacers, then use the two spanners to tighten the cone and locknut together so that they wedge firmly onto each other. Test the adjustment – it is rarely right first time. The axle should spin freely with little resistance.

Step 10: Hold the wheel so that the end of the left-hand side of the axle faces towards you and rock the axle from side to side. There should be no play at all – you should not be able to feel the axle knocking from side to side. If the adjustment isn't correct, hold the left-hand cone still and undo the left-hand lockring a turn.

Step 11: Hold the axle still with a spanner on the right-hand lockring and adjust the left-hand cone – clockwise if there's knocking, to reduce the space between cups and cone, and anticlockwise if the axle is stiff, to give the bearings space to spin freely.

Step 12: Holding the left-hand cone in its new adjustment, tighten the left-hand locknut against it. This often changes the adjustment, so play with the adjustment to compensate – a satisfactory adjustment often takes several goes, but it's just a case of trial and error. Once you're happy, replace any seals and refit the cassette and skewer. Refit the wheel, tightening skewers firmly.

Toolbox

Tools for adjusting front cones
- Cone spanner – almost always 13mm

Tools for adjusting rear cones
- Cone spanner – almost always 15mm
- Locknut spanner – an ordinary 17mm spanner will work on most – however, those locknuts with two flats rather than six will need a 17mm cone spanner

Tools for servicing hubs
- Spanners for hubs as above
- Good-quality bicycle grease, for example Finish Line or Phil Wood
- Degreaser and clean cloth to clean hub surfaces
- Replacement bearings – almost always ³⁄₁₆ inch (5mm) front and ¼ inch (7mm) rear – if in doubt take your old ones to the shop to size-up fresh ones

Sealed bearing hub service

Sealed bearing hubs use a pair of cartridge bearings pressed into the hub in place of the traditional cup-and-cone arrangement. The cartridges are more expensive than ordinary ball bearings, but the advantage of this set-up is that the cartridge unit consists of both the bearing and the bearing surface – replacing the cartridge means that you've effectively got a new hub.

In some ways, servicing a sealed bearing hub is a lot easier than maintaining a cup-and-cone hub service because there's no adjusting – you just pop out the old bearing, clean or replace it and fit a new one.

Selecting the correct bearing size can be awkward because there are so many similar, but different, sizes. Bearings are identified by three measurements – the diameter across the outside of the cartridge, the diameter of the hole in the middle and the thickness. The size is printed on the side of the bearing. When buying them from bike shops, ask them to reorder replacements from your hub manufacturer, which will guarantee that you get the correct replacement. Bearings are also available from specialist bearing and engineering shops, but it's well worth taking the old one along as an example.

We take a front hub; rear hubs work in the same way, apart from the fact that you have to remove the cassette to get at the axle properly. You may find that the axle covers have a small Allen key bolt that locks them onto the axle – undo the Allen key a couple of turns to release it from the axle, then treat as a push-fit axle cover. Once you've serviced the hubs, refit the axle covers as normal, then retighten the Allen key bolts gently – they won't need a huge amount of force to keep them in place.

The instructions specify a rubber mallet or a plastic hammer. If you don't have either of these, a block of wood works fine, but don't be tempted to use a metal hammer. It's not the same thing at all and you will inevitably damage the ends of the axle.

You'll need to support the hub while you knock through the axle. My preferred tool for this job is a short piece of plastic plumbing waste pipe. The plastic is strong enough to support the hub but soft enough not to damage it, and it's just the right size for the hub to sit on, with a hole in the middle into which the axle can fall. Plumbing supplies shops usually have discarded scraps that they'll give you if you wander in and smile at them. Perfect.

When refitting the new bearing, take care to ensure that it fits flat into the hub so that an even gap shows all the way around the edge of the cartridge. The bearings will wear very quickly if fitted crookedly.

Check the condition of your axle at the same time. It will be specific to your hub, and a replacement for a damaged one will have to be ordered from the hub manufacturer by your bike shop. Cartridge-bearing axles seldom snap, since they are well supported by the cartridge, but the cartridge support shoulders and the axle ends can get worn. If the new bearings fit loosely onto the axle or can be wiggled about once you've seated them onto the axle, then the axle must be replaced.

SEALED BEARING HUB SERVICE

Step 1: Pull the axle covers off the axles. They will often come off by hand. If they're stiff, lever them off gently by sliding a small screwdriver underneath and easing them upward. The aluminium is soft, so work patiently to avoid damaging the cover.

Step 2: Stand the waste pipe on end, then balance the hub on top. Tap the top end of the axle through the hub. The axle has a raised section in the middle – the shoulder of this section rests against the inside of each bearing, so that as you tap the axle from one side, it pushes the bearing out from the other.

Step 3: The axle comes out with one bearing still attached. Place the axle in a vice, with the long end hanging through the jaws of the vice. Protect the jaws with wood or cardboard, then close the jaws so they almost clamp on the axle, but not quite. Tap the axle through the bearing to release it. Slide the axle back through the bearing that's still stuck inside the hub and use the axle to tap out the bearing, supporting the hub again on your plastic tube.

Step 4: The axle will probably be stuck on that bearing now, so pop the axle back in the vice and tap it out again. You should now have two axle covers, an axle and two bearings. If you're replacing the bearings, take the old ones to your bike shop to get the right size replacements. If you're measuring them to order new ones, you will need to know the outside diameter, the inside diameter and the thickness of the old bearing.

Step 5: Clean the inside of the hub thoroughly. Compare the depth of the bearing seat to the thickness of the bearing, so that you know how much of the bearing seat shows when the bearing is properly seated. Each bearing needs to sit flush with the bottom of the bearing seat. Dry the inside of the hub well. Spread a very thin layer of Loctite on the bearing seat; it helps to keep moisture out and holds the bearing in place without creaking.

Step 6: The new or regreased bearings now need to be tapped carefully into place, but it's important to support the bearings carefully as you do this to avoid damaging the bearing surfaces. You need to find a couple of bearing supports that sit on the outer ring of the bearing, with a hole in the middle wide enough for the axle to pass through. Sockets from a socket set are often perfect, as are bottom bracket fitting tools.

Step 7: Support the hub on your plastic pipe, then tap one of the bearings into place, using your bearing support to ensure that only the outer ring of the bearing is under load. Turn the hub over and rest the bearing on the bearing support. Tap the axle through the bearing you've fitted.

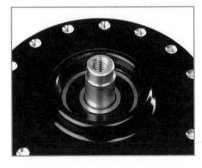

Step 8: Place the second bearing over the axle. Now comes the tricky bit: keeping both bearings lined up on their supports so that only the outer ring of each bearing is under load. Tap the second bearing into place, making sure both bearings are equally recessed into the hub, and that any gap at the top of the bearing is what you expected from your measurement of the bearing-seat depth.

Step 9: Refit the axle covers. If they were a press fit, simply slide them on by hand. They will get squeezed properly into place when you refit the wheel and tighten the skewers. If the axle covers have grub screws, fit them by hand, refit the wheel in the bike, tighten down the quick-release skewers, then tighten the grub screws.

Toolbox

Tools for sealed bearing hub service

- Allen keys for axle cover grub screws – most are press fit, though
- Rubber mallet, plastic hammer or block of wood
- Replacement bearings
- Socket to support bearing – same size as outer diameter of bearing
- Loctite
- Hub support – plastic waste pipe or similar
- Vice with soft jaws, or improvised jaw protectors – scrap of cardboard or carpet

The importance of cleaning and regreasing sealed bearings

Worn cartridge bearings have to be replaced, but if they're just sticky and dirty, a quick service will keep your wheels running smoothly. Check whether they're worth servicing before you take the wheels apart – hold the wheel flat and rock the axle gently from side to side. If you can feel movement, or the axle knocks from side to side, the bearing is due for replacement. Otherwise, follow the steps for a clean and regrease.

The old grease inside sealed bearings can often be caked firmly onto the bearings and bearing surface; anything that finds its way in past the seal has no way out again, so it just becomes compacted onto the bearing surface. You will generally need to use degreaser to clean this stuff up.

Once the seals have been removed (so that the dirt has an exit route), soak the cartridge in degreaser. Ideally, pop cartridges in a small pot and cover them in degreaser, so that they're completely submerged. Leave for an hour, replace the degreaser and soak for another hour, shaking occasionally. This should loosen all the old grease. Use a stiff brush to scrub the bearings clean. A toothbrush is perfect. Flush again with degreaser, repeat until the bearings come up shiny and you've got all the old grease out of the gaps between the ball bearings. Check your degreaser instructions – if it has to be flushed off with water, use plenty.

Drying the cartridge

Dry the cartridge. Properly, this should be done with compressed air, but nobody I know has a compressor at home. Fine substitutes are hot-air hand-dryers and hairdryers. If the person you borrow the hairdryer from doesn't know what you're going to be doing with it, it's well worth cleaning greasy fingerprints off it very, very carefully before returning it.

Once dry, the bearings must be regreased immediately – the degreased surface is vulnerable to rusting because you've just stripped off its oily protective coating.

Good quality grease is well worth it – you don't get into the cartridge very often so it doesn't need much. Waterproof grease is best; I like the green Phil Wood stuff for this. The consistency is perfect. Pack the grease into the cartridge but don't overfill – you need to leave the bearings enough room to move.

CLEANING SEALED BEARINGS

Step 1: Place the cartridge flat on a clean surface. Hold it still with your finger, press hard, so it doesn't slip. Use a very slim blade to lift the edge of the seal, taking care not to bend it or cut the plastic. Make sure you direct the blade away from you – this sounds obvious, but I've carelessly and stupidly cut my fingers doing this too many times. Pull the seal off completely and repeat on the other side.

Step 2: Flush the bearings with degreaser. Use a small brush to get all the old grease out – an old toothbrush is ideal. Rinse the bearings to remove all the degreaser and dry them. Repack the bearing with fresh grease. Don't overfill the bearing – there should be a little space for the balls to move in.

Step 3: Push the seals back over the bearing with your thumbs. The edges of the seals fit under the lip of the casing of the bearing. The fit is tight, so ease them carefully into place. When you've finished, there shouldn't be creases or folds in the edge of the seal. Wipe excess grease off the outside of the cartridge.

Removing and refitting cassettes for rear-hub services

Servicing rear hubs is trickier than servicing front hubs, since the right-hand side of the axle is concealed under the cassette. It is possible to service the hub without removing the cassette, but it's much more difficult – the bearing surface is behind the cassette, so it is tricky to clean properly. Use these steps to remove the cassette, then replace it after you've cleaned and regreased the hub.

Almost all cassettes use the same fitting method and the same tool, making cassettes easily interchangeable between hubs of different makes. The main body of the cassette slides over the freehub on 'splines' – the freehub has long parallel grooves all the way around it, which fit into the identically shaped grooves on the inside of the cassette. When you pedal, forcing the chain around, the sprockets are supported all the way around by the leading edge of each spline. The cassette is held onto the hub with a lockring, that screws into the end of the freehub. Once this is removed, the cassette will slide easily off the freehub.

The standard fitting means that one tool will fit all lockrings. The tool also has a set of splines, which fit into matching slots in the lockring. The best type of tool for hollow, quick-release axles has an extra rod that extends out from the middle of the tool. This supports the tool under pressure, stopping it from slipping out when you turn it.

You'll also need a chain whip to hold the cassette still while you turn the lockring and an adjustable spanner to turn the tool. You won't need the chain whip for refitting the cassette – the ratchet inside the freehub will stop it from turning. See the transmission chapter for more details about cassettes.

◆ Remove the skewer completely. Fit the cassette tool over the end of the axle so it engages with the splined hole in the centre of the cassette. Seat it firmly, so it doesn't slip off. If the tool has a rod poking out of its centre, insert this into the hole in the end of the axle. If the tool has a hole in the middle, refit the skewer and use it to clamp the tool onto the wheel. Otherwise just seat the tool firmly.

◆ Stand the wheel on the floor at your feet with the cassette facing away from you. Take the chain whip in your left hand. Wrap the loose end of chain around the top sprocket of the cassette, so that it passes across the top of the cassette and back around the bottom, leaving the handle sticking out horizontally to your left.

◆ Fit a large adjustable spanner onto the cassette tool so that it sticks out horizontally to your right. Lean over the wheel and push down on both tools, steadying the bottom of the wheel between your feet. The chain whip will stop the cassette from rotating, so that the cassette tool can undo the cassette lockring. There will be a horrible crunching noise as it undoes. Don't panic, this is perfectly normal!

◆ Once the lockring is loose, undo it completely. Now you can slide the cassette gently off the freehub body – the sprockets simply pull straight out from the wheel. Some of the outer sprockets are separate; take them off carefully and keep them in order, together with any accompanying washers.

To refit the cassette after servicing the hub:

◆ Look at the freehub body, which the cassette slides onto, and the hole in the middle of the cassette. You see there are splines on the outside of the freehub body and matching ones on the cassette. One of the splines is slightly fatter than the others. Line up the fat spline on the freehub body with the fat slot on the cassette, and slide the big chunk of cassette onto the freehub body. Fit any loose sprockets with a washer if there was one originally.

◆ Refit the lockring, starting it off by hand. Align it carefully – its easy to cross-thread as the thread is very fine. Once it's too stiff to turn, refit the cassette tool into the splines and use a large adjustable spanner to turn it. It makes the crunchy noise as it tightens – again, this is fine. It still needs about a half-turn after the noise starts.

Removing and refitting Shimano freehubs

We will only deal with the Shimano freehub here. This is the single most common type and the most commonly available replacement part. You have to remove the rear axle for the job, so it's worth servicing the hub at the same time. A freehub doesn't last forever and can get clogged up with muck. It can also suffer badly if you catch it at the wrong angle with a jet hose.

The first sign of trouble is usually a regular slight slipping as you pedal. This feels very similar to a worn chain and cassette, so check those first, but if you measure your chain and it's in good condition, the freehub is the next suspect. Take your back wheel off the bike and turn the cassette gently anticlockwise. You will hear the pawls of the ratchet click. Try to turn the cassette clockwise again – you should feel the pawls catch and stop you from turning the cassette. If the pawls catch, turn the cassette another click anticlockwise and test again. You should be able to turn the cassette a complete turn anticlockwise, testing after every click, and the pawls should catch every time. If they slip, so that you can turn the cassette clockwise more than a tiny bit, you have sticky or broken pawls in your freehub body. Replace your freehub.

Follow the instructions for servicing a rear hub (see pages 192-3). Once you've removed everything – locknuts, cones, axle and bearings – follow these steps to replace the freehub. Then finish the hub servicing procedure.

Compatibility between freehub bodies

Back in the early days, back wheels had old-fashioned freewheels with six sprockets. After a few years, this standard was replaced by a stronger design – a freehub with wider-spaced bearings and seven sprockets. Space was found within a couple of years for an extra sprocket by making the freehub body longer.

Seven-speed cassettes would not fit on the longer eight-speed freehub, nor would eight-speed cassettes fit on seven-speed freehub bodies. However, since the distance between each sprocket was the same, the two types could both work with the same width chain.

The next sprocket, increasing the cassette from eight to nine speeds, happened in a different way. Nine-speed sprockets are narrower, with less space between each one. So nine-speed and nine-speed cassettes will fit on the same freehub, but the nine-speed system uses a narrower chain that it fits into the reduced gap. Eight-speed chains won't work on nine-speed sprockets, nor will nine-speed chains work on eight-speed sprockets.

REMOVING FREEHUBS

Step 1: The freehub is bolted into the wheel with a 10mm Allen key bolt (**A**). The bolt is recessed deep in the hub, so you'll have to wiggle the Allen key in there carefully from the right-hand side of the hub. Engage it securely.

Step 2: The freehub bolt should be done up very tightly, so you'll need to be firm with it to undo it. Stand with the wheel at your feet with the freehub facing away from you. Turn the wheel so the Allen key is horizontal, on your right-hand side. Hold the wheel with your left hand and push down hard on the Allen key with your right hand. You may find that you need more leverage. If you can find a tube that fits over the Allen key, use that for extra help.

Step 3: Once the freehub bolt (**B**) is loose, undo it completely and pull it out. Clean it; you can reuse it for the fresh freehub (**C**). Clean the area exposed behind the freehub, line up the new one and pop the bolt through. Tighten it really hard – as tightly as the one that came off. Use your 'extension tube' again if you need it to get the bolt off.

Which tyres?

Your tyres are the only part of your bike that touches the trail or road. When you actually start to think about it, the contact patch is frighteningly small, in some cases only a couple of thumbprints. These tiny patches of rubber have to transmit the force of your pedal strokes to propel you along, steer you around corners in all kinds of loose and slippery conditions and bring you to a swift, controlled stop at the drop of a hat. So it's worth spending a little time thinking about them and paying them a bit of attention.

Puncture resistance

The single factor that's encouraged so many people to get back on their bikes in the last few years hasn't been fancy gears or radical frame materials/ design – it's been an unseen strip of puncture-resistant material woven into the fabric of tyres, under the tread. Mosty used in road tyres, a puncture-resistant strip will stop the majority of nasty little sharp things worming their way through to your tube. They make the tyre slightly heavier and more expensive, but it's worth it.

Quality

A good-quality tyre will be made of stickier rubber, which will grip the road or trail better.

▲ Smoother tyres mean more grip on tarmac

Pressure

Pressure is critical. The correct amount of air in your tyres is the single thing that makes a difference to how long they will last. The correct pressure is printed on the sidewall of the tyre as it's a legal requirement to include it. You'll need a pressure gauge to check the pressures at first. After a while, you get a feel for what the correct pressure feels like when you pinch the tyre, but it takes a while to learn. Many pumps come with a pressure gauge included. These are worthwhile, although the number given by gauges on cheaper mini pumps should be treated more as an indication than an exact reading.

Tread

If you're riding off-road on trails, the shape, depth and layout of the knobbles is critical. If you are riding in muddy conditions then broad tyres, with widely spaced bars running across the rear tyre, grip where nothing else can. For harder terrain, using something with closer knobbles that has less rolling resistance. Heavier riders need a wider tyre; lighter people can get away with something narrower. But for tarmac, you generally just need to maximise the amount of rubber in contact with the road, so the smoother the better. If you're going to be riding on towpaths and the like as well as tarmac, it helps to have a smooth raised central ridge, with knobbles at the side.

Condition

Tyres are in constant contact with the road or trail. It is inevitable that they will wear out, so inspect them regularly and often. For road tyres, take a minute every week to just go round each tyre and pick out any bits of glass or other stuff, you'll halve the number of punctures you have. It takes a while for stuff to work its way through your tyre to the tube and, if you catch it before it gets there, you'll save yourself a tube and some hassle. Slashes and holes in the surface of your tyre are an ideal shortcut for glass. Once they've begun to accumulate, replace the tyre. On mountain bikes tyres, the edges of the knobbles start to wear down. This has an impact on the level of grip the tyre can offer – no matter what tyre you choose, a fresh tyre will always grip better than a worn one.

UST tubeless tyres

UST (Universal Standard for Tubeless) mountain bike tyres do away with the inner tube and seal the tyre against the wheel rim for airtightness. No inner tube means lower rotational wheel weight (ideal for racers) and no more pinch punctures (where the inner tube pinches against the wheel rim and gets cut). Tubeless tyre set-ups are available for road bikes, too.

Rims and rim tape

Punctures that happen because some sharp thing has worked its way through the outside of your tyre and punctured your tube are annoying but fairly inevitable. On the other hand, those that happen because your tube has been punctured by your rim wall, or because your valve has shifted around in the rim and torn itself, are completely preventable.

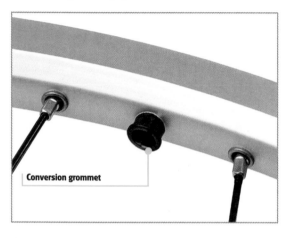

Conversion grommet

▲ Schraeder to Presta rim-converting grommet

Valve holes

Valves come in two sizes. The narrower Presta valve fits through a 6mm (¼ inch) hole in the rim, while the wider Schraeder valve fits through an 8.5mm (⅜ inch) hole.

If you ride with low pressure in your tyres (which slows you down but increases grip), you will find that the tube shifts about inside the tyre. Since the valve is held in place by the valve hole, the area near the valve gets stretched and can tear. The retaining ring on the valve stem will help by reducing the amount of movement in the valve, but this is often not enough if you're using Presta valves in Schareder-sized holes. A better solution is to buy one of the plastic or rubber rings that fit into Schraeder-size holes to reduce them to Presta size. This helps support the valve stem and stops water getting into the gap between valve and rim. They're properly called 'Schraeder to Presta conversion grommets', but are more usually identified by a description of what they do: 'those little black things you put in your valve holes if you run Presta tubes'.

Some rims come with a narrower valve hole that is only big enough to take a Presta valve. You can drill these out if you want to run Schraeders – use an 8.5mm (⅜ inch) drill bit and drill through from outside. Cover the hub and cassette with a cloth so they don't get covered in swarf. File off sharp edges around the valve hole or they will cut into the valve stem.

Rim tape

Rim tape sits around the inside of the rim to stop the heads of the spoke nipples cutting holes in the tubes. Make sure the tape sits evenly across the well of the rim, but that it doesn't run up the sidewall anywhere because this stops the tyre seating properly. I like the thick plastic ones; they don't move around on the rim as you fit the tyre and have to be stretched over the rim to fit.

Once it's fitted, check that the rim tape completely covers all the spoke holes – if there are any gaps at all, the tube will creep into them as you inflate it. The sharp edges of the spoke hole and rim tape will cut gradually through the tube, puncturing it. This may not happen straight away – it's more likely that your tube will last until the furthest point of a long loop, just before it starts to snow.

When you've fitted rim tape, you will often find that the valve hole in the tape doesn't line up with the hole in the rim. Stick a screwdriver under the rim tape, lift it a little and push it over to rest across both rim walls with the tape stretched over it. Roll the screwdriver around the rim until the holes line up and remove the screwdriver.

Cloth tape is heavier than plastic tape, but it is a better solution for high pressures because it's less flexible. Thinner rim tapes will bulge into the nipple holes as you put pressure in your tyres. If the rim tape has bubbles at every spoke hole, replace it with a thicker one. Don't double up the rim tapes, though – if you put one on top of the other, they fill up the rim well, making it tricky to remove and refit tyres.

Wheel-truing: the science of keeping your wheels in balance

You get better at wheel-truing with practice. These instructions start you off and they can rescue you if your wheel is too buckled to ride on. See page 70 for more detailed instructions in post-crash basics.

Rest the bicycle upside down, then remove the buckled wheel. Strip off the tyre and tube. This makes it easier to see what you are doing, and also releases pressure on the rim, making it easier to true accurately. Replace the wheel in the frame. Spin the wheel and look carefully at the part of the rim that passes between the brake blocks. If the wheel is too badly buckled to pass between the brake blocks, slacken off the brakes as much as possible with the barrel-adjuster on the brake lever or unit. In extreme cases, remove one or both brake blocks.

Before getting out the spoke key, have a look at the rim to confirm what you're aiming to do. Look at the part of the rim nearest you, as well as the parts of the hub you can see behind it. You will also see spokes leaving the rim and heading for the hub. There are an equal number of these, connecting alternately to the left and right sides of the hub.

Tightening a spoke that connects to the right side of the hub pulls the small portion of rim that it's connected to across to the right. Tightening a spoke that attaches to the left side of the hub pulls that part of the rim to the left. The rim is held in tension between the right spokes pulling to the right and the left spokes pulling to the left.

Slackening a left spoke allows the right spokes to pull the rim over – just as with a tug-of-war team one team, can move the central flag by pulling harder, but the same effect can result when the other team is tired and isn't pulling as hard. The aim of truing wheels is to balance the tension in all the spokes so that the lefts are pulling the same as the rights, holding the rim exactly central.

With this in mind, spin the wheel gently while watching the gap between the brake blocks and the rim. As the wheel spins, you will see that the rim moves from side to side. Imagine the centreline the rim ideally runs on, an equal distance between the brake blocks. Identify the area of the rim that has the biggest buckle.

Centre of the buckle

Look closely at the buckled area and identify the spoke at the centre of the buckle. You have to adjust the tension in this spoke to encourage the rim to sit more centrally. If the buckle pulls the rim to the right of the imaginary centreline, then spokes that go to the right-hand side of the hub must be loosened, and spokes that go to the left must be tightened.

Adjust the nipple at the centre of the rim by a half-turn. The spokes are laced alternately to the left and right sides of the hub; if one spoke goes to the left, both its neighbours must go to the right. So, once you've adjusted the spoke at the centre of the buckle by half a turn, adjust both its neighbours by a quarter-turn in the opposite direction. Spin the wheel again and look for the next biggest buckle. It may be in the same place or somewhere else. It's better to work slowly, adjusting three spokes then checking progress by spinning the wheel.

Working out which way the nipple turns to tighten or loosen the spoke catches many people. If you get it wrong and turn the nipples the wrong way, you make each buckle worse rather than better. Eventually, if you persist, the wheel collapses. If you see things are getting worse and not better as you true, stop and think carefully about what you're doing.

Looser or tighter

When I was learning, I had to think about which way to go all the time. Eventually, I drew two circles on a piece of paper, one with a clockwise arrow that said 'looser' in the middle and one with an anticlockwise arrow saying 'tighter.'

It lived in my toolkit for ages, and every time I had to true wheels, I put it on the ground underneath the wheel. I would spin the wheel to identify the buckle, then turn it so that the area I had to work on was at the bottom, over the paper. That way, I always knew which way to turn the nipples.

After a while, your hands remember, and you don't have to think about it any more. It's a good idea to get into the habit of using the spoke key in this position, since if a spoke breaks as you turn the nipple (which happens), it hits the ground harmlessly. Don't turn the wheel so you can see the head of the nipple you're turning, as this puts your eyes and face in the firing line.

It's possible you may not get the wheel completely straight. If the wheel stops improving, stop. As long as it passes through the brake blocks, you can ride the bike somewhere to get it dealt with properly.

Fitting a new spoke so that your wheels maintain their tension

Spokes usually break as the result of a crash, but they also break from being worn out. When you look at the wheel, it usually has one area with a big buckle. Run your fingers gently over the spokes and one may come away in your hand. It's important to fix it as soon as possible. Wheels rely on even spoke tension for strength. A broken spoke weakens the entire wheel structure, which then falls further out of true quickly.

Replacing broken spokes

If you have a broken spoke, remove the wheel, then the tyre, tube and rim tape. For rear wheels, remove the cassette (instructions on page 199). Locate the broken spoke and remove it. If it's broken near the head, pull the spoke out through the nipple hole and push the head out through the flange of the hub. If it's broken at the nipple end, push the nipple out and weave the spoke back so that you can pull it out of the hub. You may have to bend it to get it out.

Measure one of the other spokes to determine the length you need. Make sure you measure one from the same side of the same wheel as the broken one – lefts and rights can be different lengths. The spoke length is measured from inside the elbow where the head curves over to the very end, which will be inside the rim – look at adjacent spokes from the outside of the rim to estimate how far they protrude through the rim. The replacement spoke must be no more than 2mm (⅛ inch) longer or shorter than the others.

It's vital to weave your spokes back in in the right order. Look at your hub: you'll see that alternate spokes are 'heads in' and 'heads out'. 'Heads out' spokes on the flange nearest to you appear as circles because you can only see the heads (perhaps with the manufacturer's logo stamped on them), whereas 'heads in' appear through the flange so that you can see the elbow of the spoke, which then points off toward the rim. Your new spoke must follow the pattern.

'Heads in' spokes are the easiest to fit. Start from the far side of the hub, post the spoke across the hub and through the hole. It will now dangle on the outside of the wheel, with the head between the flanges. Pull it gently all the way through so that the head of the spoke butts up the inside of the hub. Wiggle it around so that the spoke points toward the rim. It's important to ease the elbow of the spoke gently through the hole in the hub. The hole is only just big enough for the spoke, so that it can't shift about in use, which can make it awkward to get the elbow of the spoke seated in the hub hole without bending it.

The spoke pattern

The pattern repeats every four spokes, with all the 'heads in' spokes on each side of the rim radiating out in the same direction. Pick out the next similar spoke and use it as a guide. Your new spoke crosses three others on its way to the rim. The first cross is over the adjacent spoke – the 'heads in' one. These two spokes are very close so that the hub flange is between the two spokes. The new spoke passes over the next spoke it meets, but then has to be woven under the third. Try to curve it gently, rather than bending it, and avoid scratching the rim with the sharp end of the spoke. Line the spoke up with the empty hole in the rim, checking that the adjacent spokes in the rim head off to the opposite side of the hub.

'Heads out' is trickier – and more common! Post the new spoke a little way through the near side of the hub. Don't push it all the way through yet – it will end up stuck between the second and third spoke crossings on the opposite side of the wheel. Curve it gently outwards from the hub and guide the end of the new spoke out of the far side of the hub, beyond the spoke crossings. It will need to be quite curved, and so will not slide easily through the hole in the hub. Push the head through with one hand, while maintaining the curve on the spoke with the other.

As with 'heads in' spokes, the pattern repeats itself every four spokes. Count along three from your new spoke, in either direction, and use this one as a guide. Your new spoke crosses the adjacent spoke at the hub, passes under the next one it meets, and then has to be woven so that it passes outside the third. Line the spoke up with the empty hole in the rim, checking that the adjacent spokes in the rim head off to the opposite side of the hub.

For both types, put a drop of oil on the thread, post the nipple through from the outside of the rim and thread the nipple onto the spoke. Take up the slack with a spoke nipple, and go to page 203 to true the wheel.

What makes spokes break?

Spokes usually break on the right-hand side of back wheels. The back wheel takes more of your weight than the front, since you sit almost on top of it. Derailleur gears mean the cassette sits on the right-hand side of the hub, so the spokes on the right approach the rim at a steeper angle. They have to be tighter to keep the rim central in the frame, so they are the most vulnerable to breakage.

They are also the most awkward to replace; the cassette has to be removed to fit a standard spoke into the holes in the flange. These spokes frequently get damaged by the chain.

A badly adjusted derailleur may allow the chain to slip into the gap between cassette and spokes. If you're pedalling hard at the time (which is quite likely, since you were already in a low gear), the chain acts like a saw on your spokes, cutting through them. If you have to take the cassette off to replace a spoke behind it, inspect the others at the same time for chain damage. Replace any that have been cut or torn. It's best to swap them one at a time, so that wheel tension and shape are retained. Tighten the nipple on each replaced spoke enough to support the rim before removing and replacing the next damaged spoke. The plastic spoke protectors that sit behind your cassette are ugly, but they do prevent the chain from dropping into the gap – always replace the spoke guard after fitting new spokes.

Rim damage

Rim damage is frustrating, and often happens as a result of punctures. If the tyre deflates fast, there may not be enough time to stop before you're running on your rims. This is particularly damaging if the wheel is heavily loaded or if you're bouncing down a rocky hill. The rim sidewalls can dent, ticking constantly on the brake blocks and making the bike difficult to control during braking. Sometimes the whole rim gets a flat spot so that, as the wheel turns, and the flat spot passes between the brake blocks, the blocks rub on the tyre. Tyre sidewalls are very soft, and the brake blocks soon wear through them and the tube, causing blowouts. One of the advantages of disc brakes is that your braking isn't affected by buckled wheels in the same way, but flat spots and bent rims will still weaken the rim.

Bent sidewalls can be bent back as an emergency measure, although they will be weakened and should then be replaced as soon as is practical. A small adjustable spanner is an ideal tool; clamp it tightly onto the bulge in the rim and ease it straight. If the bulge is big, do it in several stages, working inward towards the centre from either side of the bulge.

If the rim has a flat spot, check that brakes are clear of the tyre sidewalls. If not, adjust the blocks downwards, so there is clearance even when the tyre is at its lowest relative to the blocks. It's important to check with the tyres pumped up because at higher pressures the sidewalls can bulge, throwing themselves into the path of the blocks. Once the wheel has a big flat spot, there's little you can do to correct it – if the rim bends inward more than a couple of millimetres ($\frac{1}{8}$ inch), you're looking at rebuilding the wheel with a new rim.

Toolbox

Tools for wheel repairs – post-crash wheel true:
- Spoke key – individual ones are better than those that come on multi-tools, which can be awkward to use

Tools for wheel repairs – tools for replacing spokes:
- Spoke key – as above
- Tyre-levers – to remove and replace tyre
- Pump – to reinflate tyre
- Rear wheel – cassette tool plus chain whip to remove and replace cassette

Wheel words: learn the jargon

There is a proliferation of ready-built wheels on the market, but you still get the best value by attaching a hub to a hoop with a bunch of spokes yourself. If you do the weaving and tensioning yourself, you can spend the extra you save on a rim upgrade.

Your first attempt at building a wheel often takes some time, but it is a very satisfying experience. Once you've managed your first one, it gets easier every time. Don't be tempted to start with a second-hand rim and old spokes; it's much harder to true a secondhand rim, which will probably be dented and buckled, so will be frustrating since you find yourself doing the right thing without any effect.

Lacing, attaching the rim to the hub with all the spokes in the right place, comes first. This is easier than it looks. Next comes truing up the wheel so that it is round, flat and centred. This looks easier than it is and requires a fair bit of patience and care.

Front wheels are easier to start with than back ones. Back wheels have the cassette fixed on one side, which means the rim doesn't sit centrally to the hub. Therefore, the spokes on the cassette side have to be tighter than those on the other side. So begin your wheelbuilding career with a front wheel if you can to ease yourself into it.

Disc brakes often come with recommended spoking patterns. This is because braking applies force to only one side of the wheel, so it's important that the spokes stressed by braking are those that best support the braking force. The lacing pattern given here works best for disc brake bikes and fine for the rest, so use it for everything.

Crossing patterns

Most wheels are built 'three-cross' (3x). To see what this means, look at a wheel and follow a spoke from the hub to the rim. The spoke passes either under or over others on its way. If it crosses three other spokes, it's a standard three-cross wheel. The other common lacing pattern is 'radial', where the spokes go directly from hub to rim without crossing any others. It is also known as a zero-cross (0x) pattern.

Radial spoking is used almost exclusively for front wheels. A crossed pattern is more suitable for the back wheel; you're using the pedals to force the rear hub to turn. The spokes transfer this rotation to the rim and tyre. A crossed pattern means that the spokes leave the flange at an angle, which reduces the stress on both flange and spokes.

3 crosses

For both radial and crossed patterns, alternate spokes are connected to opposite flanges. This enables you to adjust the position of each section of the rim, moving it to the right by tightening spokes that connect to the right flange or loosening spokes that connect to the left flange, and moving it to the left by tightening left spokes or loosening right ones.

In crossed patterns, the spokes divide into pulling spokes and pushing spokes. The pulling spokes get tighter when you pedal and pull the hub around, dragging the rim behind them. The pushing spokes provide a counterbalancing force, thereby keeping the wheel in its strong, round shape.

When you're braking, the opposite happens – the pushing spokes suddenly have to do all the work, with the pulling spokes supporting them.

◀ **Three-cross is the standard pattern**

Spoke length

Whether you're building a new wheel or replacing a broken spoke, you need to choose the correct spoke. The length needs to be exactly right – a spoke that's more than 2mm (⅛ inch) too long or too short will not fit. Minor differences in flange size (the wider part on either side of the hub, with holes through which to thread the spokes) and rim profile will affect the spoke length.

When replacing a broken spoke, check the length by measuring another on the same side of the same wheel. Spokes are measured from the very end of the threaded end to the inside of the elbow of the head end. When measuring a spoke that's laced into a wheel, you have to take the rim tape off and look into the rim from outside to estimate how much of the spoke is inside the rim.

Spokes that are too long will protrude up inside the rim, where they can puncture the tube. You can file the ends off, so that they're flush with the top of the nipple, but that's still not good enough – only the end of the nipple is threaded, so if the spoke is too long, the nipple will have to cut its own thread on the unthreaded section of the spoke. This usually just damages the nipple thread, which then won't hold spoke tension securely.

Spokes must be long enough that they're threaded most of the way onto the nipple – if the nipple is only hanging onto the spoke by the last few threads, it will pull through as soon as the spoke is stressed.

When you build a new wheel, you start from scratch. You can work out the correct length using three-dimensional trigonometry, but it's hard maths. It's easier to ask your bike shop to look it up for you – shops have tables of common hub and rim combinations, or computerized spoke-length calculating programmes. Choose a quiet time, not a busy Saturday in July. The shops are most likely to help if you buy the spokes at the same time. In order to work out the correct length, the shop needs to know the hub model, rim model, number of spokes and crossing pattern, so either take along the components you're using, or buy them at the same time.

If you're building a wheel, buy a couple of extra spokes, so that you have spares later. Don't forget to pick up nipples at the same time – they don't automatically come with spokes.

Spokes come in two types: 'rustless' – meaning they are cheap – or 'stainless'. Always build with stainless. (The savings kept from using rustless will just be spent on more spokes sooner.) Good makes include DT and Sapim.

Spoke gauge

Spokes are usually either plain gauge (the same 2mm diameter all the way along) or double-butted (2mm at the ends where they normally break, and 1.8mm in the middle to save weight). Although spokes aren't a heavy component, saving weight here is particularly significant – wheels spin around their own axles, so weight saved here makes a big difference in how easily the bike accelerates. For heavier riders, plain-gauge spokes are less stretchy, so they help keep the wheel in shape when you bounce up and down on it.

The holes in the hub flanges are only just big enough for the spokes to fit through. If the fit is very tight, the spokes are more awkward to fit, but the wheel will stay true longer. Baggy hub holes allow the spokes to shift about, wearing the holes and releasing spoke tension. The width of the flange is also important. Once again, there's a compromise between ease of assembly and wheel longevity – if the hub flange is only slightly narrower than the elbow of the spoke, it will be tricky to ease the bend in the spoke through the hole. However the whole width of the spoke elbow will be supported by the inside of the hub hole, reducing the chance of spoke breakage. Some spokes are a smaller diameter at the threaded end. This does save a little weight, but means that you must use special 1.8mm nipples; while normal 2mm nipples will fit, they will work loose, usually over the first few miles that you use the nipples. Since a spoke gauge does vary from manufacturer to manufacturer, it makes sense to use the same make of nipple and spoke – even if they are supposed to be the same size, wheels built from mix-and-match components don't stay true as long.

Number of holes

Mountain bike wheels have mostly settled at 32 holes at the moment. The norm used to be 36, but as rims have become stronger, it's been possible to save weight by losing some spokes. Today, 28-spoke wheels are becoming more common, while 36 holes is still a good idea for heavier riders, or for those prone to trashing lots of wheels. The movement in expensive wheels is toward fewer spokes, but these are harder to build because, as you reduce the number of spokes, the tension in each becomes greater and the precision balance between the tension in each spoke becomes critical. If you've not built one before, I recommend getting good at 32- and 36-hole wheels before moving onto the fancy stuff! Road bike rims can have as few as 16 holes on the front and 20 on the rear.

▲ **Rims with double eyelets stay true longer**

Eyelets

Rims are made of aluminium, which is light but relatively soft. Good-quality rims have an eyelet pressed into the rim at every spoke hole. These spread the pressure from the tension in the spoke over a wider area of the rim and provide a smoother surface for the underside of the nipple to turn on. Single eyelets **(A)** sit on the inner surface of box-section rims. Double eyelets **(B)** are shaped to spread the pressure over both inner and outer surfaces, making the rim stronger but adding a bit of weight.

Lefts and rights

Once only rear wheels had awkward right and left sides, but the advent of disc wheels has sent fronts that way too. The lacing pattern is important because disc brakes are much more powerful than rim brakes. The spokes need to be arranged so that the strongest are lined up to resist the braking force. It's fine to build non-disc rims in the same way.

When you're building the wheels, there are lots of right and left directions. Discs are always attached on the left of the hub, cassettes on the right. Non-disc front hubs are the same both ways, but it's traditional to build them so that if you were sitting on the bike and looked down at the label on the hub, it would be the right way up. Rim labels are usually laced so that they can be read from the right-hand side. Again this doesn't really matter but it's a nice touch.

Off-centre rims

There are several different makes of off-centre rims, including Bontrager and Ritchey. Take care when building them – they are confusing. The spoke holes are not central but are set off to one side. Build front disc wheels so that the overhang is biggest on the left; for rear wheels the overhang should be on the right. The overhang compensates for the dish that the wheel is forced to take on because of the extra stuff on the hub – either the cassette or the disc mounting. Reducing this dish makes a stronger wheel. There will always be an arrow on the rim to help you get the right direction.

Deep-section rims

Deep-section rims are good for heavier riders because they keep their shape well, but they can be awkward to build. Good-quality rims are made of a shaped tube, bent around into a circle. With deep-section rims, it's easy to drop the nipple into the tube by mistake, instead of in one side and out the other. Once they're in there, you have to get them out, otherwise the nipple will roll around inside the rim, forever rattling. Sometimes the nipple will come out if you can shake it around until it's near the valve hole, otherwise you have to tease it out by poking it through of one of the holes with a spoke.

If the rim you're using is deep, screw the top of each nipple a couple of turns onto an extra spoke, and use that to insert the nipple through the rim hole. Unscrew the extra spoke, then screw the nipple onto the laced spoke. If you build lots of deep-section wheels, you can get a special little deep-section rim nipple screwdriver that grips the head of the nipple so you can pass it safely through the rim. (It's one of those special tools that seems extravagant to everybody except the person who has to use it . . .)

Nearing the end of the build, you have to bend spokes to manoeuvre them around those already fitted. This is fine, but ensure they don't get kinked. A gentle bend over most of the length of the spoke is far better than a sharp kink. You'll always need to bend the spokes slightly when lacing them onto the rim, but building with deep-section rims means fitting shorter spokes into a smaller space, so the bend must be tighter.

Disc wheels

Disc wheels are no more complex to build than non-disc wheels. The flanges are usually bigger, which makes it easier to lace them, but the front wheel must be slightly dished to allow space on the left-hand side for the rotor. The amount of dishing is minor, though, so the tension on each side of the wheel remains fairly even.

Building your own set of wheels is not as difficult as you might think

Wheelbuilding is often treated as a mysterious art, unfathomable to mortals. It's actually not as difficult as it's made out to be. Producing a perfectly tensioned set of wheels that will run true for years in half an hour does take a lot of practice, but with a bit of patience, and a free afternoon, you should be able to make your own wheel out of a set of spokes, a rim and a hub.

Building your own wheels is a satisfying achievement, impressing other cyclists more than most other bicycle-fixing tasks. It breaks down to two parts: lacing and tensioning. Lacing – weaving all the spokes so that they join the hub to the rim – looks complicated, but is easy. Tensioning – tightening all the spokes so that they hold the rim round, true and central – looks easy, but is complicated.

Follow the lacing steps carefully – they look confusing, but as long as you don't panic, you'll be fine. The key to lacing wheels successfully is remembering that there are four sets of spokes, each of which follows the same pattern. For each set, get the first spoke in the right place, then follow the pattern around the wheel until you come back to where you started. You really only have to think carefully about four spokes – not 32 or 36. On each side of the wheel, alternate spokes face in and out of the flange, and radiate clockwise or anticlockwise from the hub to the rim. At the rim, alternate spokes are connected to opposite sides of the hub.

Spoke key

Buy a nice spoke key with which to build wheels. The small ones on multitools are great for emergencies, but are awkward to use for more than a few rough nipple twists. Big dedicated spoke keys are more comfortable than little cheap ones that make the nipples hard to turn when putting the final bits of tension on, leaving you with sore fingers. There are two different common nipple sizes, refered to variously as 'Japanese' and 'American', 'small' and 'large'. 'Red' and 'yellow' refers to the colours used to differentiate between the two sizes of the most popular spoke key, made by Buddy. These are great for wheelbuilding: they hold the nipple on all four sides, so that the flats don't get damaged. Check your nipples fit neatly into the spoke key before you buy it.

Wheel jig

Your most essential tool for learning to build good wheels is a wheel jig. A basic £50 model is fine for learning to build wheels on, although average workshop models cost £400. It is possible to build wheels without a wheel jig, using your bicycle frame as a guide, but it's a difficult way to learn. Splash out on a jig or borrow one if you can.

The wheel jig holds the wheel steady between two clamps. Different makes have slightly different features, but all work in the same way: an indicator arm comes out from the jig and sits beside the rim. The distance between the indicator and the rim can be adjusted, and is set so that the rim just touches the indicator. The roundness of the wheel is checked by spinning the wheel and watching how the gap between the rim and the indicator changes. The tension in the spokes is adjusted where the gap is smallest or greatest to reduce the total amount of wobble in the rim. The indicator is then moved closer, and the process is repeated until the rim is straight. Cheaper, more portable and storable models have an indicator on just one side of the rim, whereas more expensive types have an indicator on both sides.

Wheels are surprisingly heavy once they're spinning. If you can clamp or bolt the jig onto a workbench, it will help to stop it from wobbling around, making it easier to see the gap between your rim and the indicator gauge on the jig. Plenty of light also helps, as does a piece of white card or paper under the jig, so that you look through the gap onto the card.

These wheelbuilding guidelines take you through building a front and rear wheel in the most common three-cross style. If you want to know more about wheelbuilding, get a copy of *The Bicycle Wheel* by Jobst Brandt. It's packed with technical information, explaining how spoked wheels actually work, how to build wheels in other patterns and how to know when you should use other patterns.

The delicate art of lacing up the spokes for a new front wheel

We start with a front wheel, because they are much easier. The wheel is built up in four groups of spokes, one set radiating out in each direction from each side of the hub. Divide your spokes up into four equal batches before you start: four batches of eight for a 32-spoke wheel, four batches of nine for a 36-spoke wheel and so on . . .

Assemble all components. If you're reusing a hub, clean it up, taking special care with the spoke holes. If they are dirty, the fresh spokes you push through them will get grit in the threads and become difficult to turn on their nipples. Oil each of the spoke holes in the hub and all of the holes in the rim, so the nipples can turn easily. Oil the spoke threads too. Hold the hub so that the right side of the hub is upwards.

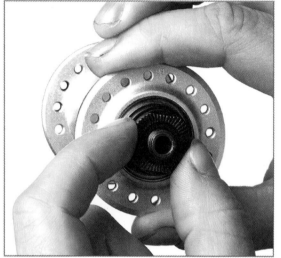

Servicing the hub

If you're rebuilding on an old hub, check that the axle spins freely, with no side-to-side movement. If the axle feels rough or knocks, service the hub before you start lacing the spokes onto it. It's easier to manipulate and clean the hub on its own, and this is a good time to check the condition of the hub.

It's better to discover that the hub is almost worn out before you start building than to realize that you've got a perfectly tensioned rim attached to a pepper grinder. Check the condition of the spoke holes in the flange too. They should be neat and round. Worn holes will have been pulled into a teardrop shape. Replace hubs once this happens – the spokes in your newly built wheel won't retain tension.

◀ **Check that the hub spins smoothly, with no side-to-side play**

LACING A FRONT WHEEL

Step 1: Take the first group of eight spokes and drop them down through every other hole in the upper flange of the hub. The heads of the spokes go on the outside of the flange.

Step 2: Take any one of the spokes. This is the first spoke of the group, so you must get it in the right hole. Hold the hub vertically, with loose spokes hanging down. Hold the rim flat, label upside down. The correct hole is immediately to the left of the valve hole. Pop the spoke through the hole and trap it by screwing on a nipple a couple of turns.

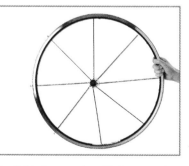

Step 3: Take the next spoke anticlockwise around the hub. Moving anticlockwise around the rim, miss three holes, then pop the spoke in the next one. Trap it with another nipple. Take the next anticlockwise spoke, miss three holes and take the next. Continue until you arrive back at the valve hole. Because each wheel consists of four sets of crossed spokes, the ritual of fitting the spoke into every fourth hole holds true regardless of the number of holes in the rim.

Step 4: Keep the rim facing toward you. See the far side of the hub has the same number of holes as the near side, but they are offset; each far-side hole falls between two near-side holes. Find your first spoke again, next to the valve hole – we'll call it spoke 1. Hold the wheel upright, with the valve hole at the top. The next spoke drops into the flange hole just left of spoke 1, and laces onto the rim on the next hole to the left of spoke 1.

Step 5: Drop a spoke through alternate holes on the further flange, and follow the pattern around the rim, fitting a spoke in every fourth hole. Now, starting with the valve hole and moving anticlockwise, you should have spokes in the next two holes, then two gaps, then two spokes, two gaps, all the way round. You should be able to see the heads of all the spokes. Hold the rim still, and twist the hub anticlockwise so it looks like this picture.

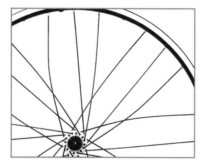

Step 6: Turn the wheel so the other side faces you. Shake the hub lightly to settle the nipples into the rim, but make sure you keep the twist in the hub. Drop a spoke through all the remaining holes on the flange nearest to you. Take one of these spokes. It will currently be hanging down between two of the pairs of spokes already laced, but you have to send it clockwise around the rim. Curving it gently, ease it between the spokes.

Step 7: It crosses three spokes on its way to the rim, passing under two and over the last one. The first one it crosses, near the flange, is its neighbour. It goes under the next one too. Weave it gently over the next spoke. Check where this crossing spoke meets the rim – your spoke fits in the hole that's two further around clockwise. Complete the pattern, fitting in each spoke four holes on. N.B. Count all holes with or without a spoke, but never count the valve hole.

Step 8: Without turning the wheel over, drop a spoke through all the remaining holes on the far side of the hub. Lift up each one in turn. It passes over the first two spokes it meets, starting with its neighbour, and under the third. It should be obvious which hole it fits into, because there aren't many left. It's the one 'two further on' from the last one it passed over.

Step 9: Complete the pattern, weaving each spoke at a time over two and under one. You're all laced now. Starting at the valve, tighten each spoke until the thread just disappears inside the nipple. A screwdriver or a spoke key speeds this up. Now you are ready to put tension into the spokes. Go to the truing and tension section on pages 214–6.

Toolbox

Tools for wheelbuilding
- Decent, well-fitting spoke key
- Wheel jig – basic models are fine
- Oil for spoke threads
- Threadlock to be applied to spokes after final tensioning (optional)
- Fresh rim tape if necessary

Lacing a back wheel

Now you're ready for the next step. If you can build a front wheel, you can build a back one, but there are complications because of the cassette.

The right-hand flange (the shoulder on the hub with holes for the spoke heads) has to be shoved over toward the centre of the hub to accommodate the sprockets, so that the spokes on that side are doing a harder job. That's why when you break a spoke, it's usually on the drive side, where the cassette is attached. It makes sense, therefore, to start with shorter spokes on the drive side. The length difference is usually about 2mm (⅛ inch), which may not seem a lot, but it matters.

That there are two lengths of spoke makes things a little more complicated when lacing the wheel; you must be careful not to mix up the spokes. It helps to make up the four groups before you start lacing, two batches of shorter ones for the drive side and two batches of longer ones for the non-drive side. Each group has a quarter of the total number of spokes, so if you're building a 32-hole wheel, each group has eight spokes; if you're building a 36-hole wheel, each group has nine spokes. The ritual of lacing is slightly different for a back wheel.

Step 1: With the drive side (the side on which the cassette fits) of the hub facing upward, drop the first batch (7, 8 or 9) of shorter, drive-side spokes into every other hole in the top flange.

Step 2: Hold the rim upright. For extra points, make sure any labels are facing towards you. Take any one of the spokes and put it through the rim hole immediately to the left of the valve hole. Trap it with a nipple.

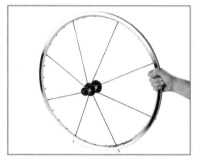

Step 3: Working round in an anticlockwise direction, fit each successive spoke into every fourth hole, i.e. miss three holes, fit a spoke, etc. Count all rim holes with or without a spoke, but never count the valve hole. Turn the wheel around so that the non-drive side of the hub faces you, keeping the valve hole at the top.

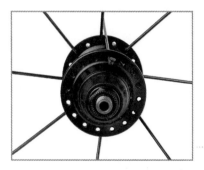

Step 4: Take a batch of the longer, non-drive side spokes. Look at the alignment of the holes in this side. You'll see that each hole on the far side falls between two holes on the near side. Choose a hole in the near flange, so that when you push a spoke through, it hangs to the right of the spoke already fitted next to the valve hole.

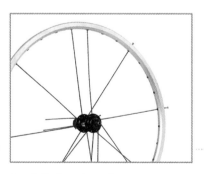

Step 5: Fit this spoke to the right of the spoke beside the valve hole. Secure it with a nipple. Drop longer spokes through every other hole around the hub.

Step 6: Follow the spoking pattern clockwise, missing three holes then fitting a spoke until you reach the valve hole again. Check the pattern – starting at the valve hole and, working around clockwise, you should have two spokes, then two gaps, all the way back around to the valve hole.

Step 7: Without turning the wheel around, drop the next batch of shorter spokes through the remaining holes in the far flange so that the heads are between the flanges. Take the hub and twist it clockwise while holding the rim still.

Step 8: The spokes you've already fitted radiate out anticlockwise from the rim. The next spoke has to go the opposite way. The first spoke it crosses is its immediate neighbour – they cross with the flange between them. Keep outside the next spoke, then weave the spoke under the third. Check where this spoke meets the rim. The adjacent rim hole clockwise will already have a spoke in it – fit your spoke into the next hole clockwise.

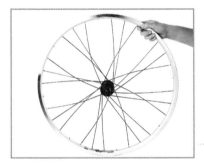

Step 9: Repeat with the rest of this group, fitting each successive spoke four rim holes on from the last, counting rim holes whether they have spokes in or not. Check your pattern again. Starting at the valve hole and working clockwise, you should have three spokes then a gap, all the way back around to the valve.

Step 10: Take the final set of longer non-drive side spokes. Push them through the final set of holes from the drive side so that their heads are between the flanges. The hub area is quite crowded now, so ease the spokes through the flange holes as carefully as you can with a minimum of bending.

Step 11: Facing the non-drive side of the wheel, this spoke radiates out clockwise. The first spoke it crosses is its immediate neighbour, with the flange between the crossed spoke. This spoke passes over the next spoke it meets. Curve it gently to pass under the next one. Pop it into the next available hole and keep it in place with a nipple. Repeat with the other spokes in this group, fitting the spokes into the remaining holes.

Step 12: When you come to truing, the rear wheel takes a little longer than the front. Take it slowly, in very small steps. The drive side spokes end up a lot tighter than the non-drive side; typically, the non-drive side will have two-thirds the tension of the drive side. Dishing is also an issue; the wheel wants to start further to the left, and you have to pull it back.

Spoke-lacing – quick guide

Rear wheel:
- Drive side up, drop spokes through top flange
- Hold rim upright, valve hole at top
- Hold hub drive side toward you, lace any spoke in rim hole adjacent to and left of valve hole
- Continue pattern anticlockwise, lacing spokes into every fourth hole
- Turn wheel around so non-drive side faces you
- Feed spoke through nearest flange so that it passes immediately to the right of top spoke on far side of hub
- Fit this adjacent to and onto the right of the first spoke you fitted, on the far side from the valve hole
- Continue pattern clockwise
- Twist hub clockwise
- Keep wheel same way around, push spokes through remaining holes in further flange
- Turn wheel over, then take any spoke, cross it over its neighbour (with the flange between the two), over the next spoke and under the third
- Count two from the last spoke you crossed and fit the spoke in the next hole
- Continue the pattern with the rest of this batch
- Push spokes through remaining holes in far side of flange
- Turn wheel over, then take any spoke, cross it over its neighbour (with the flange between the two), over the next spoke and under the third
- Count two from the last spoke you crossed and fit the spoke in the next hole
- Continue the pattern with the rest of this batch

Building your own wheel: tensioning and truing the spokes

This is the part that looks easier than it is. The spokes must all be tight, so that the wheel is strong and perfectly balanced and the rim runs true. The balancing comprises four separate operations: correcting the true, correcting the hop, correcting the dish and correcting the tension. Part of the reason wheelbuilding has always been considered difficult is that adjusting one of these factors affects all the others.

The four operations listed above break down as follows:

True

The spokes are laced alternately to the left and right sides of the hub. For example, a zone of the rim that is too far to the left can be corrected by tightening the spokes that go to the right. Since every other spoke is connected to opposite sides of the hub, this can be broken down into a series of very small steps, always truing just the part of the rim with the worst bulge.

Hop

The rim must be an equal distance from the centre of the hub all the way around. If it isn't, the brake blocks will be hard to set up and you will kangaroo down the road, your wheel falling apart in no time at all. If a section of the rim hops outward, i.e. is too far from the hub, it can be drawn inwards by tightening two or four spokes centred around the peak of the hop. Tighten the same number of right-hand side spokes as left. Adjusting the hop always throws the wheel slightly out of true, but try to minimize the effect.

It's easier to correct an outward hop, where a section of the rim is too far from the hub, than it is a flat spot.

Dish

The rim must end up centred between the locknuts, so that when you put the wheel into the bicycle frame, the rim runs evenly between fork legs, between seat and chainstays and between swingarms. Tightening all the spokes on the right-hand side will move the entire rim to the right; tightening all the spokes on the left will move the entire rim to the left. The rear wheel has a cassette bolted onto the right-hand side so that the heads of the spokes on that side are closer to the centre of the hub. This means that the right-hand spokes have to be tighter than those on the left, in order to keep the rim central – that's why they're more likely to break than those on the left-hand side of the rear hub.

Front disc hubs also have to allow a little bit of extra space on the left-hand side, but the dishing required is minor.

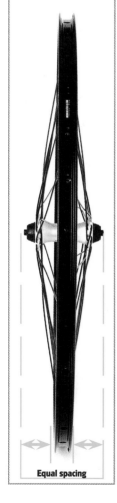

◀ **Dish: these two distances must be the same in width**

Equal spacing

Tension

Tension is tricky to get right. You can easily destroy a rim by overcranking the spoke tension until the rim collapses. For the home mechanic, the easiest way to ensure the tension is correct on the wheel you're building is by comparing with another set of wheels.

Take hold of a pair of almost parallel spokes on a completed, functioning wheel and squeeze them. Then do the same with a pair of almost parallel spokes on a working set. Be sure to compare like with like; front-wheel spokes have lower tension than backs, and the right-hand side of back wheels has higher tension than the left when the dishing is correct.

Tightening the spokes

Once your wheel is laced, the next step is to tension it. It's important to take this in small steps, increasing the tension gradually and evenly, while constantly checking that the wheel remains round. The most common mistake is to crank up the tension too fast, without straightening the rim between each round of spoke tightening.

Follow steps 1–6 below for a wheel that is fairly round, true and dished. Then start again at the valve hole, and go methodically around the rim, tightening each spoke a quarter-turn. Repeat steps 3 to 6, truing the wheel more precisely. Go round again, tightening each spoke a further turn.

Refer to a set of working wheels, so that you can compare spoke tension. Keep tightening all spokes, then correcting true, dish and hop. Once you get close to the tension in the working wheels, stress-relieve the spokes; see page 216.

TIGHTENING THE SPOKES

Step 1: If you've just built your wheel, most spokes will be loose. Give all spokes an even amount of tension. Tighten each nipple until the spoke thread just disappears. Set wheel in the jig and spin. Pluck the spokes with a fingernail. To start the truing process, most need to be tight enough to get a note from. If most do, skip to next step. Otherwise, start at the valve hole and tighten each one a quarter-turn. Repeat until the wheel has some tension.

Step 2: Once you have a degree of tension in the wheel, you can start truing it. Spin the wheel again. It probably doesn't look round at all. Your jig has an adjustable indicator – set this so that when you spin the wheel, the indicator only touches the side of the rim in one place. This is the most out-of-true section.

Step 3: Find the centre of this biggest bulge. Loosen the spoke at the outside of the bend a half-turn, and tighten the spokes on either side a quarter-turn. This won't make much difference, but that's okay. This step has potential for going horribly wrong, so we'll take it in very small stages to maximize our chances of success.

Step 4: Repeat the procedure. Spin the wheel, identify the worst bulge, loosen the spoke at the centre, tighten those at both sides, until the wheel moves from side to side no more than 10mm ($^1/_8$ inch). This can mean working repeatedly on the same area; don't worry as long as you are always attacking the biggest bulge.

Step 5: Once you have the wheel vaguely true, spin it and check for hops. Move hop indicator on your wheel jig as close as it will go; watch the gap vary as wheel turns. It's easier to draw rim nearer to the hub than force it away, so concentrate on areas where rim hops outward. As with truing the wheel, work on the largest hop. When you find it, tighten the two spokes at its centre a half-turn. Repeat until the total hop in the rim is less than 3mm ($^3/_{16}$ inch).

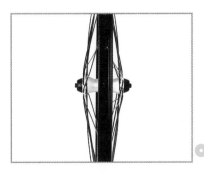

Step 6: Check the dish is correct; see page 166 for details if you're unsure how dish works. Turn the wheel over in the jig or in the bike without moving the indicators. If the wheel is perfectly dished, the rim sits in the same place again. If it's off to one side, it moves over in the jig. Correct by tightening all the spokes on the outer side one quarter-turn. If this is not enough, loosen all the opposite spokes a quarter-turn. Repeat until the wheel sits centrally.

Wheelbuilding: how to make sure the tension in your spokes is right

When you put tension in the wheel and true it, the spokes can get twisted. Instead of the nipple turning on the spoke thread, it can twist the whole spoke. The tension may look correct, but the first time you cycle down a bumpy road on your new shiny wheel, the twisted spoke will unwind as the tensions in the spokes change, and the wheel will immediately drop out of true.

▲ **Squeeze hard to stress-relieve the spokes**

When your wheel is almost fully tensioned, it's a good idea to go around the wheel and relieve the stress in the spokes. Start at the valve hole, and choose a pair of nearly parallel spokes from the same side of the hub. Squeeze them firmly together. Work around the wheel, first from one side of the wheel, then the other.

You may hear the spokes creaking or pinging as you do this. Once you get back round to the valve hole, check the wheel again for side-to-side wobble. You may need to true and then stress-relieve several times. The wheel is ready when you can stress-relieve all the spokes without affecting the truth of the wheel and the tension is similar to that of a functioning wheel. Some people swear by standing on the rim at this point as a final stress-relief procedure. I say don't do this – it's excessive and unnecessary.

Freshly built wheels last longest if given two or three trues as they settle in; it's worth popping the wheel back into the jig after 100 miles to keep it exactly straight.

Spoke length.................. L

Effective rim diameter .... D
Flange hole circle diameter..... d
Flange width.................. W
Flange hole diameter.......... S
Crossing pattern.............. X
Number of spokes............. N

Work out first:
$T = 360 \times X/(N/2)$
$A = (d/2) \times \sin(T)$
$B = D/2 - ([d/2] \times \cos[T])$
$C = W/2$

Spoke length:
$L = \sqrt{(A^2 + B^2 + C^2)} - \dfrac{S}{2}$
Alternatively, to save time, look on the Net.

Spoke-length mathematics

♦ Effective rim diameter – this is the distance directly across the rim, measured from the underside of a nipple head to the underside of the opposite nipple head. This is tricky to measure directly, as the underside of the nipple head is inside the rim. I measure the length of a nipple, from under the head to the end; i.e. the total length minus the head. For DT nipples, this measurement is 10mm (⅜ inch). Then drop the nipple through the rim and measure the amount that's exposed. Take one from the other, which gives you the length of nipple inside the rim. Measure across the inside diameter of the rim, between opposite spoke holes, and add twice the concealed nipple length – once for each end. This gives you the effective rim diameter.

♦ If you look at the hub from one side, the hub holes make a circle. Measure across this circle for the flange hole circle diameter, from the middle of a hub hole to the middle of the opposite hub hole.

♦ The flange width is measured across the hub, from the centre of one flange to the centre of the other.

♦ The flange hole diameter is the size of the spoke holes in the hub – usually about 2mm (⅛ inch).

Troubleshooting wheels

Symptom	Cause	Solution	Page
Bike feels slow, you feel tired after short rides	Cones too tight on front or rear wheels, or both	Adjust cones so that wheels spin smoothly	191
Bike feels uncertain when cornering	Cones too loose – wheel will wobble from side to side on the frame	Adjust cone so that the wheel can't rock from side to side in the frame	191
	Wheel is buckled	True wheel so that rim runs true and doesn't wobble from side to side as the wheel spins	203
	Insufficient tyre pressure	Inflate tyre to minimum pressure marked on the sidewall of the tyre	N/A
Rim brakes – rim rubs on V- or cantilever brake blocks	Wheel is buckled	True wheel, so that rim runs true and doesn't wobble from side to side as the wheel spins	203
Brake blocks wear quickly	Rims dirty	Clean rims with degreaser	78
	Rims worn	Check rims for scours, grooves or ridges – replace rims or wheels	88, 209-16
Spokes loosen repeatedly	Rim buckled	Uneven spoke tension in buckled wheels causes spokes to loosen – rebuild wheel with new rim	209-16
Frequent punctures	Tyre still has sharp things stuck in it	Check tyre carefully, feeling around the inside for protruding thorns or glass – fold the tyre inside out, so that you can see more clearly	61
	Spokes poking through the rim	Run your fingers around the inside of the rim, checking for sharp spoke ends – file sharp ends off	N/A
	Rim tape shifting, exposing spoke holes	Replace rim tape with wider, tighter one	202
UST tyres leak	Tyres need pumping before every ride	This is normal! Fit tubes for normal riding, take them out again on race days – an unexpected training bonus!	62

7 – Suspension

Suspension, in the form of either front forks, rear shocks, or both, is standard on mountain bikes and some road bikes, too. It is designed to iron out lumps and bumps on the trail or road. This chapter gives you an overview of some of the most common types of suspension units but to cover every type would need a whole book on its own. You'll need to use these instructions in conjunction with the owner's manual, which you can download from your manufacturer's web site. Most procedures aren't as complicated as you might think.

Suspension: why you need it and how it works

Suspension technology is a key part of mountain biking. What is currently state of the art is actually more likely to be part of a great work in progress than the final form. One happy result of this is that good, reliable designs constantly get cheaper and better. It's easy to forget how much better suspension forks are now than, say, six or seven years ago, and to realize that for the same amount you paid for the fork back then, you can now get a whole bike with a better fork.

Many people originally resisted suspension forks – the extra weight was a high price to pay for the clunky suspension, which seemed to need an hour of servicing for every hour it was ridden. But even the early forks made bikes feel so much faster, and helped them stick to the ground much better.

Although we now see fewer completely weird designs, radically different approaches continue to evolve, and there is no sign of suspension shaking down into just one clear 'best design'. In fact, sometimes the easiest way to tell what the next favourite design will be is by checking which one is currently being slagged off as outdated.

You would have thought that once we'd decided to fit suspension to bicycles, we could borrow the technology from other disciplines. But it didn't seem to work out like that. Although many of the best designers working on the problems come from other areas, like John Whyte from Formula One racing cars and Keith Bontrager from motocross, the bicycle seems to need to be thought about in different ways.

One reason is that the power source – the rider – has a low output, and you can't just slap on a bigger engine. The other is that rider weight makes up a big proportion of the suspended weight, but that weight might vary considerably from one rider to another, even on the same-sized bike.

Suspending disbelief

So, what does it all matter? You can hardly buy a decent mountain bike with rigid forks any more, and full suspension goes up in quality and down in price all the time. All those people who used to say, 'It's all very well for the kids, but it's so heavy you can't climb at all on it'. used to be right. Early suspension was heavy and bounced so much when you climbed that you might as well be trying to hop up on a pogo stick. Some people are still saying this, but we can't hear them any more because we've left them behind at the bottom of the hill.

Full suspension is light enough to climb on now and good design means that full suspension helps you climb by keeping the back wheel pressed down into the ground, finding whatever grip there is to help you up hills. Suspension isn't just for people who want to jump off roofs – it allows you to blast over rough ground without carefully picking a line as you would with a rigid bike.

Suspension does need more care and attention than other parts of your bike. The first surprising thing is that when it's new, it needs attention straight away. When you buy a new fork, or a new bike with forks and a rear shock, you need to spend a little time adjusting it. The adjustments are very personal – nobody can set it up for you because adjustments must be done to your weight and reaction speed. It takes maybe upward of half an hour – and you need to take your bike somewhere you can play safely without traffic. Follow the instructions in the sections on setting up your forks (page 228) and setting up your shocks (pages 237–8).

Once your suspension is set up correctly, check and clean it regularly – shocks don't respond at all to neglect. A check and clean needs no special tools and is easy to do, but it should be done regularly. There's no harm in checking shocks after every ride, but they also need a thorough inspection once a month – see pages 230–34 for forks and pages 239–41 for rear shocks.

Doing a full service on suspension forks and shocks is more advanced and often requires special tools particular to the make and model of your bike. Previously, the instructions that came with forks were very comprehensive – manufacturers positively encouraged everybody to get in there and get dirty – but in the last few years there has been a clear move away from this. Indeed, most manufacturers now take the opposite stance, with clear injunctions for you to not go further than the basic maintenance and regular inspection set out in the owner's manual. However, your forks and shocks still have to be serviced frequently, so either go to your bike shop or post the fork or shock off to a shock servicing specialist – see contact details in the back of the book. The strip-down of a fork on page 230 is to show you the kind of thing that happens when an authorized agent services them.

The same applies to rear shocks – you are expected to keep them clean and lubricated, but not to delve too deeply into their innards, as this will void your warranty.

Remember to increase the frequency of servicing if you ride in sandy, salty or muddy conditions, if you cover a lot of miles, or if you have a reputation for breaking bits of your bicycle.

Part of the mystery of suspension is that talking about it demands all kinds of jargon: terms for the parts, for the adjustments and for how the fork reacts to the terrain. Much confusion arises because most of the words have both a real-world meaning and a suspension-world meaning, which, while not altogether different, is a lot more precise.

Vital elements

Everybody claims their design is the best and most unique, but all suspension does the same job. A fork needs only two elements to work: a spring, which allows the wheel to move so you don't have to, and damping, which controls the speed at which the spring moves.

The spring can be a chamber of air, a coil spring, a rod of springy elastomers or a combination of all three. The spring performs the visible function – shock absorption. When you hit something, the spring gets shorter, absorbing the pressure. The stiffness of the spring controls how far it moves when you hit something – a soft spring gives a lot; a stiff spring gives a little.

The more mysterious element is damping. Damping is vital because it controls the speed of the spring action. Pogo sticks are an example of springs with no damping – if you bounce on them, they keep bouncing. This is great fun on a pogo stick but rubbish on a bike. Damping controls the speed of the spring movement. You may be able to control the speed of the damping with external knobs, or it may be factory-set. More expensive forks allow you to control the speed of the fork compression separately from the speed at which the fork rebounds.

Buttons, bells and whistles

More controls doesn't always mean better. One of the problems with buttons bells and whistles is that there are as many wrong positions as right ones and, if you're not systematic, you can make things worse rather than better.

The least familiar function is lockout, which does exactly what it says on the packet. It locks out the suspension, so the bike doesn't bob around and is particularly useful for smooth climbs and road riding, where you don't need the suspension. Most useful for climbing are forks that lock out in the compressed position, which helps you to keep your weight over the front wheel on steep bits.

Learn the language: travel

Travel is one of those suspension jargon words that means exactly what it says: how far your fork travels from its most extended to its most compressed position.

Many early suspension forks were proud of travelling all of 63mm (2½ inches). Today, 100mm (4 inches) is a common fork travel, and travel of 150mm (6 inches) or so is not uncommon.

These longer travels come at a price though – they're always heavier because you've got more fork material, and they have also to be beefier, otherwise they flex too much. Flexible forks are no good because they don't corner confidently, and they waste your pedalling energy. The other advantage of shorter forks shows up when you climb: long forks lift the front of the bike up, making it difficult to keep the front wheel on the ground during steep ascents. Similar compromises exist for rear suspension: loads of travel is great for jumping off things, but it is not as handy for climbing up them.

Forks with 130mm (5 inches) or 150mm (6 inches) of travel are for freeride and downhill use, as the long springs will absorb big landing forces without too much stress.

Adjustable travel

This is an effort to reconcile the compromises between long travel, which is great for absorbing big bumps, and short travel, which is more efficient for climbing. Certain kinds of suspension forks and shocks are available that allow you to change your travel on the move without getting off the bike, although personally I prefer not to be fiddling around with travel-adjust knobs while whizzing along. Including adjustable travel in a fork adds cost, but it's worthwhile for versatility. Be aware that in some forks the adjustability in the travel is obtained by preloading the spring, leading to a higher spring rate for shorter travel settings. This should be an advantage – stiffening the spring in its short-travel, climbing mode – but some people don't like the way it changes the feel of the bike. Test-ride adjustable travel forks through their range before you commit yourself.

Learning the language of suspension: sag and preload

Your suspension is there to do a simple job – taking short, sharp shocks and turning them into smoother, more controllable forces. This allows you to travel fast over uneven terrain, maintaining as level a path as possible, saving your energy. and allowing you to pick shorter, quicker lines on the trail.

Sag

Suspension moves up and down as you go over lumps and through potholes in the trail. Since the ideal is for your body to move in as straight a line as possible, ironing out the irregularities, it makes sense for the resting position of your suspension to be around the middle of its travel – so it can extend into dips as well as compressing over bumps. If the fork extends into dips so that you don't fall into them, you don't have to ride out of them, saving you some energy.

Sag is the distance that your fork or shock compresses when you sit still on your bike in your normal riding position. It's worked out by measuring the length of your fork or shock with and without you on the bike, then subtracting one number from the other. This tells you how much your weight has compressed the fork or shock.

The amount your forks compress when you sit on the bike depends partly on how much you weigh, and partly on the geometry of the bike, so it needs to be set up individually for each person on his/her own bike. For those who can't be bothered to measure and adjust, new forks and shocks are supplied preset with an average amount of sag, but your suspension will work much better when tailored to you and your bike.

Each suspension fork manufacturer recommends an ideal amount of sag for your particular fork. There's no hard-and-fast rule, and suggested starting points range from 10 to 40 per cent of your total travel. A longer fork will always need to be set up with more sag than a shorter fork.

You also need to take into account what kind of ride you want – if you race, you set your forks up with a little less sag to minimize the amount of energy lost bobbing up and down. If you ride all day, you set them up with slightly more sag so your bike is comfortable to ride, absorbing trail noise so you don't get as tired. Rougher trails need still more sag and, if you jump around, you set your forks soft to absorb the force of landing.

Preload

This is the adjustment you make to the spring to alter the amount of sag. Increasing preload by pumping air into an air spring or compressing a coil spring will make the spring stiffer, keeping you higher in the air – less sag. Reducing pressure in an air spring, or unwinding the preload on a coil spring, reduces the sag and sits you lower down.

Altering the preload is the single most important adjustment for you to make on your forks or suspension because it sets the fork or shock up to match your weight and bike geometry. With coil forks, you may need to replace the standard bone spring with a harder or softer coil to get the perfect preload setting.

Coil springs will keep their adjustment once you've set it, but air spring forks tend to leak slowly, so they need to be checked every couple of months. You need a shock pump to measure and adjust the air pressure. Occasionally air forks come supplied with a pump, but it's more common for you to have to buy one separately. Shock pumps have narrow barrels and pressure gauges so that you can set the pressure accurately.

Topping out and bottoming out

Both these terms mean 'hitting the end of your available travel'. Bottoming out is when you hit something hard, and your forks or shock compress completely. Topping out is when your fork or shock extends and reaches the limit of its travel. First generation suspension forks used to let you know this in no uncertain terms – the end of the stanchion hit the inside of the fork with an alarming thwack. This was so unsettling that fork manufacturers soon designed a form of stop at each end of the travel, so that now you run into the buffers at the end of the track rather than crashing into the barrier. It's often considered a bad thing to top or bottom out – but don't be concerned. Ideally, your forks should be set up so you bottom out about once every ride – otherwise you're not using the full extent of your fork or shock travel. Put a ziptie loosely around the shaft of your shock or the stanchion of your fork, and push it down to the seal before you ride. The fork or shock will push it up again as it travels, and show you how far the shock is moving.

Learning the language of suspension: the spring thing

The spring in your fork is in many ways the simplest component – when you compress the fork, the spring resists the compressing and it re-extends the fork as soon as you release the compressing force.

Air springs, coil springs, elastomers

It may be freely available, light and highly adjustable, but air can be pesky because it doesn't like being trapped inside the fork. The fork manufacturer has to spend your money ensuring it doesn't leak. An air spring works by trapping air in a chamber at the top of the fork leg. As you compress the fork (by riding into an obstacle), you squash the air into an even smaller space, which it resists, responding by pushing out the fork again to make more space for itself and acting like a spring.

Coil springs are very simple, and neither leak nor get affected by temperature. But if you want to change their springiness much, you either have to buy a new one or exchange it. If you buy a bike or a fork with a coil spring, make sure it's the right stiffness when you buy it by checking that you can adjust the sag for your weight. You can tune in a small amount of stiffness by altering the preload, but you can't make major changes – the spring has to be the right stiffness from the beginning. Exchanging steel springs for titanium ones is expensive but saves a little weight.

Elastomers used to be the most common spring type, but they have been largely superseded by coil springs. Elastomers are made of rods of urethane, usually in different colours to denote their stiffness. Elastomers are a cheap spring medium, but their spring rate is affected by temperature, so they become much stiffer when cold and much softer when warm. Fine-tuning tricks for the first generation of elastomer-sprung forks included drilling holes across the elastomers to make them softer.

Your forks may have springs in both legs, but it's also common to have springs in one leg and a damping mechanism in the other. If there are springs in only one leg, they will almost always be in the left leg, nearest the disc brake. This keeps the damping mechanism farther away from the heat generated by the disc brake, which will affect the viscosity of the damping oil. Having springs in just one leg doesn't make the fork unbalanced – the two sides of the lower legs still work together as a unit.

To get the best of both worlds, some forks use a combination of air and coil springs.

Spring rate

This is a measure of how much the suspension moves under pressure. Under the same force, a spring with a higher spring rate compresses less than one with a lower spring rate. If you are lighter, you use a spring with a lower spring rate than someone heavier.

Progressive spring rates

All suspension depends on the spring, either air or coil. Both types perform the same function: when you press on the spring, it shortens slightly. When you ride along on your bike, and you hit a rock, force is applied to the fork, which then compresses. One difference between air and coil spring forks is how they behave through their stroke. Coil spring forks are linear – that is, it takes roughly the same amount of force to compress the second half of the coil as it does to compress the first.

Air springs behave differently. When you pressurize your fork, you put a lot of air into a small space. The air dislikes being compressed in the first place, so when you hit a bump and compress the fork, squashing the air even more, it resists and pushes the fork back out again – doing the spring thing. But, as the fork compresses, the space that the air is in gets even smaller, and it dislikes being compressed even more. In other words, the beginning of the stroke takes less force to compress than the end. The disadvantage is that air forks are less active over small bumps.

Negative air springs

As well as the regular positive air spring, many forks (including most models from Rock Shox) have a second air spring, a negative one, which sits at the top of the fork leg and compresses upward (rather than downward). This allows you to tune the reaction of the fork to small bumps. Less negative air pressure makes the fork stiffer at the beginning of its travel, so that it doesn't bob so much when you climb out of the saddle. More negative air pressure allows the fork to move more at the beginning of its travel, soaking up small bumps.

Learn the language of suspension: damping

Whenever you hit a bump, your fork and rear shock (or both) compress, absorbing the shock. When you've gone over the bump, they spring back out again, ready for the next bump. But you don't want them to spring out quickly and bounce you off your bike (if we wanted to play that game we'd return to rigid bikes), so we 'damp' the movement, by making the rebound extension happen more slowly than the original compression.

This is a good thing. However, you can take it too far. If the rebound happens too slowly, and you ride over a series of bumps, the fork compresses when you go over the first bump and will not have had time to extend again by the time you hit the second bump. As you go over the series of bumps, the fork gets shorter and shorter, doing less and less suspending, until you're riding on a very short, rigid fork. This is called 'stacking up' and can be avoided by reducing your rebound damping. Damping adjustment affects your steering too – forcing your front wheel around a corner compresses your fork and, if you have too much damping, the fork stays compressed through the turn, tucking under the handlebars rather than helping to turn.

Suspension forks are designed so that you can control the speed of the movement, adjusting the damping to find the middle ground between too fast and too slow. At the ideal setting, your fork is always ready to respond to fresh forces, but it never moves more quickly than you can, so that you're always in charge. Ideal damping setting is an individual preference.

Early attempts at damping control were very basic. One design had what the manufacturers referred to as 'friction damping', as if this was an asset. What it actually meant was the elastomers that did the springing rubbed against the insides of the tubes they were trapped in, slowing down the movement. I had a pair like this – they cost me a week's wages and wore out in three months – and I thought they were fantastic.

Each generation of suspension since then has become more sophisticated. Oil is the universal damping medium now. The same principle is used by all manufacturers, regardless of what three-letter acronym they use to convince you that their product is radical and innovative. I'll describe the process for suspension forks, but shocks work in exactly the same way.

Your fork contains damping oil that sloshes about in the fork leg. While your forks are extended, the oil remains at the bottom of the chamber. As the fork is compressed, the stanchions get pushed down through the oil. But between the two is a piston, a disc that blocks the flow of oil. Holes in the piston allow the oil to pass through, but oil doesn't really like being forced through holes, and it won't be hurried. The fork can only compress as fast as the oil will pass through the holes.

Once the fork is fully compressed, the springs start doing their job, and act to force the fork to extend again. In order for the fork to re-extend, the oil has to pass back through the holes in the piston – once more, only as fast as the oil will flow through the holes. The key to effective damping is controlling the speed of the oil through the holes. This is done by changing the thickness of the oil – see the oil weight section opposite – or more easily by changing the size of the oil-flow hole. A bigger hole equals faster oil flow equals less damping.

Turning the damping adjustment knobs on your forks will open or close the oil ports, changing the speed at which the oil can pass through the piston, and so altering the speed at which your forks can respond to shocks.

Ideally, we'd like to control the movement of the oil through the holes separately in each direction, so that we can alter the rebound speed without affecting the compression speed. One way to do this is by mounting a thin, flexible washer on one side of the piston so that it covers a set of relatively large piston holes. When you hit a big bump, the fork compresses, pushing oil through the piston towards the washer. The force bends the washer out of the way, allowing the oil to flow freely. Once the spring begins to re-extend the fork, the direction of oil flow is reversed. From this side, the pressure of the oil will flatten the washer against the piston, blocking the holes and preventing oil flow. The addition of the washer means that the piston acts like a turnstile, allowing free flow of oil in one direction and not in the other.

However, you don't want to block the flow of oil completely, as this would simply lock the forks out. So a smaller hole is set in the middle of the piston, where it won't get blocked by the washer. This allows the oil to flow back, but it does so much more slowly. Controlling the size of this hole adjusts the rebound speed. The most common control set-up is a needle that gets pushed into the central hole as you turn the rebound adjustment knob. It makes the hole effectively smaller, and increases damping, so that the forks re-extend more slowly.

Piston

Hole in
damping shaft

▲ Damping shaft

Rebound damping

After the preload adjuster, the most common adjustment that you'll find on forks is a rebound adjuster that controls the speed at which the fork re-extends after it's been squashed by hitting an obstacle. Here's an example of a rebound adjusting mechanism – this piston sits inside the fork stanchion. The rebounding oil is forced to flow through the hole in the damping shaft. The size of this hole is controlled by turning the rebound damping knob, which pushes a rod up through the centre of the shaft, gradually closing off the hole to reduce oil flow, thereby increasing the damping and slowing down the fork.

Compression damping

Compression damping affects how quickly the suspension responds to being compressed – if there is very little damping, the suspension reacts to every bump, which is good, but it will reach the end of its travel very quickly, bottoming out when you hit something big. The damping in forks is often controlled by damping oil being forced through a small hole as the fork compresses. A larger hole, or thinner oil, allows the fork to compress more quickly.

All forks have some kind of compression damping. As they get more expensive, this is more likely to be adjustable externally. The compression damping mechanism can also be used to lock out (turn off) the fork or shock, so it doesn't bob when you climb. Turning the lockout knob closes the hole through which the oil passes, effectively stopping the fork compressing. This design almost always 'blows' – or automatically releases if it's put under a lot of pressure – if you forget to turn off the lockout and hit something big. This is to stop the fork getting damaged (and hopefully helping you out in the process).

Oil weight

Oil resists being forced to flow through small holes. The speed at which it moves depends on two things – how big the holes are and how thick the oil is. Large holes and thin oil means fast oil flow. Small holes and thick oil means slow oil flow. The thicker oil is, the less it likes squeezing through small holes.

The thickness of the oil is called its weight (wt). Thicker (gloopier) oil, say 15wt, is more reluctant to pass through small holes, and so it increases the rebound damping. Thinner oil, say 5wt, is lighter. This makes your forks faster. However, each fork is made for a specific weight of oil, and changing the performance of the fork by altering the weight is a precise science. Unless you are particularly heavy or light, use the oil weight recommended by your fork manufacturer, and adjust the damping speed by changing the size of the flow holes with the damping adjustment knobs.

Extreme temperature affects how runny the oil is. Heat makes the oil runnier, and it flows through the holes quicker, reducing damping. Very cold weather has the opposite effect. So increase the oil weight for very hot climates and reduce it for cold ones. A change of 5wt should be enough, but you have to experiment.

Damping oil does get worn out over time. It picks up dirt and moisture from the insides of your forks. It needs to be changed periodically. It should last two years with normal use, more frequently if you're hard on your forks. New forks will sometimes have tiny metal scraps left over from the manufacturing process, which get picked up by the fork oil, so it's a good idea to schedule an initial oil change after six months or so.

Front suspension

Fork servicing isn't magic. It isn't even difficult, but it does need care and patience. It often needs very specific parts, which usually have to be ordered – there must be at least a million different spare suspension part numbers out there now. Don't assume you'll get spares for older forks. Some companies stock a longer back catalogue than others, but if your forks are more than about three years old, you're on sketchy ground. That counts from when they were first made, so if you picked them up as a cheap end-of-line model, you'll arrive in obsolete land even sooner.

Steerer tube

Crown

Valve cover

Top cap

Compression Damping

Remote spool for pop-lock

Stanchions

Lower legs or sliders

Rebound adjusting knob

▲ **RockShox Reba**

Forks are generally harder to repair than to maintain – once something goes wrong or breaks, they need special parts and usually special tools as well. This is often best left to your bike shop or the fork manufacturer. If your bike shop doesn't do fork repairs, you can send your forks off to be serviced. I have included a sample fork strip to demonstrate the principle of what your shop does as part of a service.

There are several designs of fork. There isn't space here to go through a complete strip-down of every kind of fork, so I've included just a couple of examples. The main reference text is always the owner's manual. If you don't have the one your fork came with, print a new one off the Internet. Make sure you get exactly the right year and model – even if the fork looks the same, small details change from one year to the next.

How far should you go? Use the manual for guidance – be aware that stripping down your fork further than recommended may invalidate the warranty. Take extra care with any fork that uses an air spring. Always be sure to release all the air pressure from the fork before you take anything apart. This is easy to forget but vital to remember – start undoing things under pressure, and they rocket off. If they don't hit and hurt you, you'll probably lose something vital.

You should be able to service forks while they're on the bike, but you'll probably find it easier if you remove them. Follow the instructions on pages 230–34 – and you might as well service the headset while you're there. Either way, you'll need to be able to clamp the forks upright to add oil to the tops, and to inject oil horizontally into the bottoms of the fork legs.

The most important constant maintenance for forks consists of only three things:

◆ Keep them clean, but don't jet-hose them. The most common cause of death for forks is dirt that works in between stanchions and seals, leaving scratches.

◆ Be conscious as you ride of any changes in the ride characteristic – nothing trashes forks faster than being used when something is a little loose.

◆ Ride them regularly. Forks get cantankerous if they're not ridden for a while.

There are two good reasons why people should carry out mild maintenance on their bikes more often than most do. The first is economic: the more expensive forks are to buy, the more expensive they are to fix. Catch a problem sooner rather than later and you save yourself money. The second reason is safety. Suspension is good at keeping your wheels on the ground, maximizing your grip and steering, but if parts work loose and break free, you can be left with no control over your bike.

The very best time to clean your forks is just after your last ride, not just before your next one! Forks left dirty do not last as long as forks cleaned between rides. Find something wrong and you have time to fix it before going out next.

How suspension parts fit together

Fork designers keep us all on our toes by changing the locations of damping and preload-adjusters from year to year and model to model. Here's a couple of examples, but refer to your owner's manual to find which knob does what on your forks. Sometimes, generous designers label the knobs on the forks for you – this makes life a lot easier!

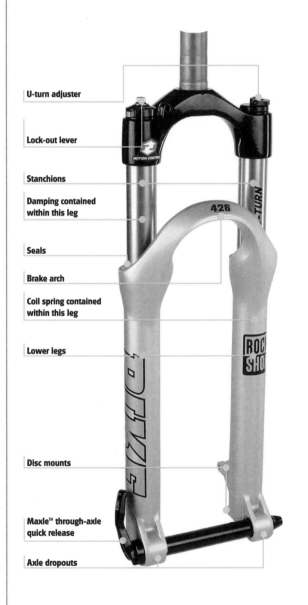

U-turn adjuster

Lock-out lever

Stanchions

Damping contained within this leg

Seals

Brake arch

Coil spring contained within this leg

Lower legs

Disc mounts

Maxle™ through-axle quick release

Axle dropouts

▲ RockShox Pike

Floodgate adjuster

Valve for preload adjuster

Stanchions

Air springs contained within this leg

Brake arch

Lower legs

Disc brake mounts

Dropouts

Rebound damping adjusting knob

▲ RockShox Reba

Setting up your forks properly

I still get shocked by how many people happily spend a chunk of cash buying a new set of forks but can't find an hour to set them up properly. It's not difficult and it makes an expensive fork ride like an expensive fork.

Basic forks allow you to set the preload, which you use to alter the sag. As forks get more expensive, you are also able to adjust the rebound damping, the compression damping, the travel and you can temporarily lock out the fork to make it rigid. All the different manufacturers put the controls for these adjustments in different places – say, the rebound knob at the top of the left leg or at the bottom of the right leg. Before you go any further, dig out the owner's manual for your fork and identify the adjustments you can make on it, and locate where the adjusters are.

When setting up and tuning your forks, it's important to change only one thing at a time. Don't be tempted to twiddle all the knobs and see what happens: you are as likely to hit upon a 'just wrong' place as a 'just right' place. Keep a note of the adjustments you make, so that once you find the adjustment to suit you can return to it.

Sag

First set up the sag, which is where the fork compresses a little under your weight. The best information about how much sag your fork needs should come from your owner's manual – as I mentioned earlier, if you haven't kept it, you can usually print another off the internet. As a general guideline, start with 20–25 per cent of your total fork travel for cross-country forks, and 30–35 per cent for all-mountain/freeride forks.

This is only a rough guide; your fork is designed for a specific amount of sag. There are still plenty of diehard XC racers who consider they have made enough of a concession by fitting suspension forks and run them so they hardly move at all. I don't understand this – it makes no more sense than fitting a nine-speed cassette and adjusting the end-stop screws so that only the middle five gears work. The worst part is that these guys do it to good-quality, lightweight, adjustable forks. Oh well.

Page 229 takes you through setting up your fork sag; page 238 describes setting up your shock sag.

Rebound damping

Once the sag is sorted, adjust the rebound damping. You'll need to take your bike outside and ride around for this bit. People like to lean on suspension forks, watch them spring back and nod knowledgeably, but there's no substitute for getting out and seeing how your fork reacts to being properly ridden.

Most manufacturers have a pretty good idea of a starting point for you and will recommend it in the manual. I like to set my rebound damping as fast as I can before it's so fast that the bars come back up quicker than I do. I think that's the key – to match the fork's reaction speed to yours. The faster it is, the less often it gets caught out by a series of bumps, hitting the next before recovering from the last. But it's a very personal adjustment. Your rebound damping setting affects the bike's feel when cornering – if you have too much rebound damping, the fork stays compressed as you turn, digging the wheel into the corner rather than pushing you around it.

Find a baby dropoff that you can ride over repeatedly – 10cm (4 inches) or so is about right. Set your fork to the slowest rebound damping position (i.e. maximum damping equals slowest movement) and ride over the dropoff. Reset to the fastest damping position (least damping equals fastest movement), and ride off again. You'll feel your bike react differently, with the handlebars springing straight back toward you.

Repeat the dropoff, slowing the rebound damping down a little at a time – if your adjuster has distinct clicks, go one click at a time. You're aiming to find a position where you're completely in control throughout the cycle of the fork, but with as little damping as possible. Once you've found the right place, write down the adjustment so that you can find it again. I use a marker pen to draw a line on the fork and the knob so that I can find the adjustment again by lining up the two marks.

High- and low-speed compression damping

If you have a compression damping adjustment, set this last. This adjustment affects how fast your fork compresses when it hits an obstacle. Again the right setting is tied up with your reaction speed. If you set up the preload correctly and are still bottoming out, you don't have enough compression damping. If the fork doesn't respond to small obstacles, you have too much compression damping. With many forks, your compression damping is preset and cannot be adjusted. I don't think this is a great loss, I've always found the preset levels to be fine. If you have both front and rear suspension, set up the front forks first, then set the back end to match. Set yourself a time and place where you can ride safely without looking where you're going, ideally somewhere fairly flat with a single obstacle you can ride over repeatedly without too much effort. You need to ride over the identical object a number of times to see the effect the adjustments are having.

Setting your sag for the best possible results

Use the steps below to measure your sag, and adjust the preload to give you the recommended sag. Remember that this is just a starting point though – you may want to fine-tune the preload for your riding style.

Once you've followed the steps, ride your bike to see how it feels. If you hit something hard, you'll go all the way through the travel of the fork to the point where the top part thuds against the bottom part. This is 'bottoming out the fork'. It's not a bad thing – if you don't hit that point during normal riding, you aren't using all the available fork travel. Play with the initial sag setting to aim to bottom out about once a ride.

SETTING YOUR SAG

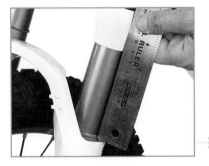

Step 1: Work out your travel. If it's written in your owner's manual or as here, handily printed on the fork, use that measurement. Manuals for air shocks often give you a recommended air pressure for your weight, but it's worth testing the actual sag you get on your bike because it depends on your position on the bike and the configuration of your shock.

Step 2: If you don't have the manual, work travel out like this: with the fork fully extended, measure the distance from the bottom of the fork crown to the top of the lower leg seal, i.e. check how much stanchion is showing.

Step 3: Release air pressure in air forks or remove coil springs in coil forks, and push the fork right down as far as it will go. Measure the same distance again. Take the second number from the first. This is your total travel. Replace coil springs, reinflate air chambers.

Step 4: Take a ziptie and loop it around one of your fork stanchions so it's fairly tight but can still be pushed up and down easily. Push it down so it sits just above the seal. Your fork may also have an O-ring installed on one of the legs for this purpose. Or markings printed on the leg.

Step 5: Lean your bike against a wall and mount it carefully. Sit still on the bike, in your normal riding position. Don't bounce up and down. Get off the bike. Your weight on the bike has compressed the forks, pushing up the ziptie. Now measure the distance between the ziptie and the top of the seal. This is the sag.

Step 6: Adjust the air pressure or the coil-spring preload until the sag is the required proportion of the total travel.

Inspecting and maintaining your forks for fun and profit

Regular, careful fork maintenance will save you money – keeping your forks clean will help reduce servicing frequency. It's also a good time to inspect them, allowing you to pick up and sort out potential problems quickly.

All fork maintenance starts with a good clean. Disconnect the V-brakes and drop the wheel out of the frame, so that you can get to the forks properly. For disc brakes, push the brake spacer that came supplied with the callipers (you kept it, right?) or a wedge of clean cardboard between the disc pads, so that you don't accidentally pump the brake pads out of the callipers. Go through the steps below; if you find worn or broken components, it's time for a fork service. Don't ride damaged forks – they may let you down without warning.

Stanchions

Wipers/seals

426

Lower legs

Disc mounts

Dropouts

RockShox Pike 428

◆ Start by washing the lower legs, stanchions and fork crown. Plain water is fine, although if they're really grimy, use Muc-Off or other similar bike-cleaners. With magnesium lower legs, check carefully for bubbling paint – this is usually an indication that it's time for a new fork. If in doubt, get to your local bike shop for a second opinion.

◆ As you wash the dirt off, inspect the forks carefully and methodically. Start with dropouts. Check for cracks around the joint between the fork leg and the dropout, inside and out.

◆ Take a look at the condition of the surfaces that your wheels clamp onto, inside and out. These grip the axle and stop the wheel popping out of the fork. The serrations on the quick-release and axle make dents in the fork – make sure that these are clean, crisp dents, rather than worn craters that indicate the wheel has been shifting about.

◆ Check each fork leg in turn. You're looking for splits, cracks or dents. Big dents will weaken the fork and prevent the stanchion from moving freely inside the lower legs. Cracks and dents both mean that it's new fork time.

◆ Take a look at disc and V-brake mounts. Check disc mounts for cracks and check that all calliper fixing bolts are tight.

◆ Check the bolts at the bottoms of the fork legs – these hold everything together, so make sure they're not working loose. Look for signs that oil has been leaking out from under the bolts.

◆ Clean muck out from behind the brake arch – grit has a tendency to collect here.

◆ Inspect the wipers that clean the stanchions as they enter the lower legs. Tears or cuts will allow grit into the wipers, where they will scour your stanchions. The tops of the wipers are usually held in place with a fine circular spring that should sit in the lip at the top of the wiper.

◆ Check the stanchions. If grit gets stuck in the wipers or seals, it will be dragged up and down as your fork cycles, wearing vertical grooves in the forks. These grooves in turn provide a new route in for more dirt.

◆ Check all the adjuster knobs. They often stick out so that you can turn them easily, but this does make them vulnerable.

◆ Refit the wheel and reconnect the V-brakes. Pull the front brake on and hold one of the stanchions just above the lower leg. Rock the bike gently back and forth. You may be able to feel a little bit of flex in the forks, but you should not be able to feel the lower legs knocking. Lots of movement here means you need new bushings.

◆ Push down firmly on the bars, compressing the forks. They should spring back smoothly when you release the bars. If they stutter or hesitate returning, it's time for a fork service.

◆ Finally, finish off by polishing the lower legs. It makes the forks look better, which is important in itself, but also leaves a waxy finish that means dirt doesn't stick so well to the fork.

Cleaning and lubricating the stanchions

Wipers are the black rubber rings at the top of the lower legs into which the stanchions disappear. Your forks bob up and down constantly as you ride, and on a muddy day your stanchions will be constantly bombarded with grit. If this grit can work its way down into your seals, it will get dragged up and down by the action of the forks, scouring long vertical grooves in the stanchions, which will allow dirt into your fork and oil out of it.

The wipers serve as a first line of defence against unwanted grit, helping to keep it off the seals. Regularly clean any build-up of dirt off the wipers to stop dirt from working its way down to the seals, which are found below the wipers where they are pressed into the top of the lower legs.

Fork seals have to flex with the movement of the stanchions, forming a tight-fitting barrier to prevent dirt getting in or oil getting out. The seals mustn't fit too tightly though, or they will stop the fork from moving smoothly. Good seals are one of the most important qualities in a fork. Seals need to be replaced regularly, so ensure that this is done when you get your forks serviced.

Forks used to all come with fork boots, which are flexible rubber gaiters that were supposed to keep the stanchions clean. Besides being ugly, they had a tendency to trap moisture in the area around the top of the lower leg, just where you need it least. Very few forks come with boots now – wipers have replaced them and seals have become much more effective.

Wiper care

After cleaning the fork externally, spray the stanchions lightly with a light oil like GT85, and cycle the forks. This is a fancy term that means, stand next to the bike and push and release on the bars a few times to spread around the oil you've applied to the upper part of the stanchion. Then, use a small pick to carefully peel back the top of the wiper and drop in a couple of drops of a heavier oil. Whatever you're using for your chain will be about right – I prefer something like Finish Line Cross Country. Run the pick gently around the circumference of the wiper, following the pick with a trail of oil. Cycle the fork again and use a clean cloth to wipe away any dirt that emerges.

It's important not to scratch the stanchion while you're doing this. If where you normally ride is muddy, it's worth taking the time to custom make yourself a tool for the task. An old, thin-bladed screwdriver, ready to be put out to pasture, can be usefully repurposed and recycled – clamp the last couple of centimetres (1 inch) in a bench vice and bend over at 90 degrees. Clean the blade really carefully and pop into your toolbox. An old spoke, bent at the end and hammered flat, will also serve well. You can buy specially made tools for this purpose, but I can imagine no reason why you'd want to.

Don't be tempted to use degreaser on the stanchions, even if they're caked in dirt. It will find its way into the gap between the stanchion and the wiper, and break down all the lubricant inside your fork. So you'll be nice and clean, but with no bounce.

Cheap forks have chrome steel stanchions. Although heavier than their more expensive anodised aluminium stanchions, chrome steel is smoother and more resistant to nicks and scratches. Some forks are made with both options – for example, a RockShox Recon has the same controls as a Tora, but the stanchions are upgraded to lighter aluminium versions.

RockShox Reba:
50- and 100-hour service

All forks respond better to persistent nurturing than intermittent guilt-ridden frenzies.

Sadly there isn't room to include all the popular fork configurations here but this should give you an idea of the kinds of thing that go on inside. I've used the RockShox Reba as an example, since they're widespread and respond well to attention.

The fork has an air spring in the left leg and a damping assembly in the right leg. The rebound adjusting knob is on the bottom of the right leg, with the compression damping adjuster and lockout at the top of the right leg, and both lower legs have an oil bath for lubrication. This arrangement keeps the entire damping mechanism as far away as possible from the heat of the disc brake, mounted on the left leg.

Damping performance depends on the viscosity of the damping oil, which is affected by temperature. If you ride in extreme temperatures, get to your local bike shop for a recommendation on oil weight. The damping oil level and condition is critical, so check it twice a year and replace once or twice a year depending on your mileage.

There are three levels of servicing:

◆ **Level 1**: Every 50 hours, take the fork apart, cleaning the lower legs and stanchions, and reassemble with fresh oil. Follow steps 1–5 to disassemble, then steps 13–14 to reassemble.

◆ **Level 2:** Every 100 hours of riding, the air and damping chambers will need to be cleaned and filled with fresh oil. Follow the procedure all the way through steps 1–14. If you're not confident about this level, take the fork to your bike shop and ask them to do it.

◆ **Level 3:** A specialist suspension tuner can customize your damping internals to suit your weight and riding style. Either take your forks into your bike shop or send them away to one of the service centres listed on page 240.

Before you start servicing your forks, make sure all external surfaces are clean. All lefts and rights are given as if you were sitting on the bike looking at the forks.

ROCKSHOX REBA

Step 1: Before you start, make a note of the air pressures and rebound setting you're currently using. Remove the valve cap from the bottom of the left fork leg. Release all negative air pressure by depressing the central stalk in the Schraeder valve, as show. Repeat with the positive air pressure, at the top of the left fork leg.

Step 2: Pull off rebound damping knob from bottom of right fork leg. Look at the forks from below. Undo the 5mm Allen key bolt on the bottom of the right fork leg five complete turns. On the left leg, use a 10mm socket wrench to undo the nut on its shaft until the top of the nut is flush with the end of the shaft.

Step 3: Have a container handy to catch the oil as it drains out of the bottom of the fork legs. Place a 5mm Allen key into the bolt in the bottom of the right leg. Tap the Allen key gently with your plastic hammer to free the damping shaft from the lower legs, releasing oil. Repeat on the left leg, with your 10mm socket placed over the nut to protect it.

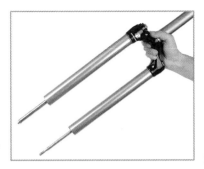

Step 4: Pull the stanchions out of the lower legs gently, keeping the lower legs over the container to catch the old oil. Leave the lower legs draining while you clean and inspect the upper legs.

Step 5: Clean and check for scours on the stanchions. Badly scratched stanchions need replacing – get a second opinion from your bikeshop if you're unsure. Clean the insides of the lower legs by wrapping a clean rag around a stickand winding it down in there – repeat until it comes out clean. If you're only doing a lower legservice (every 50 hours) go directly to step 13 on page 234. Otherwise continue with step 6.

Step 6: Double check that you've released all the positive air pressure via the valve at the top of the left fork leg. Remove the air cap carefully with a 24mm socket and drain any oil on top of the air piston.

Step 7: Remove the circlip with your circlip pliers from the underside of the left leg. Pull out the air shaft, catching any oil that comes out. At this point, you can change the travel if desired by adding or removing the black plastic spacers below the piston. Clean the air tube and air shaft, then reassemble, pouring 5ml of 15wt oil onto the air piston through the crown. Then refit the top cap.

Step 8: Remove Floodgate adjuster with a 1.5mm Allen key then remove either the lockout lever or lockout remote spool (depending on your fork model) with circlip pliers. Undo the top cap with a 24mm socket.

Step 9: Remove the Motion Control damper and clean.

Toolbox

Tools for 50hr service
- 5mm Allen key
- 10 socket wrench
- Plastic hammer
- 15wt suspension oil
- Syringe to pour oil into lower legs

Tools for 100hr service
All of the above plus:
- 24mm socket wrench
- 1.5 and 2mm Allen keys
- 5wt suspension oil from your bike shop
- A tray to catch the old oil and clean cloths to mop up spillage
- Isopropyl alcohol or disc brake cleaner

If you're using the opportunity of a service to alter the travel on your forks, you'll need to get your hands on the appropriate spacers before you begin. New forks usually come with an extra 20mm spacer kicking around in the box, but if you didn't keep it, or need another, check your local bike shop or RockShox dealer.

Tips for servicing forks

◆ Circlips always need to be fitted back into their groove with the sharp edge facing outwards. Run your finger over either side – you'll feel the sharp edge. This catches on the groove that it sits in, keeping the assembly securely attached.

◆ You may have been supplied with a random 20mm black C-shaped spacer along with your fork. These can be inserted under the air piston to change the overall travel of your fork (see step 6). Reduce the travel for a steeper geometry and crisp race-day steering, increase travel for more control on fast downhills. The spacers are also available in 15 or 25mm lengths from your local dealer. For full suspension bikes, as a general rule it's not worth having more than 20mm more travel on your fork than you've got on your rear shock.

◆ Always reassemble lower leg bolts with blue Loctite 243, to ensure they don't shake loose. It's also worth while fitting new crush washers onto these bolts at every service – your bike shop may have to order them for you, but they're very cheap. Fit these in step 13.

◆ If you're planning on servicing your own forks regularly, invest in a torque wrench to tighten bolts accurately (see page 53). All the correct torque setting will be available on the manufacturer's website – check those that apply to your particular model.

REPLACING THE DAMPING OIL

Step 10: Upend the fork and pour the damping oil into your pan, cycling the damper shaft to help it out. Remove the circlip on the underside of the stanchion, catching remaining oil. Remove and clean the damper shaft. Clean the interior of the fork legs carefully with a twist of clean cloth – it may need a couple of goes. Reinsert the damper shaft. Reinstall the circlip in its groove, sharp edge outwards.

Step 11: Inspect the O-ring seal at the top of the Motion Control damper and replace if there are any cuts or tears. Refill the damping chamber, from the crown, with 110ml of 5wt oil.

Step 12: Refit the Motion Control damper. In order to overcome the resistance of the oil, gently twist as you push the damper towards the threads. Then do up the top cap firmly and refit the lockout lever or lockout spool and circlip. Refit the Floodgate adjuster, with a 1.5mm Allen key.

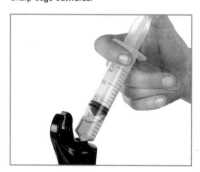

Step 13: Slide the stanchions carefully onto the lower legs, past the seals. They'll slide on a little way, then you'll have to wiggle them to get them through the upper bushings inside the fork leg. Get the stanchions through the bushes (gentle wiggling!) but don't push them fully home yet. Up-end the fork and inject 15ml of 15wt oil carefully through the holes at the bottom of each leg with your syringe.

Step 14: Wait five minutes while the oil runs into the fork, so that it settles between upper and lower bushes. Keeping the forks upended, push the lowers carefully home, wiggling past the lower bushings. The air shaft will appear through the hole in the bottom of the lower legs. Install crush washers, then firmly refit the 5mm Allen key onto the damper shaft and the 10mm nut onto the air shaft.

Step 15: You noted your air pressures before you started – reinflate the positive air spring, then the negative air spring. Recheck all nuts, bolts and controls, with a torque wrench if possible. Refit the rebound damper knob and valve caps.

Rear suspension

Mountain biking – being highly competitive in sporting, technology and commercial terms – boasts as many different rear suspension designs as it does bike companies. And each proud designer knows their beautiful baby blows the others away. While the models differ in detail, it is possible to divide the majority into three types: cantilever, linkage, and URT (unified rear triangle). All three rise and fall in popularity over time. Within each type, there are bikes that have been designed with computer-aided wotsits and cutting-edge doodahs but still ride like dogs. Meanwhile, those you heard a convincing argument against last week still feel fast and furious.

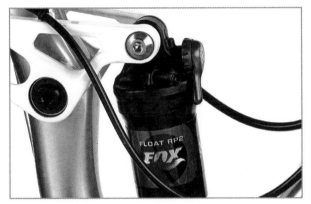

▲ Fox Float suspension unit

Choosing a suspension bike can be stressful. Anybody with any experience has an opinion on what suspension you should consider, and they're all different. However, out there is a bike designed by someone who wants the same from a ride as you do. My advice is try to ride as many different designs as you can before making a decision.

The appropriate design for you depends on your build and riding style. Some people sit in the saddle as long as possible, using their energy economically (they might have a road-bike background). They may generally dislike designs where the position of the rear end affects the chain length, snapping back as they pedal. Others, maybe with a BMX or trail bike background, are up and out of the saddle with little excuse, using their shoulders and their body weight rather than their legs to propel the bike. They may waste loads of energy, but they like great short bursts of power.

Rear suspension design has two elements: frame shape and shock characteristic. All frames are based on the principle that the rear part of the frame is hinged so that the rear wheel moves relative to the main body of the frame. A lot of thought goes into manipulating the pivot and strut positions that make up the rear end in order to control the axle path (or, the position of the axle relative to the frame as it moves through its travel).

Trail forces come from different directions. When you land from a dropoff you apply force directly upwards, and if this were the only force on the rear wheel the equation would be much simpler. But you're also driving the back wheel by pedalling, applying force to the wheel along the horizontal, along the chain from chainring to sprocket. If the hinge between the back and front of the bike lies between the chainset and the rear axle, then pedalling activates the suspension. The movement of the rear end as it reacts to the terrain causes movement in the pedals – 'chain reaction'. This isn't always a bad thing; in climbing, the pedalling tends to extend the suspension and dig the back wheel into the ground, giving you extra grip. Chain reaction is not so alarming, as long as it isn't huge. Your feet get familiar with dealing with the effect quickly, until you don't notice it. Successful suspension design makes the rear axle as responsive as possible to uneven terrain, while minimizing the extent to which pedalling compresses the shock and wastes your energy.

Once the frame has been constructed, the task of the rear shock is to control the speed at which the rear wheel moves along its axle path under force. The spring in the shock absorbs force, while the damping ensures that the spring re-extends at a controllable speed and doesn't buck you off the saddle. A perfect shock responds to small forces instantly, making the bike feel supple and helping to find whatever grip there is. It can also take a big blow without reaching the limit of travel.

This is a lot to pack into the back end of a bicycle, especially when, at the same time, people want everything to be light, strong, stiff and painted this week's hot colour. Small wonder there are as many different 'perfect' designs as there are designers. The evolution of suspension design has taken place in fits and starts, with some folks charging down cul-de-sacs and others beavering away to refine proven designs. There is no right answer, and thus it would be a shame to waste too much riding time wondering if your pivots are in the 'right' position.

Why do all full suspension bikes look different?

While it's difficult to categorize full suspension bikes precisely, most fall into one of two broad categories – cantilever and linkage. There are examples of both types that are a dream to ride and others that are a nightmare.

Cantilever

Early full-suspension bikes were a cantilever design: the rear wheel is connected to a swingarm rotating around a single pivot near the bottom bracket, with the shock connected directly to the main frame. The design's strong advantages – a single pivot and few moving parts – make the frame light, durable, stiff and strong without costing the earth. It is still in use – see the Santa Cruz Bullit.

The disadvantage of the cantilever design is it is difficult to control the effects of chain reaction. Wherever you place the pivot, the rear wheel moves in an arc around it so that, as the axle moves through its travel, the distance between axle and chainset changes appreciably.

Linkage

The addition of linkages adds extra pivots, changing the shape of the rear end of the bike as it moves through its travel. Linkage bikes come in a few types, including, 'four bars' and 'faux bars' and Active Braking Pivot. All rely on smooth-running pivots, which appreciate regular cleaning and lubrication and suffer badly if subjected to jetwashing.

Faux bars are essentially link driven cantilever systems, as the chainstay or swingarm still moves around the main pivot in an arc. The advantage of adding linkages to drive the shock is that this allows the designer to fine-tune the leverage ratio – the relationship between shock movement and wheel displacement.

Faux bar bikes can be identified by the position of the rearmost pivot, just above the rear axle. Manufacturers currently using this design include Kona and Commencal.

Four-bar bikes have the rearmost pivot under the rear axle. This is often called a Horst link, after the designer who pioneered it. In this position, the linkage works as a parallelogram, giving the rear axle a near-vertical axle path. This effectively isolates pedalling and braking forces from the suspension action. An enduring example is the Specialized FSR.

A newcomer design comes from Trek, and is called the Active Braking Pivot. In this set-up, the rearmost pivot rotates around the rearmost hub. This isolates the suspension even further from braking and pedalling forces, but requires a custom rear through-axle or quick release.

Short link four bar designs utilize two very short linkages between the main frame and the rear triangle to create a parallelogram. Tinkering with the configuration of each link allows designers to customize the path the axle will take under vertical load, varying the extent to which braking and pedalling forces interact with the suspension reactions. Examples include VPP (Virtual Pivot Point) models from Santa Cruz and Intense, Giant's Maestro system and Marin's Quad-Link system.

Types of shock

As with suspension forks, rear shocks come in several different styles, while the two main components remain the same – some form of spring and some form of damping. The spring can be air or coil, and the damping can be air, oil or a mixture of oil and gas.

An air spring is stiffened by pumping more air into the spring chamber. The volume of air is small, so adding a tiny amount makes a big difference: use a suspension pump with a gauge for the job. Bleed air off either by using the bleed valve on the pump (if you have one), or by removing the pump and depressing the pin in the middle of the Schraeder valve, then using the suspension pump to go back up to the right pressure. Don't overpump the shock, you will damage it. The maximum pressure the shock will take is almost always printed on the shock body, otherwise check your manual.

Coil springs have a steel spring wound over a damping unit. The preload is adjusted by turning the plate that supports one end of the shock along a thread, squashing the spring. Springs don't have a huge weight range and work much much better if you don't put too much preload on them. Don't be tempted to crank up the preload-adjuster on a spring that's too soft to get the right sag. As a general rule, use no more than two turns of the preload-adjuster to get the right sag, unless your manual specifically says that you can use more.

Air shocks are slightly lighter than coil spring shocks, although using titanium springs rather than steel ones can decrease the weight difference. It is easier to adjust air shocks for a wide range of rider weights, whereas coil springs are only adjustable within the range of the spring – riders who weigh more or less than average will need to swap springs, whereas air can simply be added or released.

Coil and air shocks do feel different though. Coil springs are very supple and are often the preferred choice. I like air springs because I don't weigh much. If you carry a shock pump with you, it will cancel out most of the difference in weight between air and coil.

Suspension: measuring total travel

Travel is the total distance your suspension unit can move, from fully extended to fully compressed. More travel means that your shock unit can absorb larger shocks, stretching out the short, sharp impacts so that you can maintain control over your bike. Longer travel allows people to do stuff on bikes that would never have been possible five years ago – jumping off things and onto things, in ways that would previously have resulted in broken bikes and broken bones.

Longer travel isn't all good, though. Frames have to be beefier and heavier to maintain stiffness, as well as to withstand abuse. The shape of a long travel frame changes through the travel, making it tiring to ride long distances or to take on steep climbs. Cross-country frames with a medium amount of travel seek to find a compromise between soaking up uneven terrain, maximizing grip by keeping the rear wheel glued to the ground, and providing a comfortable, stable pedalling platform. Microtravel suspension – where the rear triangle moves 5cm (2 inches) or so – will absorb harsh trails, adding a bit of comfort with the minimum of weight penalty.

Like front suspension, rear shocks need to be set up so that when you sit on the bike the suspension settles slightly. This is important – it means that your rear wheel can drop down into dips, as well as fold upwards to pass over lumps and obstacles in your path. This keeps you floating in a horizontal straight line, rather than climbing in and out of every irregularity on the trail, saving you energy.

Each manufacturer has their own ideas about how much of your total travel should be taken up by this initial sag, so you'll need to consult the shock handbook or the manufacturer's website to find out their recommendations. Since the sag is always given as a proportion of total travel, you'll need to know the travel as well before you can start setting your sag. If you don't know it already, use the steps below to measure it.

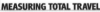

MEASURING TOTAL TRAVEL

Step 1: Stand the bike up and measure the distance from centre to centre between the shock eyelets. This is the extended length.

Step 2: Release the spring: for an air shock, take the valve cap off, push down the pin in the middle of the valve, pump the bike up and down a couple of times and push the pin down again to release the rest of the air. For coil shocks, back off the preload-adjuster, as far as it will go, so that the spring dangles loose.

Step 3: Push the bike down to compress the shock and measure the distance between the eyelets again. Subtract the second measurement from the first, and that's your total available travel.

Setting up sag

Once you've worked out how much travel your bike has, put a small amount of air back in the shock or remount the coil and put in a single turn of preload.

10% sag = total travel divided by 10	
15% sag = total travel divided by 7	
20% sag = total travel divided by 5	
25% sag = total travel divided by 4	
33% sag = total travel divided by 3	

The next step is to calculate how much sag you're aiming to have. Different bike shapes and shock models work best with different amounts of sag, but as a rule, for cross-country racers it's 15–25 per cent of total travel; for general cross-country, it's 20–30 per cent; and for all mountain/freeride, it's 30–35 per cent. These are guidelines only – refer to your shock manual for recommendations. This gives you a starting point to use to tune to your preferences. Don't worry about that now, we take that into account at the test stage.

Now work out what sag you would like.

Coil shock

You'll need a friend to help you with this. Measure the distance between the shock mounting bolts. Sit on your bike, in your normal riding position (it helps to lean against a wall for this), and get your friend to measure the same distance again. Get your friend to repeat the measurement between the centers of the shock eyelets. Subtract this new measurement from the original unloaded shock length, and you have the sag. If the amount is more than you expected, add preload to the coil spring. If it's less than you expected, back off the coil spring, or bleed out air, until you have it about right.

Air springs are adjustable throughout the range of what you need, but coil springs have a much narrower range. For example, Fox Vanilla springs are designed for up to two turns of the preload-adjusting ring. Crank them up too much and they won't work properly. Leave them too loose and they bang around. Ideally, with the exact spring rate, you shouldn't need to use preload at all. If you can't get the adjustment you need from the spring you have, get a softer or a harder spring. Give the bike shop the details of your bike (make, model and year) and spring (spring rate and travel as printed on the spring), as well as your weight, so that they can work out the correct spring for you.

Air shock

You can work out the sag on an air shock without press-ganging an assistant to measure for you – the travel O-ring on the shock shaft will get pushed down as you compress the shock, and will then remain there when the shock re-extends, making it simple to measure how far you squashed the shock by sitting on the bike. You'll need a shock pump to add air and to measure the pressure inside the shock.

AIR SHOCK

Step 1: For air shocks, push the travel O-ring right up the shaft of the shock, so that it rests against the air sleeve.

Step 2: Sit in your normal position on the bike in normal riding clothes. Just sit, don't bounce or twiddle. Get off the bike. Your weight will have compressed the shock, pushing the travel O-ring along the shaft. Measure the gap between the air sleeve and the O-ring. This is your sag.

Step 3: If the measurement is less than you expected, release a little air from the shock. If it's more than you expected, add a little air – screw the shock pump onto the valve, enough so that you can hear a little air escaping, then half a turn more. Add a little pressure. Remove the shock pump and test again. Make a note of what pressure you ended up with!

Testing and adjusting rebound damping for the best setting

If you don't have this adjustment, it doesn't mean you don't have rebound damping, but rather that the manufacturer has decided what works best and they don't want you fiddling with it . . .

First, get a feeling for the effect of the rebound damping adjustment before finding the right setting. Find a place where you can repeat a simple five-minute loop – nothing special, a car park will do fine. Ride the loop twice at the two extremes of the rebound damping adjustment to get a feel for the effect of changing the settings. Then set the rebound damping in the central position; for example, if it has a total 12 clicks, start with six clicks.

Find a clear, flat space without cars with a single baby dropoff – 50mm (2 inches) or 100mm (4 inches) or so – to ride repeatedly. The idea is you ride over the dropoff, the shock compresses, rebounds further than it started, and returns to its original position. If the shock springs back and kicks you on landing, the rebound is too fast, and you need to increase the damping. If you wallow on landing, it's too slow and needs to be reduced. At first you may want to make radical changes to the adjustment to learn its effect. Whatever you do, remember to keep a clear and constant note of all changes you make, and resist the temptation to fiddle randomly with combinations – if playing with the rebound damping, leave the sag alone.

Now for the test ride. Go out and play. You should bottom out the shock about once every ride. If not, you are not using the full travel, which is a waste. Play with the sag, a little at a time. This is where your personal taste and riding style come into play. If you stand a lot, up and out of the saddle, you may prefer a stiffer ride, at the lower end of your recommended sag range.

Maintaining rear suspension

Rear shocks have two levels of servicing: they need to be kept clean; and the moving parts need regular lubrication. The bushings that allow them to move must be kept clean and must be replaced when worn. They need to be checked regularly to ensure they're working properly. You can kill a shock very quickly by continuing to ride when something internal is broken. All this can be done with a few simple tools, and it is worth learning to do regularly.

Rear shocks often sit directly in the firing line for mush thrown up by your back wheel and their performance deteriorates quickly if you ignore them. Conversely, keep them clean and greased and they last a whole lot longer – see page 240 for air shock servicing.

Deeper, internal servicing and tuning must be carried out by a shock servicer. Don't be tempted to continue ripping inside the shock once you are confident with the outer parts. Depending on make, the internal parts may be filled with nitrogen or stored under high pressure. Don't get involved. It's too easy to hurt yourself, and the action voids the warranty. Post the shock to the service centre.

Luckily, there are enough specialists to do the job and, luckily again, once you've taken the shock off the bike, it is small enough to post easily. If there's one thing you can do to help this process, clean the shock before packaging. It is cleaned at the other end, but it's polite to wipe off last weekend's fun before putting it in a box. The correct service centre depends on the make of shock. Servicers are quick too. You can usually get a shock back in the time between weekends.

Maintenance commandments

◆ When opening up the shock for regreasing, clean the bike before you start. Otherwise mud drops into the body of the shock – the rebound characteristics of mud are notoriously variable.

◆ Air shocks: DON'T forget to discharge all the air in the shock before you start working it. Open a unit that is still pressurized and it releases suddenly, flying into the air. Usually it hits you because you are undoing it. It hurts and you feel stupid.

◆ DON'T open up the damping cartridge inside the shock.

◆ Occasionally, air shocks get stuck in the squashed position. Let all the air out of the valve, then reinflate to the maximum pressure the shock is rated for. If this doesn't work, deflate again and send to the servicer. DON'T open the air sleeve – let the specialist deal with it.

Coil springs have a pair of numbers printed on the coil: the first is the spring rate (stiffness); the second is the travel in inches. You need to know the vital statistics of your spring to change it for a stiffer or softer one.

Fitting and adjusting a Fox Float Air

I like the Fox Float Air shock. It works well, adjusts easily and is simple to keep clean. Don't be tempted to go further than the level of servicing below. For that, send it to an authorized service centre or you void the warranty. The damping chamber is charged with pressurized nitrogen, which makes it dangerous to open and impossible to refill without a cylinder of nitrogen.

All types of shocks, both coil and air, are well worth keeping clean and well greased – it costs less to service if you don't let the internal parts wear out. Most shocks are centrally mounted above the rear wheel. Any mud, grit and sand left over after your back wheel has sprayed a stripe up your back gets dumped onto your shock body. Clean this off regularly; grit will work its way in past any seals, scouring grooves in the central shaft, in turn allowing in more dirt.

This particular shock model allows you to adjust rebound-damping and travel, but other combinations are common on other bikes – preload and rebound is the most useful, although lockouts are great for climbing and roadwork. Some people like to be able to adjust their compression damping. Compression damping affects the speed at which the shock compresses; and rebound damping, the speed at which it springs back.

Greasing air sleeve

If you're happy with how your shock performs – it soaks up uneven terrain without consistently bottoming out – then measure and record the pressure before you start maintenance, so that you can reinflate to that pressure when the shock is reassembled. It's also worth checking and noting the rebound settings – count the clicks back to fully open (it's easy to knock the adjusting wheel during work). As ever, when working with air springs, release all air pressure before starting work.

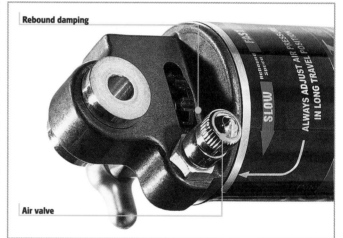

Rebound damping

ALWAYS ADJUST AIR PRESSURE IN LONG TRAVEL POSITION

SLOW

Air valve

Fox Float suspension unit ▶

GREASING AIR SLEEVE

Step 1: Release air from the shock by removing valve cap and pressing down pin at centre of valve. Pump bike up and down a couple of times through the whole stroke of the shock to expel air from the negative air spring. Release the air at the valve again. Undo the pivot fixing bolts at either end of the shock, usually using an Allen key and socket, or two Allen keys. Pull the aluminium reducers out of each end of the shock and clean them.

Step 2: Clamp the body end of the shock (the end with the air valve and any adjusting knobs or dials) into a vice. Protect the eye bolt with wood – otherwise you damage the shock. Take care not to crush the valve, or the lockout switch, or anything else down there. Stick a screwdriver, or similar, through the top eyelet to stop the air sleeve flying off when unthreaded.

Step 3: Undo the air sleeve by hand. This has a normal thread and undoes anticlockwise. A little gadget called a gator (available from auto shops) can grip the sleeve if stiff, as can the mats that help to remove jam jar lids. Don't use grips or pliers, which can damage the sleeve. The threads are very fine, so they take ages to unscrew. Persevere until you pull the sleeve free. Remove the screwdriver and pull off the sleeve, along with the travel O-ring.

Step 4: Now the parts have been separated, clean them carefully. If things look fairly clean, just wipe with a clean rag. If things are a mess, you need to clean and degrease (check your degreaser is O-ring-friendly, something like Finish Line Ecotech 2 should be fine). If there's no grease at all, or the grease is discoloured and dirty, you need to clean-and-grease more frequently.

Step 5: Next, grease. Good-quality, clean grease is essential. I like Pace grease, but there are plenty of alternatives – RockShox Judy Butter is great. There are three sets of O-rings. The two outer sets, at either end of the air sleeve (currently attached to the shock, just below the air sleeve threads), both need a light smear of grease – just a little, but ensure a constant bead all the way around.

Step 6: The same goes for the bearings and seal at the end of the air sleeve. The air sleeve threads also need a smear of grease. Make sure the beads run all the way around with no gaps.

Extra grease

Step 7: Be more generous with the O-ring and bearing in the middle of the shock, the one that sits in the middle inside the air sleeve. Pack an extra layer of grease into the shoulder above the body bearing, which gets dragged onto the bearing and O-ring during the shock cycle.

Step 8: Slide the air sleeve loosely back onto the body of the shock. Air will become trapped in the sleeve, so slide the thin end of a ziptie (not anything metal!) under the seal – see the arrow in the picture, allowing air to escape. Push the air sleeve all the way onto the shaft. Once the threads are engaged, remove the ziptie, then tighten the air sleeve firmly by hand.

Step 9: Refit the travel o-ring. Clean and refit aluminium reducers, with a drop of oil on the outer faces. Apply LocTite to the fixing bolts, then refit the shock to the bike, in its original orientation. Tightening both fixing bolts securely. Inflate the shock to maximum pressure (printed on the shock and in the owner's manual), then release air to the correct pressure. Refit the valve cap, recheck all nuts and bolts.

Toolbox

Tools for cleaning and greasing air shaft

- Allen keys to remove shock from bike – usually a 5mm or 6mm
- Screwdriver
- Plenty of good-quality shock grease, such as RockShox Judy Butter or Pace RC7
- Plenty of clean cloth or kitchen towel
- Shock pump to reinflate once you're done
- Thin zipties

Fitting new reducers and bushings

Your shock is held in place by pivot bolts at either end. These need to move smoothly, so that the shock can rotate with the rear end of the bike as the shock moves through its travel. If the pivots become stiff, the shaft of the shock is forced to slide in and out of the shock body at an angle, wearing the seals and the shaft. Loose, sloppy pivots make your bike feel uncertain, since the back end hesitates before following the front end around tight turns.

Checking pivots for slop

◆　Check the pivots for slop by holding the main frame still and rocking the back end of the bike. There should be no lateral movement, and definitely no knocking or clunking noises. If the pivots are worn, order fresh ones before you start, so you can refit them as you go along. See page 243.

▲ **Check for play by rocking the back end of the bike sideways**

▼ **Replace worn reducers**

It makes sense to replace the bushings at the same time as the reducers, while everything is open. This takes a little more work, but it is worth the effort.

◆　Undo the bolts at either end of the shock using either an Allen key and socket, or two Allen keys.

◆　Release the spring:
For air shocks. Make a note of the pressure in the shocks so you can reset it at the end. Then release all air pressure.
For coil shocks, back off the preload nut, so that the spring is baggy.

◆　Check the orientation of the shock so you can refit it correctly later. Remove the shock from the bike. The bike folds up when you take out the shock – support it so that no hoses or cables are stretched or kinked, and that your vulnerable paintwork is protected.

◆　Pull the reducers from either side of each eyelet. The bushing is the part that lines the inside of the eyelet. You need to use the new one to push the old one out, installing itself in the process. It's atight fit, so you need a vice for controlled force. I've seen this done with a hammer, but it wasn't pleasant.

◆　Support the far side of the eyelet with something hollow for the old bushing to push out into. A socket is ideal. Choose one where the hole is slightly bigger than the bushing, so the bushing does not touch as it pushes out.

◆　Look closely at the eyelet. The bushing is slightly shorter than the width of the eyelet, maybe 0.5mm (¹⁄₅₀ inch). This creates a shoulder to rest the new bushing on, aligning it precisely. Sit one of the old reducers in the new bushing for protection.

◆　Set up the shock in the vice, with all the parts in order: socket lined up with shock eyelet, shock, new bushing, old reducer.

◆　Carefully close the jaws of the vice. This pushes the new bushing in through the eyelet, forcing out the old bushing in the process so it ends up inside the socket. Leave the new bushing exactly flush on one side with a shallow shoulder left on the other side, so you can repeat the process next time.

◆　Refit or replace the reducers. Grease the part in contact with the bushing.

◆　Refit the shock to the bike, checking direction and orientation. Refit the bolts, using Loctite on the threads. Reset the sag by preloading the spring or by refilling with air.

Pivot maintenance

The performance of the rear suspension depends utterly on the free movement of the pivots that join the struts and swingarms to the frame. All the hard work that went into designing and building the frame and shock is completely wasted unless you keep the pivots clean and lubricated. There are as many designs as designers, but they have one common enemy – the jet-wash. Never directly jet-wash at the side of your bike – you blow any lubrication out of the bearings.

Check the pivots twice a year by hanging the back of the bike up, taking off the back wheel, removing the rear shock completely and moving the back of the bike through its travel. Don't kink or bend hoses or cables. Rock the back end of the bike sideways. There should be no movement.

If there's pivot slop, or if the rear end of the bike doesn't swivel freely, it's time for pivot maintenance. Details depend on your frame, so check the owner's manual. Usually pivot maintenance is not at all difficult.

Undo the bolts through the pivots and disassemble carefully. Make a note of the position and orientation of any washers. Remove and inspect bushings or bearings. Bushings have to be ordered from your frame manufacturer, but sealed bearings are almost always common sizes so your bike shop or an auto supply shop can supply fresh ones. You can also service bearings; use a sharp knife to peel off the plastic seals on both sides of the bearing, degrease, rinse, dry and repack with fresh grease. Refit the seals, pressing them gently into place with both thumbs. Hold the central part of the bearing and rotate the outer part to check they run smoothly. Refit into the frame. Use Loctite on the bolt threads to stop them rattling free. Retighten the bolts firmly. Once you've refitted the bearings, and before you refit the shock, move the rear end of the bike through its travel again to check you've cured the problem. Check the fixing bolts are still snug after your first ride.

Troubleshooting forks

Symptom	Cause	Solution	Page
Forks have correct sag, but stop working over a series of bumps	Stacking up – forks haven't had time to re-extend between two obstacles	Reduce rebound damping	228
Knocking from the front end of bike	Bushes worn (check also headset adjustments and calliper bolts)	Replace bushings – send to service centre	242–3
Forks spring back with a jolt after an impact	Insufficient damping	Increase rebound damping	228
Forks suddenly start recoil too quickly, even though the adjustment is unchanged	Damping mechanism damaged	Replace damping mechanism – send to service centre	231–4
Forks rebound slowly, even with minimum rebound damping	Insufficient lubrication	Replace or replenish lubricating oil	231–4
	Oil weight too high	Use lower weight oil – try 5wt less than current	172
Forks leak oil from top of fork legs	Seals worn or damaged	Replace seals – send to service centre	N/A
Forks leak oil from lower-leg fixing bolts	Fixing bolts working loose	Check tightness of fixing bolts	243
	O-rings on fixing bolts torn or missing	Replace O-rings	172
Air shock bottoms out repeatedly	Not enough preload	Increase air pressure or spring weight	238

8 – Bottom brackets and headsets

Bottom brackets and headsets are the two major bearings on your frame. The bottom bracket runs through the frame, connecting your cranks together and transferring the vertical force that you input through the pedals into rotational motion that drags your chain around your chainset. The headset connects your forks to your frame, keeping the front wheel securely attached while allowing you to rotate the bars to steer the bike. Both run uncomplainingly for years but will eventually need replacing.

Routine maintenance of the bottom bracket

The bottom bracket is the large main bearing that passes through your frame, between the cranks. Actually, it is a pair of bearings, one on each side bolted into threads cut on both sides of the frame. Like all the sealed parts of the bicycle, water and dirt will get in with enough time and abuse. This slows you down and wears out the bearings, so your bottom bracket needs regular, say annual, changing.

Back in the beginning, bottom brackets were sold in their separate parts: the axle that ran through the middle, the cups that bolted into the frame, and the bearings that sat in the gap between the two. The advantages of this system were that the gap between the bearings could be adjusted so that the bearings ran smoothly with no drag and that the parts could be regularly disassembled, cleaned, regreased, reassembled and adjusted. But we were all too lazy to do this often enough, so now almost all bottom brackets are sealed-in cartridges. They stay cleaner and, when they wear out, they have to be replaced as a unit.

Bottom brackets have a reverse thread on the right-hand side, so the cup on the chainset side of the bike has to be turned clockwise to remove it and counterclockwise to fit it. This is true of all mountain bikes and almost all other bikes. The exceptions are a few fancy Italian road bikes, which have a standard tighten-clockwise thread on both sides. These bikes serve to demonstrate why the reverse thread is necessary – bottom brackets with the Italian threading are prone to unravel under pressure from the pedals and require special attention from mechanics to stop this happening.

Different types of bottom bracket

Around the late 1990s, we'd finally come to settle on a standard fitting to attach cranks to bottom bracket axles when somebody came along with another improvement. History is now repeating itself with the appearance of a new bunch of designs. The standard for a while was called 'square taper', which worked fine. Newer bottom brackets are splined and are generally lighter. Your bottom bracket type must match your crank type. There is no compatibility at all between the different types; you cannot exchange cranks or bottom brackets between systems.

Square taper

A square-shaped axle fits into a similar hole on the crank. Since the axle and the hole in the crank are both tapered, as you tighten the bolt on the end of the axle, you push the crank farther onto the axle, wedging it firmly in place. The idea is simple, but if the crank comes just a little loose on the axle, it tends to loosen more, damaging the soft metal of the crank at the same time. This problem is particularly marked on the left-hand side – since the crank bolts both have a standard thread, the one on the left has a tendency to loosen as you put pressure on the pedals, whereas the right-hand one generally tightens itself. Check the bolts regularly.

Square taper

Cup

ISIS

ISIS stands for International Spline Interface Standard. This is the type of bottom bracket used by Bontrager, Race Face, Middelburn and others. There are 10 splines on each side. The chainset has matching splines. To fit the chainset to the bottom bracket, slide it over the splines and tighten until the back of the chainset butts up firmly onto the shoulder on the bottom bracket axle.

Take care lining up the second crank – the cranks fit just as easily into each of the 10 splines, so make sure your cranks point accurately in opposite directions before you tighten down the bolts.

ISIS

Crank bolts

Cup

Shimano Octalink

This is the Shimano splined bottom bracket. It has eight splines, rather than 10 as on an ISIS bottom bracket. ISIS bottom brackets and chainsets are not compatible with Shimano ones. When refitting chainsets, always carefully clean the splines on the chainset and bottom bracket, otherwise the chainset will work itself loose as you pedal. Retighten the crank bolts after the first 50 miles.

Octalink

Cup

2.5mm spacing washers

External bottom bracket

External

The standard, pioneered by Shimano but adopted now by a raft of others, external bottom brackets use a wider, stiffer, hollow axle that's attached permanently to the chainset and bolted to the left-hand crank. The bearings are larger and sit outboard of the frame. Replacement is straightforward and they fit into the same frame threads as square- and splined- style bottom brackets.

BB30 and Press Fit

First developed by Cannondale, BB30 bottom brackets have very large bearings that press directly into the frame of the bike. Shimano have their own version, the Press Fit system.

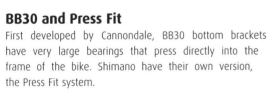

Shimano Octalink

External bottom bracket

Square taper

ISIS

Bottom brackets: regular checking for play and wear

The bottom bracket suffers from being invisible much of the time. It is an essential bearing and is expected to turn smoothly even when you stamp on the pedals yet, because it can't be seen, it tends to be ignored. But a worn bottom bracket slows you down without noticing and also makes your chain and chainset wear quickly. Check regularly for play; the bottom bracket should spin freely and shouldn't rock from side to side at all.

Crouch on the right-hand side of the bike. Line up the right-hand crank with part of the frame – chainstay, seat-tube, down-tube, whatever. Hold the crank (not the pedal) in one hand and the frame in the other. Rock your hands gently toward and away from each other. You should not hear or feel any knocking or play between the crank and frame – no side-to-side movement at all. Repeat at other angles, lining the crank up each time with a part of your frame and rocking across the bike – you might get more knocking at one angle than another. Repeat on the other side.

Once you've checked both sides, you'll have to work out whether the play comes from the crank moving on the bottom bracket axle, from the bottom bracket moving in the frame or from worn bottom bracket bearings.

If you can only feel knocking from one crank, most likely the crank is loose. For square taper and splined axles, tighten the crank bolt on the knocking side very firmly – usually an 8mm or 10mm Allen key, for older models a 1mm socket. Tighten the other side for good measure. You'll need an extra long Allen key to get enough leverage – a trail tool is only sufficient for emergencies.

For Hollowtech bottom brackets, check the left-hand crank pinch bolts, and tighten if loose. These need care, as the bolts will strip if overtightened – if you've invested in a torque wrench, congratulate yourself now.

If that's not the problem, check whether the bottom bracket cups are moving in the frame. Watch the left-hand cup closely as you rock the cranks – there should be no movement at all between cup and frame. If they shift about, you may be able to solve the problem by removing the cranks and tightening the cups in the frame – see page 250 for square taper and splined axles, and 256 for Hollowtech. In either case, the cups need to be fitted really snugly in the frame, to eliminate movement. However, if the cranks aren't shifting on the axle, and the cups are snug in the frame, your bottom bracket is worn out, and you'll have to replace it. Don't be daunted – this isn't a huge deal, apart from choosing the correct size for replacement – if in doubt, take the old one out and take it to your bike shop for them to match you up a fresh one.

Next, check that the bottom bracket bearings spin freely. Change into the smallest chainring at the front, then reach around to the back

of the chainset and lift the chain off the smallest chainring. Drop it into the gap between the chainset and the frame below the front derailleur, so that the chain is not connected at all to the chainset. Spin the pedals. They should spin freely and silently. Grinding or crunching noises, or resistance mean it's time to change your bottom bracket. Lift the chain back onto the top of the smallest chainring and pedal forward slowly to re-engage the chain with the chainring.

◀ **Checking for bottom bracket play**

Creaking noises

This kind of noise from the bottom bracket area can spoil a perfectly good ride. Like all creaking sounds, investigate it straight away – bicycles rarely complain unless something is loose, worn or about to snap. If your bicycle has the courtesy to give you warning creaks, it's worth your time to pay heed.

Fat-tubed aluminium bikes amplify the smallest sound. Anything with any tube fatter than you can get your hand around is, basically, a soundbox, and it will do its best to ensure you hear everything. The end result is that you start lusting after a narrow-tubed Italian steel racing bike, then suddenly you're visiting your mother for Christmas in full Lycra, duck shoes and aero helmets. Tighten your cranks instead.

Try these decreaking measures, and then test to see if the creaking has gone away. If nothing works, note that frames transmit noises strangely, so creaks can sound as if they come from somewhere else. Common causes include handlebar and stem bolts, and rear hubs.

SORTING OUT NOISES

Step 1: Tighten both crank bolts clockwise. They both need to be tight – you will need a long (at least 200mm Allen key; not just a multitool. The 8mm Allen key on multitools is for emergencies only.

Step 2: If that doesn't work, remove both crank bolts, grease the threads and under the heads, and refit firmly.

Step 3: Tighten both pedals. Remember that the left-hand pedal has a reverse thread – see the Pedals section (page 279) for more details.

Step 4: If that still doesn't work, remove both pedals, grease the threads and refit firmly. This sounds far-fetched, but it does the trick more often than you'd imagine. Dirt or grit on the pedal threads will also cause creaking, so clean the threads on the pedal and inside the crank.

Step 5: Take hold of each pedal and twist it. The pedal should not move on its own axle. If it does, it could well be the source of the creak and needs stripping and servicing (see the Pedals section section – page 279). Spray a little light oil, like GT85, on the cleat release mechanism. Don't use chain oil – it's too sticky and will pick up dirt.

Step 6: Remove the crank and chainset, loosen the left-hand bottom bracket cup, tighten the right-hand cup firmly (remember it has a reverse thread so tightens anticlockwise), then tighten the left-hand cup (normal thread, tightens clockwise). Refit crank and chainset, and tighten bolts firmly. See pages 250–51 for more details.

Removing and refitting the cranks: square taper and splined bottom brackets

Start on the left-hand side of the bike. Remove the Allen key bolt or 14mm Allen key that holds the crank on. Check inside the crank and remove any washers in there. Look into the hole to determine the kind of axle.

If the bike is an older or entry-level model, you will see the square end of the axle. Alternatively, you will see the round end of a splined axle.

Use the appropriate crank-extractor – splined axles are fatter, so an older crank extractor, designed for square taper cranks, cannot push out the axle. It disappears down the hole into the middle of the axle instead. Crank extractors for splined axles have a fatter head and do not fit into older square cranks. If you do have a splined axle and an older crank extractor, Shimano makes a little plug to slip into the end of your splined axle, so that the square taper crank extractor will work: a TLFC15. Sometimes one comes packaged with new chainsets. If your crank extractor is designed for fatter, splined axles, it will not work at all with square taper axles.

REMOVING A CRANK

Step 1: The crank bolts should be tightly fitted, so you will need a long Allen key (or 14mm socket) to undo the bolt. If you find the bolts come off without too much effort, tighten them more firmly next time!

Step 2: Hold the handle, or the nut end of the inner part of the crank extractor and turn the outer part of the crank extractor. You will see that turning one against the other means that the inner part of the tool moves in or out of the outer part.

Step 3: Next, back off the inner part of the tool so that its head disappears inside the outer part of the tool.

Step 4: Thread the outer part of the tool into the threads in the crank that you've revealed by taking off the bolt. The crank is soft in comparison to the tool so take care not to cross-thread the tool and damage the crank, which will be expensive. Thread on the tool as far as it will go.

Step 5: Start winding in the inner part of the tool. It will move easily at first, but will then meet the end of the axle and stiffen. You need to be firm with it. Once it starts moving, turning the tool gets easier as it pushes the axle out of the crank.

Step 6: Once you've started the crank moving on the axle, the crank will come off in your hand. Pull it off the axle and remove the tool from the crank.

The crank extractor has two parts. The outer part threads onto the crank; the inner part threads through the outer part and bears on the end of the axle. As long as the outer part is firmly fitted into the crank, as you thread in the inner part, it pushes the axle off the crank. The inner part of the tool will either have an integral handle, like the Park one in the picture on page 250, or it will have separate flats for a spanner. Either version works fine.

If at any time the outer part of the tool starts to pull out of the chainset, stop immediately. If you continue, you will strip the threads out of the chainset, and it will be difficult to remove the chainset without destroying it. Remove the tool from the crank and check that you've removed all bolts and washers. If there are any accidentally left in there, remove them and try again. If you can find no reason why the threads are stripping, this might be a good time to beat a retreat to your bike shop and get your mechanic to have a go.

Once you've got the left-hand crank off, repeat the procedure for the chainset side, which works exactly the same way. Once you've done whatever you need to do in the bottom bracket, you need to refit the chainset and cranks. It's worth giving the area that's behind the chainset a good clean while the rings are off, and you might as well give the chainset a good scrub with degreaser too. Rinse it off well afterward. There's no need to oil it.

Refitting the crank and chainset

The same procedure is used to fit both crank and chainset. Fit the chainset first. Before starting, clean the axle and the hole in the chainset thoroughly. Make sure there's no dirt left on the tapers or between the splines, or you will get creaking. Apply antiseize to any titanium parts.

There are two different opinions about whether the axle should be greased before you fit the cranks onto it. Proponents on both sides of the discussion are often fiercely loyal to their points of view. The advantage of greasing the axle is that the lubrication allows the crank to be pulled further onto the axle, fitting it more tightly. Those who prefer not to grease the axle say that the grease layer allows the two surfaces to move against each other, leading to potential creaking and then allowing the parts to work themselves loose. Personally, I can be convinced by either argument, but have found that it makes more difference whether the axle and crank surfaces are clean than whether they are greased. New bottom brackets often come with antiseize already applied to the right-hand axle; this should be left on.

Inspect the surface of both the axle and the holes in the cranks. Square taper axles should be flat with no pitting. The crank hole is the place you're most likely to find damage – the hole needs to be perfectly square and must fit smoothly over the axle. The most common problem is where loose cranks have rounded themselves off on the axle, smearing the shape of one or more of the corners of the square. Splined cranks will also be damaged by being ridden loose. Each spline should be crisp and clean. Replace damaged cranks immediately – they will never hold securely and will cause expensive damage to your bottom bracket axle.

Slide the chainset over the end of the axle. Line it up with the square or splined axle and push on it firmly. Grease the threads of the fixing bolts and add a dab of grease under the head of the bolt, which may otherwise creak. Fit the bolt and tighten firmly.

For the last part, line the crank up with the Allen key/socket spanner, so they are almost parallel. Hold one in each hand and stand in front of the chainset. With both arms straight, use your shoulders to tighten the crank bolts. (This uses the strength of your shoulders and reduces the chance of stabbing yourself with the chainring if you slip.)

Next, fit the crank onto the other end of the bottom bracket axle. Line it up so that it points in the opposite direction to the one on the other side. This is simple with square tapers but takes a little care with splined designs – the bike feels very strange if you fit the crank to a neighbouring spline. Tighten that crank on firmly too.

It's worth retightening all types of crank bolts after the first ride – you often find they work themselves a bit loose as they bed in. Both types of crank, square taper and splined, depend on the shape of the hole in the crank being exactly right. Riding with loose cranks stretches the shape, so the cranks will never fit firmly enough again, leaving replacement the only option. The material of the crank is softer than that of the axle, so it wears first, but if the worn crank is not replaced, it also eventually wears down the shape of the end of the bottom bracket axle.

◄ **Hold crank steady, retighten crank bolt firmly**

One-key release

Some chainsets come with one-key release as standard. You can also buy them separately – they fit into standard crank threads.

These releases were invented so you could get the cranks off without using a crank extractor. They can also seize easily and can be fiddly.

The one-key release comes in a bag with no instructions. The large diameter washer (usually black) fits under the bolt head; the smaller one (usually white) sits on top between the bolt and the one-key release cap. The white one is vital; it allows the top of the bolt to turn easily against the inside of the one-key cap. The one-key release cap fits over the top of this washer so that the washer ends up trapped between the bolt and the cap. Both washers should be greased to help the bolt turn easily when fitting and removing the cranks.

Some one-key release bolts use a 6mm Allen key rather than the standard 8mm size. You'll need to get an extra long one from your bike shop to get enough leverage, or you can extend a standard one by sliding it into a longer tube.

FITTING A ONE-KEY RELEASE

Step 1: Start with the chainset side. When you come to fit the left-hand crank, make sure it lines up so that it points in exactly the opposite direction – this is easy on square tapers but takes a little more care with splined axles.

Step 2: Your one-key release kit comes with two washers. One fits neatly over the head of the bolt, the other sits underneath the bolt. Choose the washer that fits snugly over the threaded part of the bolt and sit it in the crank with a dab of grease.

Step 3: Thread the bolt into the axle, with the second washer pushed over the head of the bolt. This will also need a dab of grease to help the bolt turn against the one-key release cap when you come to take the crank off.

Step 4: Tighten the crank bolt firmly using an Allen key with at least 200mm (8 inches) of leverage. Hold the end of the Allen key and the end of the crank so that you get maximum leverage, and tighten very firmly. Otherwise your crank will work loose and fall off.

Step 5: Grease the threads of the one-key release cap and the inside surface, and tighten into the crank threads. A small peg spanner is perfect for this, but you can also use circlip pliers. If you have the special Shimano tool for tightening the backs of chainset bolts (TL-FC20), it has a one-key release cap spanner on the other end.

Step 6: To remove the crank, simply undo the crank nut. It will turn easily briefly, but will then jam against the inside of the one-key release cap. As you continue to turn, the bolt will push the crank off the axle.

Internal bottom brackets: what size do I need?

With internal bottom brackets, every model of every make of chainset is designed to work with a specific-length bottom bracket, which determines how far out from the frame the chainset sits. If it's too close, the chainrings will rub on the frame; too far out and the front derailleur will struggle to reach the outer chainring.

Aligning the chainset correctly minimizes that angle of the chain in the outer rear sprockets, reducing chain wear.

Before removing your old bottom bracket, inspect it to see whether it is the right length. Even new bikes sometimes come fitted with the wrong-length bottom bracket, so it's worth checking rather than automatically replacing it with the same length again.

- ◆ Check the chain line by shifting into your middle chainring and middle sprocket, and looking along the chain from behind the cassette. The chain should run straight, without an obvious kink where it meshes onto the sprocket and chainring teeth.
- ◆ Check the gap between the chainstay and chairings – there needs to be 2–3mm (around ⅛ inch) clearance to allow for chainring flex under pressure. If the chainrings rub on the chainstay, they'll wear it away.
- ◆ Shift into the smallest chainring and check the back of the front derailleur does not touch the frame. You need enough clearance here to adjust the front derailleur.
- ◆ Shift into the middle chainring and the smallest chainring at the back. If the chain rubs on the bottom of the outer chainring in this gear, the chainring needs to move outward.

If your current bottom bracket is the right length, replace with the same length. Estimating what length to use to correct any of the above problems can be tricky – it's worth taking your bike to your bike shop for help. Take your cranks off to measure the size of your current bottom

bracket; once you've done that, you can measure your bottom bracket while it's still in the frame. Bottom bracket shell width **(A)** is measured across the part of the frame that the bottom bracket fits into. Measure only the frame, not the flange of bottom bracket overlapping the edge of the frame. For example, if the frame is blue, measure across only the blue part, not across the silver bottom bracket. The two most common sizes are 68mm and 73mm. If your frame measures up any other size, measure again; there are other widths, but they are very unusual. The total axle width **(B)** runs from one end of the axle to the other (including the amount that sticks out each side) and is measured to the nearest millimetre. The differences between sizes are quite small – for square taper axles, Shimano make 107mm, 110mm, 113mm, 115mm, 118mm and 122mm lengths.

These may seem like a lot of similar sizes, but the difference between one size and the next will radically affect your shifting.

Toolbox

Square taper and splined (internal) bottom brackets
Removing and refitting chainsets and cranks:
- Crank bolt spanner - 8mm or 10mm Allen key, or (for older bikes) a 14mm socket. For all styles, you'll need one with a long handle - around 200mm - so that you can apply sufficient leverage. The bolts will be firmly fitted, and need to be firmly refitted
- A crank extractor - choose the correct type for your crank. Those with a smaller head are designed for smaller cranks, those with larger heads for splined cranks
- Grease for refitting the crank bolt threads

Removing and refitting bottom bracket cups:
- A splined bottom bracket cup remover. For ISIS bottom brackets, you'll need the version with the larger hole in the middle, to accommodate the fatter axle - this will also fit fine on Shimano square taper and splined versions
- A big spanner to drive the bottom bracket tool. You'll need lots of leverage here, so a long-handled spanner will help. If you're struggling, find a suitable length of tubing and slide it over the spanner handle to increase its effective length

One-key release kit:
- Circlip pliers, small peg spanner, or the reverse end of the special tool (TL-FC20) that Shimano make for holding the backs of chainring bolts steady while you tighten the Allen key (It took me years to work out the function of the other end of my chainring bolt tool)

Internal bottom bracket: removal

The key here is remembering that the right-hand cup has a reverse thread, so it undoes backward. This is the same for all mountain bikes and most road bikes.

Before starting, check what kind of bottom bracket you have so you know the tool you need. Check the fitting. Almost everything is now a Shimano-type splined fitting with 20 narrow splines in each cup. ISIS bottom brackets use the same size spline, but the hole in the middle of the tool must be bigger to fit over the fatter axle. ISIS tools work fine on Shimano-type bottom brackets, though. Many of these bottom brackets have eight notches on the outside of the cup, and a few have only the notches.

If your bottom bracket has both internal splines and notches around the outside of the bottom bracket, always use the internal splines to remove and refit – they make a more secure fitting and the tool is less likely to slip and damage your frame or the notches.

REMOVING BOTTOM BRACKETS

Step 1: Start on the left-hand side. Clean out all the splines on the bottom bracket cup so that the tool fits into them firmly. It's worth getting a little screwdriver and picking the dirt out of all the splines before you start – they're right down near the ground and tend to pick up all sorts of rubbish, which can stop the tool from engaging with the full depth of the slots.

Step 2: Insert the tool, firmly clamp on a large adjustable spanner and turn the tool anticlockwise to loosen the cup. It may be very firmly fitted. Take care not to let the tool slip off – it will damage the splines and it's easy to hurt yourself. If the cup won't come out easily, clamp the tool onto the bottom bracket. This calls for ingenuity; you need to fashion a washer of a size that allows you to bolt the tool on with your original crank bolt.

Step 3: Remove the left-hand cup completely. Check the condition of the splines and the threads, especially the cheaper plastic cups. These work fine and are light, but the splines can get damaged easily.

Step 4: Shift the tool onto the right-hand side and fit it firmly into the spline. Remove the tool by turning it clockwise. It can be tough to turn. Clamp on the tools if necessary. Bottom brackets often seize on, so a release agent like Shimano Get-a-Grip could be handy. If you use a release agent, make sure you're in a well-ventilated place. Spray or drip on, and leave the release agent to do its chemical magic for half an hour before you try to shift the cup again.

Step 5: Remove the body of the bottom bracket. Don't throw it away immediately – you will need to measure it to get the right size for your new one.

Step 6: Once both sides are out, take a look at the inside of the frame. Clean it out carefully. If it holds lots of debris, work out where the dirt is getting in and block up the hole. Make sure there are bolts in all the water bottle bosses, even if they have no cage mounted to them.

Internal bottom bracket: refitting

Check the new bottom bracket. The fitting threads are either metal on both sides, or metal one side and plastic the other. Grease the threads that will take a metal thread, but do not grease those that take plastic. All titanium threads need a generous coat of antiseize.

Generally, the cups are marked 'L' and 'R.' Usually, the body of the bottom bracket is the right-hand side, with a loose cup that attaches from the left. This is not universal though. If it's the other way around, reverse the fitting order. The bottom bracket threads are very fine, so it's important to take care when fitting that you don't 'cross-thread' (thread in crookedly) the cups. Start each side by hand so that you can't force the threads to start unless they fit properly. Riding with a loose bottom bracket will damage the threads. New frames, and those that have been resprayed, may have paint stuck in the threads that prevents fitting the new bottom bracket. If the threads are damaged, get the frame to your bike shop. Unless they are really badly damaged, they can be recut with a tap (a big tool with the same size and shape thread as the bottom bracket, but with hard, sharp cutting blades instead of a plain thread).

REFITTING THE BOTTOM BRACKET

Front of bike

2mm

Step 1: Roll the left-hand cup a couple of turns into the thread on the left-hand side. Start fitting the right-hand side – the main body of the bottom bracket – into the right-hand side of the frame, tightening anticlockwise by hand. Once you've got it in a couple of turns, look from the left-hand end of the bottom bracket, to check that the axle is coming out exactly in the middle of the hole in the cup you just fitted.

Step 2: Tighten anticlockwise. It needs to be fitted really firmly – you need about 300mm (12 inches) of leverage and a good grunt home. Once the body of the bottom bracket is fitted firmly, tighten up the left-hand cup. Take care with plastic cups – they need to be fitted fairly firmly, but won't take as much force as the main body of the bottom bracket. Overdo it and you damage the plastic splines and make it difficult to remove next time.

Step 3: Refit the cranks as on pages 250–51. If you fit a new bottom bracket, watch as you fit the chainset side. Even if you've measured carefully, it's worth checking that the chainset doesn't jam on the chainstays as you tighten the crank bolt. You need at least 2mm (1/8 inch) of clearance between the chainset and the chainstay – if there's not enough, remove the bottom bracket and fit a longer one.

Stubborn bottom brackets

Sometimes bottom brackets get wedged in hard. Usually, it means they weren't fitted with enough grease or antiseize in the first place, or that they've simply been in there too long. Living by the sea in a salty atmosphere, doesn't help either. Try the following measures:

A good dose of release agent helps in three or four applications over a couple of days – especially if, in the middle of proceedings, you put everything back together and go for a good hard ride. A light spray like WD40 will work as a basic penetrant, although you can get something tougher at your hardware or auto shop. You can also get bike-specific release agent from your bike shop – Shimano makes one called Get-A-Grip that is frighteningly effective. All release agents contain various nasty chemicals, so use sparingly in a well-ventilated space and don't get any on your skin. Check once again that you are trying to turn the tool in the correct direction – it's easy to get confused. Looking from the right-hand side of the bike, the right-hand cup is removed by turning it

clockwise – a reverse thread. Looking from the left-hand side of the bike, the left-hand cup is removed by turning it anticlockwise – a normal thread.

Once you've soaked the bottom bracket thoroughly, try using as long a lever as possible on the tool. Find a tube that fits over the end of your adjustable wrench, and use that to increase your leverage, bracing yourself carefully so you don't slip and hurt yourself when the tool starts to move. Clamping the tool in place helps stop the tool slipping off and damaging you and the splines. You need to fiddle with the washers to clamp it successfully. Use the crank bolt and find a washer that stops the crank bolt from slipping into the hole in the centre of the tool without interfering with the wrench flats.

If you have a vice and assistance from a friend, take off the wheels. Drop the tool into the vice and clamp it so the bike is held horizontally over the workbench. Use the bike as a lever and turn it to undo the tool.

External bottom brackets

External bottom brackets have replaced internal (square tapers and splined) versions on higher end models. They are marketed as stiffer, lighter and easier to work on, and fit into standard frame configurations so can be fitted as an upgrade to bikes that currently have square taper or splined bottom brackets. You can't mix and match between internal and external elements – it's one or the other, because with external bottom brackets the axle is integrated onto the chainset as a single piece. Fitting and removing the assembly is relatively simple. You'll need the specially shaped tool for the preload cap and bottom bracket cup, as well as a 5mm Allen key. The pinch bolts need care when refitting – they're bolted into the soft aluminium of the cranks and will strip easily if overtightened. However, if they're left too loose the crank will work loose and fall off. It's tricky to judge exactly how tight is just right, which is where an investment in a torque wrench pays off. These can seem like overkill, but the payoff for our hunger for lighter bike parts is that modern components have less margin for error. They come in a variety of sizes – choose one with a range from around 2-20Nm. Most of the small nuts and bolts on your transmission, suspension and braking systems will need a torque in this range. The standard Shimano versions of external bottom brackets are not serviceable – once the bearings are worn out, the cups have to be replaced. However, manufacturers like Race Face market serviceable versions, and the tools needed to get them apart and back together. Worth considering if your mileage is high or you ride in especially harsh environments. These instructions cover Shimano versions from XT downwards – the XTR setup is different, with a more complex preload adjusting arrangement.

REMOVING BOTTOM BRACKETS

Step 1: Undo pinch bolts on left- hand crank using a 5mm Allen key. If the bolt heads are dirty use a small brush or screwdriver to pick out any detritus so you can insert the Allen key snugly into the bolt head. They'll need to undo a few turns each.

Step 2: Undo and remove the preload cap. You'll need a Shimano Hollowtech II tool for this. It should come off easily. Tuck it somewhere safe, I always lose small black plastic things.

Step 3: Use a small screwdriver to gently lift the small black plastic safety tab that sits in the slot in the crank. It's the side furthest from the bike that should come away. The other end is held captive by the innermost bolt – leave it in place. The tab is there to stop your axle falling off if the fixing bolts fail.

Step 4: The crank arm should come away with a gentle wiggle, exposing the splined end of the axle. Use a plastic hammer to tap this gently through the frame. A wooden block is an acceptable alternative, a hammer is not. Deforming the splines would be an expensive error. Support the chainset whilst you tap, so it doesn't pop right out. Once the drive side comes away from the frame, pull it gently free by hand.

Step 5: Remove the left-hand (non-drive) cup first, anticlockwise with the correct Hollowtech II tool. Steady the tool against the cups, as shown, so that it doesn't slip off and damage the cup (or you). You'll need to use the full length of the tool to get sufficient leverage. The cup will be fitted firmly in the frame – if it comes away easily, it wasn't tight enough. Set aside any spacers.

Step 6: Repeat with the right-hand (drive-side) cup, but note that this side of the frame has a reverse thread, so releases clockwise. Note the positions of any spacers and set them aside you'll need to replace them in the same places when you come to fit the new bottom bracket.

Refitting the bottom bracket

Since there are no user-servicable parts inside Shimano bottom bracket cups, this is generally only a job you'd do when replacing the bottom bracket. The bearings are integrated into the cups, you can't replace them separately. If you're replacing an old external bottom bracket with another external bottom bracket, this shouldn't be a daunting task, provided you've armed yourself with the correct tools. However, there's a slight caveat if you're using the opportunity to upgrade from an internal (square taper or splined) bottom bracket to external. The latter need to seat securely on the face of the bottom bracket shell, which must therefore be very flat and smooth. If your bike was designed for an external bottom bracket, this will have been taken into account already. If not, it's worth getting your bike shop to 'chase and face' the bottom bracket shell. This involves screwing a special tool into the bottom bracket frame threads (which incidentally cleans them out) then milling a very thin slice off each side of the bottom bracket shell, until it's nicely flat. The tool is expensive, and you'll probably only ever need it once, so get the shop to do it for you. No reason not to do the rest of the job yourself though – strip out the old bottom bracket, take the frame to be faced, then refit your new bottom bracket.

REFITTING BOTTOM BRACKETS

Front of bike

Step 7: Now you can get a good look into the bottom bracket. Clean it out thoroughly – plenty of clean cloths work fine. Be particularly picky about the threads and the face of the bottom bracket shell – the thin circle of frame that you can see if you look through the bottom bracket area from the side.

Step 8: Grease the threads on your new bottom bracket cups, then insert the drive-side cup (with the sleeve attached) into the right-hand side of the frame, with original spacers. Start off by hand, to avoid crossthreading. Tighten anticlockwise until the cup is flush with the frame. Repeat, tightening clockwise, with the left-hand (non-drive) cup. Then use the full length of the tool to tighten both very firmly (40Nm).

Step 9: Push the axle through from the drive side. Refit the crank arm, ensuring it points in exactly the opposite direction to the other crank. Refit the black safety tab, then fit the preload washer and tighten by hand with the special tool. It doesn't need any more force than hand-tight. Take up slack on the pinch bolts, then tighten them alternately to 12–14Nm, preferably with a torque wrench.

Toolbox

External bottom brackets

- For the crank bolts – 5mm Allen key
- For the preload bolt and cups – Shimano Hollowtech preload cap and cup tools. Park make a nice combination version, with the preload tool at one end and cup tool at the other, with a comfy blue handle in between
- The pinch bolts need to be tightened with care – the aluminium crank material they're threaded into is relatively soft, and will strip easily if you're overenthusiastic. So, if you're contemplating a torque wrench, now's the time to invest, so you can tighten them just so (12–14Nm)
- Grease or antiseize for the splines of the new bottom bracket axle, and the internal threads

External bottom brackets – where do the spacers go?

The number of spacers and their position depends on the width of your bottom bracket shell (see page 253) and the type of front derailleur you have. Band-on derailleurs are bolted to your seat tube, e-type derailleurs are mounted on a bracket that's clamped onto your bottom bracket shell with the right-hand bottom bracket cup.

- 68mm shell, band-on front derailleur: 2 x 2.5 spacer on the drive side, 1 x 2.5mm spacer on the non-drive side of the bottom bracket
- 68mm shell, e-type derailleur: 1 x 2.5mm spacer against bottom bracket cup, mounted outside the e-mount bracket. 1 x 2.5mm on non-drive side
- 73mm shell, band-on derailleur: 1 x 2.5mm spacer on drive side.
- 73mm shell and e-type derailleur: no spacers

Troubleshooting: bottom bracket

Internal bottom brackets

Symptom	Cause	Solution	Page
One crank rocks from side to side, the other is firm	Loose crank bolt	Tighten crank bolt	249, 251
Both cranks rock from side to side	Bottom bracket unit loose in frame	Remove both cranks, tighten bottom bracket in frame, replace both cranks	250–51, 255
	Bottom bracket worn out	Replace bottom bracket	254–5
Cranks loosen repeatedly	Crank bolt loose	Tighten firmly – use a longer wrench for more leverage	249, 251
	Crank mating surface worn by being ridden loose	Replace crank	250–51
	New crank still loosens repeatedly	Replace bottom bracket	254–5
Creaking noises from bottom bracket area	Dry or loose interface between components	Remove cranks, clean interface between cranks and axle, replace, retighten firmly	249–51
	Bottom bracket loose in frame	Remove both cranks, tighten bottom bracket in frame, replace both cranks	249–51, 255
Bottom bracket works loose constantly	Insufficiently tightened in frame	Use a longer wrench on the bottom bracket tool for more leverage	249–51
	Bottom bracket shell stretched by riding with loose bottom bracket	For minor stretching, use Loctite threads to fill gaps. For major stretching, the only option is to replace frame	N/A
Front derailleur won't shift on to largest chainring	Bottom bracket too long	Replace with shorter one	254–5
Chainrings rub on frame	Bottom bracket too short	Replace with longer one	254–5
Chainring clearance looks fine but chainrings rub under pressure	More clearance needed to allow for chainring flex	Fit longer bottom bracket	254–5
	Chainring bolts loose or missing, allowing chainring to flex excessively	Tighten or replace chainring bolts	172

External bottom brackets

Left-hand crank works loose	Loose pinch bolts	Torque to 12–14Nm	257
Creaking from bottom bracket area	Bottom frame cups loose in frame	Remove cranks and tighten cups firmly	256–7
	Chainring bolts loose	Remove grease threads and under bolt heads, replace firmly	172
Axle shifts in cups when cranks rocked from side to side	Bottom bracket worn out	Replace bottom bracket	256–7

Headsets

Your headset is the pair of bearings at the front of your bike that connects the forks to the frame. Like the bottom bracket, it's an 'out of sight, out of mind' component, frequently ignored in favour of more glamorous upgrades – but it makes a huge difference to how your bike rides. Incorrect headset adjustment and worn bearings both mean uncertain steering. A tight headset makes your steering feel heavy and wear quickly. A loose headset will rock and shudder as you brake, compromising control.

Types and styles

A Headsets are the predominant style of headset system now for almost all types of bike. They're simple to adjust and maintain, needing few special tools. A pair of bearings sit on the top and bottom of the bike's head tube. These are trapped securely in place with a pair of shaped cones. The lower one is fitted tightly to the steerer tube just below the lower bearing, whilst the upper cone sits just over the upper bearing, and can slide on the steerer tube.

To adjust the play in the bearings, the stem bolts are released so that the stem can move on the steerer tube. Then, the bolt that sits on top of the stem is adjusted. This is bolted into the top of the steerer tube, so when you tighten it, it pushes the stem, the washers below the stem, and then the top bearing cone down the steerer tube, squeezing the bearings. Once the adjustment is correct, the stem is retightened, locking the adjustment. All A Headset type systems are adjusted in a similar way, but there are a couple of variations in the way that the bearings are mounted on the frame. In a conventional set-up, a simple cup is pressed into the top and bottom of the bike's headtube, with replaceable bearings sitting in each cup. When the bearings are worn, they can be replaced. When the cups finally wear out, they would be drifted out of the frame and a new set accurately press fitted – a job for the bike shop.

There are now a couple of variations on this theme. Integrated headsets are designed with a shoulder cut into the top and bottom of the head tube, into which a cartridge bearing is placed directly by hand. This eliminates the need to press separate cups into the frame. The shoulder is cut to a very precise size, so that the correct size and shape of cartridge fits exactly, which are designed to take the cartridge bearing. When the idea first caught on, there was the usual competing flurry of sizes, however two 'standards' quickly emerged for the cartridge size – Cane Creek (36/45), and Campagnolo (45/45). Although neater, this design does require precise machining for the cartridge seat. If this becomes damaged, the only solution may be to replace the frame.

Internal headsets are designed so that both the bearing and the headset are pressed into the head tube as a unit. Bearings can be replaced easily, but if new cups are required, again this is one for your local bike shop.

Threaded headsets

There are still a few of the older threaded headsets knocking around – you'll recognize them by the two large nuts between the stem and the frame. The lower of the two is an adjustable bearing race, used to alter the amount of space the headset bearings have to roll about in. The upper is a locknut, used to hold the correctly adjusted bearing race securely in place. The stem height is adjusted separately, with an Allen key on the top of the stem.

CHECKING HEADSET ADJUSTMENT

Step 1: Pick the bike up by the handlebars and turn the handlebars. The bars should turn easily and smoothly, with no effort. You should not feel any notches.

Step 2: Drop the bike back to the ground and turn the bars 90°, so the wheel points to one side. Hold on the front brake to stop the wheel rolling and rock the bike gently back and forth in the direction the frame (not the wheel) is pointing. The wheel might flex and the tyre yield a bit, but there should not be any knocking or play. Turning bars sideways isolates headset play, avoiding confusion with movement you may have in your brake pivots or suspension.

Step 3: Sometimes it helps to hold around the cups, above and below, while you rock the bike – you shouldn't feel any movement at all.

Aheadsets: adjusting bearings

The bearings are adjusted for no play at all, while allowing the fork and bars to rotate smoothly in the frame without resistance. Use the steps on page 259 to check the adjustment if they're tight or if there is play. You wear your bearings really quickly if you ride them either tight or loose.

It's vital to check that your stem bolts are tight after finishing this job – it's easy to get carried away with doing the adjustment and forget to finish the job off. Some people will tell you to leave your stem bolt slightly loose, so that in the event of a crash your stem will twist on the steerer tube rather than bending your handlebars. You should not do this. The consequences of your stem accidentally twisting on your steerer tube as you ride are far too serious and dangerous. Always tighten your stem bolts firmly. It is fine to slacken the topcap bolt off though – it's only needed for headset adjustment and can be a handy emergency bolt if something else snaps!

ADJUSTING AHEADSET BEARINGS

Step 1: Loosen the stem bolt(s) **(A)** so the stem can rotate easily on the steerer. Undoing the top cap **(B)** makes the headset turn more easily; tightening it eliminates play. Approach the correct adjustment gradually, testing for rocking. It is easier to get the adjustment right by tightening a loose headset than by loosening a tight one. If the headset is too tight, back off the top cap a few turns, hold on the front brake and rock the bars gently back and forth.

Step 2: Slowly retighten the top cap, checking constantly, and stopping when you've eliminated all the play. Remember to check for play with the bars turned to one side, so that you can be sure that any knocking you feel is the headset, rather than the brake pivots or fork stanchions.

Step 3: Once you have the adjustment correct, align the stem with the front wheel and firmly tighten the stem bolts. Check the stem is secure by holding the front wheel between your knees and twisting the bars. If the stem shifts on the steerer, the stem bolts need to be tighter. Check the adjustment again and repeat if necessary – sometimes tightening the stem bolt shifts everything around.

Toolbox

Adjusting bearings
- Allen key to fit stem bolts
- Allen key to fit top cap

(Both of these are almost always a 5mm or 6mm Allen key, although you may occasionally come across a 4mm Allen key fitting)

Adjusting stem height
- The same Allen keys as above, to fit your stem bolts and top cap

Servicing:
- Allen keys as above
- Tools to disconnect your brake cable, lever or disc calliper – almost always the same Allen keys as above – 4mm, 5mm or 6mm Allen key
- Degreaser to clean bearing surfaces
- Good-quality grease – preferably a waterproof grease such as Phil Wood

- Fresh bearings: ball bearings for headsets are generally 4mm (5⁄32 inch), but take your old ones to your bike shop to match them up

(Bearing races can be replaced by loose bearings, which are more fiddly to fit but roll more smoothly and last longer)

(Cartridge bearings should be taken to the shop to be matched up for fresh ones – there are a few different types in use, all of which look very similar)

(The most common type, for Shimano bearings, also fits in headsets made by other manufacturers)

Cutting down steerer tube
This is the most tool-intensive job you can do to your Aheadset!
- All the servicing tools above
- Hacksaw
- Vice to hold steerer tube while you cut it
- Soft jaws or an improvised tube clamp to protect steerer tube from vice

Aheadsets: adjusting stem height

If your bars are set at the correct height, you'll be more comfortable, stable and in control.

There are a couple of ways of changing the height of your bars. Easiest is to swap your stem out for another model , see page 274. There are countless options for length and angle so you should be able to find the perfect set-up. However, for minor height adjustments, a cheaper option is to use the stack of washers that sit between your stem and your headset. If you take off your stem, and a couple of the washers, and refit the stem, it'll sit at a lower position. The washers you've removed will then have to be repositioned above the stem, as they're used to push the stem down the steerer tube when you tighten the top cap. It's a quick, free upgrade!

You'll end up with a neat stack of washers sitting above your stem. Ignore them until you're sure you're happy with the new position, then use the instructions on page 264 to cut off the excess steerer tube. Don't do this until you're sure you won't want to raise the stem back up again – it's relatively easy to make the steerer tube shorter, but you can't make it longer again!

You'll need to readjust the headset bearing again once you've reassembled everything.

ADJUSTING STEM HEIGHT

Step 1: Remove the top cap. You'll need to undo the top cap bolt all the way and wiggle the cap off. This reveals that star-fanged nut inside the steerer tube. Lift off any washers that were sitting between the top cap and the stem. Check the condition of the top cap. If it's cracked or the recess where the bolt head sits is distorted, replace it.

Step 2: Loosen the stem bolts so that the stem moves freely on the steerer tube. Pull the stem up and off – you may need to twist it a little to help it on its way. Tape the entire handlebar assembly to the top tube so that hoses and cables don't get kinked under the weight of the bars.

Step 3: If you've hung the bike in a workstand, keep a hand on the forks so that they don't slide out of the headset. Add or remove washers from the stack under the stem. If you're adding washers, you can only add washers that came off above the stem.

Step 4: Replace the stem, then any leftover washers – everything that came off the steerer tube should go back on. The washers are all necessary because as you tighten the top cap, they push down onto the stem and then the bearings, adjusting the headset.

Step 5: Check the height of the washer stack above the top of the steerer tube. There should be a gap of 2–3mm (around $\frac{1}{8}$ inch). If possible, this should be a single washer, not a stack of thinner ones as individual washers have a tendency to get caught and stop you adjusting the headset properly. Add or remove washers from the top of the stack to achieve the desired gap.

Step 6: Replace the top cap, and go to 'Aheadset: adjusting bearings' on page 260. Once you're satisfied with the adjustment, **ensure the stem bolts are securely tightened**.

Headsets: regular maintenance to ensure a smooth ride

Headsets are remarkably simple to service, needing no special tools at all, just one (or two) Allen keys, degreaser or other cleaning agent and good-quality grease.

Headsets, like bottom brackets, are frequently ignored, gradually deteriorating without you noticing. Regular servicing will help keep them turning smoothly and will make your bike feel more responsive. Cleaning the dirt out and replacing the grease with fresh stuff will help make the bearing surfaces last as long as possible. With the ball type, it's worth replacing the bearings at every service – new ones only cost a couple of pounds. Cartridge bearings are more expensive and can usually be resuscitated – see page 268 for help servicing them. If they need replacing, always take the old cartridge bearings along to your bike shop to match up new ones. The size and shape are crucial.

Check carefully for pitting on bearing races once you've cleaned out the headset. Even very tiny pits are a sign that your headset needs replacing. The surface that suffers most is the crown race, the ring at the very bottom of the headset that's attached to your forks. Your bearings will quickly wear a groove in this, showing you where they run. The crown race should be completely smooth. You should be able to run a fingernail around the groove without it catching in any blemishes on the surface.

Headset replacement is a job for your bike shop. The new headset needs to be pressed into your frame, with the top and bottom surfaces exactly parallel; otherwise the headset will wear very quickly and bind at some handlebar angles. The cups are a tight fit and so must be pressed in carefully to avoid damaging the shape of the head tube. Ignore anybody who tells you that it's OK to fit new headset cups by bashing them into the head tube with a block of wood.

Headset hints

Before you start, remove the front wheel altogether. It's easiest to do this job if you disconnect either the front brake lever from the front brake or the front brake lever from the handlebars. This way you won't damage the cable or hose when you remove the forks.

With cable brakes, disconnect the noodle from the brake (don't undo the fixing bolt, just quick-release it), line up the slots on the barrel-adjuster with the slot on the lever, pull the cable gently out and wiggle the nipple free from its nest inside the brake lever.

With disc brakes, have a look at the lever. If it's fixed on with two bolts on either side of the handlebar, simply remove them both, untangle the hose from the other cables and tape the lever to the forks to stop the hose getting snagged on anything. Otherwise, remove the handlebar grip on the front brake side, loosen the brake-fixing bolt, and slide the brake lever off the end of the bars.

Untangle the hose from any of the other controls and tape or tie to the fork leg.

SERVICING HEADSETS

Step 1: Undo the Allen key on the very top of the stem, the top cap bolt. Remove the top cap completely, revealing the star-fanged nut inside the steerer tube. Undo the bolts that secure the stem while holding onto the forks, and the stem should pull off easily.

Step 2: Tape or tie the stem to the top tube out of the way (protect the frame paint with a cloth). Pull off any washers and set them aside. Pull the forks gently and slowly down out of the frame.

Step 3: The fork may not want to come out. Lots of headsets have a plastic wedge that sits above the top bearing race and that sometimes gets very firmly wedged in place. Release it by sliding a small screwdriver into the gap in the plastic wedge, and twist slightly to release the wedge. You could also try tapping the top of the fork with a plastic or rubber mallet. Don't hit it with a hammer – that's not the same thing at all.

Step 4: Catch all pieces as they come off and note the orientation and order of bearing races and seals.

Step 5: Once you've got the fork out, lay out all the bearing races and cups in order. Check the bearing cup at the bottom of the head tube for any bearings or seals left in there. Clean all the races carefully: the ones attached to the frame top and bottom, the loose one off the top chunk of bearings when the fork came out and the crown race still attached to the fork. If you have cartridge bearings, see the section on servicing the cartridges.

Checking the condition of the steerer tube

While you've got the forks out, it's worth checking the condition of the steerer tube. This will break if abused, so it is worth inspecting regularly. Adjustment of the bearings also depends on the stem being able to slide easily up and down the steerer tube when the top cap is tightened or loosened.

Step 6: Look carefully at the clean races and check for pits or rough patches. Pitted bearing races mean a new headset. This needs special tools and so is a job for your bike shop. Otherwise, clean all the bearings and seals carefully. If you used degreaser, rinse it off and dry everything. Grease the cups in the frame enough that the bearings sit in grease up to their middles. Cartridge bearings just need a thin smear to keep the weather out.

Step 7: Don't grease the crown race on the fork or the loose top head race. Fit a bearing ring into the cups at either end of the head tube and replace the seals. The direction the races face is crucial, so replace them facing the same direction they were. Slide the fork back through the frame and slide the loose top race back down over the steerer tube. If it had a plastic wedge, put it on next, followed by any washers or covers in the order they came off.

- Hold a ruler up to the steerer tube. The side of the ruler should lie flat against the length of the steerer. Any bends in the steerer will show up as gaps between it and the ruler. Gaps greater than 1mm ($\frac{1}{16}$ inch) mean that the steerer is bent and should be replaced.
- Feel along the surface of the steerer with your fingers. There should be no bulges, dips or irregularities in the diameter of the steerer.
- Check for cracks, especially down at the bottom of the steerer tube, near the crown race.
- Check that the crown race is a tight fit on the forks – you should not be able to move it with your fingers.
- Check the area that the stem bolts onto. It's important that this is clean and smooth. Some stems will damage the steerer if overtightened – replace if it is distorted.
- The top of the steerer must be smooth. If you've cut down the steerer, file the cut surface so that there are no overhanging snags of metal – these will get caught in the stem and prevent you from adjusting the bearings.

Step 8: Refit the stem and any washers from above the stem. Push the stem firmly down the steerer tube.

Step 9: Make sure there's a gap of 2–3mm (around $\frac{1}{8}$ inch) between the top of the steerer tube and the top of the stem, adding or removing washers if necessary. Refit the top cap, then adjust bearings (see page 266). Tighten the stem bolts securely, then refit your brake lever or cable and your front wheel. Check your stem is tight and facing forward. Also check that your front brake is working properly.

Aheadsets: cutting off excess steerer tube

With your stem at its maximum height, your stem top cap will sit directly on top of your stem. If you decide to move your stem downwards, removing washers from below the stem, you'll have to replace them above the stem, so that they bear down on the top of it when you adjust the top cap. Excess steerer tube will then protrude above the stem.

Mechanically, this works perfectly well, but it's not particularly attractive and will hurt if you land on it in a crash. It's a bit of extra weight that you don't need to carry around, too. So, once you're sure that you prefer the new, lower stem height – and do be sure because cutting off excess steerer tube is easy, making it longer again means buying a new pair of forks – cut off the protruding part. You'll also need to do this when fitting a new pair of forks – they are always supplied longer than you would ever need and are then cut down to length – this is much cheaper for suppliers than making a selection of different steerer lengths.

Start by very carefully marking the place to cut. It's easy to get confused and cut off too much, leaving you with a useless pair of forks. Marker pen works well. Assemble the fork completely, including the stem. Mark the point where the steerer tube comes up out of the top of the stem. Draw the line all the way around the top of the stem. Remove the forks from the bike again.

If you are shortening previously fitted forks, you need to check the position of the star-fanged nut inside the steerer tube. You can see it if you look down into the steerer tube from above – a short length of thread mounted in a domed, fanged plate. The fangs point slightly upward, so that, as you tighten the top cap, they are forced into the inside wall of the steerer tube. This means that the more you tighten the top cap, the firmer the star-fanged nut wedges itself in place.

The star-fanged nut needs to sit just inside the steerer tube so that the top of the nut is about 10mm (⅜ inch) below its top. When cutting down forks, you will often find that the current position of the nut is just exactly where you want to cut the tube. If this is the case, it's best to move the nut down the tube so that you can reuse it. Thread a long 6mm (¼ inch) bolt into the star-fanged nut and tap it down gently with a hammer until it lies about 10mm (⅜ inch) below the level of the line you've marked. Be careful to knock it in straight, don't let it drift to one side.

Cutting the steerer tube

Now you're ready to cut the steerer tube. I like to hold the forks up against the bike as a final check that I've measured correctly before I start cutting.

The forks will need to be clamped securely while you cut them, but it's vital not to squash the steerer tube. Soft vice jaws, made of wood or plastic, work fine as long as you're careful not to overtighten the vice. If you have a scrap of wood (a 50mm (2 inches) cube is perfect) and a drill, cut a hole that's about the same diameter as the steerer tube (25mm (1 inch) should be fine) through the length of the wood. Then cut the wood in half across the middle of the hole and along its length. You will end up with two blocks of wood, each with a semicircular channel. Place these on either side of the steerer tube so that you can clamp the steerer tube firmly in the vice without squashing it.

You need to cut the steerer tube 2–3mm (around ⅛ inch) shorter than the mark you've made. Draw a new line, all the way around the steerer tube – it's important that the cut is flat and square. Cut carefully, checking that you're not trying to cut through the star-fanged nut as well – you may find that you need to knock it through a little further. File off sharp edges because the stem needs to be able to slide freely over the steerer tube without scratching. Clean off any metal shavings and filings; these will play havoc with your headset bearings if they work their way in there.

If you're fitting new forks, or you cut the star-fanged nut off, you'll need to fit a new nut. They have two parallel-toothed plates. Both plates are slightly curved – the nut sits in the fork, so that the teeth point upward. Screw the new star-fanged nut onto a long (45mm or so) bolt – the usual size is 6mm, but some nuts take 5mm. Protect the dropouts at the bottom of the fork by standing them on a piece of wood. Take special care if you have adjuster knobs or valves protruding from the bottom of the fork legs – support the forks so that these parts don't come into contact with hard surfaces, as they will bend or break. Tap the top of the bolt, knocking the star-fanged nut into the top of the steerer tube. Take care to keep it vertical. It should sit 10–20mm (⅜–¾ inch) below the top of the steerer tube.

Threaded headsets

The big advantage that the older style threaded headset has over new Aheadsets is that it is very easy to adjust the stem height without replacing any parts.

Adjusting stem height

Follow these instructions to change your stem height. Then check that the stem is tight by standing in front of the bike, holding the front wheel between your knees. Try to twist the bars around. If you can move them, the stem bolt is too loose. Retighten. If the stem is tricky to tighten, it may indicate that the steerer tube (the central part of the fork that extends up through the frame and onto which your stem is bolted) is damaged. Alternatively, the wedge at the bottom of the stem, the one that is pulled upward when you tighten the stem bolt, may have become twisted in the steerer tube. Either way, if you can't tighten your stem, get your bike shop to have a look at the stem and steerer tube, and to replace the forks if necessary. Also make sure that the front wheel is pointing straight forward; if not, loosen the stem bolt, twist it so the wheel and bars are at 90 degrees, and retighten.

ADJUSTING STEM HEIGHT

Safety mark

Step 1: Undo the expander bolt at the top of the stem. This almost always needs a 6mm Allen key, but you might need to prise off a rubber bung first. Undo it in four complete turns.

Step 2: As you turn the bolt, the head rises up out of the stem. Tap the Allen key with a rubber mallet or block of wood, so that the Allen key drops down flush with the stem again. This releases the wedge that holds the stem in place.

Step 3: Once the stem is loose, you can adjust its position. Make sure you don't raise it above the safety mark – an arrow or a row of vertical lines around the stem. They should not be visible; instead they should be hidden inside the headset. Retighten the 6mm Allen key bolt firmly.

Toolbox

The main reason for the demise of the once ubiquitous threaded headset is that it requires a pair of expensive spanners to adjust it – unlike the Aheadset, which can be adjusted with an Allen key.

Tools for threaded headsets: adjusting stem height
- 6mm Allen key
- If the expander bolt is wedged firmly, a plastic hammer or a block of wood is needed to knock it down

Tools for threaded headsets: adjusting bearings
- Ideally, two headset spanners – the most common size is 36mm, although older, 1-inch headsets need 32mm spanners – it is possible to use an adjustable spanner on the top lock nut instead of a headset

spanner, but take time to tighten the spanner carefully onto the nut flats, since they are soft and easily damaged

Threaded headsets: adjusting bearings

You need two spanners to adjust the bearings. The most common size, for 1⅛-inch headsets, is 36mm. You may also come across 1-inch headsets, which need a 32mm spanner, and even the rare 1½-inch headsets, which need a 40mm spanner. The adjustable nut is quite narrow, so you will need a special narrow headset spanner. The top nut is wider, so use an adjustable spanner if you only have one headset spanner.

To check your headset, pick the bike up by the handlebars and turn the steering. The bars should turn easily and smoothly, with no effort. You should not be able to feel any notches. Drop the bike back onto the ground again and turn the bars 90 degrees so that the wheel points off to one side. Hold on the front brake to stop the wheel rolling and rock the bike gently backwards and forwards – in the direction the frame points, not the direction the wheel points. The wheel might flex and you may feel the tyre giving a bit, but you should not feel or hear any knocking or play. Sometimes it helps to hold around the cups, above and below, while you rock – you shouldn't feel any movement.

The top of the fork steerer tube is threaded and held into the frame with two big nuts. The lower of these has a bearing surface on the bottom in which the top set of bearings runs. Tightening the nut draws the fork up into the frame, squashing the bearing surfaces closer together and eliminating play between fork and frame. Loosening this nut increases the space the bearings sit in, allowing them to turn more smoothly. The correct adjustment is found by turning this nut to a position that eliminates play while still allowing the forks to rotate freely. Once you've found this magic position, the top nut can be locked down onto the adjusting nut, holding it firmly in position so that it doesn't rattle loose as you ride along. Once bearings have been correctly adjusted and the top nut firmly locked down, they should not work loose over time, so they will not need frequent readjustment. However, the bearings often settle a little bit after servicing, so they will often need readjusting. If you find yourself having to readjust your bearings often, check that the threads on the forks and the headset are in good condition. The threads will suffer if the headset is ridden loose, when both nuts will rub constantly over the fork threads.

Remove the stem, then the top locknut. Have a look at the threads inside the nut. They should be crisp and distinct, with sharp edges. The fork threads should be the same. Unscrew the lower adjusting nut and check the threads on it, as well as the fork threads that were concealed by the adjusting nut. If the threads are slightly damaged, reassemble the headset with Loctite on the threads to prevent the nuts from working loose. A new top locking nut will also help. However, if either the fork threads have been badly worn or the nut has worn grooves in the surface of the fork, the fork should be replaced immediately.

ADJUSTING BEARINGS

Step 1: Hold the adjusting nut still with one spanner and undo the top nut a couple of turns with the other. The two will be firmly locked together, so you have to be firm with the spanners to get them moving. Once the top nut is loose, use the spanner to adjust the position of the adjusting nut – tighten clockwise to eliminate play in the headset, loosen anticlockwise to allow the bars to rotate freely.

Step 2: Ideally, you are looking for the place where the adjusting nut is as loose as possible, without allowing the forks to rock in the frame. Turn the adjustable cup clockwise to eliminate rocking – anticlockwise to allow the headset to turn more freely. Test by holding the front brake on and rocking the bike forwards.

Step 3: Once you've found the right place, hold the bottom nut still with the spanner to maintain the adjustment, and lock the top nut firmly down onto it. Test the adjustment again – you often find that locking down the top nut changes the adjustment, and so you have to repeat the procedure. Take care as you do this not to overtighten the adjusting cup – if you wedge it down onto the bearing surface, you damage the bearings.

Threaded headsets: servicing

Headsets will thank you for regular servicing. Pick up the bike by the handlebar, and twist it – the bar should move freely, with no crunching noises.

Check before you start that it's not too late for a service – leave it too long and you have to replace your headset. Replacement is a job that needs expensive and special tools, so it is worth getting your bike shop to do it for you.

Turn your bars gently from one side to the other. If the headset is pitted, you will feel a notch as the headset passes through the 'straight ahead' position – almost as if the headset is indexed. If this happens, it's new headset time. Otherwise, it's worth trying to service.

Release the front brakes, and free the cable from the front brake lever so that it hangs free. Take the front wheel off (you take the forks out in a while, and the wheel makes them heavy and unwieldy). Remove the stem – loosen the expander bolt on the top of the stem four turns, then knock the head of the bolt gently with a block of wood or a rubber mallet. Pull the stem up and out of the steerer tube, and tie or tape it to the top tube to keep it out of the way. Now you're ready to service the headset.

SERVICING HEADSETS

Step 1: Remove the top nut. It is wedged tightly against the lower nut, so you need two spanners of the right size: one to hold the adjusting nut still, one to loosen the top nut. Slide off any washers. Lay out everything you take off in order so you know how to put them back together.

Step 2: Hold the fork still and undo the adjusting nut. When you've removed it, you should find that you can slide the forks out from the bottom of the frame. Make sure you catch any bearings or seals that come off, and note which direction they were facing in. Be particularly careful with bearing races – they must go back together in the correct order.

Step 3: Clean cups, bearings and seals carefully. To remove compacted grease and mud, scrub them with an old toothbrush and some degreaser. Rinse and dry afterwards. Inspect the bearing surfaces carefully. Any kind of pitting means replacing the headset, a bike shop job. Pay particular attention to the crown race, the part that usually suffers first. If the bearings are dirty, replace them – fresh bearings make your headset last longer. Make sure you get the correct size.

Step 4: Grease the cups at either end of the head tube. There should be enough grease to cover the bearings up to their middles. Cartridge bearings are the exception: you do not need to grease the cups. Grease the threads on the adjusting and top nuts, and dab a little on the bottom surface of the top cup.

Step 5: Pop bearings and then seals into the cups, paying attention to the direction of the bearings. Slide the fork up through the frame and trap it in place by threading on the adjusting cup. Make sure it's flat as it goes on – it's easy to cross-thread by mistake. Tighten until the fork doesn't rattle around in the frame – no tighter for now.

Step 6: Replace any washers. If the fork has a slot cut down through the thread, orientate any washers with a tab so that the tab fits in the slot. Fit the top nut and tighten it down until it touches the adjusting nut. Grease the inside of the steerer tube and replace the stem. Check that it points straight forward and that the safety mark is inside the frame. Tighten the Allen key bolt at the top of the stem firmly. Replace front wheel and front brake, then adjust bearings as on page 266.

Headset bearing types and servicing cartridge bearings

When headsets are new, it makes little difference how they are made. As long as they are properly adjusted, cheap ones feel about the same as expensive ones. The difference shows up after a bit of hammering.

A major advantage of better headsets is usually in the sealing: cheap headsets allow in rain, mud and dust, and then deteriorate quickly. Once headsets start to get sticky, they retain everything that gets trapped in them as a paste. Soon this wears pits in the bearing surfaces, and then the bearings fall into the pits as you turn the bars, rather than rolling smoothly. This is new headset time! Basic headsets use two rings of ball bearings, sealed above and below with a rubber washer. If you have this type and ride in wet or muddy conditions, build up a regular servicing habit to keep your bike running smoothly. Consider servicing your headset twice in winter and once more in summer.

A variation on the loose bearing idea is the needle bearing. Instead of a ring of balls, these use a ring of small rods fanning out from the center and sitting at an angle. Some people swear by them. Personally, I like my ball bearings round. If you have needle bearings, treat them in the same way as standard round bearings.

Cartridge bearing

Needle bearing

Ball bearing

Cartridge headset bearings are more expensive. Instead of loose bearings, the bearings are set top and bottom in cartridges that fit into the headset cups. The advantage of this system is that when you replace the cartridges, you replace the bearing surface as well as the bearings themselves. It's a very good idea for headsets, since replacing the cartridges is equivalent to replacing the headset. They are more expensive than buying ball bearings, but less expensive than buying a headset, especially when you take into account the extra time it takes to fit new headset cups, or to pay someone to do it for you.

There are several different types and shapes of cartridges, so take the old cartridge to the shop when you buy a new one. They can be serviced though – see below. The bottom race is worked harder than the top race, so swap the top and bottom races every service to get maximum life from them. Cartridge bearings can be replaced easily, with the advantage that as well as replacing the ball bearings, you also replace the bearing surface on which they run. If you can catch them before their condition gets too bad, they respond well to a cleaning and regreasing. This is only easy if they have a plastic seal – otherwise replace them.

SERVICING CARTRIDGE BEARINGS

Step 1: Using a very sharp knife, carefully peel back the seal on one side of the bearing. Take care not to bend the seal or cut it. Keep the knife as parallel to the seal as possible. Always push the knife away from your fingers. It's easy to slip and cut yourself – take care. Once you've lifted the seal, run the knife carefully around the seal, lifting it off without bending it. Repeat on the other side.

Step 2: Soak the bearing in degreaser and scrub all the old grease out. An old toothbrush is perfect for this. Dry the bearing; hairdryers work fine (I strongly recommend cleaning off all the grease and putting it away when you've finished and will not be held responsible for any failure to do so). Clean the seals.

Step 3: Pack the bearing half-full with good-quality bicycle grease. Spin the bearing to spread the grease evenly around the bearings. Refit the seals, easing them into place with both thumbs. Wipe excess grease off the outside of the bearing.

Troubleshooting headsets

Symptom	Cause	Solution	Page Aheadset	Page Threaded
Steering sluggish, unresponsive	Headset too tight	Loosen headset	260	266
	Headset clogged	Service headset	262–3	267
Front of bike rocks when braking	Headset loose	Tighten headset	260	266
Bike uncertain when cornering	Headset loose	Tighten headset	260	266
Headset rotates in distinct steps rather than smoothly	Bearings dirty or worn	Service headset, replace bearings	262–3, 268	267, 268
Headsets don't last long, wearing out frequently	Bearing surfaces pitted	Take to bike shop for new headset	N/A	N/A
	Headset cups not parallel in frame	Take to bike shop to have headset repressed into frame	N/A	N/A
		Take to bike shop to have faces of head tube reamed flat	N/A	N/A
Creaking noises when bars turn	Brake and gear cables flexing in cable stops	Check that all sections of casing have ferrules and oil ferrules	N/A	N/A
	Headset dry – insufficient or contaminated grease	Service headset, repack with plenty of good quality grease	262–3	267
Aheadset – top cap won't tighten any more, but headset still rocks	Not enough washers on steerer tube, so that top cap tightens directly onto top or steerer	Remove top cap, fit an extra washer above or below the stem, replace top cap, readjust, tighten stem securely	261	N/A
Aheadset – bearings work loose after adjustment	Stem bolts not tightened enough	Remove, clean and regrease stem fixing bolts, tighten firmly	261	N/A
	Steerer tube too slippery to grip stem	Remove stem, clean off excess grease, refit securely, test for stem tightness	261	N/A

9 – Components

This is the part of the bike where you get to express yourself! When you buy a new bike, the manufacturer makes guesses about what size and shape you'll be and chooses the 'finishing kit' – handlebars, stem, seatpost and saddle – accordingly. These are really personal items, though, and getting the right size and shape for your needs makes a big difference to how much you enjoy your riding. This chapter will help you when you are swapping components, fitting them securely and adjusting them.

Handlebars

Renew your bars regularly, whether they show signs of cracking or not. Of all the components you use, these are the ones with a short shelf life. I like to use lightweight bars because I don't weigh much, and I like how they feel. I exchange bars every couple of years, but if I was heavier or harder on equipment, I'd replace them once or twice a year.

Removing and swapping bars whatever their shape means taking off bar tape, grips, shifters and levers. The key is remembering not to scratch the bars. It's tempting to twist and pull, leaving a spiral scour all the way along. But if you want to break a handlebar, the easiest way is to scratch it, then stress the bar repeatedly. Sound familiar?

The other damage to watch out for is crash damage – especially if you ride with bar ends. Any bending at all means they must be replaced. Both ends of the bar should be exactly the same shape and point in completely opposite directions.

Also beware of causing scratches or cracks where the stem bolts onto the handlebars. Creaking noises are a warning – always take them seriously. Sometimes the sound is caused by dirt trapped between bars and stem; sometimes it means something is about to break. Check the section on stems for help cleaning out the stem.

The standard clamp diameter is now 31.8mm – older (smaller) diameters are becoming difficult to find.

A different-shaped bar makes a surprising difference to how the bike feels. Straight, flat bars keep the front end of your body low, spreading your weight evenly between the front and back of the bike. The aerodynamic advantage is minimal unless you ride a lot on the road, but many people find this a comfortable position.

A little extra rise, say 20mm (¾ inch), makes the steering feel more precise. A slight sweep back on the bars, say 5 degrees, is easier on your wrists and shoulders. When you fit the bars, roll them until the sweep points up and back towards your shoulders. You can raise them, but don't go too far – too much height at the front end makes climbing difficult because you struggle to keep the front end of the bike on the ground.

When you refit the brake levers and shifters, spend a little time getting the angle right. I like mine set so that the brake levers are at 45 degrees to the ground, with the shifters tucked up as tight as possible underneath – but it's personal preference.

Manufacturers often save money by fitting heavier own-brand or no-brand bars on new bikes, so bars are a good place to start upgrading if you want to shave a little weight. Lightweight thin-gauge aluminium bars absorb vibrations from your bike, which helps stop your wrists from getting tired on long rides.

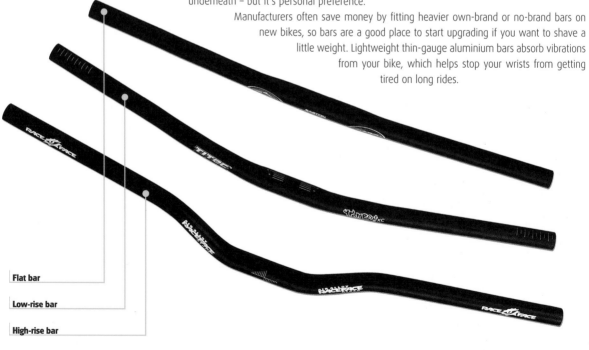

Flat bar

Low-rise bar

High-rise bar

Fitting new handlebars

Bars that have been bent in a crash need to be replaced immediately – they'll be weakened and will let you down when you least expect it. You may also be upgrading your bars for lighter or stronger ones – or for a new shape like a higher rise for more downhill control or a flatter bar to keep your weight over the front wheel when climbing.

Carbon bars are popular because they're stiff, light and strong. They need to be looked after though – a scratch on the surface will weaken them significantly. Take care when fitting and adjusting.

Next, remove the grips. Slide something underneath so that you can lift the grip up a little. It's tempting to use screwdrivers because they're the right size and handy, but it's all too easy to scratch the bars with them. Chopsticks, being made of wood, are much better. Use hairspray, spray degreaser or warm soapy water to lubricate the undergrips. Twist and pull to get the grip off.

Unbolt and remove the shifter and brake lever. Take care not to scratch the bars at all because cracks can grow from tiny scratches, especially on carbon bars. If the levers and shifters don't slide off easily, remove the fixing bolts altogether and open up the clamp very slightly with a screwdriver – just enough to slide off the levers. Don't bend the clamps, though!

▲ **Ease the clamp open slightly to avoid scratching the bars**

You may find that cables or hydraulic hoses are too short to slide the levers off without kinking them. Don't wrestle with them: undo the bolts that hold the handlebars onto the stem and slide the handlebars along in the stem so the levers don't have to travel as far to slip off the end. Remove the handlebars.

Clean the face of the stem that the bars fit into – if dirt has worked its way in between the two parts, the bars won't clamp firmly onto the stem and will creak as you ride. Lubricate the central part of the new bars – grease for aluminium bars, carbon prep for carbon bars.

Next, clean and grease the bolts that fix the bars onto the stem. The threads in the stem are soft and will strip easily if treated badly – this is expensive neglect because once you've stripped the threads, your only option is to replace the stem. So clean dirt out from the bolt threads and under the bolt head, then grease the threads and bolt head.

Fit the new bars loosely onto the stem, then slide the brake and gear levers onto the bars. If the cables or brake hoses are short, you may need to pass the bars from one side to the other through the stem to get the controls onto the bars without kinking the cables. Next, refit the grips. They need to be a tight fit so that they don't suddenly slide off the ends of the bars as you ride (this sounds like it would be a comic moment, but is actually disastrous and painful). You'll have to lubricate them to slide them on, but whatever you lubricate them with then needs to stick the grips to the bars. The ideal product is motorbike grip glue, but it's often hard to find. Alternatives include isopropyl alcohol, disc brake cleaner and artists' fixing spray. Don't use spray oil because it never dries properly. Set the bars in the centre of the stem, tighten the stem bolts enough to hold the bars in place, then sit on your bike to work out the most comfortable angle for the bars to sit at. If the bars are swept or curved back, a good starting place is pointing the sweep up and back towards your shoulder blades. Small rotations of the bar can make a big difference, so take a bit of time playing with the angle. Once you have the bar position, rotate brake levers and shifters to a comfortable angle. You need to be able to grab and operate them with as little effort as possible. Experiment with different brake-lever angles. Set the levers so that you don't have to lift your fingers too far up to get them over the lever blades.

Once you have everything in place ergonomically, go around and tighten all the fixing bolts. If your stem has a removable front face, be sure to tighten the bolts evenly so that there is an equal gap above and below the bars.

Bars are usually supplied wide, so that you can cut them down to suit your tastes. Check the manufacturer's recommendations for carbon bars before you start – if they tell you not to modify the length, follow their instructions.

Fitting a new stem

The length and angle of the stem make a big difference to your comfort and sense of well-being, as well as to how well the bike steers.

Longer stems have the same effect as big steering wheels on cars: when they are too long the steering feels lazy, which is great for cruising but hard work for fast singletrack. Very short stems make the bike twitchy; the smallest hand movement translates into movement of your wheel, which is great for technical stuff but tiring for longer rides. The right stem length depends on your top tube length, your riding style and your body shape. Women are often more comfortable with a slightly shorter stem than men of the same size. Almost all stems are now the Ahead type. One advantage is you get two different-shaped stems in one: take it off, turn it over and refit it for a higher or lower position.

First check how the stem fits to the handlebar. It will either be a front-loader with two or four bolts or a single-bolt type. Front-loaders are the easiest to deal with: the front of the stem can be completely removed, allowing you to change or flip the stem without too much fuss. With older single-bolt stems, the handlebars can only be removed if you strip all the controls off one side of the bars.

Single bolt/quill stems

Remove the grip on one side by sliding a chopstick between grip and bar, lubricate with a squirt of light oil and twist to slide off. Loosen the bolts on the shifters and brake levers and slide them off without scratching the bars. If they're a tight fit, lever the clamps gently open with a screwdriver, without bending the clamps. The cables will often be too short to allow you to slide the controls off the end of the bar. Loosen the bolt that holds the stem to the handlebars and slide the bar sideways in the stem so that you can remove the controls without kinking the cables. Undo the bolt at the top of the stem four turns and knock it back into the stem with a rubber mallet or block of wood. This releases the wedge nut at the bottom of the stem. Twist and pull to remove it. Clean carefully inside the steerer tube. Clean the central part of the handlebars, then smear a little grease on the part that will be trapped between bars and stem. Fit the new stem to your bars. Grease the inside of the steerer tube generously and fit the bars. Make sure they're pointing directly forward, then tighten the bolt at the top of the stem firmly. Gripping your front wheel between your knees, twist the bars to check that the stem bolt is tight. If the bars rotate out of line, retighten the stem bolt. Slide the shifters and brake levers back onto your bars, then twist the grips back onto bars, lubricating with hot water if necessary. Slide the controls back up to the end of the grip and tighten the fixing bolts.

Front-loader stems
Removing
These clamp onto the handlebars with two bolts, or a bolt and a hinge. When you've undone and removed the bolt(s), you can take the front of the stem off or fold it out of the way, releasing the handlebars completely.

REFITTING

Step 1: Clean both the stem and the handlebars where they clamp together. Any dirt left at this interface can cause annoying creaking. Once both are clean, spread a thin layer of grease or carbon prep on the part of the handlebar that's to be clamped in the stem. Grease the bolt threads with an extra dab of grease under the bolt head. Titanium bars, stems and bolts need a generous dab of copperslip.

Step 2: It's important to do bolts up evenly. With two-bolt stems, tighten both bolts until there is an even gap between the main part and the front of the stem, then tighten each bolt one turn at a time until both are firm. With four-bolt types, tighten in a cross pattern as shown above.

Step 3: Once the bolts are tight, check that the gap is even top and bottom and, for four-bolt types, that the gap is also even either side. This matters because the bolts will go in straight and be stronger. If one side has more gap, bolts enter the main part of the stem at an angle, stressing them and making them more likely to snap. If the front of the stem is hinged, fold over the hinge and tighten the bolt firmly.

Seatposts

Seatposts must be sized very accurately: the 30 different common sizes come in increments of 0.2mm. One size too big won't fit your frame; one size too small will fit but rock slightly at every pedal stroke, slowly destroying your frame. If you have your old seatpost, the right size is stamped on it. If in doubt, get your bike measured at the shop.

All seatposts have a minimum insertion line. This is usually indicated by a row of vertical lines printed or stamped near the bottom of the seatpost. The vertical lines must always be inside the frame. If you have to lift your seatpost high enough to see the marks, you need either a longer seatpost or a bigger bike. In the unlikely event that you have no markings on your seatpost, you need a length at least 2.5 times the diameter of the post inside the frame. Seatposts that are raised too high will snap your frame.

ADJUSTING SADDLE POSITION

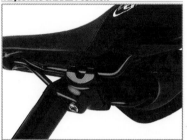

Step 1: This is the most common type of saddle fixing. The saddle rails are clamped between two plates with a single bolt. The bottom of the lower plate is curved to match the top of the post. Loosening the bolt (6mm Allen key) allows you to slide the saddle backwards and forwards or to roll it to change the angle. Start with the top of the saddle horizontal, clamped in the middle of the rails. Remove and regrease the fixing bolt regularly.

Step 2: This design allows you to control the angle of the saddle precisely. To tip the saddle nose downwards, loosen the back bolt slightly and tighten the front bolt firmly, one turn at a time. To lift the nose, loosen the front bolt one turn and tighten the back bolt. To slide the saddle along on the rails, loosen both bolts equally, reposition the saddle, then retighten the bolts equally. A ball-ended Allen key is handy here, as the front bolt can be tricky to access.

Step 3: This design has two small Allen keys at the back of the clamp. Loosen both to slide the saddle rails in the clamp or to roll the clamp over the curved top of the post.

SADDLE ANGLE

Step 1: Saddle angle is critical for a comfortable ride. Pedalling in this position, with the nose of the saddle tipped upward, will push you off the back of the saddle, lifting the front wheel off the ground when climbing. For hardtails – sitting on the bike compresses the fork, dropping the saddle angle – you'll have to start with a slight rise so the angle levels off with your weight on it.

Step 2: This position can help relieve the discomfort of a saddle that doesn't suit you, but it tips you forward toward the bars, causing wrist and shoulder pain. This position is also often a sign that your saddle is too high – try levelling it off and dropping your seatpost a few millimetres into the frame.

Step 3: A level saddle position is always the best starting point for full suspension bikes.

Suspension seat posts

These have become a lot more common and are now frequently fitted to new hybrids. They used to be a bit of a gimmick to comfort people who thought they were missing out on the whole suspension revolution. In the meantime, they've quietly got better and are actually quite a good idea. They work best if you have a fairly upright riding position, which puts most of your weight onto your saddle. The suspension takes the edge off the constant jolting in and out of potholes.

Suspension seat posts often help if you get a sore back and shoulders through cycling. They are even more effective in combination with a good-quality saddle.

Getting the seat height right can take a little bit of getting used to. When you sit on the saddle it squashes the post a little bit. This is called 'sag' and is supposed to happen. It has a side effect, however, since when you get off the saddle, it pops upwards a little bit, making it seem like it's set too high. You just have to get used to lifting yourself up a little higher to get up onto the saddle. The alternative is to set it to your normal height, so that it's easier to get on to but, once you're aboard, the slight sag means you're sitting too low down so your legs never get to have a proper stretch.

The standard pattern seat post – there is remarkably little variation in design – works by trapping a spring between two telescoping parts of post. The bottom part of the post that fits into the frame looks normal. The top section of the post is narrower and slides into the bottom part. This top part may be covered with a flexible rubber boot to keep the dirt out. The spring lives inside between the two parts and may either be a long metal coil spring or an elastomer rod.

Before you ride, the sag in the seat post has to be set up so that it settles into place the correct amount under your weight. The post is supposed to give a little bit so that it's got room to spring upwards, supporting you if the bike drops into a dip. It has to be able to compress as well, so that if you hit a bump the bike can ride upwards, without kicking you upwards with it. The ideal is to set the preload on the spring inside the post, so that, when you sit on the bike, the natural resting point of the saddle is some way between the two extremes.

The total travel on seat posts isn't a great deal of distance, usually around 40mm (1½ in), so you're looking for the seat to sink about a quarter of that when you sit on it – about 10mm (⅜ in).

You'll need assistance for this bit as you have to sit on the bike and then let someone else measure how much difference you've made.

ADJUSTING SAG FOR SUSPENSION SEAT POSTS

Step 1: Lean the bike against a wall and measure from the top of the seat post – where the post meets the clamp – to the bottom of the knurled nut. Take a note of the measurement. Leave the bike against the wall and climb on. Sit still in your normal riding position. Get a friend to measure again between the same two points as before. The difference between the two measurements should be around 10mm (³/₈ in).

Step 2: If the sag isn't right, undo and remove the clamp holding the seat post into the frame. Turn the post upside down. You'll be able to fit an Allen key in the cap in the bottom. If you've got more than 10mm (³/₈ in) sag, the spring is too soggy – turn the Allen key clockwise, adding preload. If you've got less, the spring is too firm – turn the Allen key anticlockwise, reducing preload. It's important not to undo the cap so far it protrudes out of the end of the post.

Step 3: You'll have to refit the post in the frame and repeat the measurements to check that the amount of sag is correct. It may take several goes to find the right place. Once you're confident about the sag, you'll need to reset your seat height. If you're not sure about how to work out the correct height, use the instructions on page 23.

Care of suspension seat posts

Suspension seat posts seem to be one of those things that people ignore – perhaps because they come fitted to new bikes rather than having been specifically chosen, or perhaps because their performance deteriorates so slowly that you don't really notice until the moment when they actually stop working completely.

The most common problem is that the knurled nut that holds the two parts of the post together has a tendency to work itself slowly loose. The spring that's trapped between the two parts then finds itself with plenty of elbow room.

When this happens, the spring isn't compressed at all by your weight and just rests at the bottom of its travel without supporting you in any useful way at all. If the knurled nut continues to work itself loose, the top part of the post can become completely detached from the bottom part.

Normally they don't separate of their own accord, because the top part rests inside the bottom part, but if your bike falls over or you bump off a deep kerb, they will soon part company.

You do get some warning when this starts to happen – instead of absorbing bumps smoothly as you ride, the post will sink slowly to the bottom of its travel, resting at its lowest point. You'll start to feel every bump you ride over, and you may even feel the post knocking as you go round tight corners.

The other problem that can occur is that the interface between the two telescoping parts of the post can corrode, so that they don't slide easily over each other and, however strong the spring is, the post won't respond to bumps. It doesn't happen all of a sudden. There will be a period when the movement of the post starts to feel lumpy and the saddle shifts in discrete jerks rather than with a smooth flow. If you catch it at this stage, there's hope as you can give the post a new lease of life by taking it apart, cleaning it and re-greasing it. The steps below show you how to do this. If you leave it much longer, the spring will become embedded in the post. The simplest and cheapest solution at that point is usually to replace the post.

It's worth getting the post out of the frame regularly and re-greasing the outside of the post as well as the inside of the frame. You don't need to use anything particularly fancy; ordinary bike grease will do the job just fine. If you don't do this and simply leave the post in the same place for years at a time, it will end up stuck (seized) within the frame. Parking your bike outside frequently will mean it's exposed to the weather, which will greatly increase the speed of corrosion.

A seized seat post is not an immediate problem as long as you never want to change its height, but you won't be able to access the bottom of the post to adjust the spring preload. Moreover, you'll be stuck if you ever want to lend the bike to someone who's a different height, or to sell it.

SERVICING SUSPENSION SEAT POSTS

Step 1: Ensure that the knurled nut at the top of the bottom section of the post is screwed down securely. These often work loose without anyone noticing. You'll have to lift the black rubber boot up and out of the way to turn the knurled nut. Keep turning the nut – if you stand over the saddle the nut must turn clockwise although you won't actually be able to see it because the saddle will be in the way.

Step 2: Remove the seat post from the frame. There's a cap on the bottom of the post. Note how deeply the cap is recessed and then use an Allen key to remove the cap. The spring will drop out. Clean it since it will be greasy and sticky. Once it's clean, spread a generous dollop of fresh grease all over it as the sides of the spring rub inside the post and need lubrication. Replace the end-cap, taking care that it goes in square, not cross-threaded.

Step 3: Tighten in the end-cap so it's as deeply recessed into the frame as before you removed it. The end of the cap must not protrude beyond the end of the post. Clean the outside of the post and the inside of the frame, then smear grease on the outside of the post. Refit the post. Insert it far enough into the frame so the 'min insertion' marks – a band of short parallel lines – disappear. If your saddle is too low, the seat post is too short and should be replaced.

Bar ends and grips

Bar ends (suitable for flat handlebars) went through a flourish of popularity some years ago when everybody owned a pair and everyone famous had a signature model. There are less about at the moment. I'm sure it's an aesthetic thing: they look a little odd on riser bars.

Bar ends are most useful for climbing because moving your weight forward over the front wheel helps keep it on the ground. They're great for short bursts of standing up on the pedals too – the angle is more comfortable, allowing your shoulders to open out so that you can get loads of air into your lungs. And it's nice to have a variety of hand positions when you're out on a long ride so that you don't get stiff and locked into a single position.

The profusion of shapes available can be confusing. Generally, choose short, stubby ones for climbing and longer, curved types for altering your riding position. I like ones with a machined pattern on the metal for extra grip.

The extra leverage that bar ends give you can be enough to twist your handlebars in their mounting – always check that your stem bolts are tight after fitting bar ends. Test that they will hold by standing in front of the bike with the front wheel between your knees. Push down hard on both bar ends. They shouldn't move on the bars, and neither should the bars move in the stem.

The end of your bar end, like handlebars, should always be finished off with a plastic plug. This protects you a little bit if you land on the end of your bar or bar end in a crash – an open end will make a neat round hole wherever it encounters parts of your body.

Just as vital for handlebar comfort are grips. There really are a lot of different choices here, so many that it's confusing rather than helpful. The most significant variable is grip thickness. Slim versions are lighter but less comfortable. Thick ones absorb more vibration, but this makes your bike feel less responsive – it's harder to feel what's going on if there's too much cushioning.

Your hand size also matters here. If you've got small hands, choose thinner grips. Dual density compounds, which have a softer, spongier layer over a firmer core, are a good compromise. Deep-cut patterns are better if your grips tend to get muddy and if you tend to ride when it's very hot, as smooth grips get slippery when you sweat onto them.

Grips that bolt on rather than stick on, like those made by Yeti, are a little more expensive but they are more secure and are easier to get on and off if you swap bars frequently. Each end of the grip has a locking aluminium collar that you tighten on with an Allen key.

Carbon bars need a little extra care – check whether your manufacturer recommends them, and follow any indicated torque settings carefully.

REFITTING BAR ENDS

Step 1: Undo the bar-end fixing bolt (almost always a 5mm Allen key). Slide the bar ends off the bars. They usually come straight off easily, but if they don't, ease the clamp open by removing the fixing bolt completely and opening the gap with a screwdriver. This avoids scratching the bars.

Step 2: Inspect the end of the bar and the bar end. Bar ends provide enough leverage for them to damage bars in a crash. If the end of the bar has been bent or dented, either replace the bar or choose not to refit the bar ends. Clean the interface and grease under the bolt head.

Step 3: Refit the bar ends, tightening the bolt just enough to keep them in place. Sit on the bike in your normal riding position and rotate the ends into a comfortable position. (It can help to close your eyes.) Check that both are pointing in the same direction, then tighten firmly. Stand in front of the bike and push down on the bar ends to check that they don't rotate on the bars and to see that the bars don't rotate in the stem under pressure.

Pedals and how to look after them

Clipless pedals are the standard for almost all speed-orientated bikes. They're also commonly known as SPD pedals, after the original Shimano version. (SPD stands for Shimano Pedalling Dynamics.) There are many versions available from different manufacturers. There isn't a standard-shaped cleat, so only use the cleats made by your pedal manufacturer – you can sometimes make others clip in, but you might not be able to clip out in a hurry.

Treat the threads of the pedals with grease or antiseize before fitting them. This treatment helps you to remove them and stops the cranks creaking as you pedal. Screw the pedals on firmly, or they will work loose and strip the threads, an expensive mistake to rectify. The thread that fixes the left-hand pedal is reversed, which means it screws on anticlockwise, and removes clockwise. This also means that the left-hand and right-hand pedals are not interchangeable.

This standard helps prevent the pedals from working loose and was originally adopted for fixed-wheel racing bicycles. Still in use today for track racing, these bikes have no ratcheting mechanism in the back wheel, so you can't freewheel. You brake by slowing down the pedalling. The reverse thread was vital. If the pedal bearings seized, the pedal, still being driven by the back wheel, would unwind from the cranks instead of snapping your ankle.

Pedals usually need more attention in the winter; seals are fine for summer but dirt works in as soon as it gets cold and muddy. Check by spinning the pedals on the axles. They should spin around at least twice with a good start. If not, it's time for a bearing service. Somehow, people neglect pedal bearings. I often come across otherwise well-cared-for bicycles with a pedal that almost needs a wrench to turn it. You might as well ride with the brakes dragging on the rim.

Often, one pedal continually needs more attention than the other. This is the side you fall off most, the side that gets stuck in the ground and picks up muck. Most mud falls off, but the rest is dragged in past the seals. Mud is not a good lubricant. I usually do both pedals in the same session, rather than just the sticky one. Once you have the tools out, doing both sides doesn't take much more effort than doing one.

Jet-washing destroys pedals faster than anything other than crashing. This is partly because people usually jet-wash from the side – the perfect angle to drive water and mud past seals that weren't designed to withstand pressure – and partly because the bindings accumulate mud so the pedals get extra spraying.

Pedals also suffer more than most other bearings. They get pushed as hard and are turned as often as bottom brackets, but in comparison their bearings are tiny and close together.

Toolbox

Tools for component upgrades
- Allen keys – 4mm, 5mm and 6mm
- Degreaser to clean interfaces and bolts
- Grease
- Chopstick to remove grips
- Grip glue or hairspray
- Cloth or paper towel for cleaning

Tools to cut bars down
- Hacksaw
- Tape measure
- File to clean off cut ends

Pedal tools: to remove and refit pedals
- Almost universally: long 15mm spanner
- For older Time pedals: long 6mm Allen key
- Grease (or antiseize for titanium axles) – otherwise your pedals will creak, and will seize into your cranks

Pedal tools: Time Alium pedals
- 6mm Allen key
- 10mm socket wrench
- New cartridge bearing – order this from your bike shop
- Degreaser to clean axle
- Grease

Pedal tools: Shimano PD-M747 pedals
- 15mm pedal spanner
- Shimano plastic pedal tool
- Shimano bearing adjustment tool or 7mm spanner and narrow 10mm spanner
- 24 2.5mm ($\frac{3}{32}$ inch) bearings
- Degreaser to clean bearing surfaces
- Good-quality bicycle grease

Time Alium pedals

These nice pedals clear mud quickly, and the cartridge bearings can be replaced without using any special tools. Before you start stripping the pedals down, check the condition of the pedal-release mechanism. The wide wire springs that clip around the cleat do eventually wear out, but luckily Time supply all the separate parts as individual spares – so you can rebuild worn pedals. I like this attitude.

Check for bearing wear by holding the pedal body and twisting it. The pedal should feel firm on the axle and should not knock from side to side – worn bearings won't turn smoothly under pressure, wasting your energy with every pedal stroke. Spin each pedal on its axle. They should turn silently and keep spinning half a dozen times. If the bearings are loose or binding, pick up a pair of new cartridges and rejuvenate your pedals.

REPLACING TIME ALIUM BEARINGS

Step 1: Remove the pedals from the cranks, remembering that the left-hand pedal has a reverse thread. The original Time pedals had to be removed with an Allen key, which was a pain, but current models use an ordinary 15mm pedal spanner. Remove the bearing cover at the end of the pedal.

Step 2: This exposes the pedal bearing which is held in place with a 10mm nut. Hold the axle steady with a pedal spanner, and use a 10mm socket spanner to undo. Remove the nut, which untightens anticlockwise on both pedals.

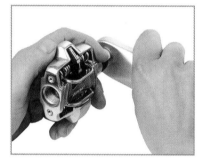

Step 3: Pull the axle out of the pedal body. You may have to screw the axle back into the crank and pull on the body firmly to get it off.

Step 4: There are very few parts inside this pedal. Clean the axle, the seals and the inside of the pedal body. Pay particular attention to the bearing surface at the inboard end of the pedal body. Replace or service the cartridge bearing. Cartridge bearings are not expensive, so replacement is a better option if the bearing doesn't spin easily.

Step 5: Replace the seal on the axle, with the soft flange facing toward the pedal. Grease the wide, shiny section of the axle and slide it back through the pedal body. Push the cartridge bearing in from the other end. Spread a thin layer of grease on the surface of the bearing to help keep out the weather.

Step 6: Refit the nut, holding the axle still with your 10mm spanner. The nut has a plastic ring above the threads. This stops the nut from working loose but makes it stiff to turn as soon as the plastic engages with the axle threads. Tighten it down onto the axle but not so far that the pedal won't spin freely. Replace the axle cover. Don't overtighten: it holds nothing on, is made of plastic and will shatter easily.

Shimano PD-M747 pedals

Check pedal bearings by holding the pedal body and twisting it sideways. The pedal should feel firm on the axle and should not knock from side to side. Spin each pedal on its axle. It should turn silently and keep spinning freely.

If the pedals are knocking or binding, it's new bearing time. They're an unusual size: ³⁄₂ inch. If your bike shop doesn't have them, try a bearing shop. If the bearing surfaces or cones are pitted or otherwise damaged, replace the whole axle. Take care not to swap the plastic sleeves between pedals – I usually do one pedal at a time to avoid confusion.

Remove both pedals from the bike, remembering that the left-hand pedal has a reverse thread and comes off clockwise. Follow the instructions below to replace the bearings. The final readjustment of the bearings can be a bit tricky – you have to reassemble the pedal and refit it to the cranks before you can be sure that your adjustment is correct. Sometimes it takes a couple of goes – adjusting the pedal bearings, reassembling the pedal and checking the adjustment – before you're satisfied.

REFITTING THE PEDALS

Step 1: To strip the pedal, you need the Shimano grey plastic pedal tool, that you can order through your bike shop. Clamp the tool in a vice and turn the pedal in the direction of the arrow printed on the tool. Wrap a cloth around the pedal for extra grip if necessary. The threads are plastic and strip if forced backwards, so check the direction carefully.

Step 2: Pull the pedal right off the axle. Take the axle out of the vice, remove the plastic tool and clamp the pedal axle back in the vice, narrow end upwards. You see the top row of bearings **(A)** trapped under the cone. The second set is between the steel tube and the washer below it.

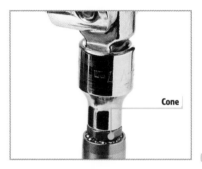

Step 3: The top of the pedal has two spanner flats, 7mm and 10mm. Shimano has a neat cone-adjusting tool, which makes the job easier, but you can use ordinary spanners. The 10mm must be narrow to fit in the space. First remove the locknut, then the cone; the lower one is the cone and takes a narrow 10mm spanner, the upper one is the locknut and needs a 7mm spanner.

Step 4: Remove the lock nut and cone. Pick off all the bearings, then pull off the steel tube. Pull the rubber spacer off the axle, then lift off the lower washer complete with bearings. Pull off the plastic sleeve and the rubber seal. Clean all parts carefully and check for pitted bearing surfaces. If they're worn out, replace the axle. **(B)** Rubber sleeve; **(C)** Lower washer; **(D)** Locknut; **(E)** Cone; **(F)** Steel washers.

Step 5: Refit rubber seal and plastic sleeve. Dry the curved washer so that the grease sticks, and grease it. Place 12 ³⁄₃₂ inch bearings carefully on the washer, then slide it gently over the axle to rest on top of the plastic sleeve. Refit the rubber spacer. Grease the bearing surface in one end of the metal tube, then pack another 12 bearings onto it. Slide carefully over the axle.

Step 6: Tighten the cone, curved side down, onto the axle by hand. Make sure it traps all bearings. Refit the locknut loosely. The cone must be tightened onto the bearings, so there is no play between the axle and the metal tube but so the tube can still turn freely. Holding the cone still, tighten the locknut onto it. This is fiddly: you may have to repeat the action several times to get it right. Refit the axle assembly into the pedal body, then use the grey tool to tighten firmly.

Choosing the right gear

Kit is the fun bit. You always find that some buys make a permanent place for themselves in your life, whereas other stuff, which once seemed a good idea, is more trouble than it's worth.

Liquid

Cycling is hard enough work without being thirsty as well. A litre an hour is often thrown about as a guideline, but you should increase this in hot weather. Water bottles on your frame are a great low-tech solution, but protect the drinking nozzle if your trails take you through farms – muddy bottles don't bother me, but I don't like the thought of drinking farmyard detritus.

Luggage

Most people carry everything on their backs or round their waists. I like to make an exception for tools, which I think are best carried in a seatpack under your saddle. They're usually oily, so you don't want them knocking around in your bag with clothes and sandwiches. And if you fall off, the last thing you want to land on is your toolbag. For day rides, hydration systems with luggage capacity – as pioneered by CamelBak – are great. If you live somewhere wet, make sure you get something waterproof – no point in carrying an extra layer all day then having to wring it out before you put it on. For hot climates, concentrate on getting enough air circulating between bag and back to keep you as cool as possible. Larger bags take heavier loads, so look for wider breathable straps. Bags with lots of little pockets are more expensive, but it is worthwhile having different compartments so you can keep spare socks separate from sandwiches.

Mudguards

If you live somewhere dry and dusty, skip this section. I do like cycling in all those places that don't have mud, and I agree it can be fun, but I always worry that it's just not real. So, for real cyclists who get dirty, a word about mudguards.

Full-length mudguards are tried and tested bits of kit for road bikes but for mountain bikes, there are a lot of options. I think that a front 'crudguard' – a piece of plastic strapped securely to your downtube (or equivalent) – is an essential piece of kit. I have eaten too many pieces of tyre-grated cowpie in my life already, and if not eating any more comes at the price of fixing an ugly piece of plastic to my bike, it's worth it. The guard also helps to stop bits of stuff from your front tyre getting flicked up into your eyes. Even if you wear glasses, the angle of approach from the back of your tyre is perfect to slip lumps of crud under the bottom of your glasses. Strap on a front guard today. If you can't bear to spend hard cash on a plastic moulding, cut a waterbottle in half, punch some holes in it and ziptie it on. Guards can also make great emergency shovels and, with a good wash, make a lovely camping plate too.

Back mudguards aren't quite so useful, but if it's cold as well as wet, they make the leap into the essential items basket. I can't bear spray from my back wheel hitting the gap at the top of my jacket collar, trickling cold rain down my back. Again, I will put up with ugly plastic on my bike if it helps keep me warm and dry. And when I get home, I won't give up my place by the fire to a colder person with a prettier bike.

Computers

I'm definitely in two minds about these. I go cycling to escape things like computers, so I will only attach them to my bike reluctantly. On the other hand, they are very useful for map reading, allowing you to pace off distances and to estimate how far you have to go before looking for a turning. They can also be useful for structured training routines and all that kind of thing. The simpler models usually have everything you need. You can get models that will read your altitude and heart rate, but mostly I'd rather not know about these things. It's up to you though – if it matters to you, you need one.

Lights

Night rides are fun. They bring on some kind of ancestral night vision that often lets you ride sections faster at night because all the extraneous information your brain normally processes is invisible. I like it best when there's enough moon to see by – otherwise you'll need lights. The faster you go, the more powerful you need your lights to be – you need to be able to see far enough ahead to have time to react to things that appear in your pool of light before you arrive at them. And here's a safety message – don't do anything dangerous. If you can't see there, don't go there!

With lights under 5W in power, you have to move fairly slowly, even if there's a bit of moon. All batteries also contain a heap of environmentally unpleasant stuff, and we use far too many of the disposable ones as it is, so treat yourself to at least 600 lumens of rechargeable units. Make sure they're strapped on securely.

Fitting a rack

Follow the steps here to ensure your rack ends up flat, level and secure. Once this is done, you can either hang panniers off it or bungee your load to the top.

If your frame doesn't have the special lugs which are needed for bolting the rack to, you'll have to take your bike to the shop and investigate brackets.

As well as the p-clips mentioned on the opposite page, there is a whole range of specially made little gadgets for bolting the rack to the frame. The most common is a monostay adapter bracket, which allows you to bolt a rack onto the type of frame where the seat stays merge into one tube above the rear wheel. Rack-mounting seat collars can also save the day, especially on smaller frames. These replace the ring that you tighten to adjust your seat height, with a similar version that has additional threaded holes for the rack to bolt onto.

FITTING A RACK

Step 1: Work out which end is the front – more confusing than you think! The stays will bolt onto holes in the top of the rack. The holes on the back are for attaching reflectors and lights to – in this picture, you can see a separate plate on the back. You may have to spread out the legs of the rack slightly to fit over the frame – the rack stays go on the outside of the frame on either side of the back wheel.

Step 2: Bolt the legs of the rack to the outside of the frame, just above the back wheel axle. Use a washer under the head of each bolt. Take special care on the right-hand side of the bike as the bolt must not protrude through the frame, where it may interfere with the sprockets. If it does, either use a shorter bolt or take the bolt out and add extra washers directly under the bolt head. Don't tighten the bolts yet.

Step 3: Next, attach the stays loosely to the front of the rack. Two common kinds consist of a pair of thin, flexible stays or a stiffer pair of stays with a selection of different-length extra sections to be bolted on. The stays bolt into slots rather than holes, so that you can adjust the position of the rack to suit the shape of your bike. If you're using shake-proof washers, you'll need a spanner to hold them while you tighten the bolts.

Step 4: Next, fit the front of the stays loosely onto the frame. If you've got flexible stays, bend them gently so that you can get the bolts into the frame – take care not to crossthread the bolts. If you've got a selection of joining pieces, choose a length that allows the stays to reach the frame.

Step 5: With all the bolts loosely attached, you should now be able to pull the rack into place so that the top of the rack is level with the ground. Look from above too and check it's pointing straight forwards. You may have to twist it into place.

Step 6: Once it's in place, go round systematically and tighten all the bolts – on the bottoms of the legs, on the stays and where the stays join to the frame. Check again that the bolts on the bottoms of the legs don't protrude through to the insides of the frame and interfere with your sprockets.

Fitting panniers

Once you've got your rack fitted, you're ready for panniers. These need to be attached securely since, if you pack them full of stuff and it starts shifting about while you ride, it makes your bicycle feel very unstable. The worst case scenario is your pannier partially bouncing off the rack and getting caught in your wheel... or bouncing somewhere into the distance when you go over a pothole. The chances are that you won't notice this happening...

Each pannier will have a pair of hooks that loop over the tubing of the rack. Better versions have a secondary clip that hooks under the tubing, so the pannier won't come off unless you release it. You'll generally find the rack is longer than the width between the pannier hooks, so you can choose how far back along the rack the pannier should sit. Keeping the weight as far forward as possible will maximise stability. However, if the panniers sit too close to you, you'll bang your heels on them every time you pedal – this is really irritating. You should be able to shift the position of the hooks sideways on the bag, choosing a position that prevents the bag shifting. As well as keeping your load stable, this helps to prevent the pannier hooks wearing through the rack tubing by constantly shuffling back and forth.

The bottom part of the bag must also be secured to the rack. This may seem superfluous when the bike is standing still, but out in the real world it's essential. If the back of the bike bounces around, the bottoms of the panniers flap outwards and may become dislodged.

Before you ride off, ensure that you've got any straps or bungees neatly tucked away. If they dangle down, they will inevitably flap about and get tangled in the back wheel, bringing you to an unexpected halt. If you're going to be carrying a lot of weight, just take a moment to check your rear-tyre pressure. A well-inflated tyre will give your wheel a bit of extra protection.

With panniers, it may seem tempting just to get one big one and stuff everything into it. But I would suggest two smaller ones rather than one big one. Although it's slightly more expensive, it's worth it for a couple of reasons. The first is that it's a lot easier to be organised if you've got two separate panniers – put your work papers in one side, and your sandwiches in the other. It's also less tiring to ride with an evenly loaded pair of bags than a single, heavy one. You rock from side to side as you pedal, so the bike dips slightly over to one side, and then down on the other. Evenly weighted bags will bob across like a pendulum, counterbalancing each other, whereas a single bag will have to be dragged back upright with every revolution of your feet.

POSITIONING A PANNIER

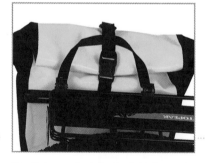

Step 1: Pop the panniers on the rack and sit on the bike. Put your feet on the pedals in their normal pedalling position, with the ball of your foot directly over the pedal axle and pedal backwards. Move the pannier until your heel just clears the bag. Check your rear light is still clearly visible. Push the backs of the bags in towards the wheel and check that they won't go far enough to get caught in the spokes.

Step 2: Loosen the bolts that hold the pannier hook in place and slide the hooks so they trap the cross-struts of the rack or the rail across the back of the rack. This prevents the bag from sliding forwards and backwards on the rack. Retighten the hook bolts.

Step 3: The bottom of the pannier needs to be attached to the rack stays, so that it can't flap outwards. In this case, a plastic tab must be positioned so that it hooks behind the rack leg. Other options include a strap or loop of elastic that hooks around the bottom of the pannier leg. The pannier may come with a hook to loop the strap around. You'll have to undo the bolt that attaches the rack to the frame and refit it with the hook underneath.

Fitting dynamos

Many people who are otherwise quite confident about their mechanics get daunted by dynamos and all that goes with them. They're not that complicated though – there must be a unit generating the electricity, which must then have an uninterrupted route out to each light and back. The easiest way to achieve this is to use dual-core wire – the type that often connects speakers to amps. The electricity runs to each lamp unit along one of the strands of the dual-core wire and then earths back to the generator along the other.

◆ It always makes sense to start by fitting the dynamo body to the bike. If you're using a hub dynamo, this can be easily accomplished by fitting the front wheel. Take care with orientation – they are designed to roll in one direction, which will be printed on the hub flange. Shimano dynamo hubs also come packaged with a circle of card slotted around the axle. Align the wheel so that the arrows point forwards.

◆ Bottle-type dynamos, which run on the sidewall of the tyre, are a little more complex. They require a bracket to fit them to the bike, which as often as not doesn't come supplied with the dynamo body. The dynamo bottle will work equally well on front or back wheels, but the bracket needs to hold the dynamo body so it sits forward of its mounting. The bottle is sprung to hold the head in onto the tyre. If it's mounted backwards, the tyre pulls the bottle constantly closer to the wheel, causing excessive drag. There's a particularly neat dynamo bracket made by Busch and Miller that fits the brake mounting boss on the front fork and holds the bottle safely out of the way in front of the front brake.

◆ The angle that the bottle sits at is crucial for smooth running and minimum drag. If you look at the dynamo from the side and imagine a straight line running directly through the centre of the bottle, the bottle should be rotated on its bracket so that the straight line also passes through the wheel axle. Once you've decided on the correct position, secure the bracket. Since you're using dual-core wire with a separate earth, it's not necessary to ensure there is a bare metal connection between the dynamo body and the frame.

◆ Next, secure the lamp units. Set them so that they're as high as they can practically be for maximum visibility and so that they're not obscured by any of your other baggage.

◆ Now, start with the front light. Measure out sufficient dual-core wire – leave enough to wrap the wire around the frame to secure it with plenty to spare as there's no harm in a little slack. Make sure there's enough slack for the handlebars to turn in both directions without stretching the wire. Secure to the frame with tape or zipties.

◆ Separate the last 10cm (4 in) of the dual-core wire into two separate strands – the joining web is thin and soft and will simply pull apart. Strip the last 5mm (¼ in) of plastic coating off each end of each wire.

◆ One of the two wires will be marked – usually with a pale line or a ridge in the insulating plastic. Connect the marked line to the live terminal on the lamp and the live terminal on the dynamo bottle. Then repeat, with the unmarked line attached to the earth terminals on the lamp and the bottle. You may find that there isn't a specific earth terminal on the lamp, the bottle or both. If this is the case, the stripped end of the wire must be trapped under a metal part of the bracket, either where two parts of the bracket clamp together or where the bracket clamps to the frame. It is essential that an electrical connection is made, so bare metal must touch bare metal.

◆ Repeat with the rear lamp unit, remembering, if the bottle runs off the front wheel, to leave enough slack in the cable for the front wheel to turn. Strip off the last 5mm (¼ in) of insulating plastic from each end of each wire and attach both ends of the marked wire to the live terminals and both ends of the unmarked to the earth terminals.

Now, spin the wheel to test. Both lamps should come on. If not, investigations should proceed in the following order:

◆ If one of the lamps works and the other doesn't, it's the bulb or the wiring. Check the wiring carefully, especially at the terminals. Then try replacing the bulb. Note that front and rear bulbs have different power rating, so you can't just swap them.

◆ If neither lamp works, try disconnecting first one then the other. If one light suddenly starts working when the other is disconnected, the other has a wiring fault – check that both earth and live wires are connected correctly. If neither lamp works, even when they're disconnected one at a time, the generator is either faulty or worn out – replace it.

10 – Conclusion

It can sometimes feel like bicycles change all the time, with designers thinking up new ways to make them lighter, stronger and faster. However, underneath the surface gloss, the principles stay pretty much the same – a couple of wheels, a couple of brakes, some gears, a seat to sit on, and something to point you in the right direction. Once you've worked out how derailleurs work, for example, the same procedures apply whether you're dealing with seven sprockets on your cassette or 10.

Glossary: the language of bikes

From Aheadset to Ziptie, this list covers most of the odd word and phrases that you are going to need in order to talk about bicycles and their mysteries. It's easy to get confused since many of the names that refer to specific parts also have more general meanings. Stick with these definitions and you should be okay.

- **Aheadset:** The bearing that clamps the fork securely to the frame, while allowing the fork to rotate freely so you can steer. The now-standard Aheadset design works by clamping the stem directly to the steerer tube of the forks, allowing you to adjust the bearings by sliding the stem up and down the steerer tube with an Allen key.

- **Air spring:** Used in both suspension forks and shocks, an air spring consists of a sealed chamber pressurized with a pump. The chamber acts as a spring, resisting compression and springing back as soon as any compressing force is released. Air has a natural advantage as a spring medium for bicycles – it's very light.

- **Antiseize:** This compound is spread on the interface of two parts, preventing them sticking together. It is vital on titanium parts, since the metal is very reactive, and will seize happily and permanently onto anything to which it is bolted.

- **Axle:** The axle is the central supporting rod that passes through wheels and bottom brackets and around which they can rotate.

- **Balance screws:** These are found on V-brakes and cantilevers and allow you to alter the preload on the spring that pulls the brake away from the rim so that the two sides of the brake move evenly and touch the rim at the same time.

- **Bar ends:** Handlebar extensions that give you extra leverage when climbing and permit you to use a variety of hand positions for long days out.

- **Barrel-adjuster:** This is a threaded end-stop for the outer casing. Turning the barrel moves the outer casing in its housing, changing the distance the inner cable has to travel from nipple to cable clamp bolt, and so altering the tension in the cable.

- **Base layer:** A close-fitting vest worn in cold weather, that wicks perspiration away from your skin, keeping you warmer, drier and more comfortable.

- **Biscuit:** (1) Useful things, like odd nuts and bolts, you keep in an old biscuit tin for emergencies; (2) A suitable offering you can take to your bike shop in exchange for past and future favours.

- **Bleeding:** The process of opening the hydraulic brake system, allowing air to escape, and refilling the resulting gap with oil. Bleeding is necessary because, unlike brake fluid, air is compressible. If there's air in your system, pulling the brakes on squashes the air, rather than forcing the brake pads onto the rotors.

- **Bottom bracket:** The main bearing connects the cranks through your frame. Often ignored because it's invisible, the smooth running of this part saves you valuable energy.

- **Bottom bracket cups:** These threaded cups on either side of the bottom bracket bolt onto your frame. The right-hand cup has a reverse thread and is often integral to the main body of the bottom bracket unit.

- **Bottoming-out**: This suspension term means that the fork or shock has completely compressed to the end of its travel. Sometimes accompanied by a loud clunk, bottoming-out is not necessarily a problem – if you don't do it at least once every ride, you're not using the full extent of the travel.

◆ **Brake arch:** On suspension forks, this is a brace between the two lower legs that passes over the tyre and increases the stiffness of the fork. It is called a brake arch even if your brakes are down by your hub.

◆ **Brake blocks:** These fit onto your V-brake or cantilever brakes. Pulling the brake cable forces them onto your rim, slowing you down.

◆ **Brake pads:** On disc brakes, these hard slim pads fit into the disc callipers and are pushed onto the rotors by pistons inside the brake calliper. They can be cable or hydraulically operated. Being made of very hard material, they last longer than you'd expect for their size, and, unlike V-brake blocks, do not slow you down if they rub slightly against the rotors. Contamination with brake fluid renders them instantly useless.

◆ **Brake pivot:** This is the stud on the frame or forks onto which cantilever or V-brakes bolt. Brakes rotate around the pivot so that the brake blocks hit the rim.

◆ **B-screw:** This component sits behind your derailleur hanger and adjusts its angle. Set too close, the chain rattles on the sprockets; set too far, your shifting is sluggish.

◆ **Burn-in time:** New disc brake pads need burning in; they never brake powerfully fresh from the box. Burn new pads in by braking repeatedly, getting gradually faster, until the brakes bite properly.

◆ **Cable stop:** This part of the frame holds the end of a section of outer casing but allows the cable to pass though it.

◆ **Cable:** This steel wire connects brake and gear levers to shifters and units. It must be kept clean and lubricated for smooth shifting and braking.

◆ **Calliper**: This mechanical or hydraulic disc brake unit sits over the rotor and houses the brake pads.

◆ **Calliper brakes**: Found on road bikes, these are simple and light. A horseshoe-shaped brake unit holds a brake block against the rim on either side.

◆ **Cantilever:** (1) This older rim brake type connects to your brake cable by a second, V-shaped cable; (2) A suspension design that sees the back wheel connected to a swingarm that pivots around a single point. These designs are simple and elegant.

◆ **Cantilever brake:** See cantilever.

◆ **Cartridge bearing:** These sealed bearing units are more expensive than ball bearings, but they are usually better value since the bearing surface is part of the unit, and so is replaced at the same time.

◆ **Casing:** Usually black, this flexible tube supports cables. Brake and gear casings are different: a brake cable has a close spiral winding for maximum strength when compressed; a gear casing has a long spiral winding for maximum signal accuracy.

◆ **Cassette:** This is the cluster of sprockets attached to your back wheel.

◆ **Cassette joint**: Not to be confused with a cassette, this is a fiddly metal contraption fitting over the sprocket of Shimano hub gears. Rotating the cassette joint, using the gear cable, selects one of the internal gear ratios.

◆ **Chain-cleaning box:** This clever device makes chain cleaning less of a messy chore, increasing the chances of you doing it. (Now you just need a chain-cleaning-box-cleaning box.)

◆ **Chainring:** This is one of the rings of teeth your pedals are connected to.

◆ **Chainset:** See crankset.

◆ **Chainsuck:** A bad thing! When your chain doesn't drop neatly off the bottom of the chainring, but gets pulled up and around the back, it jams between chainring and chainstay. Usually caused by worn parts, chainsuck is occasionally completely inexplicable.

◆ **City bars**: Curving upwards and backwards towards you, these handlebars are comfortable and allow you to sit quite upright – the style of bars often seen on Dutch town bikes.

◆ **Clamp bolt:** This holds cables in place. There is usually a groove on the component, indicating exactly where the cable should be clamped.

◆ **Cleat:** Bolted to the bottom of your shoe, this metal key-plate locks securely into the pedal and releases instantly when you twist your foot.

◆ **Clipless pedal:** This pedal is built around a spring that locks onto a matching cleat on your shoe. It locks you in securely and releases you instantly when you twist your foot.

◆ **Coil spring:** Usually steel but occasionally titanium, coil springs provide a durable, reliable conventional spring in forks and rear shocks.

◆ **Compression damping:** This is the control of the speed at which forks or shock can be compressed.

◆ **Cone:** This curved nut has a smooth track that traps bearings while allowing them to move freely around the axle without leaving room for side-to-side movement. The amount of space available for the bearings is adjusted by moving the cone along the axle, which is then locked into place with the locknut.

◆ **Crank:** Your pedals bolt onto cranks. The left-hand one has a reverse pedal thread.

◆ **Crank extractor:** This tool removes cranks from axles. There are two different kinds available – one for tapered axles, the other for splined axles.

◆ **Crankset:** The crankset is made up of three chainrings that pull the chain around them when you turn the pedals.

◆ **Cup-and-cone bearings:** These bearings roll around a cup on either side of the hub, trapped in place by a cone on either side. So that the wheel can turn freely with no side-to-side movement, set the distance between the cones by turning the cones so that they move along the axle threads.

◆ **Damping:** Damping controls how fast a suspension unit reacts to a force.

◆ **Derailleur hanger:** The rear derailleur bolts onto this part. This is usually the first casualty of a crash, bending when the rear derailleur hits the ground. Once bent it makes shifting sluggish. Luckily, hangers are quick and easy to replace, but there is no standard size; take your old one when you buy a new one, and get a spare for next time too.

◆ **Disc brake:** This braking system uses a calliper, mounted next to the front or rear hub, that brakes on a rotor or disc bolted to the hub. Hydraulic versions are very powerful. Using a separate braking surface also means the rim isn't worn out with the brake pads.

◆ **Dish:** Rims need to be adjusted to sit directly in the centreline of your frame, between the outer faces of the axle locknuts. Adding cassettes or discs to one side or other of the hub means the rim needs to be tensioned more on one side than the other to make room for the extra parts.

◆ **Dishing tool:** This tool allows you to test the position of the rim relative to the end of the axle on either side of the hub.

◆ **DOT fluid:** The fluid used in DOT hydraulic brakes. Higher numbers – i.e. 5.1 rather than 4.0 – have higher boiling temperatures.

◆ **Drivetrain:** This is a collective name for all the transmission components: chain, derailleurs, shifters, cassette and chainset.

◆ **Drop bars**: These curve forwards and downwards and are usually seen on road bikes. The brake-and gear-levers are combined into one unit for fast and instinctive shifting.

◆ **Duct tape:** Like the Force, it has a dark side and a light side, and it holds together the fabric of the universe.

◆ **Dynamo bottle**: A small generator that runs off the sidewall of your tyre, making electricity for your lights.

◆ **Elastomers:** This simple spring medium is usually found only in cheap forks now.

◆ **End cap (cable end cap):** This is crushed onto the ends of cables to prevent them from fraying and stabbing you when you adjust them.

◆ **End-stop screw:** Used on derailleurs, this part limits the travel of the derailleurs, preventing them from dropping the chain off either side of the cassette or chainset.

◆ **Eye bolt:** On cantilever brakes, the stud of the brake block passes through the eye of the bolt. Tightening the nut on the back of the bolt wedges the stud against a curved washer, holding the brake block firmly in place.

◆ **Ferrule:** This protective end cap for outer casing supports it where it fits into barrel-adjusters or cable stops.

◆ **Fixed wheel**: Without a ratcheting mechanism in the back wheel, the pedals must keep turning with the back wheel. Beloved of cycle messengers, they allow you to control the speed of your back wheel precisely.

◆ **Freehub:** This ratcheting mechanism allows the back wheel to freewheel when you stop pedalling. It's bolted to the back wheel, and has splines onto which the cassette slides. This is the part that makes the evocative 'tick tick tick' as you cycle along.

◆ **Freewheel:** This older version of the sprocket cluster on the back wheel combines the sprockets and ratcheting mechanism in one unit. Freewheels are rarely used for multispeed bikes now; the cassette/freehub set-up is far stronger, as it supports the bearings nearer the ends of the axle. Freewheels are often found on singlespeed bikes.

◆ **Front derailleur:** This part moves the chain between the chainrings on your chainset.

◆ **Gear ratio:** Calculated by dividing chainring size by sprocket size and multiplying by wheel size in inches, the gear ratio determines the number of times your back wheel turns with one revolution of the pedal.

◆ **Guide jockey:** The upper of the two jockey wheels on the rear derailleur, this part does the actual derailing, guiding the chain from one sprocket to the next as the derailleur cage moves across beneath the cassette.

◆ **Hop:** This term describes a section of the rim where the spokes don't have enough tension and bulge out further from the hub than the rest of the rim.

◆ **Hub gears**: Also known as internal gears, these have a single sprocket and chainring, with three, four, seven, eight, 11 or 14 gears concealed within the rear hub. The added bulk of the rear hub means they're affectionately known as 'tin can gears'.

◆ **Hydraulic brakes**: Usually disc brakes, these use hydraulic fluid to push pistons inside the brake calliper against a rotor on the hub. Because brake fluid compresses little under pressure, all movement at the brake lever is accurately transmitted to the calliper.

◆ **Indexing:** The process of setting up the tension in gear cables so that the shifter click moves the chain across neatly to the next sprocket or chainring.

◆ **Instruction manuals:** Often ignored or junked, these contain vital information. Keep them and refer to them!

◆ **International Standard:** This term refers to both rotor fitting and calliper fitting. International Standard rotors and hubs have six bolts. International Standard callipers are fixed to the bike with bolts that point across the frame, not along it.

◆ **ISIS:** This is a standard for bottom brackets and chainsets and has 10 evenly spaced splines.

◆ **Jockey wheel:** These small black-toothed wheels route the chain around the derailleur.

◆ **Lacing:** This technique is used to weave spokes to connect the hub to the rim. This part of wheelbuilding looks difficult, but it is easy once you know how.

◆ **Link wire:** Used in cantilever brakes, this connects the pair of brake shoes to the brake cable. It is designed to be failsafe; if the brake cable snaps, the link wire falls off harmlessly rather than jamming in the tyre knobbles and locking your wheel. You are still left with no brake though . . .

◆ **Lockring:** Used on bottom brackets and barrel-adjusters, this is turned to wedge against frame or brake lever to stop the adjustment you've made from rattling loose.

◆ **Lower legs:** The lower parts of suspension forks, these attach to brake and wheel.

◆ **Mineral oil:** This hydraulic brake fluid is similar to DOT fluid and must only be used with systems designed for mineral oil. It is greener than DOT, and less corrosive.

◆ **Modulation:** This is the ratio between brake lever movement and brake pad movement, or how your brake actually feels.

◆ **Needle bearing:** Similar to a ball bearing, a needle bearing is in the shape of a thin rod rather than a ball. Since there is more contact area between bearing and bearing surface than with the ball type, they are supposed to last longer, but they can be tricky to adjust. They are usually found in headsets, although some very nice bottom brackets also use needle bearings.

◆ **Nest:** This hanger or stop in a brake lever or gear shifter holds the nipple on the end of the brake or gear cable.

◆ **Nipple**: (1) This blob of metal at the end of a cable stops it slipping through the nest; (2) This nut on the end of a spoke secures it to the rim and allows you to adjust the spoke tension; (3) This perfectly ordinary part of a bicycle causes the pimply youth in the bike shop to blush furiously when asked for it by women.

◆ **Noodle:** This short metal tube guides the end of brake cable into V-brake hanger.

◆ **Octalink:** This is the name of the Shimano eight-splined bottom bracket/chainset fitting.

◆ **One-key release:** The combination of axle bolt and special washer fits permanently to the bike and doubles as a crank extractor.

◆ **Overshoes**: Nylon or Gore-Tex bootees that fit over your cycling shoes to keep the weather out. They're quite bulky, so you feel slightly foolish in them, but it's better than feeling stylish with cold feet.

◆ **Pannier**: A bag or bags that sit either side of your rack.

◆ **Pawl:** This part allows you to freewheel: a sprung lever inside ratcheting mechanism in the rear hub is flicked out of the way when the ratchet moves one way, and catches on the ratchet teeth the other way.

◆ **Pinch bolt:** In this version of a clamp bolt, the cable passes through a hole in the middle of the bolt, rather than under a washer beside the bolt. Occasionally it is found on cantilever straddle hangers.

◆ **Pinch puncture:** This happens when the tyre hits an edge hard enough to squash the tube on the tyre or rim and puncture it. It is also known as snakebite flat because it makes two neat vertical holes a rim width apart. Apparently this is what a snake bite looks like, although I've never had a problem with snakes biting my inner tubes.

◆ **Pivot:** (1) This bearing on a suspension frame allows one part of the frame to move against another; (2) this is also a rod or a bearing around which part of a component rotates.

◆ **Post mount:** Brake callipers are mounted with bolts that point along the frame, rather than across. These are less common than the alternative, the International Standard mount, but easier to adjust.

◆ **Preload:** This initial adjustment made to suspension springs to tune forks or shock to your weight is usually made by tweaking the preload adjustment knob, or by adding or removing air from air springs.

◆ **Presta valve:** Also known as high pressure valves, these are more reliable than Schraeder valves, which are designed for lower pressure car and motorbike tyres. Their only disadvantage is that they cannot be inflated on gas-station forecourts.

◆ **Puncture-resistant tyres**: These contain a strip of tough, pliable material under the tyre tread, preventing almost all of the glass and shards on the road from getting through to your tube.

◆ **Rapid-rise (low-normal):** In this rear derailleur, the cable pulls the chain from larger to smaller sprockets, then, when cable tension is released, the spring pulls the chain back from smaller to larger sprocket.

◆ **Rear derailleur:** This mechanism is attached to the frame on the right-hand side of the rear wheel. It moves the chain from one sprocket to the next, changing the gear ratio, when you move the shifter on your handlebars. It makes odd grinding noises when not adjusted properly.

◆ **Rebound damping:** Rebound damping controls the speed at which the fork or shock re-extends after being compressed.

◆ **Reservoir:** This reserve pool of hydraulic damping fluid is housed in a chamber at the brake lever. Having this reservoir of cool fluid a distance away from the hot rotor and calliper helps to minimize fluid expansion under heavy braking.

◆ **Reverse thread:** The spiral of the thread runs the opposite way to normal: clockwise for undoing; anticlockwise for tightening.

◆ **Rotor:** Bolted to the hub, this is the braking surface of a disc brake.

◆ **Sag:** This is the amount of travel you use sitting normally on your bike. Setting up suspension with sag gives a reserve of travel above the neutral position.

◆ **Schraeder valve:** This is a fat, car-type valve. The inventor, Franz Schraeder, is buried in a magical spot at the Cirque de Gavarne in the French Pyrenees.

◆ **Seal:** A seal prevents dirt, mud and dust from creeping into the parts of hubs, suspension units, headsets, bottom brackets and any other components where the preferred lubricant is grease rather than mud.

◆ **Seatpost clamp:** These plates and bolts connect the seatpost firmly to your saddle.

◆ **Seatstays**: A part of your frame, these connect the middle of your back wheel to the junction where your seatpost is attached.

◆ **Shim:** This thin piece of metal is used to make two parts fit together precisely. The washers between IS (International Standard) callipers and the frame are shims because they hold the calliper precisely in position.

◆ **Shimano joining pin:** Once split, Shimano chains must only be joined with the correct joining pin. Attempting to rejoin the chain using the original rivet will damage the chain plates.

◆ **Singlespeed (1x1):** This state of peace is obtained through self-liberation from the complexities of modern life by throwing away your gears.

◆ **Snakebite flat:** See pinch puncture.

◆ **Socket:** Shaped like a cup, this spanner holds the bolt securely on all the flats.

◆ **Splines:** These ridges across a tool or component are designed to mesh with a matching part so that the two parts turn together.

◆ **Split link:** This chain link can be split and rejoined by hand without damaging the adjacent links.

◆ **Sprocket:** This toothed ring meshes with the chain to rotate the rear wheel. The cassette consists of a row of different-sized sprockets.

◆ **Stanchions:** This upper part of the suspension forks slides into the lower legs and contains all the suspension extras, including springs, damping rods and oil.

◆ **Standard tube:** For those who don't need tubelessness, this normal inner tube is designed to fit into a normal tyre.

◆ **Star-fanged nut (star nut, star-fangled nut):** This nut is pressed into the top of the steerer tube. The top cap bolt threads into it, pushing down on the stem and pulling up on the steerer tube.

◆ **Stationary pad:** In disc brakes with one piston, the piston pushes a pad against the rotor, which in turn pushes the rotor against the stationary pad, trapping the rotor between moving and stationary pads.

◆ **Steerer tube:** This single tube extends from the top of the forks through the frame and has the stem bolted on the top.

◆ **Stem**: The component that connects your handlebar to the top of your forks.

◆ **STi**: A combined brake-lever and gear-shifter.

◆ **Stiff link:** The plates of the chain are squashed too closely together to pass smoothly over the sprockets, and they jump across teeth rather than mesh with the valleys between teeth.

◆ **Straddle wire:** This connects the two units of a cantilever brake via a straddle hanger on the brake cable.

◆ **Stress relief**: You can achieve this by squeezing the spokes to settle them into place as you build a wheel.

◆ **Swingarm:** This is the rear of a suspension frame, to which the back wheel attaches.

◆ **Tension jockey:** The lower of the two jockey wheels on the rear derailleur is sprung so it constantly pushes backwards, taking up slack in the chain created by the different teeth size combinations of sprockets and chainrings.

◆ **Toe-clips:** These survive today only in ghost form as the missing clip in clipless pedals. An unfortunate loss is the accompanying toe-strap, which was occasionally a priceless emergency item. (See ziptie.)

◆ **Toe-in:** To prevent squeaking, rim brakes are set up so the front of the brake block touches momentarily earlier than the back.

◆ **Top cap:** This disc, on the top of your stem, is bolted into the star-fanged nut in the steerer tube. Provided the stem bolts are loose, adjusting the top cap pushes the stem down the steerer tube, tightening the headset bearings. Always retighten the stem afterward!

◆ **Trailerbike**: These have a single wheel and clamp to the back of an ordinary bike, turning it into a mini-tandem. The trailerbike part has its own pedals and sometimes gears, too.

◆ **Travel:** Travel is the total amount of movement in the fork or shock. The longer the travel, the heavier and beefier the fork or shock must be.

◆ **Triggershifters:** This gear shifter features a pair of levers: one pulling, the other releasing, the cable.

◆ **Truing wheels**: The process of adjusting the tension in each spoke prevents the rim from wobbling from side to side when the wheel spins.

◆ **Tubeless:** In this weight-saving tyre design, the bead of the tyre locks into the rim, creating an airtight seal that needs no inner tube.

◆ **Twistshifters:** These gear shifters work by twisting the handlebar grip. Turning one way pulls through cable, while turning the other way releases cable.

◆ **Tyre boot:** Stuck onto the inside of a tyre, this patch prevents the inner tube from bulging out of big gashes.

◆ **URT:** Unified Rear Triangle. In this suspension frame design, bottom bracket, chainset and front derailleur are located together on the swingarm (rear end of the bike), so the movement of the swingarm never affects the length of the chain.

◆ **UST:** Universal Standard for Tubeless. This is an agreed standard for the exact shape of rims and tyre beads. UST tyres and rims made by different manufacturers lock together neatly for an airtight seal.

◆ **V-brake:** In these rim brakes, two vertical (hence 'V') units connected by the brake cable, hold the blocks.

◆ **Virtual pivot:** In suspension, this is when the swingarm is made of a series of linkages that combine to rotate around a position. Rather than a physical location on the frame, this position may be a point around which the frame would rotate if it was a simple swingarm.

◆ **Wheel jig:** This frame for holding a wheel during truing has adjustable indicators that can be set close to the rim to allow you to estimate how round and straight the rim is.

◆ **Ziptie:** The tool for whenever you need to connect one thing to another thing.

Index

A

adjustable spanners 45
adjustments
    balance screws 87
    brake blocks 85, 86-7, 95,
      116-17
    calliper brakes 100
    cantilever brakes 98
    disc brake callipers 106,
      121
    end-stop screws 149
    Fox Float Air 240-1
    front derailleurs 157
    gear cables 154
    handlebars 25, 77
    headsets 260-1, 265-6
    hub gears 179
    hubs 191
    hydraulic brakes 119
    preload 229
    rear derailleur cables 148
    rebound damping 228
    saddles 22-3, 77, 275
    spokes 71
    stem 77, 261, 265
    suspension seat posts 276
Aheadsets
    adjusting bearings 260
    adjusting stem height 261
    excess steerer tube 264
air shock 238
air springs 223, 236
Allen keys 25, 45
    long-handled 8mm 45, 48
    in trail toolkit 55
antiseize 51
axles
    refitting 193

B

B-screw 150
back racks 30
balance screws
    adjusting 87
    description of 88
    tools for 87
bar ends 278
bar tape 103
barbags 33
barrel-adjusters 91, 97
bars see handlebars
base layer 15
baskets 33
batteries 35, 36
bicycles
    parts of 42-3
    storage 39
bike hooks 39
biscuit box 52
bite point adjuster 121
bleed nipple 82
bleeding brakes 122, 124-6
BMX-style pedals 24
bolts
    torque on 53
bottom brackets
    description of 42
    noises from 249
    refitting 250-1, 255, 257
    removing 250-1, 254, 255,
      256
    servicing 248
    size of 253
    tools for 47, 253, 257
    troublehshooting 258
    varieties of 246-7
brake-bleeding kit 47

brake block adjusting unit 82
brake block stub 82
brake blocks (calliper brakes)
    fitting 101
brake blocks (cantilever brakes)
    adjusting 95
    replacing 95
brake blocks (disc brakes)
    cleaning 115
    replacing 114-15, 120-1
    tools for 122
brake blocks (hydraulic
    brakes)
    adjusting 119
brake blocks (mechanical disc
    brakes)
    adjusting 116-17
brake blocks (V-brakes) 82
    adjusting 85, 86-7
    choosing new 87
    replacing 83, 86-7
    safety checks 85
    tools for 87
brake cables
    casing for 159
    and gear cables 159
brake cables (calliper brakes)
    fitting 102
    outer casing for 103
brake cables (cantilever
    brakes)
    fitting 96, 102
    refitting to brake unit 97
    replacing 96
brake cables (disc brakes)
    replacing 113
brake cables (V-brakes) 46, 82
    cleaning 160

fitting 90
maintenance 90-1
outer casing for 91
safety check 84
tools for 87
brake calliper 82
brake fixing bolt 82
brake fluid 47, 122-5
brake hoses 82
clamping 122
description of 42
Hope Minis 123
safety check 75
shortening 122-3
tools for 122
brake levers
modulation 88
safety check 75
brake outer casing 46
brake pads **see** brake blokes
brake units (calliper brakes)
servicing 105
brake units (cantilever brakes)
cleaning 99
fitting 99
brake units (V-brakes) 82
connecting cable to 97
fitting 92
maintenance 92
tools for 87
brakes
bleeding 122, 124-6
cleaning 79
description of 82
disc 47
safety check 75, 89
tools for 46, 47
troubleshooting 93

broken chains 142
Brooks leather saddle 22
brush kit 50

C
cable bolt 82
cable clamp bolt 82
cable ends 159
cable locks 27
cable stops 159
cables
cleaning 79, 160
description of 42
differences between 159
gear 46, 72, 159
rear derailleur 147-8, 154
repairing 72-3
safety check 75
sealed cable kit 160
in spares box 46
tools for 169
transmission 131
upgrading 160
calliper brakes **see also** brake
blocks (calliper brakes)
and brake cables
(calliper brakes) **and**
brake units (calliper
brakes)
adjustments 100
calliper fixing bolt 82
Campagnolo, Tullio 145
cantilever brakes **see also**
brake blocks (cantilever
brakes) **and** brake
cables (cantilever
brakes) **and** brake
units (cantilever brakes)

adjustment 98
description of 82, 94
safety checks 94, 104
servicing 104
troubleshooting 93
cantilever full-suspension
bicycles 236
carbon grease 51
casing 159
cassette-remover 48, 143
cassettes 43
description of 42, 131
gear shifter compatibility
147
hub servicing 199
refitting 143, 199
removing 143, 199
for singlespeed bicycle 176
tools for 169
chain-cleaning box 48, 79,
136
chain splitter 48
chain tool 45, 55
in chain repair 64, 65, 66,
67
chain-wear measuring tool 45
chain whip 48
chainline 171
chainrings
chainsuck 172, 174
removing 172
replacing 173
tools for 169
chains
broken 142
care for 142
chainline 171
cleaning 79, 135-6

correct length 141
description of 42
fitting 68, 141
length check 64
links 46
lubricants 50-1
measuring 137
Powerlinks 46, 66, 140
rejoining 138
repairing broken 64-5, 67
safety check 75
Shimano 67, 139
shortening 69
for singlespeed bicycle 175
split links 46, 66
splitting 138
stiff links 66, 140
tools for 45, 169
chainset 43
    and chainline 171
    cleaning 79
    description of 42, 131
    one-key release crank bolt
    171, 252
    refitting 170, 251
    removing 170
    tool 48
chainsuck 172, 174
city bars 26
cleaning fluid 50
cleaning
    brake cables 160
    cables 79, 160
    chain 79, 135-6
    disc brakes 79, 115
    forks 79, 230
    front derailleurs 79, 158
    gear cables 79, 154, 160

hub sprockets 79
products for 50
rear derailleurs 152, 154
routine 78-9
sealed bearings 198
stanchions 231
cleats 14, 24, 25, 43, 46
clipless pedals 14, 24, 25
clothing
    cold weather 13
    fleece 16-17
    gloves 15
    helmets 18
    jackets 10-11, 17
    layering 16-17
    overshoes 15
    overtrousers 13
    reflective bands and strips
        19
    shoes 14
    shorts 12-13
    thermals 16-17
    tights 13
    wet weather 13
coil shock 238
coil springs 223, 236
cold weather
    gloves for 15
    layering 16-17
    overshoes for 15
    thermals for 16-17
    trousers for 13
combination locks 27
compression damping 225
    setting 228
computers 36
cone spanners 48
Cooperslip 51

cotton rags 50
crank extractors 48, 171
cranks
    refitting 170, 250-1
    removing 170, 250-21
    repairing 63
    securing 63
crescent wrench 45
cup-and-cone hubs 43, 189
    servicing front 192-3
    servicing rear 194-5
    tools for 195

D
damping
    description of 224-5
deep-section rims 208
degreaser 50
derailleurs see front derailleurs
        and rear derailleurs
disc brake callipers 43
    adjustments 106, 121
    description of 42
    International Standard 108
    Post Mount 109
    safety check 75
disc brakes see also brake
        blocks (disc brakes) and
        brake cables (disc brakes)
    axles 107
    bleeding 126
    cleaning 79, 115
    description of 82
    fluid for 51
    rotors 110-11, 115
    tools for 47, 122
    troubleshooting 127
DOT fluid 51, 82

drivetrain
    cleaning 79
drop bars 26, 33
    STi shifters on 164
dropouts 43, 176, 182
duct tape 55
dynamos 37
    fitting 285

E

earthing 37
8-speed hubs 179
elastomers 223
electrical tape 46
end-stop screws
    front derrailleurs 156
    rear derailleurs 147, 149
extension cable 27
external bottom brackets 247
    refitting 257
    removing 256
    tools for 257
    troubleshooting 258
eye bolt 82
eyelets 208

F

ferrules 46, 159
fixed wheel bicycles 177
flat bars 272
fleece 16-17
fore-and-aft positioning 23
forks
    cleaning 79, 230
    servicing 226, 230, 232-4
    springs in 223
    tools for 233
    troubleshooting 243

varieties of 227
Fox Float Air
    adjusting 240-1
    fitting 240-1
frame
    cleaning 79
freehub
    description of 42
freewheel tools 48, 144, 169
freewheels 144
front derailleurs
    adjusting 157
    cable fitting 165
    cable repair 72
    cleaning 79, 158
    description of 131
    end-stop screws 156
    fitting 157
    position of 155
    servicing 158
    tools for 169
    varieties of 156
front hubs 43
front lights 35
front-loader stems 274
front racks 34
front wheels
    lacing spokes on new 210-11
    left and right sides 208
full suspension bicycles 236

G

gear cables 46
    adjusting 154
    casing for 159
    cleaning 79, 154, 160
    fitting new 162, 163, 164,
        165, 166

gear shifters 43
    cassette compatibility 147
    description of 130
    replacing 154
    servicing 169
    STi shifters 164, 166
    thumbshifters 161
    triggershifters 147, 161,
        162, 167, 169
    twistshifters 147, 161, 163,
        168, 169
    tools for 169
    types of 147, 161
gears
    adjusting 146
    description of 133
    improving use of 154
    indexing 146-7
    proper use of 132
    for singlespeed bicycle
        175, 176
gilet, sleeveless 17
glasses 19
gloves 15, 19
Gran Sport (derailleur) 145
grease 51
griplocks 46
grips 46

H

hand cleaner 50
handlebars 26
    adjustments 25, 77
    description of 272
    fitting new 273
headsets 43
    adjusting bearings 260,
        266

adjusting stem height 261, 265
cartridge bearings 268
checking 259
description of 42
servicing 262-3, 267-8
spanners 47
threaded 259
tools for 260
troubleshooting 269
varieties of 259
helmets 18, 19
high-rise bars 272
hoods on jackets 11, 17
Hope Minis
bleeding 125
shortening 123
horizontal dropouts 176, 182
hub dynamos 37
hub gears
adjusting 179
description of 178
removing hub gear wheels 180
hub sprockets
cleaning 79
replacing 182
swapping 183
hub seals 190
hubs
adjusting 191
description of 43, 189
fitting 190
front 43
rear 199
servicing 192-3, 210
Shimano freehubs 200
spacing 190
tools for 195

hydraulic brakes **see also** brake blokes (hydraulic brakes)
adjusting 119
bleeding 124, 126
description of 118

I
indexing
front derailleur 155
rear derailleur 146-7
inner tubes 46, 55
fixing when riding 62
refitting 58-9, 60
removing 56-7
instructions 44
internal bottom brackets
refitting 255
removing 254, 255
size of 253
troubleshooting 258
International Standard callipers 108
ISIS bottom brackets 247

J
jackets 10-11, 17
jockey wheels 151, 152

K
Kevlar hoop 57
knives 45

L
layering 16-17
lights
choosing 282
dynamos 37
front 35

rear 36
link wire 96, 97, 98
linkage full-suspension bicycles 236
links
split 66
stiff 66, 140
twisted 68
locking techniques 28
locks
choosing 27
techniques for using 28
Loctite compound 51
long-handled 8mm Allen key 45, 48
long-nosed pliers 45
low rider racks 34
low-rise bars 272
lower jockey wheel 145
lubricants 50-1, 79
luggage
back racks 30
barbags 33
baskets 33
front racks 34
panniers 29, 30, 34
racks 30, 34
seat packs 33
toolbags 33
trailers 32

M
mallet 45
manuals 44
measuring chains 137
mechanical disc brakes 112
see also brake blocks (mechanical disc brakes)

description of 112
replacing cables 113
men
  saddles for 22
  shorts for 12
messenger bags 31
metric spanners 45
mid layer 16-17
mountain bikes
  pedals for 24
mudguards 38, 282

N
nipples 159
notebooks 45

O
off-centre rims 208
oil weight 225
one-key release crank bolt
    171, 252, 253
outer casing
  replacing 91, 103
outer layer 17
overshoes 15
overtrousers 13

P
panniers
  back 29, 30
  fitting 284
  front 34
  and lights 36
Park tool 47
patch kit 55, 62
pedals 43
  choosing 24
  cleaning 79

clipless 14, 24, 25
contact with 77
damaged 63
description of 43
safety check 75
servicing 279
Shimano PD-M747 281
SPD-type clipless 14, 77, 279
Time Alium 280
tools for 49, 279
pens 45
pivots 242-3
plastic lubricants 51
pliers 45
pockets on jackets 10
positions
  handlebars 26
  saddle 23
Post Mount callipers 109
Powerlinks 46, 55, 66, 140
preload 222
  adjusting 229
Presta valves 57, 62, 202
propstand 52
pumps
  track 45
  in trail toolkit 55
punctures
  causes of 59
  fixing when riding 62
  refitting inner tube 58-9
  removing tyres 56-7
  UST tubeless tyres 60-1
puncture kit 45, 46, 55

Q
quick release 43
  fitting 188

safety check 75

R
racks
  back 30
  fitting 283
  front 34
Rapid Rise derailleur 146,
    147, 165
rear derailleur hanger 43
rear derailleurs 43
  adjusting 147, 148
  alignment 153
  angle of 147, 150, 164
  B-screw 150
  cable condition 147
  cable fitting 165
  cable repair 73
  cable tension 148
  cleaning 152, 154
  compatibility 150
  cleaning 152
  description of 42, 131, 145
  destruction of 69
  end-stop screw 147, 149
  fitting new 151, 154
  servicing 152
  tools for 169
  varieties of 150
rear hubs 199
rear lights 36
rear suspension
  description of 235
  servicing 239
rear wheels
  lacing spokes on new 212-
    13
  left and right sides 208

refitting hub gear 181
removing hub gear 180
rebound damping 225
adjusting 228, 239
rechargeable batteries 35
reflective bands and strips 19,
31
rejoining chains 138
Respro bands 19
rim brakes
cleaning 79
safety check 75
rim tape 202
rims 43, 202
damage to 205
deep-section 208
eyelets 208
off-centre 208
safety checks 89
rivets
Shimano 55
RockShox Pike 227
RockShox Reba 227
servicing 232-4
rotors 43, 82, 110-11
rucksacks
choosing 31
covers 19, 31
lights for 36

S
saddles 43
adjustments 22-3, 77,
275
angle 23, 275
choosing 22
height 23
positioning 23

safety
checks 74-5, 84, 85, 89
choosing pedals 24
gloves 19
helmets 18, 19
jackets 11
reflective bands and strips
19
sag 222
setting up 228, 229, 238
Sam Browne belt 19
Schraeder valves 62, 202
screwdrivers 45, 55
seal on jackets 10
sealed bearing hub 43, 189
servicing 196-7
tools for 197
sealed bearings 198
sealed cable kit 160
seat packs 33
seatposts 43, 275
adjusting 276
servicing 277
security
choosing locks 27
locking techniques 28
security skewers 27
security skewers 27
self-adhesive patches 46
shifters **see** gear shifters
Shimano
callipers 117
chain-joining pins 46
cleats 14
derailleurs 146, 150, 152
disc brake 107, 117, 126
8-speed hubs 179
freehubs 200

Octalink bottom bracket
247
PD-M747 pedals 281
refitting chain 67
rejoining chain 139
rivets 55, 67
splined remover 47
splitting chain 139
shock tools 49
shocks 238
Fox Float Air 240-1
pivots 242-3
shoes 14, 25
shorts 12-13
shoulder bags 31, 36
sidewall dynamos 37
single bolt stems 274
single-wheel trailers 32
singlespeed bicycle 69, 175-6
size of bicycle 76
sleveless gilet 17
spanners
adjustable 45
bottom bracket 47
cone 48
headset 47
metric 45
pedal 49
spares box 46
SPD-type clipless pedals 14,
77, 279
splined removers 47
split links 46, 55, 66
splitting chains 138
spoke key 48, 209
spoke wrench 48, 209
spokes 43
adjusting 70

broken 71, 205
crossing pattern 206
gauge 207
lacing 210-11, 212-13
length 207
pattern 204
replacing broken 204
safety check 75
tensioning 214-16
tools for 48, 205
truing 214
springs
  shocks 236
  types of 223
sprockets **see** hub sprockets
square taper bottom brackets
  246
stanchions
  cleaning 231
steerer tube 263
  cutting off excess 264
stems 43
  adjustments 77, 261, 265
  fitting new 274
  safety check 75
stem top cap 43
STi shifters 164
  cable fitting 166
stiff links 66, 140
storage
  of bicycles 39
straddle cable 82, 97, 98
straddle hanger 82, 96
straight bars 26, 33
straightening wheels 70-1
sun cream 19
suspension
  damping 224-5

description of 43, 220-1
full suspension bicycles
  236
measuring total travel 237
oil for 51
preload 222
sag 222
servicing 226
tools for 49
varieties of 227
suspension fluid 49
suspension forks 43
suspension pump 49
suspension seat posts
  adjusting 276
  servicing 277

T
tape, electrical 46
tension jockey 145
thermals 16-17
threaded headsets 259
  adjusting bearings 266
  adjusting stem height 265
  servicing 267-8
thumbshifters 161
Ti-prep 51
tights 13
Time Alium pedals 280
tool libraries 44
toolbags 33, 282
tools
  biscuit box 52
  bottom brackets 47, 253,
    257
  brakes 46, 47, 87, 122
  cables 169
  cassettes 169

chainrings 169
chains 169
cleaning 75
forks 233
front derailleur 169
growth of 44
headsets 260
hubs 195, 197
instructions 44
manuals 44
pedals 49, 279
rear derailleur 169
simple kit 44-5
spares box 46
spokes 48, 205
suspension 49
tool libraries 44
trail 54-5
wheel building 209, 211
wheels 48, 205
workstand 52
top jockey 145
torque 53
torque wrench 53
Torx keys 45
track pumps 45
trail boots 14
trail toolkit 54-5
trailers 32
transmission
  parts of 130-1
  tools for 48
  troubleshooting 184-5
triggershifters 147, 161
  fitting 167
  fitting gear cables for
    162
  servicing 169

tools for 169
truing
    spokes 214
    wheels 203
tubes **see** inner tubes
tubeless tyres 60-1
twisted links 68
twistshifters 147, 161
    fitting 168
    fitting gear cables for 163
    servicing 169
    varieties of 163
Two Seconds (film) 69
two-wheel trailers 32
tyre levers 45, 55
tyres 43
    checking 58
    choosing 201
    cleaning 79
    removing 56-7
    safety check 75

U
U-locks 26
UST tubeless tyres 60-1

V
V-brakes **see also** brake
        blocks (V-brakes) **and**
        brake cables (V-brakes)
        and brake units
        (V-brakes)
    description of 82, 83
    fitting new units 93
    maintenance 83
    safety checks 84
    troubleshooting 93
valve holes 202

valves 43
    Presta 57, 62, 202
    Scraeder 62, 202
vertical dropouts 176, 182
visibility
    jackets 11
    reflective bands and strips
        19

W
wall racks 39
water bottles 282
waterproof trousers 13
wet weather
    clothing for 13
wheel building
    spoke tensioning and tru-
        ing 214-6
    tools for 209, 211
    vocabulary for 206-8
wheel jig 48, 209
wheels
    cleaning 79
    description of 42
    emergency repairs 70-1
    hole numbers 207
    lacing spokes on new
        210-11
    left and right sides 208
    refitting 188
    removing 188
    rim tape 202
    safety check 75
    straightening 70-1
    tools for 48, 205
    troubleshooting 217
    truing 203
windproof jackets 11

Wingquist, Sven 189
wipers
    lubricating 231
wire cutters 45, 47
women
    saddles for 22, 77
    shorts for 12
wool 16
workstand 52

Z
zipties 46, 55, 69